HOW TO STEER CLEAR OF DRUGS

by

Wendell Hansen, Ph.D.

Heartland Technical Publishing
A DIVISION OF
Alexander Graphics, Ltd.
Indianapolis, Indiana

Library of Congress Cataloging-in-Publication Data

How to steer clear of drugs: shocking drug facts
Hansen

Published by

Heartland Technical Publishers
125 N. East Street
Indianapolis, IN 46204

Manufactured in the United States of America

To The Family of My Life:

My mother, Anna, who in my early childhood directed me to the Lord and to a squeaky-clean life untarnished by forbidden drugs, and my father who was willing to spend much time in scout activities leadership.

To my first wife, Bertelle, who proclaimed the gospel to thousands, while helping me get an education in the dark days of the great depression. Unfortunately she was cut down in the flower of her life in child birth.

My daughter, Sylvia Marie, received her elementary home schooling on the road, starting to read at the age of three. She also then began assisting on the program as our evangelistic tours covered all states east of the rockies. Her home was a thirty foot house trailer, also housing my writing office and twenty five birds including an ostrich. She graduated from Christian Pasadena College *magna cum laude.*

The cooperation of my late sister, Evelyn.

To my present devoted wife, Eunice, who because of her editorial experience has not only given me guidance, but has taken care of the 'other things', in our lives while I devoted long hours in research, both at home and abroad.

My married son, Dean, of a different gender, continues to help in my writing, and helps make possible our evangelistic and drug prevention meetings.

TABLE OF CONTENTS

ACKNOWLEDGMENTS

To emphasize the value of rewriting, William Zinsser in *On Writing Well* mentions that E. B. White and James Thurbur "rewrote their pieces eight or nine times." In the years of writing this thesis my friends would ask, "Have you finished your book?" I would answer, "Many times."

In the course of time I would wear out, (or they moved), many excellent typist and word processors. The main ones were: Martha Crookham, Dr. Brian Aubrey, Nancy Meneely, Jackie Morgan, Sherry Johnson, Clair Robinson and Margaret Johnson, the most.

I also received valuable material from Church of the Nazarene ministers, Leslie Waltz and Keith Sparkman who gave me a copy of Dr. William Pattons' Bible Wines and got me started writing.

To be sure that my chemistry is up-to-date, I am indebted to Teresa Shahsavar G.Ph, R.Ph. of Hooks Drug Stores, now Revco, and Chemistry Professor Dr. Vickie Lynne Hess of Indiana Wesleyan University.

Priceless, helpful scholars, are introduced in the text or endnotes.

INTRODUCTION

George Allemenos moved further from the drug infested Indianapolis area into church oriented, peaceful, Hamilton County. He didn't realize that his teen age son was flirting with drugs. His son, daughter, and a friend had their throats slashed.

The Indianapolis Star, 4/20/1995, surveyed registered voters: "Forty three percent are very concerned they, or a member of their family, will become a crime victim."

Drugs and their attendant crimes have spread every where, now our nations's number one social problem.

Our government has failed to stop this drug and crime rampage.

Schools are drug infested. My wife has an M.A. in education. She taught twenty years, without one bit of anti-drug instruction.

If Christian parents find their child is into drugs, they often go to their pastor for help, but he has never had drug training. Seminarians and universities say they have no suitable materials; many of their graduates know less about drugs than the kid on the street.

In Christian Book stores I found only, *Drugs and Drinking*, by Jay Strack, Thomas Nelson, 1985. It is high time that practical drug facts become available in Christian schools and seminaries.

This study presents basic drug fighting facts for Christian schools. Aside from the Hebrew and Greek texts in the commentary for scholars, drug facts are given in simple, plain words, so the average pastor and qualified Sunday School teacher can become a specialist in the field.

In our discussion on drugs we do refer to their medical use, but we are primarily concerned with drugs taken to make people temporarily feel unnaturally good, and hypnotically give a sense of well being, but later feel bad and a need for more.

The current *assumption* is that some harmful pleasure drugs in moderation are beneficial.

The tragic result is that the one institution that is supposed to be the light of the world, has put its approval on the use of poisonal chemical substances for non-medical use as a natural part of man's normal existence.

This follows tradition. Thousands of years before Christ, the Egyptians in some periods used the 'spirits' of wine in their worship of Osiris.

The Greeks worshipped Dionysus, and the Romans Bacchus, the god of wine.

Churches were influenced by their environment just as the Hebrews were often influenced by their pagan environment. The Roman Church followed the pagan custom by partially allowing alcoholic wine in the Mass. But there were conscientious people who used only nonalcoholic wine.

Neither was there ecclesiastical disapproval when nicotine came along, except for the splinter pietist groups, the strict reformers.

The search for truth often runs contrary to both public and current predominate scholastic opinion.

A reformer is not dismayed when he has to push upstream against the current. A look at history confirms this.

How many have suffered and died for having opposed the egotistical, dictatorial 'divine rights of kings'?

How many were burned at the stake in the quest for religious liberty? Fox Book of Martyrs tells graphic stories of hundreds tortured and killed for their stand for the gospel. The religious Reformation Thirty Years' War killed a third of the population of Germany.

How many of our most valiant men died in eradicating slavery? What a struggle! Nowhere was there a specific 'thou shalt not' regarding the ownership of other human beings. The Old Testament listed the rights of slaves as slaves. Even Christ gave no specific injunction against it. The Apostle Paul asked Philemon to take back the slave Onesimus as a beloved brother. History gives a glimpse of what others said regarding slavery.

Famous religious leaders are often wrong. Richard Furman was a prominent Baptist preacher of a bygone day, and the oldest Baptist college in the South was named in his honor. He said, "Everyone who believes in the Bible would find that it approved of slavery." Theologian J. H. Thornwell, stated, "We stand on the platform of the Bible. God's word recognizes the relationship of master and slave. . . . The Church has no right to interfere directly. . . . It is not a question for the Church." In 1861, the Presbyterian General Assembly said, "As long as the Negro race, in its imperative degradation, coexists side by side with the white, bondage is its normal condition."

But in spite of such seemingly impregnable opposition, the early Quakers, the Enlightenment Philosophers, and other reformers fought on until the common consciousness and opinion regarding slavery became more aligned with Christ's gospel of love, as opposed to selfish personal benefit. Both scholars and ecclesiastics who supported slavery were defeated. Now we have this same battle with so called refreshment drugs.

We have come to realize that true scholars do not begin searching for truth with a blank sheet of paper. Each has his own innate, preconceived suppositions which color all his attempts at honest research. In translation, a Lexicon or dictionary will give several meanings. For example, fast can mean speed or to anchor solidly, or the Hebrew *BARAK* can mean to bless or to curse. So sometimes contradictory definitions exist for the same word. Scholars must make a subjective opinion based on their own knowledge or on what seems right. Sometimes the decision is based on previous influences and on personal inclinations.

A translator, then, must not use exegesis alone. But must find an additional accurate method for determining the meaning of a word. One such method is observation of the work in question according to its context. Context refers to the parts of a discourse or treatise which precede and follow a special passage, also the meaning for a Bible passage must be in harmony with the total scriptural teaching. The word selected must be based on the meaning in context as well as on all other methods. And the word selected for use must be understood in its current usage. We do not believe in regard to wine most current Bible translations are correct in regard to alcoholic use.

The word wine for thousands of years meant both alcoholic and nonalcoholic, as we shall substantiate. But the meaning of the word wine today has come generally to mean alcoholic, although in the Bible it means alcoholic only about half of the time. But copy cat translators, translate all as alcoholic, as wine in a bunch of grapes, or flowing out of the press, ridiculous.

There are many fine scholars who conscientiously believe that it is all right for Christians to moderately use refreshment drugs.

They are just as wrong as the advocates for slavery were. Unfortunately, they are generally the ones that have translated the scriptures. This has resulted usually in a tacit approval of Christianity for a chemically mind changing substance. This is at the base of our terrible socalled recreational drug problem. One of our costliest drug problems is alcohol, the gateway to other drug use.

We believe that the latest translations are pitifully out dated. There are a host of conscientious scholars who believe that the Bible teaches abstinence from addictive drugs including alcohol. Wine is used in the Bible as both a blessing and a curse. It can do this and be consistent because there are two meaning for the word wine.

I have quoted many scholars, antiquity to modern, verbatim, so there will be no misunderstanding. You will note most of those that I quote have their doctorate, real scholars in their own right. Many of these are now, or have been, in responsible position in Christian Universities and Seminaries. They have gained their spurs.

We believe this book will answer your questions on mind changing drugs including alcohol. We hope that it will inspire you to join in the eradication of such drugs, first in the church, then in the world; for one thing we need to have it safe when we drive on the highways.

Very important is our section for parents on Preventing Child Drug Addiction with practical points on prevention. How to start early to get children in an anti-drug mood, how to present dangerous drug facts with harmful side effects, and how to look for evidence of drug use. It is necessary to nip in the bud any interest to try drugs. In the event these do not keep one from a desire to experiment, try tough love. Know how to treat overdose, how to restore an addict, and the place of personal religious experience.

The book gives a list of the street drugs in alphabetical order. As to their history, their danger as how they react, their addictive power and treatment.

CHAPTER ONE

DRUG PROBLEMS - ADDICTION TO WITHDRAWAL

IS IT IMPOSSIBLE TO WIN THE DRUG WAR?

ACHIEVING VICTORY

INDIANA WESLEYAN university

Dear Dr. Hansen,

After working with your document, I have these observations.

It is as thorough and as intensive a work on this subject as I have seen in many years. I saw another book on wine from a Wesleyan writer, but it was rather less involved and exegetical than this is. So let me congratulate you on this fine piece of research. The number of cross references and citations from reliable sources makes your study particularly valid.

In His easy yoke,

Joe

Dr. Joe Seaborn
Chair, Center for Christian Studies
Indiana Wesleyan University
Marion, IN 46953

JS/bw

CHAPTER ONE
DRUG PROBLEMS—ADDICTION TO WITHDRAWAL

ACHIEVING VICTORY—IS IT IMPOSSIBLE TO WIN THE DRUG WAR?

Will It Be Safe to Walk Our Streets Again?

Impossible under our present circumstances and knowledge, says Psychopharmacologist Dr. Ronald K. Siegel. Siegel is a researcher at UCLA and a consultant to two presidential commissions, the National Institute on Drug Abuse, and the World Health Organization. He claims that "man's appetite for intoxication is as natural as that of hunger, thirst, and sex" (Siegel 8/2/1989).

In his recent book *Intoxication: Life in Pursuit of Artificial Paradise*, Siegel shows how mind-altering substances have been used by human beings and animals throughout history, in many different cultures.

Dr. Siegel is not the first expert to conclude that man's desire to alter his state of consciousness is a strong elemental drive. Harvard psychiatrist Dr. Lester Grinspoon, author of several books on drugs, says "I have come to the view that humans have a need—perhaps even a drive—to alter their states of consciousness from time to time" (Grinspoon 8/21/1989).

Coffee, my favorite addiction

Researcher Dr. Andrew Weil, of the College of Medicine at the University of Arizona, is of the same belief. "There is not a shred of hope from history or cross-cultural studies to suggest that human beings can live without psychoactive substances," he says.

"SMITHERS, THIS CONFIRMS THAT DRUG USE DATES TO ANCIENT TIMES--THIS HIEROGLYPH SAYS, 'JUST SAY NO'."

The animal world is not exempt. Some parrots and dogs prefer coffee to water. Recent experiments show that monkeys prefer cocaine to food, and would starve themselves to death, taking cocaine instead of food, if they were allowed to do so.

In other scientific experiments, hogs and rats would rather have alcohol and drugs. Siegel points out how the hawkmoth flies erratically after sucking nectar from datura flowers, the narcotic jimson weed. This plant was also used as a painkiller in the ancient Aztec civilization. Today, abstracts are used for pre-anesthetics and in childbirth. British soldiers in Jamestown became intoxicated for days after eating the poisonous narcotic datura (jimson, also known as thorn apple) leaves.

(Do some human addicts make monkeys of themselves?)

In our society, it is difficult to find anyone, (except in religious groups such as some of the Seventh Day Adventists) who does not use one or more of such mind altering drugs as caffeine, alcohol, nicotine, marijuana, opium or cocaine. Why? Is it natural?

Thirty-five million Americans were committed for drug crimes the year (1990) according to Daniel D. Benjamin, former Chief of Staff, U.S. Dept. of Labor in *Undoing Drugs*. Many of us must have thought it was all right. But half of those committed were not regular users until they spent time in prison (Benjamin, 1991, p.103).

Drugs Are Everywhere

Unfortunately, psychiatric drug users by nature tend to cause criminal behavior. One physician said every stab wound that he saw was related to alcohol (ibid, p.107).

Gilda Berger in *Drug Abuse, The Impact on Society* gives an illustration. Two girls in a parking lot break into a new sports car, and quickly rip out a radio and tape deck. They open another door, to their unpleasant surprise they see two policemen. After handcuffing them, they notice the heroin marks on their arms.

Drugs and Crime—Our Number Two Problem—Congressman Dan Burton—Survey:

This follows closely after our number one problem, the Federal Budget Deficit. Some recent surveys put drugs and crime as our number one problem. (See Survey Chapter 3, p.134). A drug addiction of several hundred dollars a day can only be supported by thievery.

Drugs and their attendant crimes are shaking our nation to its very foundation, threatening our very security. Once it was an inner city problem. Now dope peddlers are in rural schools trying to seduce children with the temporary good feelings that drugs bring. It has become a deadly plague. On our short road with six homes two were broken into.

When I was a kid we did not lock our doors. Now we have a security system. There is no security anywhere. Last week in our area five people were killed in drive-by shooting, including three innocent children, the result of drug rivalry. Children are not safe anywhere.

The cost of cocaine babies to the public is $500 million a year according to a study of the American Medical Association; the care cost of the *drug babies* with shrunken heads and brains. It takes years for them to simply be able to walk, talk, and use their arms. Always through life they are a public liability, (A.P. 9/18/91).

On our hospital birth records are Special babies. No parents are listed. Drugs are "the one social issue of our time". Dr. Robert Peterson*

Drug Lords

Elaine Shannon gives an instance of how the drug enforcement is conducted in the south. Her book is *Desperados,*

---

*Psychologist with the National Institute of Mental Health, in *Drug Abuse the Chemical Cop Out,* National Association of Blue Shield Plans.

Latin Drug Lords, U.S. Lawmen and the War America Can't Win.

The new commandant of the Mexican Federal police was feeling important. But he had a visit from a gold bedecked man. It was the wealthy powerful drug lord Rafael Caro Quintero, accompanied by his bodyguards with submachine guns.

"Are you with us," he asked of the commandant. What do you want, silver or lead?"

Humbly, the commandant, indicated silver. "He lived well after that," his agents did not bother the drug business of Caro Quintero in Mexico. (Caro Quintero was later arrested in Mexico, Shannon 1988, p.21).

"The War America Can't Win". Shocking!

"Elaine Shannon's *Desperados* is a remarkable disturbing account of America's outmanned, illfated war against the international drug lords who are threatening the very security of the United States." In this way Haynes Johnson sums up *Desperados* on the jacket cover.

As a nation it is impossible to entirely win the drug war. Individually, as Christians we can win.

Why Do People Take Drugs? To get pep, rest, intoxication.

Some argue that drug use is caused by poor housing and unemployment, which make life so miserable that people need an escape. There is certainly a relationship between drug abuse and social conditions. But it is not the whole story. The inhabitants of a miserable crack house probably have better housing than the proverbial cave dweller's hole. They survived without comfortable heat and without crack. And what about the many poverty-stricken people who shun hard drugs as they would a plague?

I also wonder about the prosperous college-educated yuppie who succumbs. The theory that drug addiction is caused by social deprivation also makes me think of the many famous and wealthy people from the world of entertainment who become addicted. One of them, a personal acquaintance of ours, died of the combination of alcohol and sleeping pills. Drug-taking is an equal opportunity addiction. It does not observe boundaries of social or economic class. Prosperity = drugs available to all.

If drug taking is not a result of our depressed economic and social environment as we have been told, why then do people start taking drugs. Is it natural? Is it all right?

To partake of mind changing drugs is to turn control of your mind over to chemicals. With two results:

1. Experience shows people under the influence of drugs are likely to commit antisocial acts.
2. The further the mind is influenced by chemicals, the further the mind gets from moral and spiritual guidance.

Whatsoever things are pure, whatsoever things are lovely, whatsoever things are of good report, if there be any virtue, if there be any praise, think on these things (Philippians 4:8).

Our Creator has endowed all creation with a euphoria of living, a will to live, regardless of the struggle. Even the lowly earthworm, that never can enjoy a beautiful sunset will strive against all odds to live, even when torn in two.

Drug taking is an attempt to substitute a chemical for the spiritual contentment, which comes from trust in God.

Study Notes

Why Then Do People Supposedly Start Using Drugs?

VS. God's wisdom.

1. **Peer pressure.** "Blessed is the man that walketh not in the counsel of the ungodly" (Psalm 1:1). Select good God-fearing friends.
2. **A desire to conform.** "Be not conformed to this world" (Romans 12:2). Better to be safe than sorry.
3. **Curiosity**—Killed the cat, and may kill you. "Lot's wife looked back . . . and she became a pillar of salt" (Genesis 19:26). In this case, "Ignorance is bliss, tis folly to be wise".
4. **Frustration and depression.** "I will give you rest" (Matthew 11:28). Drugs further frustration, often to the point of causing death.
5. **Weakness** or abnormality of character "Put on the whole armour of God" (Ephesians 6:11). By so doing it becomes the gateway to strength.
6. **Over-prescribing** by physicians. "Let all things be done decently and in order" (1 Corinthians 14:40).
7. **Just "to feel good".** "Enter thou into the joy of the Lord" (Matthew 25:21,23). I dare you to try the joy of the Lord.
8. **To get pep.** To stay awake. Drugs are not foods. What goes up must come down. They invigorate at the expense of the future. "The Lord is the strength of my life" (Psalms 27:1).

To yield to temptations without God's remedy for any of the above, can lead to the horrors of addiction.

ADDICTION DANGER

Addiction is characterized by an overwhelming desire for a drug. The person feels that he cannot get along without it. This can happen easily, to almost anyone. All it needs, according to the World Health Organization, is "an encounter, often fortuitous, between the brain of man and an addictive drug within a favorable context."

I have low blood pressure. One time, in my earlier days, I had a very grueling schedule, which resulted in a feeling of exhaustion. I was continually tired and sleepy. I went to a physician, who prescribed a delicious, pretty pink liquid. It was magic. I felt great. I wanted to work continually day and night. My saintly wife tried it and was delighted by its spark. I took it to a pharmacist to be refilled. He said it was not supposed to be refilled, but he did it. It's a good thing we lost the prescription.

It is easy to see how some of the elite, the high producers in our competitive society, become addicted to drugs. They take the uppers to give them pep and energy, then at night take downers, usually alcohol or sleeping pills, to let them rest. This unnatural use is hard on the heart and other organs, and so often leads to an early death from heart disease or other problems. For Elvis Presley it was a one way trip to Heartbreak Hotel.

"And what will be your drug-of-choice this evening, dear?"

Who Becomes Addicted?

Alcohol. There is no way to predict who will become an addict. Alcoholism can happen to an indigent wino or a U.S. president's wife, as in the case of Betty Ford. Dr. Joel Fort, in his book, *Alcohol Our Biggest Drug Problem*, says, "In spite of our present extensive knowledge of alcohol and its effects, there is no way of knowing who, in picking out a pre-alcoholic personality; that is of predicting in advance who will become alcoholic as a result of using the drug. It should be assumed it can happen to any drinker."[1] So says one who treated hundreds of addicts. The Secretary of Health, Education, and Welfare reached a similar conclusion in a report to Congress in 1971: "What will actually cause a person to become an alcoholic has not yet been fully determined, although it is known that sociological, psychological, physiological, and cultural factors are all significant and probably begin to take effect at an early age in producing a potential alcohol abuser." Statistically, it is known that from 5% to 10%, closer to 10%, of alcohol drinkers will become alcoholic; of these half will die of an alcohol induced early death, an overdose, or in an attempt of withdrawal.

Cigarette. Ninety percent of cigarette smokers become addicted. Dorothy Baldwin in *Wealth and Drugs* shows that 70% who start will smoke all their life.

Crack. Some who try crack become hooked from the start. The most tragic victims are the babies born to alcohol and crack addicts. In 1990 thirty-five percent of babies born in a Milwaukee hospital had cocaine in their blood! Some are born suffering from delirium tremens (a delirium associated with alcoholism and characterized by sweating, trembling, anxiety and frightening hallucinations, like seeing charging pink elephants). Some teenagers become addicted. It seems strange that those who have suffered from the violence of addicted parents would drink and take drugs and themselves become addicted. But they often do.

1. Fort 1973.

(Pink Elephants—Beasts of Bourbon)

The Two Kinds of Addiction

Physical addiction changes the body chemistry; the body adapts to the presence of the drug, building up a *tolerance* to it to get normalcy. But the addict doesn't want normalcy, so he requires more and more in order to get the desired high or kick. A person who has developed a tolerance for cocaine or morphine, for example, may need to take several times the amount of the drug that would kill an ordinary person.

Cobra

Coming off the drug is not easy. In some cases, as with advanced alcoholic or heroin addicts, a sudden withdrawal can lead to what is commonly known as the snakes, or hallucinations. At times it can lead to death. Such withdrawals need to be made under the care of a competent physician. Physical withdrawals are very difficult because the body has come to depend on the drug; it really needs it, and may become ill without it.

Psychological addiction does not effect much change in the body chemistry. The person may think that the drug is necessary for his physical well-being, but this is probably not so. This is the type of addiction that a coffee drinker largely has, although sometimes, with caffeine, there is a combination of physical and psychological addiction. I remember that when my mother was traveling, if she did not get her morning coffee, she would have a miserable headache for the rest of the day.

Withdrawal from a psychological drug addiction causes the body to become only slightly ill. There might be insomnia, irritability, appetite loss, headaches, and nervousness for a few days, but nothing serious.

Quit coffee cold turkey—next day, a headache. Quit heroin cold turkey—next day, cold turkey à la morgue.

Sensible people realize that the price of so much drug taking is too high. They would rather not have the suffering, health risk, and moral stigma that drug addiction brings. For them the forbidden apple can be too expensive. Many drugs create a pleasant sensation, a false and temporary sense of well-being. This masks the harm they are doing to the unwary addict.

(Weather forecast for drug users: Today's sensation will match tomorrow's addiction—Wendell Trogdon)

BRAIN AND THE NERVOUS SYSTEM

All functions, voluntary and involuntary are directed by the chemical and electrical working of the brain. Humans have learned that some brain alluring chemicals deaden the realistic awareness of the brain area and give a temporary false sense of good feeling. Some are willing to get that pleasure regardless of the price of the reaction.

Nerves are made up of bundles of nerve fibers covered with a sheath of fatty cells called myelin. They carry messages to the nerve center—the brain. Messages are carried by means of a small electrical current which is developed by chemical action, similar to a battery.

Drugs, as chemicals, upset the normal workings of the body chemicals that produce the current that transmits the messages. This is why the thinking processes of the brain gets distorted and damaged by drugs. Besides, some drugs seek out fat, and so distress the nerve cells, especially the fatty tissue of the brain. Therefore, drugs alter the way the brain works. The brain not only orders a person's actions, but also regulates the involuntary activities such as lung action, the beating of the heart, digestive organs, and sweating. It takes no Solomon to see that ingested drugs effect every single part of the body.

The Ups and Downs of Drugs

In the following diagram, the straight line represents the ordinary pleasures of a sensible life. Above the line is the added excitement that comes from drug use. But as we know from physics, every action produces a reaction. After the high of drugs, there is a low, as below the line. This soon takes its toll on the nervous system.

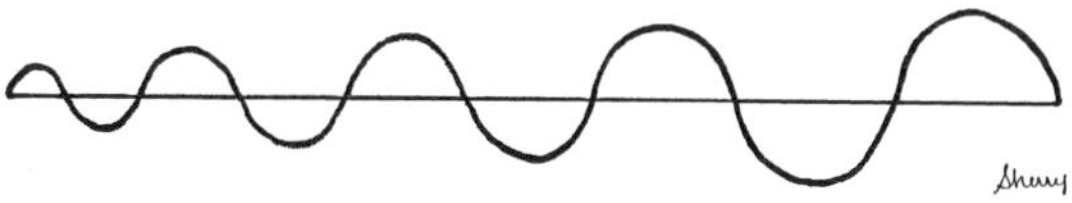

Below the line, reaction brings increasing trouble. That toll may be in brain damage, headaches, sickness, depression, weight loss, skin rash, blindness and death.

The severity of the damage depends on the class of the drugs. See chapter two.

CLASSIFICATION OF DEPENDENCY DRUGS

1. **Depressants** are the most common dependency drugs. As *downers*; they depress the nervous system, give pain relief, and produce a general feeling of well-being, but long-term use can cause depression and nervousness. Downers are: Alcohol, the most popular—can slow down the body so much that death can result. Barbiturates, narcotics, heroin, and its many derivatives, are listed in order of their strengths: heroin, morphine, delaudid, methadrine, methperedine, or demoral, codeine, tranquilizers, and sleeping pills.

2. **Stimulating drugs** (uppers) quicken the nerves by speeding up the

heart action. This gives a feeling of euphoria. These drugs include amphetamines, benzedrine, cocaine, dexodrene, methodrine, nicotine, and caffeine (the most popular).

3. **Hallucinogenic drugs.** Participants get into a dreamlike trance of bewilderment and insensibility to ordinary surroundings. (How would you like to meet such an addict on the highway?) The dream is called a good trip or bad trip. These drugs include: LSD, DMT, DOM, MAD, mescaline, psilocybin, THC (the mild marijuana), and violent PCP (Angel Dust). Frightful trips may continue after quitting the drug.

Danger. Drugs multiply. One drug plus another, even medically prescribed, does not add up to two, but the effect equals four. Ignorance of this has caused many sudden deaths, and why we need to slow the availability of drugs.

FAILURE TO PREVENT DRUG ABUSE

The Failure of Government in the Drug War

The government has lost the war on drugs. It has failed to stem the growth of drugs locally developed in illegal laboratories. It has failed to confiscate 90% of drugs coming into this country from abroad. Drugs are available to just about anyone, anytime, anywhere; and their illegal use is steadily increasing. This has resulted in a wave of drug-related crimes.

The need for jail space is growing faster than jails can be built. Drug use is responsible for this prison crisis. James Austin, executive vice-president of the National Council on Crime and Delinquency, said that drug offenders used to make up from 5% to 10% of the prison population. But in 1989 the percentage had risen to 30% of the prison

Hamilton County's Jails

Old jail with cells for 70 is at the left of the sheriff's residence, which is being restored as a museum.

Moved into new jail in April, 1977—109 cells.

Newest jail being built, room for 288.

population in many states and as high as 40% in Florida (AP 12/06/1989). As I heard one judge say, "Drugs or alcohol are involved in practically every case that comes before me." Date line Indianapolis A.P., "Indiana's prison system, filled beyond capacity and under federal court orders, won't take any more new inmates next week. Department of Justice Correction Commissioners said today, "Pendleton's new Indiana correctional unit will be full before the doors open" (Noblesville Daily Ledger, Noblesville, Indiana, 7/17/1989). Crowded jails are no cause for opening cell-elation.

On the preceding page is a pictorial jail illustration of our home county. The little white jail attached to the sheriff's residence was never full and took care of the county's needs for over 150 years. Then came the 70's and the "do your own thing and drug culture".

We can't keep up with the jail needs, one almost needs a speed reading course to keep up with the figures of drug-related crimes.

A poll showed that the public is losing confidence in the war on cocaine. "Nearly half the respondents in the Medial General Associated Press poll said drugs are a serious problem where they live. That was up 40% from ten months ago. More than four in ten Americans under 45 years old continued to say they know a cocaine user . . . 55% expect the problem to worsen" (AP 5/2/1990).

An exception to the failure of the government on drugs, is on cigarette smoking. After the campaigns of the Surgeon Generals', people quit smoking in droves.

FAILURE OF THE SCHOOLS IN THE DRUG WAR

When I went to grade school, from 1916 to 1924, we had the Bible read to us daily. But now, we Christians have allowed the Supreme Court to forbid the posting of the Ten Commandments in our public schools. In former days, tobacco and alcohol were the drugs of which we were aware. In contrast to present day smoking rooms and smoking teachers, tobacco was never allowed near our Wisconsin public schools. We had never heard of cocaine and narcotics. Our country's culture has dramatically morally deteriorated. Cartoonist Bob Thaves in Frank and Ernest says, "There is nothing wrong with your TV set. Adjust your (moral) standards down."

Many Christian parents believe the only alternatives are to put their children in a Christian school or home school them. Fine, but do those teachers and home schoolers know the facts about drugs to be able to teach them?

The *schools* can't keep up with the drug problem.

Teachers have not been taught drug facts sufficiently. My wife has an M.A. in education, but was never given training in drug prevention. Some teachers are addicts themselves.

By school age, it's getting a little late anyway. The teaching against illegal drug abuse needs to be started much earlier.

It is sadly ironic that Christianity, which is responsible for the origin of public education, has now been kicked out of public education. Until Martin Luther and the Reformation he inspired, there was no public education. The Catholic Church discouraged the reading of the Bible without a priest to interpret it. But Luther said that salvation comes by faith and faith comes from the Word of God, therefore everyone should be able to read the Word of God. Until Luther, only the wealthy, the nobility, or the clerics were educated. (The Jews, who taught their children in the synagogue schools, were an exception.) The Reformed Church, the Puritans, and the established Church of England quickly followed the Lutherans in starting Bible reading schools. The teachings of the early Protestant schools were strictly based upon the Bibles',

MARTIN LUTHER
Portrait by Lucas Cranach, the elder, Uffizi Gallery, France

morals and values, including temperance. This was protected by law.

Amendment one (1) of our Constitution says, "Congress shall make no law respecting an establishment of religion, or prohibiting the *free exercise thereof*."

The words, separation of church and state, do not appear in our constitution. This chicanery was not allowed by the founders. In my opinion, the pagan decisions of our Supreme Court have illegally legislated the Bible and prayer out of our schools, contrary to the public's desires. They are supposed to interpret, not legislate.

"80% disapprove of their banning prayer at graduation ceremonies."[2] Since 1991 the schools can no longer post the Ten Commandments, or teach that it is wrong to lie, cheat, steal, commit adultery or murder. The original Bible-teaching schools now are completely atheistic and pagan. Presently, illegally in some schools, children can no longer bring a Bible into the school or wear a T-shirt with religious symbols, but they can burn the flag. An Atlantic principal told a student who received a notice of a meeting of Christian Athletics, if he were caught again with Christian literature, he would be suspended.

Instead of Bibles, we now have drugs, knives, and guns in our schools. Students and teachers being killed. Armed police roam the schools, and sociologists wondering why there is a drug and crime wave. Ask the Supreme Court. Our schools are the devils playground. Still some Christians don't care enough to vote.

"The most dangerous place for a child to be is in a school," says Joseph Califano, U.S., H.E.W., Secretary. I presume he was not including Christian schools. While I taught at Taylor University, rooted in the Bible, we had an almost heavenly atmosphere.

2. Methvin 11/1992.

My Experience in Placing Bible Teachers in Schools

In 1859, the Iowa State Teacher's Association declared each day's proceedings should be opened with "scripture and prayer." In 1944, under the auspices of the School of Religion at the University of Iowa, with the help of the ministerial association, I put Bible teachers in city public schools. The Bible and Christian values were taught. This project was part of the requirements for my receiving a Ph.D. degree. The three towns were Lone Tree, Conesville, and Columbus City, the area that I pastored. Cooperating was the local Roman Catholic priest who taught the Catholics. A preliminary survey showed 85% in favor. By the end of the first year, that figure had increased to 100%. Complete favorable response continued in the second year. There were far less disciplinary problems; no sassing to teachers, no more fights in the school yard. The scholastic standards of the three schools greatly improved. Church attendance increased, with improved moral tone in the communities. Now many Iowa schools have reversed themselves and are *immoral and completely paganistic.*

How it must have pained Ronald Reagan, when he saw some of his appointees he had confidence in, voting contrary to his Christian ideals and principles.

Failure of the Churches in the Drug War

Do Christian Colleges and Seminaries realize the extent of our drug problem? It is high time that Christian educational institutions have courses that teach the scientific and biblical *facts* about drug abuse. Our clergy are ill equipped. Many have never had a course in drug and alcohol use. Probably, they know less than the kid on the street. They have little practical knowledge of drugs which are driving kids to hell.

Too many churches approve of the worst drug of all. Some think if it is proper in divine service, it certainly must be all right to use otherwise.

Only a tiny minority know that when the Bible was written, there were two meanings for the word wine. Just as today the words punch or cider, have different meanings; one an alcoholic and the other a nonalcoholic drink.

(Wife to husband, "You going to church today?" "Husband with hangover, "Yeah, I need a drink".)

MEDICAL VS. ILLEGAL DRUGS

The leaves of the tree were for healing (Revelation 22:2).

Our drug administration decides which drugs may be used as medicines. Medical students study the use of particular drugs for certain ailments along with the safe amount to be prescribed. The amount or dosage is very important. The fluoridation that helps drinking water is the same chemical used in killing rats.

The use of the same drugs become illegal drugs when not prescribed for an ailment by a licensed physician.

The big problem with many drugs, whether unregulated, regulated, or illegal, is their use causes a pleasant sensation, a false sense of well being, or if an upper, the drug makes one ambitious. At the same time it is self-destructive to the imbiber. It happens so easily.

From the United Nations Conference on Drugs: "Use and possession of, and traffic in, opiates, cocaine, and cannabis are illegal, except for medical or scientific purposes" (N.Y. 1961).

Some addicts go to many physicians for prescriptions, as Kitty Dukakis, the wife of the presidential hopeful did, by changing her appearance.

It was Easter Sunday morning and I had never heard our canary choir of six sing more beautifully in a church. This harmony was superb, their vigor was inspiring. But one could smell the water treatment in the hotels air. Next morning every canary was dead. From then on we carry our own well water when we travel. The amount of chemicals is so important.

OVERDOSE

Yell for help and administer first aid quickly!

Give the drug the least time to work. The victim should not be left alone. An effort must be made to keep the victim conscious, while someone should arrange for medical aid. Call 911, or police, sheriff, or fire station.

If the person is unconscious, lay the person flat on his or her back and loosen clothing, especially around the neck and waist.

If the victim stops breathing, try for artificial resuscitation. Turn the head to one side and take out false teeth or any other obstruction to breathing. Turn the head upward and tilt back, with some support under the shoulders. (See Red Cross poster next page.)

Vomit discharge should be saved for identification.

Study Notes

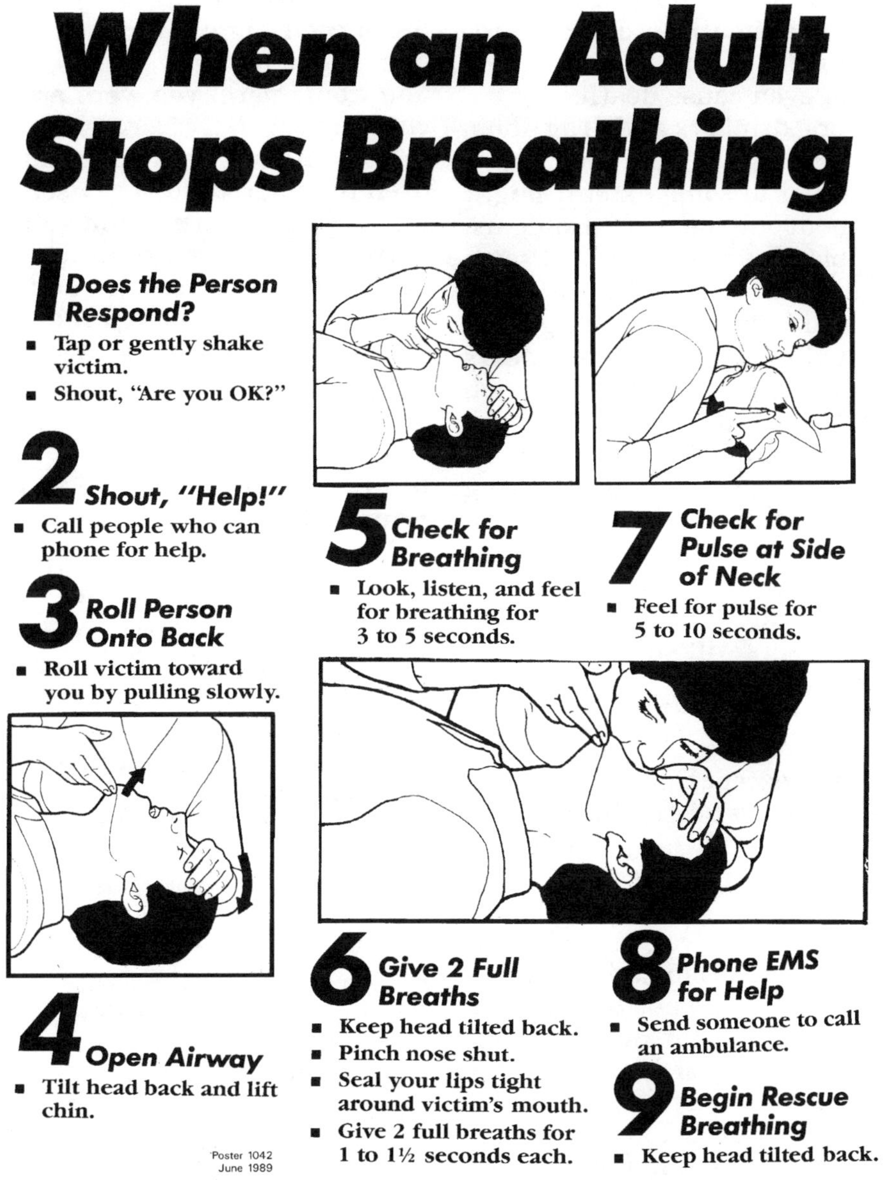

American Red Cross Poster 1042, June, 1989, by Permission

Look for evidences of pills, in the mouth or in pill boxes nearby. Check hypodermic syringes and needle marks on the inside of the forearm. If the victim is a child, get the child to vomit, being careful the throat is clear for breathing.

If the victim vomits while unconscious, be sure an air passage is left open.

PERCENTAGES

If we wanted to set up a model beautiful city, we would have to arrange for a jail. There would be a *certain percentage* of criminals.

We would want trees and flowers, but there would be a percentage who would be sensitive and suffer from hay fever.

Penicillin is normally a life-saving drug, but for a small percentage, including my wife, it can be very injurious, and can even cause death.

All smokers, drinkers and drug abusers do not end up on skid row. Many, though harmed to some extent, might get by without any serious problems. This principle of percentages, that some seem to get by and have fun, must be acknowledged from the beginning of instruction. Otherwise if kids see peers enjoying drugs, perhaps getting rich from street peddling, they will think Mom and Dad are all wrong: their efforts will have failed. But after saying that, the chances of trouble are high and important. Would we ride a roller coaster if we knew that once in twenty times it would kill? The facts are a big chance drug users will suffer.

A percentage of up to 10% of moderate alcohol drinkers will become alcoholics, others will not. The same is true of other drugs, except that a larger percentage of those who try heroin and crack lose control. Ninety percent of cigarette smokers become addicted to tobacco.

Sadly, prospective drug users look at those who do not become addicted and believe they also will not be affected.

You have heard about neighbor *Pete* who has smoked all of his life and is now apparently healthy in his nineties. How is it he didn't die before 65? George Burns, who was booked in London for a show on his 100th birthday, was interviewed in his late 90's. He was asked if it was true that he used 20 cigars a day. He answered in the affirmative. Did he drink? Yes. Is it true that he dated young girls? Yes. What does your doctor say about this? "He's dead!" Granted it happens, there are exceptions, but here again we must consider percentages. The greater percentage of heavy smokers die young, many in their 50s. Is it worth taking a chance? Would you go on an airplane flight if you knew that 5% of their flights were going to crash? You might if you were a fighter pilot. You would not if you were privileged to choose.

Percentages are important for children to understand. They see some using and selling drugs and getting away with it. They need to understand the danger of how some get addicted and how some are sent to jail or prison or killed. Defy the odds-play the percentages.

PRESENT PAGAN CULTURE

Many of Our Country's Pioneers Sought Religious Freedom

They established a Christian culture. The Supreme Court 100 years ago ruled: "This is a Christian nation" (143 U.S. 457, Feb. 22, 1892). But no more. Now, in 1992, in my opinion, pagans in the Supreme Court (which opens with prayer) rule out prayer, Bible study, and any mention of God in our schools. Confucius, Mohammed, and Satanism can be studied, but not Moses or Christ. Since morals are based on the Bible, schools may no longer teach moral values. We have become a secular, pagan nation, a conclusion sadly reached by Seminary Professor Kenneth Hamilton in his 1966 book, *God is Dead.* Hamilton is referring to our pagan culture with its "Christian atheist" theologians, and also, "Certainly our's is one which gives slight cultural support for the Christian faith".[3]

Jesus foresaw an eventual falling away. In His last fervent prayer in the garden, He prayed, "Father, I pray that they might be one that the world might believe." We are not one and the world does not believe, nor do we have a Christian culture. Hamilton is not in any way depreciating the personal relationship of sanctified Christians who

3. Hamilton 1966.

"find that the Living God is as near at hand as faith has always found its Lord to be" (1966). Hamilton ends his book with this piece of advice to Christians: "The root of the matter is that we hold fast to Christ, and not to any Christ who may happen to appeal to the contemporary religious consciousness, but to the Word made flesh, the Son of the Living God." (See Hamilton in chapter's end notes.)

Without that change in our culture, without a national religious revival, and anti-drug teaching in our schools our drug problem (and the immorality and crime that go with it) will never diminish. It will get worse.

(Entrance sign in Texas: "Our God Lives, Sorry About Yours").

Grape Juice and Hearts

Occasionally articles appear telling how a glass of wine a day may be good for your heart and prolong life. Since alcohol is a poison, and some researchers say that alcohol has no beneficial health effects, I never paid much attention to such articles. Besides ten percent of all moderate drinkers become alcoholics.

Now Dr. John David Folts, medical educator and cardiologist at the University of Wisconsin, got to the core of the matter. It is not the alcohol that is beneficial but the healthful elements of grape juice, primarily in this case the compounds of *flavonoids.** They reduce the activity of platelets, the blood cells that gather together to form clots.

In his report to the American College of Cardiology meeting in Anaheim, California, March 1997, Dr. Folts gave the results of the two studies. One was with five monkeys and the other with five humans. He found that drinking a glass of purple grape juice each day reduced by 40% the platelets sticking together helping to prevent blood clots to the brain which can cause strokes.

*See flavonoids under Tea, in Chapter 2.

Folts believes that a medicine could be made from grapes that would prevent heart attack. Such a medicine would be better than aspirin, which boosts adrenalin levels.

From the current issue of the journal, Science, June 1997, a group of University of Illinois scientists, discovered *resveratrol*—a natural substance found in raisins and grapes—appears to be a powerful cancer-fighting agent. It keeps healthy cells from becoming cancerous, while inhibiting the spread of cells that are already malignant.

Folts, research was funded by Nistricia Research Foundation of the Netherlands, and the Rennebohm Foundation of Wisconsin, and Welch Foods Inc." (Doug Lerry, U.S.A., Today).

PREVENTING CHILD DRUG ADDICTION

Get to Your Children Before Somebody Else Does

So It's Up to Mom and Dad

Who is going to train and protect the child? The government can't. The public schools won't. Society cannot, churches don't. So, it's up to Mom and Dad! But Mom and Dad often need to be trained by Christian abstinent educational institutions. Old ways no longer suffice. As popular practicing clinical psychologist Dr. Robert Schwebel writes in his greatly acclaimed book *Saying No Is Not Enough*: "Some of them [parents] grew up in an era when drugs were definitely not an option, and can't imagine that chemical substances are available to their children. They are far too removed from today's youth, including their own, to recognize what is happening."[4] The *good old days* are gone. Parents need current *factual* knowledge of our drug problem and how

4. Schwebel 1989.

to deal with it. There must be constant input like as from this book to counteract drugs in the schools and elsewhere.

How to Prevent Your Child Becoming Addicted

"Train up a child in the way he should go; and when he is old, he will not depart from it" (Proverbs 22:6). (A "proverb"—ordinarily true, but not an undeniable divine law.)

"As the twig is bent, the tree's inclined."

It is better to build a fence at the top of the cliff than a hospital at the bottom. But we have a problem:

"I was shapen in iniquity; and in sin did my mother conceive me" (Psalms 51:5). This means that it is perfectly natural for children to want their own way. They may rebel against authority when that authority is contrary to their desires. There are differences in children; but if a young child is allowed to be rebellious he will likely become unmanageable later on. Children should be taught obedience and values as toddlers, just as they learn a language. As writes Dobson, "A young child must quickly learn the meaning of NO!"[5] Later it becomes increasingly difficult, and after puberty, perhaps even impossible without professional help.

Spare the Rod and Spoil the Child

"Chasten thy son while there is hope" (Proverbs 19:18). The modern teaching which condemns corporal punishment is of the devil. It is partly responsible for our wave of addiction. God's way is perfectly clear: "Withhold not correction from the child: for if thou beatest him with the rod, he shall not die" (Proverbs 23:13). "Thou shalt beat him with the rod, and shalt deliver his soul from hell" (Proverbs 23:14).

5. Dobson 1989.

In the 1957 Detroit paddling case, the U.S. Supreme Court ruled: "Corporal punishment is a legal means of student discipline."[6] (Bad news for kids: Rebels without applause.)

Corporal punishment is not for babies, nor is it to be used by unloving parents. During and after discipline, parents must make it clear that they love the child, and that is the reason for the discipline. For whom the Lord loveth he chastens (Hebrews 12:6). "If ye be without chastisement, whereof all are partakers, then are ye bastards, and not sons" (Hebrews 12:8).

Are there *experts* who speak from theory, but have had no children? Much acclaimed Susannah Wesley was the mother of seventeen children. Included were John Wesley, evangelist, theologian, and founder of the Methodist Church, and also Charles Wesley, the Christian songwriter. She found time to pray with each one, but also had this to say:

"In order to form the minds of children, the first thing to be done is to conquer the will, and bring them into an obedient temper. For by neglecting timely correction, they will contract a stubbornness and obstinacy which is hardly ever conquered, and never without using such severity as would be painful to me and the child." I once had to deal with a student with the severity Mrs. Wesley mentions. It happened while I was the president of a Christian state accredited high school in central Indiana. We did not ordinarily take in problem students, but this time we did. He was a charming orphan who had been kicked out of many schools for stealing cars. No more schools would take him.

He settled in nicely for about a month and then one evening took some of the fellows for a joyride in the dean of men's

6. Strack 1985. *Drugs and Drinking.*

car. He pointed out some sights including where he went to church.

The dean of men, the principal, and I gave him a nasty paddling. After it was over we had prayer, during which he forgave us and thanked us. There were no more car thefts. Now a model student, he married a girl from one of the strictest and most spiritual families of the school's clientele. Deal properly with the seat of understanding, the mind gets straightened out. A paddle can send youth up right creek.

Daughter, Sylvia Hansen and Jumbo

Christian psychologist Dr. James Dobson agrees with Susannah Wesley. He writes in *Parenting is Not For Cowards,* "You must rule them with the rational mind."[7] "Grab the reins of authority early."[8]

We started teaching our two children the word *NO* along with Bible instruction. Our daughter was reading at age three. Previous to my university teaching, we home schooled our daughter during our evangelistic tours with our Bible Birds, then put her in our Christian high school. She graduated *magna cum laude* from a Christian college.

Our son also was an honor student all through high school and college. At three years of age, he started helping us on Sundays, as we traveled with our evangelistic Bible Bird programs. He still is assisting, thirty years later, as we preach the Gospel, including abstinence from drugs. He developed a computer language that his boss leased for a million dollars.

Neither of our children ever sassed or openly disobeyed us. We started Christian training and strict discipline when they were toddlers. There never was a hint of drug addiction. Do I sound like a proud papa?

When one starts early with both love and spanking, there is usually little need for spanking later. Spanking is love from the bottom up. However, continued care and concern are always necessary.

The fifth commandment is pertinent here. "Honour thy father and thy mother: that thy days may be long upon the land" (Exodus 20:12).

None of this loving correction can be used as an excuse for child abuse by unloving parents. "Provoke not your children to anger, less they be discouraged." Colossians 3:21. Evidence of child abuse should be reported to the police, district attorney or call 1-800-4-A-Child.

I was an abused child. Or so I thought when disciplined. That razor strap felt terrible. I lost my temper, my father helped me find it. Later, I was appreciative and thanked God and my father.

But authority must also dispense rewards for doing good, as well as punishment for disobedience. A reward tells a child that you like what he has done, it's more fun for both parent and child. Simple things—a bear hug and a com-

7. Dobson 1987.
8. Ibid, p.88.

pliment go a long way. Besides being a way of salvation, is not the Bible a book of blessings for doing good, as well as punishment for evil? "The memory of the just is blessed: but the name of the wicked shall rot" (Proverbs 10:7).

Practical Tips

Help a small child to understand the bad effects of drugs. Tell him about the short-term effects. Children do not live in the past, or in the future. They are only concerned about now. A child is not particularly interested in a long life. Neither are some adults. They say, "I'll die of something eventually, I might as well enjoy myself while living." I've seen that enjoyment turn into suffering. Live like there is no tomorrow . . . there may not be.

Tell the child there are good medicines, but also bad drugs.

Ask the child if he or she would like to taste a drug. Put a piece of quinine in a raisin and have the child chew it. Later, be sure to tell the child it was a drugged raisin, so as not to spoil his or her taste for raisins. Tell the child that if he or she uses drugs their teeth might get brown and ugly. They might not be able to have fun with toys. Kids get killed because they try to ride bikes after they have taken drugs or alcohol. Say they might get sick and have a sore throat and be required to take some horrible-tasting medicine. Children like to feel strong. Tell the boy tobacco will likely keep him from getting big and strong. Ask him, "Do you want to be a weakling?" Tell children drugs would make it hard for them to learn at school. They might get thrown out of school. They don't want to be dummies, do they, with nasty brown teeth and stinking breath?

Tell children that their hair, clothing, and breath will stink like an ash tray if they smoke. Have them smell an ash tray. They are getting harder to find; try a smoking section.

Dad told me that his father gave him a batch of cigars and told him to smoke them all up. He got terribly sick, and said he never smoked again.

When I was a kid my folks took me through the state penitentiary in Waupon, Wisconsin. The somber inmates were making rope in a horribly dusty and terribly noisy room. I got the point.

Jodi Freeman, in *How to Drug Proof Children*,[9] a book which I highly recommend, suggests that a child be taken to a funeral of a child killed by drugs or a drunk driver.

Kids like to play. Tell them drugs will keep them from being good at sports. Top basketball player Len Bias, and champion football player Don Rogers died from taking cocaine. No more ball playing for them.

Kids really like approval. Constantly give it to them as a reward for being good. Otherwise they may seek approval from their peers in dangerous ways.

It should be impressed on children that if they start to take drugs, drugs may capture them, so that they may not be able to stop. They may run out of money, be unable to get any more drugs, and go crazy. The drug bandwagon has no brakes.

Jodi Freeman suggests that children make a scrapbook. A sample entry might read:

I won't smoke because ___________.

Another suggestion is to have a child make a picture of what smoking does to the lungs.

Children learn:

By watching and listening. *Monkey see, monkey do.* Children should learn drug prevention just as they learn the language by listening and watching. As

9. Freeman 1989.

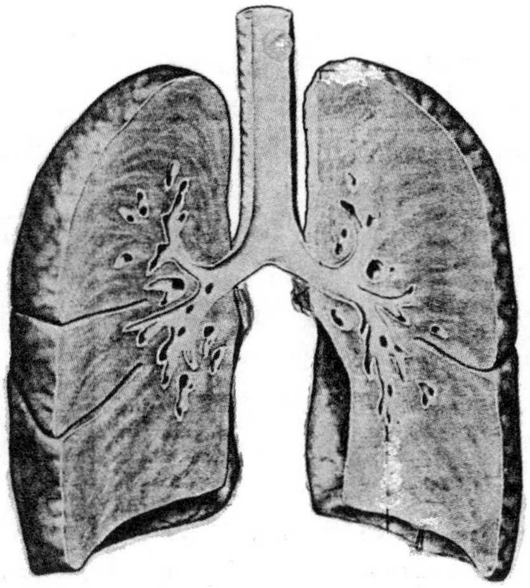

An ordinary healthy lung

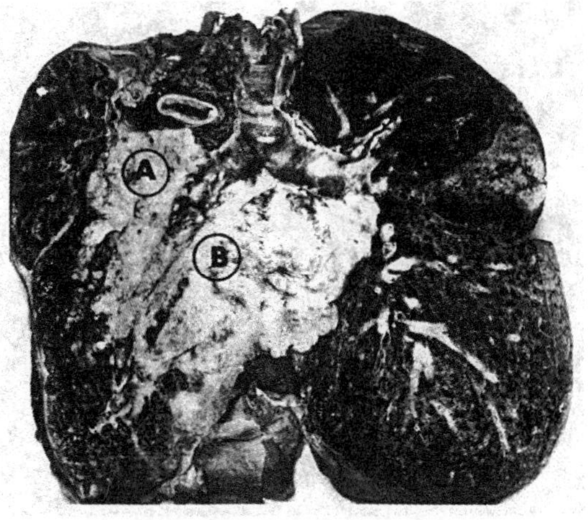

Blackened lung from smoking
(Source: American Cancer Society)

a child I saw drunks kicked out of a saloon and lying on a sidewalk across from my father's business place. I early learned not to use alcohol. Later when peers tried to get me to experiment, I had no need to experiment. I knew the answers, I said NO!

It takes some study to know the facts, to keep ahead of what the kids learn on the streets. This information is given in Chapter 2 listing each drug alphabetically. The proper names are given and also the various street names that the drugs go under.

Most drug users start with the *Gateway Drugs*, alcohol, tobacco and marijuana. Close the gates!

"Drugs! Alcohol!
Where Do Kids Get Their Crazy Ideas?"
As Gene Herndon sees it, Noblesville Daily Ledger—January 1, 1980

Self Esteem

It is believed that children with a proper self-esteem are less likely to be negatively influenced. It is easier for them to say *NO!*

In an experiment children were told that the lowest locker numbers were given to the students with the lowest ability. The numbers were given out randomly with no reference to I.Q. At the end of the year, those with the lowest numbers tended to have the lowest grades. If you would not belittle your boss to his or her face, you should not degrade your child (or spouse).

Low self-esteem is fertile ground for drug use. Self confidence can bring a reversal of peer pressure. God loves you. "I can do all things through Christ which strengtheneth me" (Philippians 4:13). "For God so loved the world, that he gave his only begotten Son" (John 3:16).

Love a child. Show love. Praise for being good.

Say No to Drugs!

We want our offspring to be smart, to be a champ; to leave drugs alone. We do not want them to be dumb, and have people take advantage of them, get their brains fried with drugs, and become dumb fools.

There is one positive, foolproof means of prevention: teach total abstinence! Don't take the first drink. Don't take the first puff. Don't take the first pill. This is a positive position.

Our former President's wife, Nancy Reagan, campaigned to say *NO* to drugs.

There is a value judgment here. If it is wrong, say *NO!* "Say No Clubs" have been very helpful. They give a positive note. They help to get rid of boredom and hopelessness with a positive outlook. Sometimes, games, sports, and physical exercise give a positive direction. Limit TV. Young people like to feel grown up. Give them chores. Encourage a part-time job. Scouting and campfire groups under good supervision are great. They take adult time. So? My dad was a scoutmaster. We had good clean instruction and fun. Kids need lots of activity. Give it to them under Christian supervision. Trips. Trips to the museum, to the zoo, to trails in the forest and parks. Young people's church conventions, etc.

A Happy Home

A government study of 47,240 households by The National Study for Health Statistics says, "Married men and women are less likely to drink heavily, smoke and engage in risky behavior."

Studies show that there is a smaller percentage of addicts where there is a cordial relationship, a pleasant atmosphere in the home. But, where there are home problems, unfortunately all too often solutions are not aggressively sought in and for the home. Rather, some try to forget about the troubles with a bottle or a pill.

How can a parent who smokes, drinks, and uses illegal drugs qualify as a proper guard against drug use? Well, an effort may be better than nothing.

There is a better way. No successful home can be built on the philosophy of doing your own thing. To make a good ho*me*, forget about the "me" in it. There must be give and take, probably more give than take. Children of part-time homes, broken homes, divorced homes, and unhappy homes are at a greater drug risk.

"Wives love your husbands. Husbands love your wives." Let there not be any gender blurring.

"A happy family is an early heaven," wrote Sir John Bowing. Where there is confusion in the home, too often children grow up with no sense of stability, or security, and they may try to find it in drugs.

A best insurance against drugs is a solid home life. Generally speaking, the more parents are involved with their children, the healthier the family, the less will be the likelihood drugs will enter the home. "So many parents seem to believe children will grow up and become solid adults without the continuous involvement of parents. Not so."[10]

Please let me get personal for a bit. My mother, as early as I can remember, taught me much about God. I was taken to Church and Sunday School.

In the *Encyclopedia Americana* is reference to the noted Juvenile Judge Benjamin B. Lensey. He once remarked, "Children who go to Sunday School and have a pet are not brought up in my court." Give a boy a dog, neither will go astray. I can vouch for the value of early Christian training, from

10. Voth and Nahab 1987.

what I saw as a Probation Officer in Minneapolis.

My father, a Sunday School teacher and Scout Master, was a good example. Every child needs a father. But it is possible, though much harder, for a lone, loving, concerned mother to ensure that a child receives proper religious training.

Psychiatrists make the point that the parents must never let down their guard in the battle against evil, against drugs. Kids will hear about the enticing use of drugs. Prepare them. Give a better alternative. Reinforce the child's good behavior and good judgments. Accentuate the positive.

"Children who go to Sunday School seldom get on drugs" (CBS TV "Series on Drugs", Nov. 2, 1990).

The parent must keep close to the child. The child should feel free to be able to commune with the parent as one who loves him. The parent should realize that the child needs a constant friend who is sympathetic; and to whom the child can go for answers instead of to the street. (A friend at home, need not to roam) Trogdon.

With such constant care we are likely to have a drug free child. However, even with all our loving care, we have to realize every child is influenced by inherited genes, and an environment other than the home. Every child has a free will and might stray. I am sure that God gave Adam and Eve the best of nurturing, but they strayed. If yours stray, when you have done your best, don't blame yourself.

Study Notes

Evidence of Drug Use

The parent should constantly be looking for tell-tale signs of drug use (see Characteristic Behavior of Addicts, under ADDICTION). If an honest child becomes an addict, he or she will likely become a liar if they know parents will disapprove. As well as the behavior, look for physical evidence of drug use.

Physical clues indicating drug use are: Small spoons for measuring, spoons blackened by heat; blood-stained cotton that has been placed over punctures; burn holes in clothing; pockets of rolling paper for marijuana; eye drops; rubbing alcohol; small plastic bags.

Addicts are very ingenious in hiding drugs and paraphernalia. You have a desire to trust your child, but if you have the slightest suspicion, you must realize that the child's very future and life may be at stake. The price of privacy may be beyond your reach. Check everything—clothes, under the mattress, in drawers, between books—everything. Have there been valuables and money missing? Or medical drugs and prescriptions? Is there incense to cover marijuana smoke? *Watch, check, watch!*

"It takes most parents a year before they realize that their child is on drugs" (National Parents Research Institute for Drug Education).

Don't take chances. Have urinary and blood samples taken.

If evidence of drug use is found, confront the child and use every possible means to get them off drugs. On an NBC talk show, one woman said it cost her $100,000 to get her daughter off drugs (12/24/1991).

Enabling? Do not enable drug use. Don't try to cover it up. Helping the child is most important. Meet it head on. Let them understand they must pay the consequences of this behavior even if it means going to jail.

Resources are available. (See Resources at the end of this chapter.) I recommend Dr. Robert Schebel's *Saying No Is Not Enough*. Get pastoral and divine help; professional help may be necessary.

To discuss complete treatment would take a whole book, but there are books available; we have recommended some.

If there is a problem, stay with the child. Don't kick him out, don't give up. There may be a ray of hope. Not all teenagers who experiment with dope develop a dependency. Too many do, but most don't. Even some regular users get along. Only a percentage get into hard, harmful use and dependency. But taking a chance is dangerous. Would a child ride a roller-coaster if he knew that one of ten rides someone would get killed? One out of 10 drug users will get hooked and possibly killed.

But every child is given a free will. No matter how much good training the child has, he or she might go wrong. If the child does go wrong, and you have done your best to train him or her, do not blame yourself. God Himself could not keep Adam and Eve on the straight and narrow.

RELIGION VS. ALCOHOLISM

One highly overriding factor is religion. From the U.S. *Seventh Special Report to Congress on Alcohol and Health*, January 1990, p. 121, we find a listing of cancers caused by alcohol: liver, esophagus, nasopharynx and larynx. Then we find these words. "The incidence of such cancers is notably lower in religious groups who abstain from alcohol use."[11]

To be disposed to alcoholism is not a predestined sentence. Don't take the first drink.

The following pages list the countries and the amount of alcohol that they import from the U.S. You will look in vain to find Moslem countries such as Saudi

11. Driver and Swann 1987.

Arabia, Iran, Kuwait or Syria. They take very seriously Mohammed's advice not to use alcohol. Because of their religion, they do not have alcoholic and drug problems as we do. Is it strange that they fear Western Christianity? Shocking?

The psychopharmacologists are probably right, saying it is impossible to win the drug war. But conscientious Christians are also citizens of the Kingdom of God. They are armed with the breast plate of righteousness (Ephesians 6:14) and following Christ's admonition, "And ye shall know the truth (including drug facts), and the truth shall make you free" (John 8:32).

From the *American Journal of Public Health* of January 1985, "Lifelong abstainers and past drinkers attend church more frequently than other categories of drinkers."[12] The study showed that the less people attended church, the more they drank. A matter of choice.

In *Winds of Change*, Dr. Ernest H.J. Steed relates how Pope John Paul II, at his official inauguration, spoke on the topic "The Virtue of Temperance," and campaigns in his travels against alcohol and other drugs.[13]

SIDE EFFECTS OF DRUGS

Most drugs, medically prescribed and those falsely labeled recreational, are poisonous and have negative side effects. Side effects are more harmful to some individuals than to others. This I recently found out.

I was suffering from a very crippling back pain, and my physician prescribed a relaxing drug. The next day, I was driving along a four-lane highway and the next thing I knew I was regaining consciousness in a hospital bed.

12. Bosley 1986.
13. Steed 1987.

I was told that I was there because of a drug reaction. A truck driver visited me and told me what had happened. He said I was driving about 45 miles per hour from one lane to the other. Although traffic usually travels at 60 miles per hour here, no one had the courage to pass me. Traffic was stretched out in a long chain behind me. The C.B. radios were buzzing about the drunk driver up ahead. The truck driver said I mostly kept to the pavements of both lanes even though I ran over a 55 mile per hour sign. But he was afraid I would cross the median and hit other cars head on.

The courageous truck driver, Jerry Durham, told me how he had pulled alongside my wagon and taken a side swipe. However, he passed me, pulled in front of my car, and put on his brakes. His poor tires were sending out smoke signals. He not only had to stop his truck, but also my pushing car. When the truck driver finally had me stopped, he got out, walked back to my car and turned off the ignition. Then, as someone called the paramedics, he took out my billfold to see who this crazy driver was. I could have killed myself and others. In gratitude, I sent a check to this good Samaritan.

No one was hurt in this extraordinary incident, although there was $4000 worth of damages to my station wagon. I will not be taking *soma 350* and *nalfon* again, no matter who prescribes them. They multiply.

U.S. Commercial Exports of Liquor by Class and Country of Destination, 1988

(In proof gallons)

COUNTRY OF DESTINATION	GRAND TOTAL	WHISKEY			NON-WHISKEY						
		Bourbon	Other	Total	Rum	Brandy	Gin	Vodka	Cordials	N.E.S.	Total
Argentina	34,262	0	34,262	34,262	0	0	0	0	0	0	0
Australia	1,880,227	1,495,182	367,801	1,862,983	0	0	0	180	637	16,427	17,244
Austria	71,257	63,728	7,183	70,911	0	0	0	0	0	346	346
Bahamas	130,889	5,506	9,490	14,996	54,296	0	0	0	15,470	46,128	115,893
Bahrain	2,204	1,255	493	1,748	0	0	0	0	0	456	456
Barbados	6,517	0	343	343	0	0	0	1,212	0	4,962	6,174
Belgium	220,961	30,626	32,539	63,165	21,690	0	16,681	71,243	47,636	546	157,796
Belize	15,589	826	0	826	4,936	1,243	0	490	0	8,094	14,763
Benin	1,617	1,617	0	1,617	0	0	0	0	0	0	0
Bermuda	46,082	982	1,169	2,151	0	0	0	35,217	3,926	4,788	43,931
Bolivia	10,354	0	0	0	10,354	0	0	0	0	0	10,354
British Pacific Islands	124	0	124	124	0	0	0	0	0	0	0
British Virgin Islands	87,843	242	1,268	1,510	33,547	3,488	1,076	13,471	237	34,514	86,333
Brazil	18,391	12,916	5,475	18,391	0	0	0	0	0	0	0
Bulgaria	7,418	7,418	0	7,418	0	0	0	0	0	0	0
Canada	1,387,417	143,404	825,530	968,934	28,548	38,759	10,177	6,661	261,050	73,288	418,483
Cayman Islands	40,628	773	970	1,743	1,902	0	228	6,130	1,367	29,258	38,885
Chile	38,491	17,575	0	17,575	12,324	0	0	6,264	2,328	0	20,916
China (Taiwan)	43,647	7,582	15,991	23,573	2,593	0	2,048	13,463	774	1,196	20,074
Colombia	39,086	0	629	629	0	2,182	1,560	7,917	10,453	16,346	38,457
Costa Rica	3,793	2,501	367	2,868	0	0	0	0	0	925	925
Cyprus	2,543	677	698	1,375	704	0	0	464	0	0	1,168
Czechoslovakia	378	378	0	378	0	0	0	0	0	0	0
Denmark	52,062	34,656	3,739	38,395	0	0	0	13,667	0	0	13,667
Djibouti	118	0	118	118	0	0	0	0	0	0	0
Dominican Republic	58,507	604	12,771	13,375	1,156	5,917	3,277	2,548	6,764	25,430	45,132
Ecuador	57,459	0	6,582	6,582	23,764	190	0	13,253	0	13,667	50,877
Egypt	2,468	178	2,088	2,266	0	0	0	0	0	202	202
El Salvador	20,875	0	9,806	9,806	5,559	878	797	2,483	1,352	0	11,069
Federal Republic of Germany	2,151,915	1,992,920	131,900	2,124,820	3,478	7,437	0	4,675	0	11,505	27,095
Finland	15,206	6,039	0	6,039	7,136	481	0	1,109	441	0	9,167
French Indian Ocean Area	272	0	130	130	0	0	0	0	142	0	142
France	531,228	361,684	130,708	492,392	0	0	0	0	3,770	35,066	38,836
French West Indies	24,414	742	756	1,498	6,275	0	0	1,296	2,000	13,345	22,916
Ghana	1,727	1,727	0	1,727	0	0	0	0	0	0	0
Gibraltar	174	174	0	174	0	0	0	0	0	0	0
Greece	95,460	55,340	28,973	84,313	3,967	2,861	0	1,528	2,218	571	11,147
Guatemala	4,932	268	3,668	3,936	0	675	0	0	0	321	996
Guinea	3,925	0	0	0	0	0	760	0	0	3,165	3,925
Guyana	802	0	457	457	0	0	0	0	0	345	345
Haiti	28,168	16,693	11,356	28,049	0	0	0	119	0	0	119
Honduras	2,448	525	949	1,474	0	0	0	974	0	0	974
Hong Kong	127,454	30,749	36,238	66,987	0	8,525	5,564	40,058	2,627	2,706	60,471
Iceland	83,926	1,325	1,423	2,748	4,788	361	1,791	70,327	3,911	0	81,178
Indonesia	6,893	0	0	0	0	931	0	5,962	0	0	6,893
Ireland	28,042	923	10,749	11,672	0	0	0	0	4,793	11,577	16,370
Israel	32,547	7,423	1,742	9,165	190	0	760	7,749	4,648	10,135	23,382
Italy	380,956	296,529	73,339	369,868	2,153	0	0	1,020	3,738	4,177	11,088
Jamaica	32,132	1,160	10,982	12,142	3,648	0	1,018	792	1,846	12,686	19,990
Japan	4,384,397	3,586,977	375,296	3,962,273	53,381	12,606	19,458	43,997	8,020	284,662	422,124

U.S. Commercial Exports of Liquor by Class and Country of Destination, 1988 (continued)

(In proof gallons)

COUNTRY OF DESTINATION	GRAND TOTAL	WHISKEY Bourbon	WHISKEY Other	WHISKEY Total	NON-WHISKEY Rum	NON-WHISKEY Brandy	NON-WHISKEY Gin	NON-WHISKEY Vodka	NON-WHISKEY Cordials	NON-WHISKEY N.E.S.	NON-WHISKEY Total
Kenya	662	331	331	662	0	0	0	0	0	0	0
Korea, Republic of	23,763	11,353	3,971	15,324	0	0	0	628	311	7,500	8,439
Lebanon	11,173	571	2,660	3,231	3,960	0	732	0	1,902	1,348	7,942
Liberia	2,735	802	1,093	1,895	840	0	0	0	0	0	840
Malaysia	18,830	11,767	3,050	14,817	0	0	0	4,013	0	0	4,013
Malta	1,471	465	665	1,130	0	0	0	0	0	341	341
Mauritania	2,030	0	0	0	0	0	0	0	0	2,030	2,030
Mexico	817,843	26,548	306,140	332,688	189,841	226,782	1,096	1,632	14,230	51,574	485,155
Netherlands Antilles	385,364	54,755	18,053	72,808	115,977	4,251	6,444	22,206	26,794	136,884	312,556
Netherlands	603,668	259,749	120,678	380,427	90,389	24,245	2,587	26,487	27,433	52,100	223,241
New Caledonia	2,327	1,049	736	1,785	0	0	0	0	0	542	542
New Zealand	153,843	118,808	28,877	147,685	2,948	0	0	2,235	975	0	6,158
Nigeria	2,161	2,161	0	2,161	0	0	0	0	0	0	0
Norway	271,482	2,979	14,607	17,586	0	0	2,101	246,355	5,440	0	253,896
Other Pacific Islands	1,262	674	588	1,262	0	0	0	0	0	0	0
Pakistan	1,612	667	0	667	0	0	0	0	0	945	945
Panama	124,300	9,963	4,768	14,731	33,228	516	0	20,032	4,683	51,110	109,569
Papua New Guinea	2,074	2,074	0	2,074	0	0	0	0	0	0	0
Paraguay	19,067	11,864	5,578	17,442	0	0	0	0	0	1,625	1,625
Peru	2,905	410	0	410	0	0	0	0	0	2,495	2,495
Philippines	42,704	5,692	5,298	10,990	8,719	8,816	5,360	2,973	0	5,846	31,714
Poland	31,223	1,778	4,539	6,317	6,206	0	16,190	0	0	2,510	24,906
Portugal	7,184	6,076	1,108	7,184	0	0	0	0	0	0	0
Singapore	119,635	29,547	18,581	48,128	0	0	0	14,646	0	56,858	71,507
South Africa	45,760	16,673	14,074	30,747	0	0	0	5,702	1,623	7,688	15,013
Spain	88,519	59,250	29,025	88,275	0	0	0	0	244	0	244
Sri Lanka	1,521	190	1,179	1,369	0	152	0	0	0	0	152
Sweden	227,895	19,228	12,425	31,653	9,014	0	0	132,722	54,506	0	196,242
Switzerland	40,348	25,132	15,003	40,135	0	213	0	0	0	0	213
Thailand	49,674	5,691	9,726	15,417	7,496	0	0	23,625	0	3,136	34,257
Trust Territories of the Pacific	12,463	972	1,162	2,134	1,077	0	0	9,019	0	233	10,329
Trinidad & Tobago	6,880	0	0	0	0	0	0	0	0	6,880	6,880
Tunisia	693	0	0	0	0	0	0	500	193	0	693
Turkey	710	710	0	710	0	0	0	0	0	0	0
Turks Island	2,822	0	0	0	0	164	0	1,121	197	1,340	2,822
United Arab Emirates	5,959	2,183	2,651	4,834	0	0	0	0	0	1,125	1,125
United Kingdom	550,726	219,172	228,412	447,584	58,030	8,325	0	13,797	1,926	21,064	103,142
Uruguay	17,391	4,675	1,494	6,169	0	0	0	0	0	11,222	11,222
U.S.S.R.	489	242	0	242	0	0	0	0	247	0	247
Venezuela	114,626	21,311	65,763	87,074	0	0	0	0	25,860	1,692	27,552
Western Samoa	374	0	0	0	0	0	0	374	0	0	374
Yugoslavia	21,012	1,663	8,876	10,539	0	0	0	0	10,473	0	10,473
TOTAL	16,055,409	9,126,999	3,089,213	12,216,212	814,117	360,008	99,692	902,361	567,084	1,095,915	3,839,197

NOTE: proof gallon equals a standard U.S. gallon of 231 cubic inches at 60 degrees Farenheit containing 50% ethyl alcohol by volume (100 proof).
N.E.S. = Not Elsewhere Specified.

SOURCE: Bureau of the Census, U.S. Department of Commerce.

DISTILLED SPIRITS COUNCIL OF THE U.S. – AUGUST 1989

The negative effects of drugs vary with their potency and their addictive force on particular individuals. I had no drug resistance built up. These sub stances can be found in the most unlikely places. Even the ordinary healthful apple a day contains a minute amount of alcohol, and sometimes has a negative chemical effect on those who are allergic to it. Your mild antiperspirant deodorant usually carries a warning: "If rash or irritation develops, discontinue use." That little "if" indicates that some people may be adversely affected.

Study Notes

WITHDRAWAL

Treatment is the last resort.

William P. Miller, Ph.D., of the University of Mexico, compares drug treatment to trying to fish people out of a fast flowing river: some are saved, some are not. Some that are saved jump back into the river.

The first step for any addiction withdrawal is to acknowledge that there is a problem. Step two—seek help from God.

Advanced cases need medical supervision with a physician qualified in the field. Some drugs can only be taken away by degrees or by prescribing a less addictive drug to be used over a period of time.

Different drugs—and different individuals—require different remedies. In some cases, withdrawal brings on sleep. After several hours the eyes and nose begin to run, and there is sweating and excessive yawning. After 36 hours the most severe cramps come in the legs, back and abdomen, with pains in the muscles. Then comes twitching, vomiting, diarrhea, loss of appetite, fever, and temporary insanity. With the best of treatment, some cannot be saved, some die a shocking traumatic death.

Those addicted to opiates will do almost anything to avoid this suffering. They get to the point where they must choose either a painful death or a torturous attempt at withdrawal. With alcoholics and barbiturate users, treatment may take many weeks in a psychiatric hospital.

The Saddest—Man's View

The saddest words by tongue and pen, "I could have been."

The Cheeriest—God's View

"Come unto me, . . . and I will give you rest" (Matthew 11:28).

"I will restore health unto thee, and I will heal thee" (Jeremiah 30:17).

Neither do I condemn thee. "Go and sin no more" (John 8:11).

Drug addiction is the attempt to satisfy the natural hunger for God with a substitute. With a healthy spiritual life there is no undesirable addiction. "But whosoever drinketh of the water that I shall give him shall never thirst" (John 4:14).

CONCLUSION OF CHAPTER ONE

We agree with the psychopharmacologist—it is impossible to win the drug war. Drugs for pleasure are endemic to humans and some animals. But personally, as a Christian, I am in a different category. We must make a distinction. I have no desire for any so-called recreational drugs. But in the world, compare it to trying to get rid of crime. There will always be those "who rejoice to do evil" (Proverbs 2:14) and those who "Fear the Lord, and depart from evil" (Proverbs 3:7). Surgeon Gen'l did help regarding smoking.

Control is always a battle; we try to control crime, drugs, mice and obnoxious insects. It is difficult. Because straight is the gate, and narrow is the way which leadeth unto life, and few there be that find it (Matthew 7:14). National prohibition did help.

With increased prosperity the drug problem will accelerate. When I was a kid, we were happy to afford a little pie occasionally with our bread. Increased drug abuse is not a result of poverty, but of prosperity. Of course, the real reason is not the external, but inward. The addicts have in their hearts rejected the peace, satisfaction and real joy that Christ brings. They pass up the churches and try to satisfy their hunger with the substitute of drugs. But it is our task to "Go out into the highway and hedges, and compel them to come in, that my house may be filled" (St. Luke 14:23).

"Give me neither poverty nor riches; feed me with food convenient for me" (Proverbs 30:8). Let Christ turn you on. Dr. Steed reports this consensus from the first United International Conference on Prevention of Drugs in 1986, "There will be no real solution to this problem until we consider and apply the spiritual dimension, and until we revive the family and moral structure. Thirty-six nations were represented by nearly 300 specialists."[14] Alcohol's use is abuse. The boozer is the loser.

14. Steed 1987.

RESOURCES

Just Say NO Foundation, 1777 N. Calif. Blvd, Suite 2000, Walnut Creek, CA 94596, 800-258-2766 in CA 415/939-6666

Students Against Driving Drunk SADD, P.O. Box 800, Marboro, MA 01752, 617/481-3568.

Drugs Anonymous, World Services, P.O. Box 473, Ansonia Station, N.Y. 10023, 212/840-1259.

Nat'l Self Help Clearing House, 33 W. 42 St., Room 620 N., N.Y. 10036, 212/840-1259.

Tobacco-American Cancer Soc., 90 Park Ave., N.Y. 10016, 212/599-8200.

CHAPTER TWO

A Cyclopedia of

Facts Regarding Specific Addictive Drugs

Arranged Alphabetically

Reflects the Facts Accurately.

Vickie Lynne Hess, Ph.D.
Professor of Chemistry
Indiana Wesleyan
University

Full of Accurate, Usable Facts.

Teresa Shahsavar, G.Ph., R.Ph.
Hooks Drug Stores, Now Revco

CHAPTER TWO
CYCLOPEDIA OF DRUG FACTS

A reference chapter where you can get specific drug facts quickly.

Get to Your Kids Before Somebody Else Does

AMPHETAMINES*

Aka: A's, Barb, Bennies, Crank, Crystal, Eye Openers, Meth, Speed, Uppers, Black Beauties, Cocaine, Crack

PLEASE NOTE: Aka—When drugs are used illegally for pleasure they usually have street aliases which we will indicate with the contraction; 'AKA' for Also Known As. Are they trying to confuse the straight world?

Amphetamines as nerve stimulants are 'uppers', the opposite of sedatives or 'downers'. They give an invigorating feeling of excitement, of being vividly conscious, just a general good feeling.

This comes from a speed-up of the electrical impulses throughout the nervous system. There is also a rise in blood pressure which results in greater alertness and a feeling that powers of concentration have increased.

Medically, strangely, Amphetamines were used to calm hyperactive children, and to help them concentrate. Formerly, they were used to help lessen the appetite in dieting, but that is now illegal. In the forms of enzedrine (Methodrene, Benzedrine and Dexodrene are brand names*) they are prescribed for fatigue or depression. They can be used with an inhaler, to lessen the swelling caused by a cold in the mucous membrane of the nose.

Illegally, amphetamines are used without a prescription as a pleasure drug for insecure adolescents, by students trying to stay awake for exams, or by truck drivers attempting to keep alert. Some take the drug to counteract the effects of the sedatives they have taken to relax. This up and down effect is very dangerous. It leads to a mental and physical disturbance that can lead to death.

"You took some 'uppers' again to help you get that 18-wheeler home, didn't you?"

Amphetamine use is dangerous because of its extreme volatility; the poison quickly becomes toxic to the whole body. The body acquires a tolerance that requires more of the drug to get the desired high effect. This may result in loss of coordination, mental and emotional control, mental illness and possible fatal poisoning. "Don't meth around," Spence.

Heavy doses may keep an addict awake for days, after which he may want to sleep continuously. Upon awakening a person will feel the need for a stimulant; the vicious cycle begins again.

* Methy-phenyl-ethyl-amine, C_9, $H_{13}N$, used in its sulphate or phosphorous form.

* Copyrighted brand names.

Withdrawal.

Except crack cocaine, stimulants are less physically addictive than depressants, so withdrawal is easier. Nevertheless, during withdrawal there are strong depression, apathy, muscle pains, and a powerful psychological craving for another dose. It takes strong will power to resist.

"Trust in the Living God, who is the Saviour (1 Timothy 4:10).

ANTIHISTAMINES

Diphenhydramine, Chlorpheniramine, Maleate, Brompheneramine

Don't Drive

Marine First Lt. Steve White felt sufficiently over his cold to go on a training flight. But he hit the flight deck at an angle, crashing into other planes and missiles. He was killed, along with 13 other crew members, and the accident caused nearly $60 million in property damages. Blood tests on White showed no evidence of alcohol or illegal drugs, but it did contain evidence of antihistamine, an over-the-counter drug. These drugs have warning labels: Do not use with alcohol, use caution, do not drive while using this product. They can cause dizziness, poor coordination, and impaired judgment.

Antihistamines counteract histamines, the uncomfortable reactions to allergies as asthma, flu, and colds. They give relief from the symptoms but do not eliminate the cause. They may lead to a dry mouth and can irritate the stomach if taken without food. Overdoses cause hallucinations, headaches, high fever, dilated pupils, convulsions, and coma.

As with all drugs, some people are more negatively affected than others. These are not mind-altering drugs taken for pleasure. We include them here as a warning. Read the label and follow directions. "Be ye therefore wise as serpents, and harmless as doves" (Matthew 10:16).

BARBITURATES

More people die from the effects of barbiturates than any other illegal drug

AKA: sleeping pills, red devils, downers, sleepers, goof balls.

Barbiturates are the opposites of stimulants. As a sedative, a downer, they reduce tension and anxiety.

Medically, barbiturates are packaged as powder in tablets, often colored. These are used to treat insomnia, nervous tension, anxiety, and epilepsy. Nembutal and Seconal act rapidly and wear off rapidly, which is why they are used for anesthesia. They are often contained in sleeping pills. These can be obtained without prescription, and can become addictive.

Barbiturates are used for conditions where formerly alcohol was prescribed for withdrawal from opiate addiction, and for stress and sleeplessness.

Taken illegally, barbiturates can lead to physical addiction, which can bring loss of emotional control, and irritability. Also, barbiturates lower body temperature, slow heartbeat, and lower blood pressure. This can lead to coma and death. Illicit use has caused many deaths. Barbiturates are sometimes used along with alcohol to commit suicide.

Some claim the derivative sodium pentothal, when injected into the bloodstream by a skilled physician, can put a person in a semiconscious state. In this state, some believe, he is more apt to tell the truth than when fully conscious.

Often barbiturate users become intoxicated, as if they had drunk alcohol. If one takes barbital and then takes sleeping pills, death often follows.

A big danger, for those who ingest, is in the sharing of needles to inject the barbital. Sometimes this can lead to tetanus, hepatitis, and AIDS.

While alcohol is not a barbiturate, it is the most popular sedative and therefore the most deadly. But when the sedative barbiturate is taken with alcohol the results are often fatal. Drugs do not add, they multiply: 1 alcohol plus 1 barbiturate does not equal 2, but rather the effect of 4.

Overdose signs: slow breathing, lack of coordination, confusion, drowsiness, slurred speech, lack of reflex, constipation, malnutrition, and coma.

Barbital is manufactured chemically from barbituric acid, $C_4H_4O_3N_2$. Other derivatives are Amytal, Nembutal, Phenobarbital, Sodium Pentothal, Gluthenimide, and Chloral Hydrate. Notice the first four end in *-al* to indicate their relation to barbital.

Treatment. Torturous withdrawal symptoms, when an addict tries to stop, include temporary insanity, hallucinations, and convulsions.

Both overdose and withdrawal may need to be handled by a qualified physician.

(There is no TREAT in TREATment)

In the case of an overdose, the stomach should be thoroughly pumped out. Dr. W. B. McNight, in his book, *The Family Doctor*, suggests that large doses of coffee (or other stimulants) be used next. The patient should not be allowed to sleep.

In withdrawal, barbiturates should never be taken away suddenly, but by decreasing amounts over a period of days or weeks. Other drugs should be given simultaneously.

If the drug has been taken because of emotional or mental problems, these troubles may need spiritual and medical attention.

A good place to get help? Try Christ. "I have come to give you rest." (Matthew 11:28). There are good Christian psychologists and psychiatrists.

Is every one allowed an occasional failure?
Consider the skydiver.

BROMIDE POISONING

Flush It

Bromide, from bromine acid, cannot exist by itself. It can only exist in a liquid, as bromine acid $HBrO_3$, or in water.

Bromide has been used in the past as a sedative for nervousness, but is no longer available as a prescription drug.

The body does not build up a tolerance to bromide, so we do not have addicts in the usual sense. However, some may be able to obtain the drug illegally to try to get rid of nervousness. There are two dangers connected with continued use:

1. The build up of poisonous bromide in the system may cause an increase in the nervousness the bromide was originally taken to alleviate.
2. The poison in the system sometimes causes headaches, irritability, slurred speech, and loss of memory. Many have become mentally ill and needed psychiatric treatment in a hospital.

Treatment

A bromide victim must quit using all bromide at once. This can easily be done since there is no physical addiction. Large doses of liquid with salt should then be administered by a physician. The physician should also try to find and treat the cause of the nervousness that was the initial reason for taking the drug.

CAFFEINE ADDICTION

The use of the mildest, most used mind-altering drug, caffeine—in coffee, tea, and cola drinks—is not regulated by law. But it is quite addictive to some.

A friend of mine has a serious heart problem. His physician told him to stop drinking coffee or he may die. But he has not been able to do so.

If my mother did not get her coffee in the morning, she would have a terrible headache the rest of the day. She did not want me to start. She said she would tell me when I got old enough to drink it. She passed away. I never got the word; never tasted it.

Caffeine is a stimulant, an upper. Of itself, it is not a food; it is not the basis of energy. Nevertheless, it works to energize. Like all activating drugs, it can be dangerous.

Research scientist Dr. Schaal says his study is the first to show that caffeine has an effect on the electrical system of the heart.

Following is a chart of the caffeine count of the various popular beverages. They are published by the Community Hospital of Indianapolis, Inc.

THE CAFFEINE COUNT CHART

Coffee (5 oz.)	Mg.
Automatic drip	110-150
Percolated	64-124
Instant	40-108
Decaffeinated	2-5
Instant	2
Tea	
Brewed, five min. (5 oz.)	20-50
Iced, in cans (12 oz.)	22-36
Decaffeinated (??)	0
Soft Drinks (12 oz.)	
Coca-Cola	33
Tab	32
Ginger ale	0
Dr. Pepper	38
Mountain Dew	54
Pepsi-Cola	38
Pepsi-Free	0
7-Up	0
Sunkist Orange	0
Non-Prescription Drugs—One Tablet	
Anacin	32
Aspirin	0
Dexatrim	200
Excedrin	65
Midol	32
No Doz	100
Chocolate	
Cocoa (6 oz.)	10
Milk chocolate (1 oz.)	6
Baking chocolate (1 oz.)	35

Overdose effects: Nausea, restlessness, frequent urination, rapid pulse, fever, delirium, tremors, convulsions and coma.

Withdrawal should be done gradually to avoid headaches.

COFFEE

Two Cups of Strong Coffee Can Kill*

The caffeine in two cups of coffee, 200 milligrams, can be life threatening to caffeine sensitive people with heart problems.

This is the result of an Ohio State University research project headed by Dr. Stephen Schaal. The research, which involved 20 patients and volunteers, was funded by the Central Ohio chapter of the American Heart Association.

Coffee Can Shock Your Electrical System

In some tests, caffeine caused ventricular tachycardia, very rapid ventricular beating. Schaal pointed out that doctors were in control of patients'

* Caffeine—a bitter alkaloid—$C_8H_{10}O_2N_4$

heartbeat during the research and could deal with any threats that arose. This rhythm change can cause sudden death.

In people with heart problems, caffeine increases blood pressure.[1] So apparently there is a medical concern regarding caffeine for people who have high blood pressure. Like all drugs, caffeine effects certain people according to their particular tolerance. My father was a coffee fiend. He seemed little affected, except for bouts of *heartburn,* stomach acidity. He would spew acid into the open range, causing flames to shoot a couple of feet high. He died at 87 as the result of an accident.

Because of the increase of heartbeat and the stimulation of nerves, caused by coffee, there is a heightening of intellectual faculties, and an increased ability to perform mental and physical work. But as with all mind-altering chemicals, there is often a price to pay. In some cases sleeplessness, nervousness, headaches, and rarely possible death from heart trouble can result.

It was found, in one experiment, that after an injection of caffeine, rats worked much faster on the treadmill. However, they had difficulty on the maze and had problems learning.

Pregnant rats were fed doses of caffeine equivalent to more than twelve cups of strong coffee a day. Many of their offspring had skeletal abnormalities, with missing toes (Newsweek 9/15/1984).

Children's young hearts are most susceptible to damage. For children, who are normally so very active, caffeine stimulation is not advised. Caffeine also crowds out milk drinking, with its essential food elements.

Coffee Drinkers. The Food and Drug Administration does not require warning labels on products that contain caffeine, but is cautioning expectant mothers regarding the use of caffeine. One Yale study found the miscarriage risk nearly doubled in women who consumed over 150 milligrams of coffee a day (two cups). "The caffeine in Mom's coffee is transferred to her breast milk," which may be low in iron. "Infants don't produce the enzymes that metabolize coffee until several days after birth. So if you are breast feeding, limit your coffee to a few sips or a cup a day."[2]

Lab scientist—"Coffee?"
White rat—"Sanka Please."

Coffee drinkers are sometimes low in vitamins. The body tends to lose the unstable water soluble Vitamin B's, because caffeine causes more blood to flow through the kidneys. Especially suspect are B_1 thiamine and B_6 pyridoxine.

Experiments have shown that caffeine can damage chromosomes. This possibly can degenerate and age the body.

The average cup contains 100 milligrams of caffeine. In some people, 250 milligrams causes diarrhea, sleeplessness, nausea and trembling. Many are now drinking decaffeinated coffee.

Waitress—"Another cup of coffee?"
Customer—"Yes please, and directions to the bathroom."

Coffee History. Arabs discovered coffee around 850 A.D. Goat herder, Kaldi, noticed the increased energy of his goats after they had eaten berries of the coffee plant. In 1555, coffee went on trial in Mecca for causing melancholy and insomnia. The resulting prohibition did not last long. For a while the Catholic Church prohibited coffee. Later, coffee was promoted by Moslems as an alternative to alcoholic wine.

While caffeine comes mainly from the coffee plant, it is also found in tea, and

1. Schaal 1983.

2. American Health Journal 1990.

the cola-nut plant used in making soft drinks. Additional caffeine is sometimes added. This is of concern for children drinking soft drinks. With their smaller bodies, they may be getting the same percentage of caffeine that causes trouble for adults.

TEA

With Lemon?

The white flowered evergreen plant, *thea sinensis,* is grown in India, Japan, and countries of a similar climate. The leaves are boiled with water. Some say one gets better tasting tea by putting tea bags with water in a clear jar and setting it in the warm sun.

Less Caffeine. As the chart shows, tea has a much smaller amount of caffeine than coffee. Besides, chemical analysis reveals that tea, with its milder oils and proteins, is a very different drink from coffee. The net result is that scientists do not give the same health warnings for tea that they give for coffee. However, when Seventh Day Adventists take membership vows, they promise to abstain from all caffeine, nicotine, and other stimulating drugs.

Andrea LaCroix, who directed a comparison study at Johns Hopkins University, had this observation, "The totality of evidence for tea reveals no

Tea Plants

"Ever since William found out that tea is relatively harmless, he indulges himself whenever he can."

association with disease, especially heart disease." Similar is the observation of Arthur L. Klatsky, Kaiser Permanent Chief of Cardiology: "Whenever anyone looks at tea, it doesn't share coffee's association with coronaries. Tea drinking . . . is not related to smoking as coffee is."

Benefits? Klatsky believes tea may be beneficial: "The general perception is that tea is a healthy beverage." James P. Henry, research professor at Loma Linda University in California, states, "We have some evidence that tea has a tranquilizing effect." While this might seem strange regarding a caffeine drink, the reason, he believes, is the presence of *flavonoids** in tea.

Some teas have a lot of fluoride. Studies of English school children showed that the tea drinkers had fewer cavities.[3]

Since tea causes more frequent urination, some experts believe it helps those with high blood pressure.

---

* Flavone—The colorless crystalline compound, $C_{15}H_{10}O_{02}$ made from certain plants or prepared synthetically, is thought to have the benefits of riboflavin, vitamin B_2.

3. Barnett 1990.

"When Toni was breast-feeding Kris, she'd drink a cup of hot tea (also milk) to get her milk to come in more plentifully. Toni would sleep oh, so soundly. Later, Kris bawled and kicked something awful. The doctor told her that even though the tea didn't affect Toni, its effects were passed on to the baby."[4]

In England, afternoon tea drinking has become an institution. In Japan, tea is always offered to guests.

Iron Problem?

Lauren S. Jackson, researcher at the University of Wisconsin, finds that tea reduces the absorption of iron, but with lemon in the tea, iron may be more available. Many restaurants, serve lemon with tea.

Withdrawal

As with all drugs, its effect varies with individuals. Withdrawal can be sudden or gradual, since there is practically no physical addiction.

"Do you feel like a cup of tea?" "No, do I look like one?"

CARBONATED DRINKS

CO_2

AKA—Soda, pop, soft drinks

Why do we call soft drinks, sodas? My father showed me how they made pop in his ice cream parlor. This was before Mr. Hires popularized commercial root beer with CO_2, the fizz.

Dad put some fruit juice in a tumbler. He added vinegar, then soda, and POW! When the soda hit the acid, the bubbles exploded. There really was a zip to the drink. My mother made and stored what she called dandelion wine in the same way, by using dandelion blossoms.

What's wrong with Pop? It depends. Is it drunk by children instead of needed milk? Is it diet, or is it loaded with sugar? China is one of many countries that has discouraged Coca-Cola because of its sugar content.

Singapore *stings* out Coke and Pepsi, and is preparing a list of drinks that contain less than 10% sugar for school canteens.

Carbonation, the fizz, is harmless to the degree that it is used in soft drinks. If it were toxic, then some people would poison themselves if they held their breath. For carbon dioxide is what is breathed out after breathing in oxygen.

(It makes the trees grow.)

It's like potatoes; alone, they are not fattening. It's the fat gravy that is put on them to make them taste good. So with a carbonated drink, the problem is with what is put in, such as sugar and caffeine. Some diet drinks have no caffeine and no sugar.

Soft drinks have the same CO_2 as the so-called sparkle in wine that helps to cover the bitter taste of alcohol. Thanks to Mr. Hires for developing root beer as a substitute for beer or alcoholic wine.

Hire's to you, brother Hires.

I remember my college chemistry professor saying that pop helps to clean teeth, without sugar, it does.

What's wrong with Pop? Nothing much. He's O.K.

COCAINE—HIGHLY PSYCHOLOGICALLY ADDICTIVE

A Bitter Crystalline Alkaloid —$C_{17}H_{21}NO_4$

"Get Behind Me Satan"

AKA—Coke, Bernice, Big C, Flake, Snow

An odorless white powder, cocaine is found largely in the leaves of the cocoa bush in the area of Columbia and Peru. The native Indians chewed the leaves to reduce hunger and fatigue. Spanish

4. Lois Costomiris.

conquerors of South America brought it to Europe. In the middle of the 19th century German chemists separated cocaine from the cocoa leaf. Chocolate and cocoa are made from the roasted and ground seeds.

Cocaine was used in early American history. It was put in wine and Coca Cola until 1906. The misguided Sigmund Freud promoted cocaine for exhilaration and euphoria.

In 1914 the Harrison Act regulated its use in medicine.

Medical Use

Medically, it is used as local anesthesia, especially of the ears, nose and eyes. Dentists use it for the mouth. The value of a local anesthesia is that physicians don't have to put their patient to sleep.

Health Dangers

Bad effects of the drug are eye pupil dilation and loss of memory. Sometimes there is sweating, nausea, confusion, dizziness, aggression, hysteria, hallucinations, and death. Such fatalities were seen in the deaths of basketball star Len Bias and pro football player Don Rogers, as well as over 2,000 others in 1986. One thousand milligrams will immediately cause death.

Cocaine Addiction

It is strongly psychologically addictive, but not generally physically addictive. At present there is strong public concern about cocaine addiction and illegal use. Cocaine gives a brief, intense feeling of elation, alertness, and euphoria. But the feeling of pleasure is followed by depression. To get rid of this depression the addict takes more and more of the drug.

As with most drugs there is a large variation in how addictive it is. Some people can take it or leave it. But about 20 percent of users become immediately addicted. The temptation to try it must be avoided.

Crack Cocaine

"Don't cry so loud," the rapist demanded of his young victim. "The neighbors will hear you." In a locked, windowless Detroit room in apartment 13, a girl of 13 years was being stripped of her innocence. She had been sold by her mother, Suzanne Barbier, to pay for a crack debt. This mother of four children, by three different men, started with pot smoking in high school, then crack got her in its grip.

The judge sentenced her to life in prison for "sinking to an intolerable level of humanity." Another judge sentenced her boyfriend, Anthony Sawyer, to 40-60 years for the rape.

Crack Addiction

The name comes from the crackling sound when smoked.

Crack is a condensed smoking form of cocaine. It can give a quick cheap high lasting for 15 to 20 minutes. Presently it sells for $10.00 for a small cube, about the size of a pea. The euphoria is so great that some people get instantly addicted. But for every action, there is a reaction. After the euphoria, a terrible depression sets in very quickly. The result is a desire for more crack, and so the endless cycle begins. Addicts will do almost anything to get a supply. As with some other drugs, including alcohol, many of the nation's 5 million cocaine users can use cocaine for years without becoming dependent. But three out of five do become dependent on crack. The drug reaches its target fast, in less than 10 seconds through the lungs.

Crack Ruins Babies

The saddest time is when crack comes to the nursery. For, like heroin and alcohol, the addiction to crack is passed from the mother to the baby. Dr. Ira Chasnoff, of Chicago Memorial Hospital, made a study of 36 hospitals. He found that out of 155,000 pregnant women, 11% had exposed their unborn babies to illegal drugs, primarily cocaine. He says, "Women who wouldn't smoke or drink, can't stay away from cocaine."

When a pregnant woman uses crack, the baby's vital flow of oxygen and nutrients is interrupted. Smaller head and brain size often result. Inconsolable, ever-crying babies are born with damaged kidneys, spinal cords, and genitals. "Babies with smaller heads," Stanford's Fulroth points out, "have lower than normal IQ levels by ages 3 to 6. [Some mothers are] so high on crack, they do not know when labor begins." Dr. Judy Howard, who has studied hundreds of crack children, says that they are hard to care for from the moment of birth. They may be either extremely irritable or very lethargic; they have poor sucking ability and irregular sleep patterns. As they grow older, they may be hyperactive, slow in learning to talk, and find it hard to relate to other people. Once taken away from their addicted mothers, it is almost impossible to place them.

Research at the San Diego University shows one third have lesions of the brain in the learning and thinking section. When it's time for the child to learn to talk, he or she often cannot. At school age some cannot distinguish between their mothers and strangers. They do not even know their names, according to the Harlem Hospital studies. According to Prenatal Addiction Research in 1989, twenty percent of the babies in the large cities were affected. The beer capital, Milwaukee, cited 40%.

Crack Damage.

Crack crime, thievery, drug-related holdups, and murders have increased.

Washington, D.C., with its convicted and imprisoned crack-using mayor, had 443 killings in 1990, up from 369 in 1989. Experts blame the killing surge on drugs, largely crack. New York Police Chief Raymond Kelly, whose city has over 1,800 murders a year, was asked why there were so many more murders in the 80's than in the 70's. His answer was, "Crack."

What of the future of our country? We have let drugs replace the Bible.

"Seek the Lord while he still may be found." He has helped multitudes.

A Plague Out of Control

Unfortunately, cocaine use has been fast increasing. According to the National Institute of Drug Abuse (NIDA) there were an estimated 647,000 users in 1985 but the figure jumped to 862,000 in 1989.

Eli Lilly Endowment funded a study of two thousand tenth and twelfth year students in Indianapolis, regarding cocaine use by male students. High school male use more than doubled between 1987 and 1988. While male use rose from 2.2 to 4.4 percent, nonwhite male use increased from 2.6 to 5.7 percent.

Withdrawal

Cocaine users must admit to having a problem. They must make up their minds to stop, and should give themselves to God. They ought to see a pastor. If it is a really serious problem, see a physician. Since the addiction is primarily psychological, there is very little sickness connected when withdrawing from its use. There is no known drug to counteract the addiction of the approximately 20% who become addicted to cocaine. The cocaine help line is: 1-800-COCAINE.

To be involved in cocaine illegally is a good preparation for making license plates.

CODEINE—A MILD DOWNER

White crystalline alkaloid, $C_{18}H_{21}NO_3$-H_2O

Codeine, is Greek for *'leaf of the poppy.'* Methylmorphine, is a weak derivative of morphine, which is a derivative of opium. Prolonged use of codeine may cause addiction. It does not cause the euphoria that opium or morphine does, and, so is less often illegally used.

Medically it is prescribed for the treatment of morphine addicts. More largely, it is used as a painkiller mixed with acetaminophen or aspirin, in dental use, and cough suppressants.

It is legally available only by prescription. A large increase in dosage is more likely to produce restlessness than quietness. But writes an author friend, "This is the only pain killer that the physicians have found that I can take for my fibromyalgia (muscle disease) terrible pains." (Lois Costomiris)

HERBS (hurb)

Congress in 1994 passed the Dietary Supplement Health and Education Act which reduced the Federal Drug Act's control over herbs.

The work of the liver is to strain out poison. When it gets over worked it gets damaged or destroyed, as cirrhosis of the liver from alcohol, resulting in possible fatality. Many herbs are dangerous to the liver. These are Germander, Sassafras, Ephreda and Comfrey. While some are causing deaths, they are legal and free from control.

For details see *Newsweek* 5/6/1996

HEROIN*—NARCOTIC

AKA: Hard Stuff, Horse, Junk, Peanut Butter, Smack, Snow

Diamorphine, a depressant or downer

How Can You Get So Low?

Heroin was a medical failure. Originally discovered and manufactured in Germany, heroin was first developed to relieve pain and coughing, and to treat opium and morphine addicts.

It was thought to be less addictive than morphine, but patients became more addicted to heroin.

Though heroin was more potent than morphine, its pain relief did not last as long. Therefore, its medical use was discontinued and its importation forbidden.

---

* Heroin, $C_{21}H_{23}O_5N$, is a German trademark for this small powder made from morphine. It is an odorless, bitter, crystalline acetyl acid-based substance. Now it can be made synthetically and need not be taken from the opium abstract of morphine.

It is often fatally addictive. Abusers sniff the drug through the mucous membrane of the nose or by injecting it intravenously. The result is terrible addiction. Heroin use gives a good feeling, but can be followed by nausea, vomiting, and constipation, because of slowed down organ functions. Overdoses result in convulsions, coma, and death. (See Withdrawal from Narcotics, p.105.)

LSD*—A HALLUCINOGEN OR PSYCHEDELIC

AKA: Dose, Acid, Hawk, Big D, Cube, Sugar, Zen

Lysergic acid comes from ergot, a parasitic fungus that feeds on wheat, rye and barley.

Medical Use. In the past, it has been used medically in the treatment of mental disorders, and alcoholics, but it has caused too many problems. One drop on a sugar cube can cause hallucinations. **Its use is strictly illegal with no current medical allowance.**

Hallucinations. If the hallucinatory trance images are pleasant, it is called, in users' jargon, "a good trip". If they are unpleasant and scary, it is called a "bad trip" or "trap", as Dr. Lindsay Curtis calls it, or a *bummer.* These may be multiplied later by horrible flashbacks that can come a long time after taking the drug, so severe they are at times fatal.

"Don't tell me, let me guess. You're having a bad trip, aren't you?"

Those who partake of this illegal drug claim it gives them clearer perception. The effect varies among individuals. What happens is, there is such a dreamy change in emotion and thinking, that all real awareness of time and space is confused, often for hours.

This confusion of the mind is used by Fakers of India to have power over devotees. LSD—*L*ast *S*o *D*amaging. One may quit LSD, "It may not quit him."[5]

Danger

Effects on the mind can possibly include deterioration of chromosomes. An LSD high is actually temporary insanity.

For some people continued use results in permanent anxiety and deep depression, insanity and suicide. Experience shows that the use of this drug ultimately brings a bad experience and unhappiness.

* A crystalline alkaloid compound, an amide of the Lysergic acid diethylamide.

5. Drugs and Alcohol, Strack 1985.

Addiction Evidence

Physical signs of addiction are: eye pupils enlarge, and the face becomes red. The body temperature rises as the heart beats faster, but the user feels chilled.

Withdrawal

LSD is usually not strongly physically addictive. Although after quitting its use, one may experience, from time to time, very uncomfortable flashback hallucinations.

"Experience is what we get, when we don't get what we want." Sanford

MARIJUANA— A MILD HALLUCINOGEN

Cannabis or Hemp

Time Weeds Out the Trivial. Sapir

AKA—grass, pot, hemp, weed, reefers, THC, dagga, gage, hooka, cannabis, Indian hemp, bhang hashish, Mary Jane, tea, or whatever else users decide to call it.

Marijuana is a wild weed, the seeds for birds, the stems to make rope.

Cannabis and hemp are correct terms. It has been said marijuana comes from two female proper names: Marie-Juana. Marijuana is made from the dried leaves and flowers of the cannabis plant, which grows wild in all of the United States and some foreign countries. As a drug, tetrahydrocannabinol, usually called delta 9 or THC, has been around for a hundred years as "hashish."

It is used medically by some physicians as a narcotic, but in a very limited way. It is ordinarily illegal to use it for pleasure in most Western Countries, including the United States, except New York. New York has bowed to many who claim that there is no harm in marijuana use. Unfortunately, this has helped to popularize the craze for the drug and other drug use. The use of drugs by young people in the U.S. is higher than any other developed country.

STUDY INDICATES MARIJUANA LEADS TO HARD DRUG USE

These were the actual headlines in the A.P. story in the St. Louis Post Dispatch on October 22, 1981. At that time some were still touting marijuana as perfectly harmless.

Dr. William Pollin, of the National Institute on Drug Abuse (NIDA), reported to Congress the results of a national study of 2,510 men aged 20 to 30. It showed that THC was a stepping stone to addiction and crime!

Of those who used marijuana at least one thousand times, three-fourths went on to try cocaine and one third to take heroin. But those who never used marijuana never took cocaine or heroin.

Tony was one of the 2,510 men studied by NIDA. A clean-cut high school junior, he prided himself that he had never smoked or drunk alcohol, but pot was different. Well-known sociologists had declared marijuana to be harmless. Pot was so nice to relax with on weekends. But tensions mounted at exam time. Others were trying cocaine, with no apparent ill effects. It really was better. Tony got hooked. Those little vials got expensive, but he had to have it. People were leaving their cars unlocked. He found a market for them at a hatchet shop. Now he could buy heroin. He never went on to be a high school senior. A prison sentence interrupted school.

Tony's story was told to the Senate Labor Committee as an example of one of the three-fourths of marijuana users who went on to cocaine and heroin. He was one of the 27% that got involved in thievery, compared to 6% of nonusers.

DANGERS OF MARIJUANA

Some have said marijuana should not be classed as illegal. It has been claimed:

1. It does not harm the body.
2. It does not harm others.
3. It is not addictive.

Recent scientific experiments have shown all three to be wrong.

Lung Harm. Dr. Sidney Cohen, a professor of psychiatry at U.C.L.A.'s Neuropsychiatric Institute, testified before congress that lung cancer is probably one of the health risks from marijuana. This was evidenced by some American soldiers stationed in Germany. Those who smoked hashish heavily, for several months, developed precancerous lesions on their bronchial tubes and colons.[6]

According to the World Health Organization (WHO), and the Addiction Research Foundation, "Marijuana has a poisonous effect on the respiratory system and the development of tol-

6. Washington AP 10/22/1981.

erance to the lung and dependence."[7] In other words, it is dangerous and addictive.

Heavy users have lung and heart damage (Home Medical Encyclopedia). In one study of pot smokers, there was a definite relationship between smoking pot and bronchitis and asthma.[8]

In an experiment on a large number of rats for one year, rats were given the equivalent of up to six joints a day. At the end the rats had irreplaceable lung damage.[9]

The American Medical Association's Scientific Council states that marijuana is a dangerous drug. A growing body of evidence from clinical observations attests to its deleterious effects on behavior, performance, and functioning of various organ systems: lung, heart, brain, reproductive organs. This is evidenced by both animal and human studies.

Brain Damage

Some experts believe that the greatest body damage from marijuana is to the brain. Like alcohol, marijuana loves fat. Because the brain contains so much fat, it is the place that the drug strikes first. But there is a difference in the effect of the two drugs. The liver quickly goes to work to get rid of alcohol. But with repeated use, marijuana piles up in the body, especially the brain. Since the brain directly effects so much of the physiology, the emotions and bodily health are affected.

Dr. Mitchell Rosenthal believes pot use damages emotional brain growth. Many young people who had smoked only pot, but not hard drugs, came for psychiatric help at the Phoenix House, where thousands were cured from their pot addiction.

M. Fink has shown on the EEG machine how marijuana actually affects the brain tissue tolerance. The more the smokers used the dope, the more it took to frazzle the brain waves, and it took more for the user to get *high,* to get satisfied. So the addict gets in deeper and deeper.[10]

Dr. R. S. Heath, of Tulane University, planted recording devices deep into the brain of a Rhesus monkey and then gave it marijuana. After being given the marijuana smoke, the brain waves were thrown out of their normal functioning. The experiment was stopped for fear of permanent damage to the brain.[11]

Pot users become estranged from their families, and often try to avoid them. There may be a loss of affection, and a tendency for complete self-centeredness. A previously active, cheerful person may change to being moody, listless, drowsy, and having a lack of care of personal appearance.[12]

(Going to a party where there will be pot smoke? Use your brain, save your brain, wear a gas mask.)

Marijuana and Addiction

The body builds a defense, a tolerance, against the drug so that it can function normally. But drug users do not want normality. They want excitement, and to get a high they must surpass the tolerance level that the body has built up. They must take more and more of the drug to get their kick. Addiction is both physical and psychological.

If it were only mental, as some say, then pigeons have been reading the wrong books, for Dr. E. McMillan and

7. World Health Org., Vol. 2, p.297.
8. Henderson 1972.
9. Fleischman 1979.
10. Fink 1976.
11. Heath 1980.
12. Voth 1987.

his associates have shown that pigeons develop tolerance to marijuana.[13]

A.E. Abel has shown the same propensity of tolerance to THC, even in newly hatched chicks.[14]

(Get close to marijuana,
she may never leave you)

13. McMillan 1970.
14. Abel 1972.

Marijuana Affects Mothers and Babies

This very sad news comes from the Third International Union of Pharmacological Sciences.[15]

"Pregnant mothers, smoking marijuana, have babies 100 to 300 grams lighter, smaller heads and brains, five times more likely to be disfigured, similar to the fetal alcoholic syndrome."

In studies of mice, R.D. Harbison found that when a toxic substance such

15. Oxford 1984.

"Some people say that marijuana can cause brain damage, but it doesn't affect me . . . affect me . . . affect me . . ."

as THC enters the mother, it poisons the unborn baby.[16] In a similar study on pregnant rats, R.M. Vardaris and his associates came to the same conclusion.[17] The fetus is correspondingly affected.

With breast feeding, marijuana poisons the baby, as shown by R. L. McGreer and A. Jakubovic.[18]

Withdrawal

The physical grip is not nearly as strong as it is with many other drugs. Since it is primarily psychological, quitting will certainly not be fatal, as quitting cold turkey can be for some drugs. So the best way is to quit cold turkey. It hurts fast, but it's over fast!

The effect of quitting varies: there probably will be sickness, but there may not be. Some quitters have experienced hot flashes, sweating, vomiting, hiccups, weight loss, insomnia, and irritability; the same as some monkeys experienced. However, for only 3 or 4 days.

Let me suggest a scientific study written so as to be easily understood by kids: *Marijuana, Time for a Closer Look.*[19]

(There is no rainbow at the end of pot).

METHAQUALONE

AKA—Ludes, love drug, quaaludes, methaqualudes

$C_{16}H_{19}N_2O$, a white crystalline powder

Medically, it was used as a sedative and hypnotic. A downer with similar effects as alcohol, it slows reflexes, slurs speech, gives poor judgment, and impairs driving ability. Because of its addictiveness it is no longer legally produced, but still is illegally available.

Taken with alcohol it may lead to homicide and/or suicide.

MDMA

Best known as Ecstasy

A synthetic designer upper stimulant designed for the illegal drug traffic. It simulates hallucinogens and amphetamines, and is strongly addictive.

Herbal Ecstacy. While MDMA is illegal, Herbal Ecstacy is still legal, but for some this psychedelic is a killer. Some Herbal Ecstacy dealers lace their product with cocaine.

MPTP

A *designer drug*, designed by a criminal chemist to make a profit. It is a deadly neurotoxin. Its users often eventually get a condition similar to Parkinson Disease.

MORPHINE*

AKA: Hard Stuff, M

From Morpheus—Greek God of dreams

Morphine, the principal derivative of opium, is a fine, odorless, feathery, bitter white powder.

Medical Use

It is prescribed for shock, heart failure, as a cough suppressant, and as a preoperative painkiller. It paralyzes the bowels to relieve diarrhea, and reduces the pain in terminal cancer. As a strong depressant, it is dangerous, and is only given to those with a severe cough, or lung problems.

Addiction

Morphine is very powerful; a small capsule would cause death to someone

16. Harbison 1941.
17. Vardaris 1976.
18. McGreer and Jakubovic 1979.
19. Jarrezek.

* $C_{17}H_{19}NO_3$-H_2O

not accustomed to its use.[20] Addicts eventually end up in the lowest state of degradation. It is difficult to detect narcotic users, since they will lie about it. A physician can determine if narcotics have been used by using another drug, N-allynmorphine. Puncture marks may be seen on the skin over superficial veins. The narcotic addict may be pale, having substituted narcotics for food.

Unripe poppy seed

NARCOTICS—OPIUM

Opium, one of the narcotics, is made from the unripe opium poppy seed. It is dark brown or black with a strong odor and a bitter taste. As a narcotic it leads to sleep and lethargy.

Addiction

A narcotic drug can become very addictive. Opium is the daddy of addictive drugs, the basis for over 20 alkaloid potent addictive narcotics.

Because of the narcotic's power to physically addict, the government attempts—but not very successfully—to strictly control it. Narcotic use is one of our most serious illegal drug problems, resulting in mental disturbance, weight loss and temporary instability.

The medical use of opium has a long history.

Three thousand years ago, the Therapeutic Papyrus at Thebes gave instructions for prescribing opium in the treatment of pain (Michael Clay–Encyclopedia American Vol. 20, 1968).

Around 600 B.C., when sick people came to the temple, Aesculapius, the physician priest, would give them opium. When the patients awoke, they would tell their dreams. The physician would prescribe medicine based on the dream, to show the link between body and mind.

In 460 B.C. Hippocrates prescribed opium for dropsy, epilepsy, insomnia, and women's diseases. In Persia in the eleventh century A.D., Avicenna devised a way to standardize the amount of opium to be prescribed.

From the 13th to the 16th century the use of opium was condemned by the Roman Catholic Church.

Medically it is now prescribed in some countries to relieve terminal pain. No other medicines are as effective as the narcotic opiates to reduce pain. Withdrawing results in a terrible sickness.

Withdrawal of A Narcotic Addiction

Dr. W. B. McNight, in his book, *The Family Doctor*, has said, "Stopping the narcotic habit is *the most possible terrifying experience*. It must be in the hands of a physician. There are few cures. One may go clean for years and then return to the addiction. Everyone should be aware of the terrible effects of narcotic addiction."[21]

In treatment, methadone is often used, given in decreasing doses. A dose will last 24 hours. Clorridine is nonaddictive but effective. Also, Natrexone may be given orally with vitamins.

To be effective, treatment must be started before the addiction has gone too far. Torturous treatment will probably take a minimum of a year, in a hospital, or other drug free environment, along with psychiatric counseling.

20. Zinn.

21. McKnight 1963.

If the addict is in poor health, withdrawal may have to be delayed. Withdrawing from a narcotic takes determination and a strong will power.

(Where there is life, there is cope.)

PCP—ANGEL DUST

AKA—Killer Weed, Elephant Tranquilizer, Embalmer, Rocket Fuel

A violent hallucinogen, phencyclidine hydrochloride is cheap and easy to produce. It is one of our fastest growing drugs, affordable by very young kids.

Murderous. Author physician Nahab, M.D., PhD., calls it "the most destructive drug known to man."[22]

A TV documentary, *Angel Death*, gives medical experiential **facts** showing how those who hallucinated after taking Angel Dust murdered their friends. It often results in suicide and self-mutilation. PCP – *P*hen *C*ap *P*erversion = Devils' Black Angel. Common results of its use are coma and death.

Medical. It was developed in the 1950's as an anesthetic, but its bad side effects of torturous hallucinations led to it being discontinued. Patients awoke screaming. It is still used as an anesthetic in veterinary medicine.

PSYCHEDELICS

HALLUCINOGENS not herein discussed in detail: **Peyote P** and **mescaline** are from the peyote cactus; psilocybin is from Mexican mushrooms and the seeds of the common morning glory.

ROOT OF THE IBOGA plant is used in certain religious cult ceremonies in Zaire and parts of West Africa.

Colombian Indians drank a juice from a *yage vint*.

North American Indians made tea from the peyote cactus buttons. With its use, colors seem brighter, objects seem to throb with light and energy.

Also, DMT, DOM, MDA.

SOLVENT SNIFFING—HUFFING —TRICHOLORETHANE

Solvents are not very popular; they are mostly used by boys between 12 and 16. Commercially, solvents are substances put into various products to keep them from turning hard. They are found in paints, glue, nail polish, cleaning fluids, cigarette lighters and spray cans, thus so easy to obtain. Small kids' drug of choice.

The sniffer has a strange floating experience, like being drunk, as the brain is quickly affected.

To get the pure fumes not diluted by air, sometimes a plastic bag is put over the head. The lack of air causes a speed up of the heart. The result has sometimes been lifelong brain damage or death by suffocation. At times there has been stomach illness, with the vomit causing suffocation, loss of oxygen and death.

Other users have sprayed solvents directly into the throat, causing sweating and even death by suffocation.

NOBLESVILLE TEEN DIES AFTER INHALING FUMES

By LAURA MUSALL, Noblesville Ledger, 10/19/1991

A 15-year-old Noblesville boy died Saturday night after inhaling fumes from a leather repellent.

He went into cardiac arrest while trying to get high. Pacherich, a critical care nurse, said within about 15 minutes the user can pass out without hope of resuscitation.

"We've had lots of deaths around the state," she said. "It's horrible; there's nothing you can do, kids are found dead."

22. Voth and Nahab 1987.

NO FAMILY IMMUNE TO TRAGEDY

By KRISTY MEYER, 5/30/1997

The Daily Ledger Noblesville, Indiana

On May 3, 1997, Tiffany Hurley died after inhaling air conditioner freon.

"Common household items that are solvent will break down the cell wall, said Roabert Meier, a psychiatric social worker from Community North Hospital. This goes immediately to the blood stream and straight to the brain."

"Inhalants are cheap and available, the symptoms are profound," Meier said. "There are changes in thought process, delayed response, depression, sleepy more, moody, problems relating, loss of appetite and withdrawn. These will happen pretty rapidly."

"He urged parents to question their kids, especially if they smelled gasoline type fumes on their clothes."

STADOL

Some people suffer terribly from migraine headaches. So Bruce Fisher, son of medical Dr. Morris Fisher was very happy to get almost instantaneous relief by a nasal spray of Stadol. This drug had been approved in 1978 for use by injection.

As a spray it was approved in 1991, but seemed to be five times stronger. The Food and Drug Administration list 654 addiction reactions and 18 deaths possibly involving Stadol. The manufacturer Bristol - Myers - Squbb with over 100 million in annual sales says it recommended to the FDA that the nasal spray Stadol be reclassified as a controlled substance. It seems that for some patients the more pain killers they take, the more headaches they get. The result, is addiction.

The FDA says new restrictions will be in force in a few months. Mean time Bruce Fisher, the doctor's son, shot himself to death, while in addiction therapy.*

STEROIDS

Medically

Steroids refer to a large class of chemical compounds. Some of these cortisone steroids are produced by the adrenal glands, the progesterone, estrogen group, and testosterone.

Dianabol was developed in the U.S. This synthetic form is of the male hormone testosterone. It is available from physicians for medical disorders.

History

While we are now hearing much regarding steroids, the use of such drugs by runners and cyclists dates back to 1865. In 1954, they were used by the Russians to compete in sports.

Now it is discovered how the East Germans in the Olympics could win more gold medals than the U.S., even though the U.S. was fourteen times its size. It was their skillful use of steroids. They partly avoided detection by taking the athletes off them the day before competition. Now the ruinous health problems are appearing.

Unfortunately, the use of steroids in sports gives an unfair competitive edge. Steroids are also being used to give a macho look of a big chest and muscles (but shrunken genitals) along with a feeling of power, endurance, and aggression *in both sexes*.

Bad side effects are dangerous and many. They include infertility, bleeding ulcers, cancer, liver problems, and personality problems. Often the result is premature death.

Women users have had their voice become like a man's, growth of facial hair, changes of menstruation, and have turned excessively aggressive.

---

* A.P., Lauran Neergaard, June 16, 1997.

Peter Gent once quipped, "Better football through chemistry." But it was no joke for L.A. Raider Lyle Alzado. After pill popping he tried to make a comeback by turning to steroids. He was once a big strong man with a booming voice, but one year later, he was just a shell of a man with terminal, inoperable brain cancer. In a weak raspy voice he said, "Steroids lowered my immune system."[23] The NFL's drug adviser, Dr. Forest Tennant, agreed.

Alzado

Everyone's Doing It!

I first met Bill Ashpaugh at a Wesleyan Church that he, along with his brothers and a friend, had founded in his hometown, Noblesville, Indiana. They wanted a more active evangelical voice for holy living. However, Bill had a personal ambition to become Mr. Indiana, the strongest man in the state. He also had aspirations to become Mr. America. I observed him cry out with pain as he wrestled the iron at the gym.

A medical physician wanted to help. Through this doctor friend Bill received some steroids. At first Bill did not feel quite right in accepting the pills. However, if they helped, and if all the competition used them, what else was he to do? He was not doing anything illegal. The pills were being purchased by prescription.

He became Mr. Indiana and was on a plane traveling to New York to try for the big one, Mr. America. But something happened on the way. An abdominal pain bothered him. He would have it checked when he returned home. He only got 15th place in New York. He wasn't at his best.

As soon as Bill arrived home he went to a physician for an examination. He was immediately put in the hospital for surgery. Steroids had done their work on him with abdominal cancer. He was given six months to live. A wave of despondency swept through his relatives and many friends. All except his younger sister.

Lois said, "Bill, you don't have to die. The Lord can heal you." She prayed for him. He made a real commitment. Bill would give his life to glorifying the Lord; whether the Lord healed him, or not.

Now, years later, he gives his testimony across the nation. Crowds come to watch him blow up and explode hot water bottles, bend steel rods in a circle, and rip large catalogues in two. And he does it all without the help of steroids.[24]

TOBACCO

"God . . . please help me."

"I haven't had a cigarette since July 4, 1982. Make no mistake about it; smoking is an addiction. After 40 years

23. Alzado.

24. Ashpaugh 1981.

of smoking from two to three packs of cigarettes a day, after being warned by a surgeon that smoking was destroying my larynx, after being warned by other doctors that I was at risk of both lung cancer and emphysema, after suffering a mild stroke, after all this and more, I was still compelled to smoke: Had to smoke.

"I closed my eyes and whispered, 'God, if there's any purpose to be served by my living, please help me.'

"Almost as if I was in a trance, I went up to my apartment and put away the ashtrays. I threw out a half-finished pack of cigarettes.

"Am I home free? I don't know. But I'm not taking any chances."[25]

Ninety percent of tobacco users become addicted to it, more than to any other drug. (A.P. Scientist, 8/3/1994)

(They are dying to get them.)

As with all addictive drugs, of which nicotine is the most addictive, there is a vast difference in the ability of different people to break the habit. For many it is the hardest habit of all to break. Ask some people if they have quit, and they may answer, "Many times."

Addiction

Finally, *Thursday, March 20, 1997, a major tobacco company has admitted what we all knew, that smoking is addictive and life threatening. In 1965, our U.S. Attorney, Luther L. Terry, proclaimed the health hazard of smoking. Ever since there have been many law suits against the tobacco companies. Billions of dollars are at stake. The tobacco companies, with slick attorneys, were often able to find means to skirt the issue.

In order to settle some 22 expensive state law suits, Liggett and Myers the makers of *Chesterfields, L & M* and *Lark* cigarettes, acknowledged the addiction and that some of the companies have targeted teens in their advertising. Liggett offered to pay 25 percent of its pre-tax profits during the next twelve years. Also to add to its cigarettes a warning that smoking is addictive, and to comply with the ban on tobacco cartoon characters.

Brief History of Tobacco

The use of tobacco is of American origin. For the Indians it was often a sacred part of council gatherings, used in the proverbial peace pipe.

With the development of fast-producing cigarette machines, cigarettes could be produced at low cost. With the high cost of these machines, the cigarette business became controlled by a few large companies. At the turn of the twentieth century, cigarette companies realized the steady market for such an addictive product. Large companies embarked on very aggressive advertising sales campaigns.

As a kid, I saw very little cigarette smoking. But after the First World War there was a change. The cigarette companies, with the help of the YMCA, distributed free cigarettes to servicemen. Many got hooked, including my infantry captain uncle. Lung cancer started to increase. My uncle paid the lung cancer price.

Until Franklin Delano Roosevelt, no important politician or president would allow himself to be photographed while smoking. (Incidentally, none since.) But then, smoking became fashionable.

There were many groups which were very concerned about this development. Among them were the Women's Christian Temperance Union, The National Prohibition Party and evangelical Christian groups, old time Methodists, especially those influenced by the Wesleyan theology, and the Calvinists, who

25. Zolotow 1985.

* Shanker Vedentam, Aaron Epstein and Bob Geiger in Night-Ridder Newspaper.

preached a *separated life.* To these groups, smoking was immoral and un-Christian.

A typical Wesleyan membership requirement: "To abstain from using or trafficking in substances known to be destructive of physical and mental well-being, such as alcoholic beverages and tobacco and from using drugs for other than proper medical purposes."[26]

In 1964, U.S. Surgeon General Luther L. Terry proclaimed the health hazards of smoking. In 1970, Congress baned cigarette advertising on the airways, beginning January 1, 1971. Then came Surgeon General Koop's crusade. Restaurants expanded their non-smoking sections; smoking was banned on airline flights. Smokers quit by the millions, down from 57% to 29%. Previously, "smoke and the world smokes with you." Now, "smoke and you smoke alone, outside."

With the decrease in smokers, Dr. Vincent T. DeVita, of the National Cancer Institute, said in 1986, "fewer people under 55 are contracting lung cancer." This year's cancer death rate dropped frm 38.2 per 100,000 to 35.7.

Unfortunately, American girls are smoking more. Their cancer statistics will show up later.

Exporting Our Cancer

According to the U.S. Dept. of Agriculture, Americans and Europeans are cutting down on smoking. But the production of cigarettes has risen from 583 billion in 1970 to 710 billion in 1990.[27] This is because cigarettes are heavily promoted in third world developing countries.[28]

26. Discipline 1992.
27. Dept. of Agriculture Handbook #456, p.31.
28. Statistical Abstinent of U.S. Plate 1262, p.149.

SMOKING IS VERY SOPHISTICATED

American Cancer Society

Damage to the Brain by Nicotine

Nicotine reaches the brain of the smoker in five seconds. Although the body is being damaged, and irreplaceable brain cells are being killed, the brain still calls for more nicotine.

I remember as a kid in the 1920's, reading in a Quaker periodical about the many poisons in cigarettes. Now over one hundred are listed. I have even read that a thousand poisons are suspected in tobacco smoke. Because of such knowledge, and the teachings of my parents and church, I never took the first puff.

Danger to the Lungs From Smoking

"You smoke, you choke, you croak," from a third grader, (MADD).

The greatest danger of smoking is its effect on the lungs by causing either emphysema or lung cancer. Statistics show that of heavy smokers, two out of five die before the age of 65. The harming of lungs by smoking also makes smokers susceptible to tuberculosis. Over one million, who have tobacco-

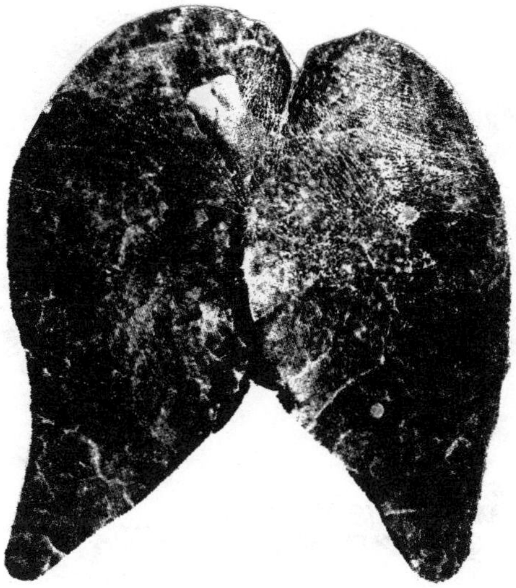

Smoke blackened lung

caused emphysema disability, are collecting Medicare or Medicaid. We all pay, as we do for many addicts. Every cigarette that is smoked reduces life expectancy by about ten minutes. A smoker is 20 times more likely to die of lung cancer than a non-smoker.[29] A pack a day will take five years off one's life.

Danger to the Lungs and Throat

The persistent smoker's cough can cause lung and throat cancer. The lungs can never get cleansed unless the smoker quits. Otherwise the lungs become irritated, inflamed, and unable to perform properly, leading eventually to death. Lung cancer grows quickly and is cured in only about 5 percent of all cases. The American Medical Association says this figure could be raised to 50 percent if the disease were caught in time.

Danger to the Heart

Naturally the heart regulates the flow of blood that the body needs. But nicotine causes a release of epeneprene, which results in an increase in blood pressure and heart rate. This makes the smoker feel good, but the unnatural heart rate is hard on the heart. Also, nicotine tends to constrict the blood vessels and to leave a layer inside them (Buerger's disease). So the heart gets a double whammy. It is forced to give higher blood pressure through less space. So smokers die more often. They die at the rate of 225,000 per year, from an overworked heart, according to the U.S. Surgeon General. Even if the heart is able to continue, Buerger's disease may prevent the legs from getting the proper oxygen. Gangrene sometimes sets in, and often legs have to be amputated.

Danger to Youth

As domestic sales dwindle, except for those to young women, the tobacco companies have been heavily promoting their product to youth in third world countries.

The earlier a child starts smoking, the greater is his or her risk of getting lung cancer or emphysema. (A father caught his seven-year-old son smoking. He told the cigarette-smoking mother. She said, "That's terrible, he's too young to be playing with matches.")

Inhaling

While there are a few smokers who claim that they do not inhale, most smokers do. Regardless of the taste, people smoke to get the energizing effects of nicotine, or to satisfy the craving that it creates. They can only get the full effect by inhaling. Most people would not want to breathe the smoke from a stove pipe or even from a campfire, but that is what a smoker puts up with just to get the kick from nicotine. The smoker breathes in ashes, tar, and many gases, including deadly carbon

29. World Book Illustrated Home Medical Encyclopedia 1980.

monoxide, which saturates the hemoglobin instead of oxygen. Toxic vaporized nicotine is also inhaled. One puff slows the cilia, microscopic hairs along the air passages. This weakens the ability of the lungs to defend themselves against infection. Some of this trash settles on the membranes of the lungs, and the bronchial tubing, causing bronchitis. The result is swollen blackened tissue that cannot bring oxygen to the blood. It also affects the voice box. A hacking cough results, as the lungs try to cleanse themselves.

"I DON'T BELIEVE ALL THAT JUNK ABOUT SECONDARY SMOKING, DO YOU?"

PASSIVE SMOKING

ETS—Environmental Tobacco Smoke

Most drugs, except alcohol, harm primarily only those who indulge. Not so with smoking. Smokers' children suffer lung infection, possibly leading to cancer. People (or animals) in a smoke-filled room breathe in as much cancer-causing smoke as a smoker does in several cigarettes.

Yale epidemiologist Dwight Janerich reported that the risk of lung cancer nearly doubled in those exposed to cigarette smoke in early life. "*Passive smoking* is now known to be responsible for the lung cancer in nonsmokers."[30]

In separate reports the U.S. Surgeon General's Office and the National Research Council firmly linked secondhand smoke to cancer. Besides, the EPA concludes that secondhand smoke is causing thousands of cancer deaths in the United States every year.

San Francisco heart researcher Stanton Glantz, along with William Parmby, concluded that living with a smoker's secondhand smoke causes 10 times as much heart trouble as lung disease, making it the third largest cause of preventable diseases in the nation.[31] Judson Wells published the same conclusion in 1988.

With cancer, heart, and lung trouble, 50,000 nonsmokers die each year from others' passive smoke. An EPA report, based on 24 epidemiological studies, concludes that secondhand smoke is a class-A carcinogen (Newsweek 6/11/1990).

Harvard researchers now give the results of their ten year study of the effects of second hand smoke on over 32,000 healthy women who never smoked.

They found exposure to others' smoking at home or work, almost doubled their risk of heart disease.*

Geographical Areas in the U.S.

Environmental Tobacco Smoke also has a geographical meaning. In general those who live closest to the major tobacco growing and processing plants have the highest risk of dying from heart disease. The 1991 edition of the American Heart Association's *Heart and Stroke Facts* showed the greater risk in geographical variation of the nation's No. 1 killer. Some of the states with the highest rates of death from

30. Janerick 6/11/1990.
31. Cowley 6/11/1990.

* May 20, 1997 Denise Grady, *The New York Times*.

The day Riverview Hospital began enforcing its new visitor smoking policy.

cardiovascular disease are South Carolina, with 258.2 deaths per 100,000 people, West Virginia, with 252.3 deaths, and Georgia, with 238.5.

The less they fume, the less we fret.

The report said those west of the Mississippi River are less likely to die of heart disease. The states with the lowest rates are Hawaii, with 159.7, New Mexico, with 161.5, Colorado, with 169.3 and Montana, with 117.1 (U.P.I. 1/14/91).

"The trends have persisted for quite a while and they probably reflect the influences of life styles and socioeconomic factors."[32]

Smokeless Tobacco

AKA—Chewing Tobacco and Snuff

Smokeless tobacco is a fairly new term. It is not listed in the book section of the large St. Louis Library. However, there are many listings in the periodical section, as it has now become an increasing health concern.

32. Lewis Kullur, M.D., Chairman of the Department of Epidemiology at the Pittsburgh School of Medicine.

While we are seriously beginning to realize the early deaths caused by the nicotine in smoking, we are overlooking the nicotine of smokeless tobacco. The amount of nicotine in the blood of those regularly chewing tobacco is much the same as those who smoke it, and is just as addictive. While there is a discoloration of teeth and bad breath, the greatest damage is mouth cancer, which has been known to eat away the whole side of a face.

A tobacco chewer might get to heaven, but he'd have to go to hell to spit.

Ralph Nader's Health Research Group found nearly all professional sport players receive smokeless tobacco from manufacturers. Its use ranges from 8% to 75% per team. In Nader's letter to major and minor teams there was the warning: "The use of smokeless tobacco causes cancer . . . there has been a phenomenal growth in the use of smokeless tobacco by teenage boys."

The Federal Trade Commission said it would request the U.S. Surgeon General to investigate, and suggested that a warning be placed on smokeless tobacco, and on radio and TV advertising (Sporting News, May 13, 1985, p. 4). C. Everett Koop, former U. S. Surgeon General, said he would investigate.

In my contact with the U. S. Alcohol, Tobacco, and Firearms Division, they report that those warnings have been put on radio and TV.

Many users of smokeless tobacco would like to quit, but this tongue in cheek, nicotine habit is tough to get rid of. Chew or snuff, it's very bad stuff.

Women and Cigarettes

"Many believed, also honorable women"
"O, London is a man's town, there's power in the air.
But Paris is a woman's town, with flowers in her hair."

I was brought up in a comparatively chivalrous age. There was a special respect for the opposite sex; there was discrimination against men. It was ladies first. Give your seat to a lady. In the Titanic sinking, it was ladies first in the few lifeboats. Hundreds of men drowned. In those days of hot dogs, baseball, apple pie, and motherhood, we did have a double standard; we expected a woman to be better.

Did you ever see a picture of an angel with a mustache? It was not only poor etiquette for a woman to be seen smoking in public, it was poor ethics; smoking was only for the lowest.

"If a woman will smoke, she'll drink, if she'll drink, she will do anything," it was often said.

Those days are long gone. With the repeal of Prohibition, women in a spirit of abandonment went into taverns. Then came feminism, and women smoking. I was given a rude awakening on women's lib. In New York, I opened a door for a woman, (not a lady) and got my face slapped. (For true equality, should I have slapped her back?)

The tobacco industry, taking a cue from the liquor people, targeted women in their advertising. One of the very first magazine ads and posters aimed at women was one by Lucky Strike, in the late twenties, of a man lighting a cigarette for a young woman. It was entitled "*Lucky in Love*". So started a campaign to get women to smoke, with the implication that it was chivalrous for men to light their cigarettes. I never learned this bit of etiquette.

Washington, 8/3/94—Scientist agreed Tuesday, nicotine in cigarettes is as addictive a drug as heroin and cocaine, possibly the first step to regulation by the federal government.

Smoking Mothers

The greatest tragedy of women who smoke is the inferiority of their off-

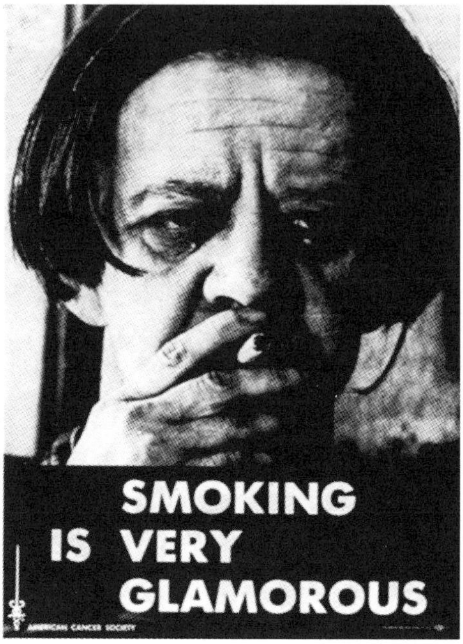

Courtesy American Cancer Society

spring. Their babies are often over five ounces (140-364 grams) lighter than babies of women who do not smoke. Mothers who smoked ten or more cigarettes a day while pregnant, had children who, at the age of eleven, were shorter. They were below the average in school work, especially in reading and in mathematics.

"A baby born of a cigarette smoking mother is sick. It may die within two weeks of birth. Sixty percent of all babies born of mothers who are habitual cigarette smokers die before they are two years old."[33]

A generation ago women smoked cigarettes and drank alcohol throughout their pregnancies and nobody looked twice, so it has been said. But since 1987, of 60 mother drug addicts there have been criminal indictments in 19 states. They have been charged with manslaughter, and child abuse. Jennifer Johnson of Florida was the first

33. Barber.

woman to be convicted on a drug delivery charge (Newsweek 4/29/91, 52). But so far this has not been extended to cover women who harm their babies by smoking.

Smoking Retards Beauty—Beauty is Skin Deep

What sort of a man is it that does not admire a beautiful woman? Back in the first book of the Bible, "Rachel was beautiful and well favoured" (Genesis 29:17).

"Seest among the captives a beautiful woman . . . Thou shalt bring her home" (Deuteronomy 21:11,12).

"The woman was very beautiful to look upon" (11 Samuel 11:2). And David got in trouble.

Cigarette nicotine causes the small blood vessels of the facial skin to shrink; this results in wrinkles, and the cheeks lose their pink color and become yellow and grayish. Nicotine also causes stained teeth, gingivitis and other gum problems.

Smoking and Advertising

There is no doubt that advertising has had a large influence in getting people to start smoking. Congress forbid advertising of cigarettes over the airwaves after January 1, 1971. The requirement that all printed advertising must display warnings of dangers to health from smoking quickly followed.*

As domestic cigarette sales started to fall, the wealthy tobacco companies started to diversify, primarily by buying up food companies. This gives them dangerous power over the press. When *Newsweek* ran an article entitled, "Showdown on Smoking", a critical look at the tobacco industry, advertising of all kinds was pulled by the tobacco companies. *Newsweek* lost a million dollars on their June 6, 1983 issue.

Tobacco advertising has been banned in Canada since May 31, 1988, and in India since 1962. In Britain cigarette ads must include warning health statements similar to those in the U.S. After 1993, no tobacco advertising will be allowed in France. In Africa, cigarette advertising is barred in Mozambique, Senegal, and Gambia. China also forbids cigarette advertising.

R. J. Reynolds was the founder of the R. J. Reynolds Tobacco Company. He was the son of a heavy smoker, who died of emphysema. When grandson Patrick saw his horrible suffering, he determined to devote his life to fighting cigarettes.

He said before a U. S. Congress subcommittee, "I believe that cigarette advertising is a promotion of a poison product and that it is moral, and good to eliminate all advertising of cigarettes."

When you see the Winston man on cigarette ads, remember David Goerlitz, the model for many years. He visited his brother in a cancer ward in a Boston hospital. Seeing so many dying from smoking, he decided to quit his high-paying job as the Winston Man. He now works for the American Cancer Society.

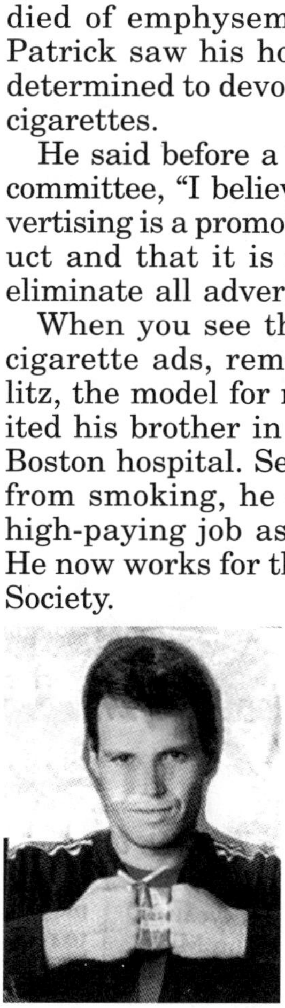

Patrick Reynolds crushing a cigarette pack. *TIME* 4/24/89

* Long before the government banned the advertising of tobacco over the air, I banned it from broadcast stations I then controlled. From the early fifties, I got control of several radio stations and a TV station. Out went tobacco advertising, along with alcoholic beverages, taverns, etc. I was told no money could be made in broadcasting that way. They were wrong. From then on the stations paid their bills.

Tobacco and the Christian

"We are a religious people whose institutions presuppose a Supreme Being," wrote Supreme Court Justice Douglas in 1952. (In my opinion, some of today's seemingly pagan justices seem ignorant of that.)

Besides Christianity's distinctive theology of salvation, Jesus summed up the Christians' aspirations: "Thou shalt love the Lord thy God with all thy heart, and with all thy soul and with all thy mind," (Matthew 22:37) and "Thou shalt love thy neighbor as thyself" (Matthew 22:39).

We take it for granted that a Christian will have nothing to do with illegal drugs. How about presently regulated semi-legal drugs, tobacco and alcohol?

Can we properly love God with all our heart, soul and mind, if we are weakening these faculties of soul and body with poison? God giveth to "all life, and breath, and all things;" (Acts 17:25) Should we corrupt that sacred breath with "an evil degrading vice habit"?[34] "Ye are the temple of the living God" (11 Corinthians 6:16).

Can we love our neighbor as ourselves while making him or her breathe in our cancer-causing poisonous gas? The law is beginning to say NO. Christians have a higher law than the legal law, LOVE.

Ways to Stop Smoking

Dr. Oski gives his experience of one easy way to stop smoking. "After finishing a cigarette he felt a terrible pain in his chest. He went to a coronary care unit in a hospital. He was put to bed for four days for absolute rest without being allowed to smoke." This, he said, "broke my habit".[35]

In contrast was the experience of James Neal, the former editor of the Noblesville Ledger. For him, there was no long term planning or retractions. He wrote a short editorial saying he got tired of the mess and bother, and quit, period!

The desire to quit must come first. I have known men to promote the *smoke-out days;* to build bonfires, and invite others to participate in burning their smoking materials. Studies show that of the 20 million that participate in the Smokeout, after ten days many were smoking again. But 20% quit for good, according to Irving Rimer, vice president of the American Cancer Society. For some it takes strong will power to ultimately succeed. Divine help is available. People who want to quit must avoid smoking friends, and any tobacco environment. Spend time in places where smoking is not allowed, such as libraries. In Church Falls, Virginia, some quitters rode a 25-foot ferris wheel, hour after hour.

GREAT AMERICAN SMOKEOUT

TAKE A BREATHER

Change habits. Keep hands busy with something. Try a new hobby, something that takes exercise. Avoid parties and social occasions where tobacco is used. Seek friends that will help rather than hinder you.

After quitting, there may be a food problem. Without nicotine, food tastes so good, especially fattening sweets. Neil Grumberg, medical psychologist at Bethesda's Uniformed Services University, makes this suggestion: Quitters should sprinkle everything from meat to poultry to fruit with a sugar substitute, to satisfy the new craving for sweets (TIME 3/25/1992, 55).

THERE IS HOPE. Said a friend, "I tried to stop for years. After I really

34. American Heritage Dictionary.
35. Oski 1984.

No. 1262. Tobacco Products—Production, Consumption, and Expenditures: 1970 to 1990

[Production data are for calendar years. Excludes cigars produced in customs bonded manufacturing warehouses. See also *Historical Statistics, Colonial Times to 1970,* series P 239-241]

ITEM	Unit	1970	1975	1980	1982	1983	1984	1985	1986	1987	1988	1989	1990
Production:													
Cigarettes	Billions	583	651	714	694	667	669	665	658	689	695	677	710
Nonfilter tip	Billions	116	80	54	47	43	39	36	33	30	28	24	23
Regular	Billions	54	36	23	21	19	18	16	15	14	12	11	11
King	Billions	62	44	30	26	24	21	20	18	16	16	13	12
Filter tip	Billions	467	571	661	647	625	630	629	625	660	667	654	687
Long and king	Billions	362	404	439	404	384	380	378	373	397	400	392	417
Extra long	Billions	105	167	222	243	241	251	252	252	263	267	261	270
Cigars	Billions	8.4	5.7	4.0	3.7	3.6	3.5	3.1	2.9	2.1	2.0	2.0	1.9
Tobacco [1]	Mil. lb.	165	152	163	163	162	163	158	147	143	142	141	142
Per capita consumption: [2]													
All products	Lb. [3]	9.7	9.1	7.9	7.5	7.2	6.9	6.8	6.6	6.3	6.1	5.7	5.5
Cigarettes	1,000	4.0	4.1	3.8	3.7	3.5	3.4	3.4	3.3	3.2	3.1	2.9	2.8
Cigars [4]	Number	60	39	24	22	21	20	18	17	15	14	14	13

dedicated my life to Christ, all desire was gone."

After quitting, the body begins to heal itself. The risk of heart disease decreases by one-half within a year of quitting. The risks of lung cancer, emphysema and strokes also decrease.

It is usually never too late to stop! Stop smoking before it stops you.

TRANQUILIZERS

These slow down the heartbeat and respiration.

The major tranquilizers are very effective in helping people with serious mental problems. They also prevent convulsions. These are patented and copyright products. Since we are concerned with addiction we will consider these first.

BENZODIAZEPINES

Valium, Xanax, Librium, Ativan, copyrighted sedatives

Side effects are drowsiness, dizziness, lack of coordination, jaundice, muscle rigidity, mental problems, menstrual problems, and a harming of mental functioning. They may cause physical addiction in spite of the fact that they are used to help users of hard drugs to be free of addiction.

ANTIPSYCHOTICS

Non-habit forming tranquilizers are:

1. Phenothiazine derivatives
   i.e. chlorpromazine, thioridazine, triflupromazine
2. Hydroxyzine

These minor ones are used in medicine to treat anxiety and other minor disorders, to aid relaxation and promote sleep, without disturbing normal mental activities.

Their deadliest effect is if taken with other drugs.

VALIUM SEDATION

"It made me feel so good, I just wanted to keep on using it." So writes the widow of our former pastor.

In a similar experience: "Here is a prescription that will make you feel much better." In his book, *From Valium to Victory,* Stan Fortenberry tells how his horrible addiction started with those words. There were five years of hopelessness. Peace and satisfaction did not come in a pill. Ordinary church attendance was not enough to give relief from "overwhelming fear, tension, and worry."[36]

Valium has become the legal drug for Christians. It does a terrific job of

36. Fortenberry 1989.

No. 197. Drug Use, by Type of Drug and Age Group: 1974 to 1991

[In percent. Current users are those who used drugs at least once within month prior to this study. Based on national samples of respondents residing in households. Subject to sampling variability; see source]

AGE AND TYPE OF DRUG	EVER USED						CURRENT USER					
	1974	1979	1982	1985	1988	1991	1974	1979	1982	1985	1988	1991
12 TO 17 YEARS OLD												
Marihuana	23.0	30.9	26.7	23.6	17.4	13.0	12.0	16.7	11.5	12.0	6.4	4.3
Cocaine	3.6	5.4	6.5	4.9	3.4	2.4	1.0	1.4	1.6	1.5	1.1	0.4
Inhalants	8.5	9.8	(NA)	9.2	8.8	7.0	0.7	2.0	(NA)	3.4	2.0	1.8
Hallucinogens	6.0	7.1	5.2	3.3	3.5	3.4	1.3	2.2	1.4	1.2	0.8	0.8
Heroin	1.0	0.5	(NA)	(NA)	0.6	0.3	(NA)	(NA)	(NA)	(NA)	(NA)	0.1
Stimulants [1]	5.0	3.4	6.7	5.6	4.2	3.0	1.0	1.2	2.6	1.6	1.2	0.5
Sedatives [1]	5.0	3.2	5.8	4.1	2.4	2.4	1.0	1.1	1.3	1.0	0.6	0.5
Tranquilizers [1]	3.0	4.1	4.9	4.8	0.2	2.1	1.0	0.6	0.9	0.6	0.2	0.3
Analgesics [1]	(NA)	3.2	4.2	5.8	4.2	4.4	(NA)	0.6	0.7	1.6	0.9	1.1
Alcohol	54.0	70.3	65.2	55.5	50.2	46.4	34.0	37.2	30.2	31.0	25.2	20.3
Cigarettes	52.0	54.1	49.5	45.2	42.3	37.9	25.0	12.1	14.7	15.3	11.8	10.8
18 TO 25 YEARS OLD												
Marihuana	52.7	68.2	64.1	60.3	56.4	50.5	25.2	35.4	27.4	21.8	15.5	13.0
Cocaine	12.7	27.5	28.3	25.2	19.7	17.9	3.1	9.3	6.8	7.6	4.5	2.0
Inhalants	9.2	16.5	(NA)	12.4	12.5	10.9	(NA)	1.2	(NA)	0.8	1.7	1.5
Hallucinogens	16.6	25.1	21.1	11.3	13.8	13.2	2.5	4.4	1.7	1.9	1.9	1.2
Heroin	4.5	3.5	1.2	1.2	0.4	0.8	(NA)	(NA)	(NA)	(NA)	(NA)	0.1
Stimulants [1]	17.0	18.2	18.0	17.1	11.3	9.4	3.7	3.5	4.7	3.7	2.4	0.8
Sedatives [1]	15.0	17.0	18.7	11.0	5.5	4.3	1.6	2.8	2.6	1.6	0.9	0.6
Tranquilizers [1]	10.0	15.8	15.1	12.0	7.8	7.5	1.2	2.1	1.6	1.6	1.0	0.6
Analgesics [1]	(NA)	11.8	12.1	11.3	9.4	10.2	(NA)	1.0	1.0	1.8	1.5	1.5
Alcohol	81.6	95.3	94.6	92.6	90.3	90.2	69.3	75.9	70.9	71.4	65.3	63.6
Cigarettes	68.8	82.8	76.9	75.6	75.0	71.2	48.8	42.6	39.5	36.8	35.2	32.2
26 YEARS OLD AND OVER												
Marihuana	9.9	19.6	23.0	27.2	30.7	32.9	2.0	6.0	6.6	6.1	3.9	3.3
Cocaine	0.9	4.3	8.5	9.5	9.9	11.8	(NA)	0.9	1.2	2.0	0.9	0.8
Inhalants	1.2	3.9	(NA)	5.0	3.9	4.4	(NA)	0.5	(NA)	0.5	0.2	0.3
Hallucinogens	1.3	4.5	6.4	6.2	6.6	8.0	(NA)	(NA)	(NA)	(NA)	(NA)	0.1
Heroin	0.5	1.0	1.1	1.1	1.1	1.7	(NA)	(NA)	(NA)	(NA)	(NA)	(NA)
Stimulants [1]	3.0	5.8	6.2	7.9	6.6	7.1	(NA)	0.5	0.6	0.7	0.5	0.2
Sedatives [1]	2.0	3.5	4.8	5.2	3.3	4.5	(NA)	(NA)	(NA)	0.6	0.3	0.3
Tranquilizers [1]	2.0	3.1	3.6	7.2	4.6	5.7	(NA)	(NA)	(NA)	1.0	0.6	0.4
Analgesics [1]	(NA)	2.7	3.2	5.6	4.5	5.5	(NA)	(NA)	(NA)	0.9	0.4	0.5
Alcohol	73.2	91.5	88.2	89.4	88.6	88.7	54.5	61.3	59.8	60.6	54.8	52.5
Cigarettes	65.4	83.0	78.7	80.5	79.6	77.6	39.1	36.9	34.6	32.8	29.8	28.8

NA Not available. [1] Nonmedical use.

Source: U.S. National Institute on Drug Abuse, *National Household Survey on Drug Abuse: 1991.*

bringing tranquillity to the temporary periods of despondency that so many people occasionally suffer.

Except the few drugs that are deliberately designed for addicts, Valium sedation use, like other possibly dangerous drugs, starts with a physician's prescription. Fortenberry's addiction got such a hold on him that he felt he would carry it to his grave.

Withdrawal.

Fortenberry's relief came with a realization that relief would come only from "an encounter with the Prince of Peace, Jesus Christ".

8 Most Questioned Chemicals in Cigarettes

The eight chemicals among cigarette additives most questioned by tobacco opponents:

- **Megastigmatrienone:** a flavoring the tobacco companies contend is found naturally in grapefruit juice and considered safe by the food industry. The FDA couldn't confirm that.
- **Dehydromenthofurolactone:** a flavoring the tobacco companies say is found in peppermint and is considered safe by the food industry. The FDA couldn't confirm that.

- **Ethyl furoate:** found naturally in coffee, kiwi and peanuts. The FDA hasn't formally ruled on the issue but said the food industry considers it safe. Last week, however, a toxicologist said the chemical can cause liver damage in laboratory animals.
- **Maltitol:** a sweetener used in chewing gum and diabetic candy. The food industry considers it safe, but the FDA hasn't ruled on a petition questioning the safety.
- **Sclareolide:** a synthetic form of a naturally occurring tobacco element. The food industry considers it safe.
- **Tobacco extract:** used to boost the flavor of reconstituted tobacco; companies say it does contain a small amount of nicotine.
- **Ammonia:** a processing aid. The FDA considers certain forms of ammonia safe in foods but couldn't comment on the type in cigarettes.
- **Methoprene:** an insecticide that toxicologists say is biodegradable and works by stopping insects from growing to adulthood. Tobacco companies say the FDA allows it in dried fruits, but the FDA couldn't confirm that.

More common items added to cigarettes: yeast, wine, caffeine, beeswax, beta carotene, chocolate and coconut oil.

Source: The Associated Press

CHAPTER THREE

I believe you have presented scientific facts. What can be more scientific than Absolute Truth?

I have read your article with more interest because I AM opposed to internal use of alcohol in all except those medications which require alcohol as solvent. Alcohol as the primary medication is totally unnecessary today and medically contraindicated because in even the alcoholic one more dose of the "Beloved Enemy" would be harmful. There is a wide range of sedatives on the market which will perform in a superior manner without the alcohol side effects.

Alton H. Ridgway, M.D.
Hospital Anesthesiologist

CHAPTER THREE ALCOHOL—OUR WORST DRUG PROBLEM

Alcohol Use Is Abuse

Alcohol claims 25 times more lives than all other drugs combined.

Source: National Institute Alcohol and Alcoholism.

National Report to Congress in 1971, "Alcohol beverage use is our country's No. 1 drug problem."[1]

Judge Harry Sauce has said, "Despite the media and the people at the state level focusing their efforts on cocaine and crack, I can assure you folks that alcohol is the most dangerous" (Sauce in the Noblesville Daily Ledger, 4/26/1990).

Dr. Joel Fort, the former consultant to the World Health Organization on Drug Abuse Problems, and the first in this country to set up a city drug program, has written a popular book entitled: *"Alcohol: Our Biggest Drug Problem."*[2] The National Commission on Marijuana and Drug Abuse confirmed Dr. Fort's statement, when it reported that, "Alcohol is indeed the biggest drug problem in the United States."

"Alcohol harms more babies than all other drugs combined."[3]

The National Institute on Drug Abuse (NIDA) representative Schuster says, "There is no question that alcoholism in terms of social cost remains *our number one problem*. We can't lose sight of that because of our emphasis on drugs."

"Twenty five times as many die from alcohol as from all other drugs together."[4]

U.S. Drug Related Deaths in 1980:

Cocaine deaths	563
Alcohol deaths	98,186

—National Center for Health Statistics

So, alcohol use/abuse is our worst drug problem.

Survey—Rep. Dan Burton, 1989

Question: "What do you regard as the number one problem facing America today?"

1. Answer number one: Deficits.
2. Drugs and crime, number two.
3. Family Values, number three.

(St. Martinsville, LA, A.P. 1/3/94): "Danny L. Burton II, son of Indianapolis Congressman Dan Burton, was arrested when a trooper found seven pounds of marijuana in the trunk of his car".

Rep. Dan Burton
Assistant Regional Whip

Drugs and crime, is our second worst American problem. Since alcohol is the worst of the drugs, then alcohol abuse has become a frightful American situation. Some surveys put drugs and crime as our number one problem.

1. U. S. Dept. of Health, Education and Welfare.
2. Fort 1973.
3. Rhine Geneticist 1986.
4. The National Institute on Drug Abuse and Alcoholism.

June 13, 1994—*Newsweek* Poll 76% believe drugs and crime, is our worst American problem and the **"United States is in a moral and spiritual decline"** (Cover story, Virtue). Why do we get into this condition? One: our Supreme Court has taken the Bible and the 10 commandments out of our schools. Some people drink and use drugs to get away from our immoral morass.

People Drink to Get Intoxicated

Alcohol is not drunk for taste—pure alcohol is bitter. Along with carbonation and flavors, there may be a pleasant taste, just as carbonation gives zest to soft drinks. But, that is not the reason people drink alcohol. Recent studies show **people drink intoxicants to get intoxicated**; a small degree of mind altering pleasure, and some relief starts with the first drink. (Almost All You Ever Wanted to Know about Alcohol, p.p. 17 and 19.) Any amount is intoxicating. "Wine makes me feel fine." So the song goes. "Drunk—intoxicated, overcome by alcohol" (Webster).

Since intoxication starts with the first drink, there is no agreement as to when one is intoxicated. There is no recipe of how much to drink. The Bible gives none, but calls it poison (Psalm 58:4). Imbibers drink to deliberately lose control.

Alcoholism is drinking to forget problems caused by drinking.

Volatility

One characteristic of alcohol is its extreme volatility. It is so volatile that as soon as it enters the mouth, some of it enters the bloodstream. As a fat and brain-seeking chemical, it first hits the fore part of the brain where social inhibitions, values, and spiritual senses are located. The numbing or temporary anesthesia lasts until the liver and kidneys and lungs clear the system of alcohol. Numbing the forefront brain cells causes the imbibers to be oblivious of their concerns, worries, and inhibitions. They feel free, uninhibited, unrestrained from drinking more, and usually happy. This unnatural phoney euphoria is the reason that the alcoholic drinker imbibes over and over causing alcoholic addiction.

(Doctor: "How did you become an alcoholic?" Patient: "Practice, practice, practice.").

A. ALCOHOLIC ADDICTION

At least one out of ten moderate drinkers will become an alcoholic. As studies show:

"One out of every ten Americans develops a serious alcohol related problem in his or her life time."[5]

Some give a higher percentage of alcoholics. The chief clinical pharmacologist of the National Institute on Drug Abuse, Jack Henningfield, states, "The nation has 106 million users of alcohol, and one in every eight is a problem drinker."

Studies by the National Institute on Alcohol Abuse and Alcoholism indicate that "Twenty-one percent of even moderate drinkers become 'psychologically dependent' on alcohol."[6]

That is 1 in 5 moderate drinkers become psychologically dependent; according to the generally accepted Gallop Survey.*

We may think of the skid row wino as the characteristic drunken bum. But alcoholism has no boundaries. It also occurs among the wealthy, the educated, and those of exalted position. Examples of this are: Betty Ford, in the White

5. Mendelson 1985.

6. Ronald Schiller, A Reader's Digest Gallup Survey.

* A drinker stumbled up to his car. A policeman said, "You're not planning on driving in that condition are you?" The drunk answered, "I'm shurr in no condition to walk."

House, the wife of one of our presidents, and Kitty Dukakis who aspired to be our first lady. Even one of our presidents? Again we say, alcoholism is an equal opportunity addiction.

Alcohol Addiction in their Genes?

Moderate drinkers do not usually intend to become drunks, they just do. Which person is likely to become addicted? As of now we cannot tell (Fort 1973). But that ten percent who become addicts may have from birth a propensity to becoming addicted. It is possibly in their genes. A couple of scientists believe they have a hint of what the suspected gene might be. Writing in the *Journal of the American Medical Association*, Kenneth Blum of the University of Texas and Dr. Earnest Noble of U.C.L.A. reported that an aberrant form of so-called dopamine D2 receptor gene was strongly associated with alcoholism in the group they studied.[7] If it's in your genes, and you start, you are a goner.

Using EEG technology, investigators have shown that alcoholics and first-degree relatives who are not alcoholics have a propensity for alcoholism. It runs in the family.[8]

They probably would become alcoholics if they drank. But one is not given a life sentence to become an alcoholic. For if one never takes the first drink, one will have no possibility of becoming a drunk. *This is the reason to be abstinent.* Blum and Noble concede that other factors can override genetic dispositions, as with religious devotees who do not use drugs. (See Religion in this chapter.)

In the light of this inherited propensity to drink, is alcoholism a disease?

Adult: "Why do you drink so much?!!"
Teenager: "It's my inheritance."

7. *Newsweek* 4/30/1979.
8. Pollook et al 1983.

This is Alcohol Equivalence.
A drink, is a drink, is a drink.
No matter what you drink or think.

Is Drug Addiction A Disease?

"Drug dependency is not strictly a disease since there is no known specific cure for the dependencies."[9]

If alcoholism (drunkenness) is a disease, it is a self-inflicted disease. This disease of choice is responsible for ruining the lives of millions of people, including the innocent killed by drunk drivers. But if one never takes the first drink, that one will never become an alcoholic. Contrary to popular belief, just a small amount of wine or beer can make one an alcoholic and kill some brain cells.

When a person starts sipping a little wine, and then finds that he or she is drinking more than is wanted, or the sipping is interfering with relationships with others, or with work, then that person is on the way to becoming an alcoholic. At the alcoholic stage there can never be a total cure. Even if there is stopping of drinking, the imbiber can never drink a little again without losing control. *When an adequate number of the brain cells that control drinking are killed, alcoholics can never curb drinking again, if they take alcohol.* "Even smelling another's alcoholic breath has been known to get a stopped alcoholic to start again" (Missionary Ann Kuhn 1993.)

9. Dr. Nahab 1987.

Kitty Dukakis, White House hopeful, stated on national TV that she started her alcohol addiction by sneaking some of her mother's reducing pills. She lost two pounds and gained an addiction (9/14/1990).

"Chronic alcoholism has come to be considered by some as a character disorder. A 'problem drinker,' that is one who cannot control his drinking, must be certainly classified as a psycho neurotic."[10] Is psycho neurosis the cause or result of addictive drinking, or both? A look at the brain might give a cue.

Hey—aren't those brain cells you are losing?

Brain damage begins with moderate drinking.[11] If alcohol were invented today, it would have the same fate as heroin. If available at all, it would be available only by prescription.

The poor fellow has tavern arthritis. Every night he gets stiff in a different joint.—Lois Costomiris.

BRAIN DAMAGE

Loss of Brain Cells

Anesthesia of brain cells is dangerous. Brain cells are not only weakened; some are killed.

"The moderate imbiber may incur some loss of irreplaceable brain cells—

60 year Alcoholic Male | 68 year Control Male

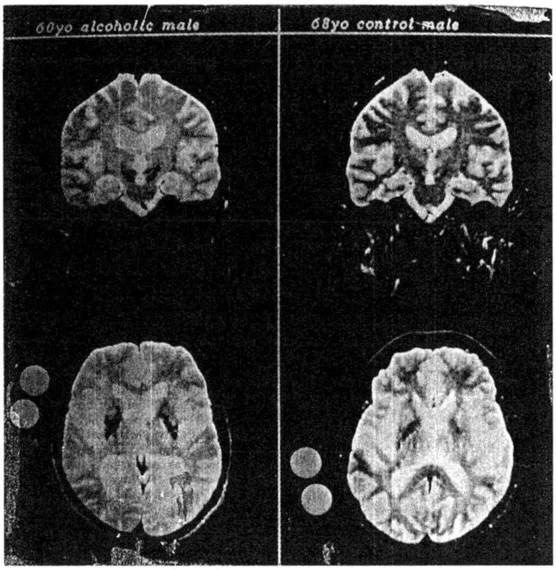

Provided by Dr. Adolf Plefferbaum.

every time he drinks." This is what Albert Q. Maisel writes in the *Reader's Digest* article of June 1970: *Alcohol and our Brain, Some News for Social Drinkers*.[12] This conclusion is based on the results of experiments conducted by Prof. Melvin H. Knisley and two young associates, Drs. Herbert A. Moskow, and Raymond C. Pennington at the Medical University of South Carolina. During my research Dr. Pennington talked with me personally on this subject.

Holes in Brain

Scientists have known of black holes in brains of cadavers where alcoholics' brain cells died. When one dies, probably some years earlier than if he or she had been a non-drinker, an autopsy of the brain will reveal enormous numbers of small areas of atrophy in which brain cells have been destroyed. In some cases, Dr. Knisely has observed that entire convolutions of the brain are so shrunken that the loss tissue can be seen the moment the brain is exposed to view.[12]

10. Dr. McKnight 1963.
11. Boston University.

12. Maisel 1979.

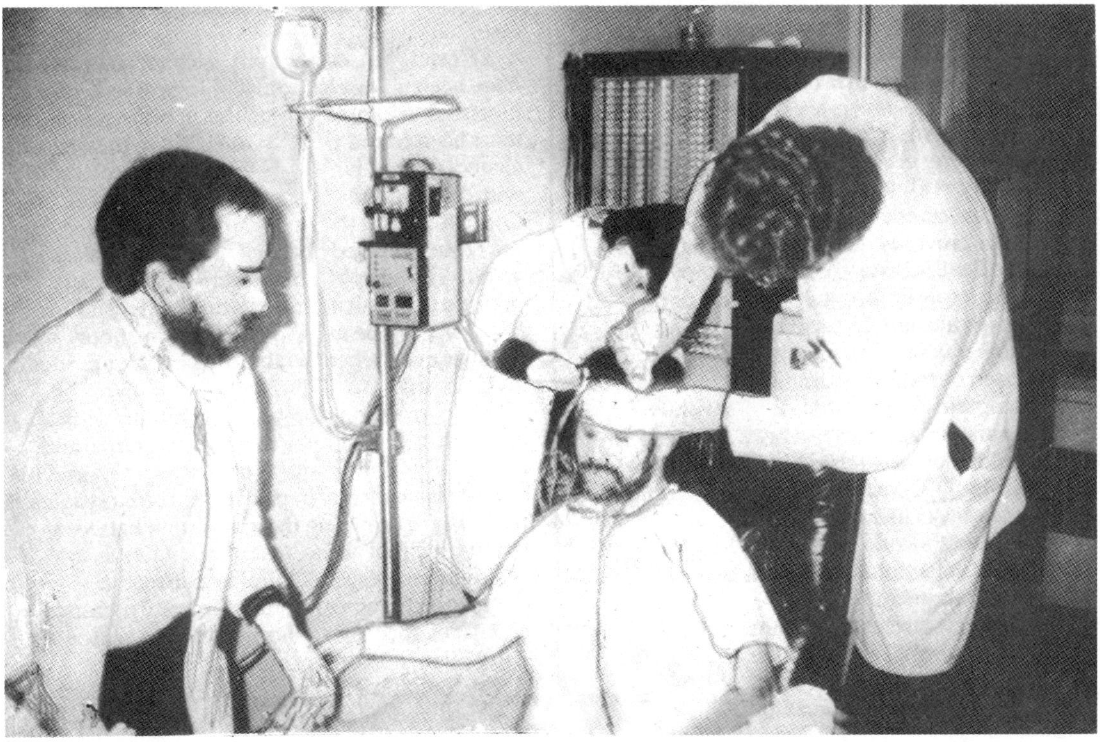

Electrodes are placed over specific brain regions on an NIAAA intramural research program control subject. Provided by Dr. Boris Tabakoff.

(A hangover is a funeral for dead brain cells).

"Moderate alcohol use diminishes brain cells."[13]

Computerized topography studies of the alcoholic brain show atrophy. There are increased spaces called "sulci," and enlargement of cavities of the brain called ventricles.

Alcoholic patients also showed loss of tissue in the mammillary bodies. This explains the short-term memory dysfunction of alcoholics. The atrophied brain of the 60-year-old alcoholic seems to compare to a blur.

With the loss of brain power, the drinker is not aware of losing brain cells.[14]

Since the brain is the center of the nervous system, when the brain is numbed, every body function is affected, but primarily the brain itself.

Galen Bosley writing in *Ministry,* May 1986, graphically shows how a steel shaft accidentally pierced the skull of Phineas P. Gage.

Gage, a 25-year-old foreman, was going to tamp blasting powder. He was distracted. The rod hit a rock, made a spark, and set off the blasting powder. The rod entered Gage's head at the jaw, and went through the top of his head, just behind the forehead.

After a time he was back on the job, but was a different man. Before the accident, he was temperate and of good character. But after the accident, according to his physician, Dr. J. M. Harlow, "The balance between his intellect and animal propensities seems to have been destroyed. He is fitful, irreverent, indulging at times in the grossest pro-

13. Geriatric Society.

14. Summers.

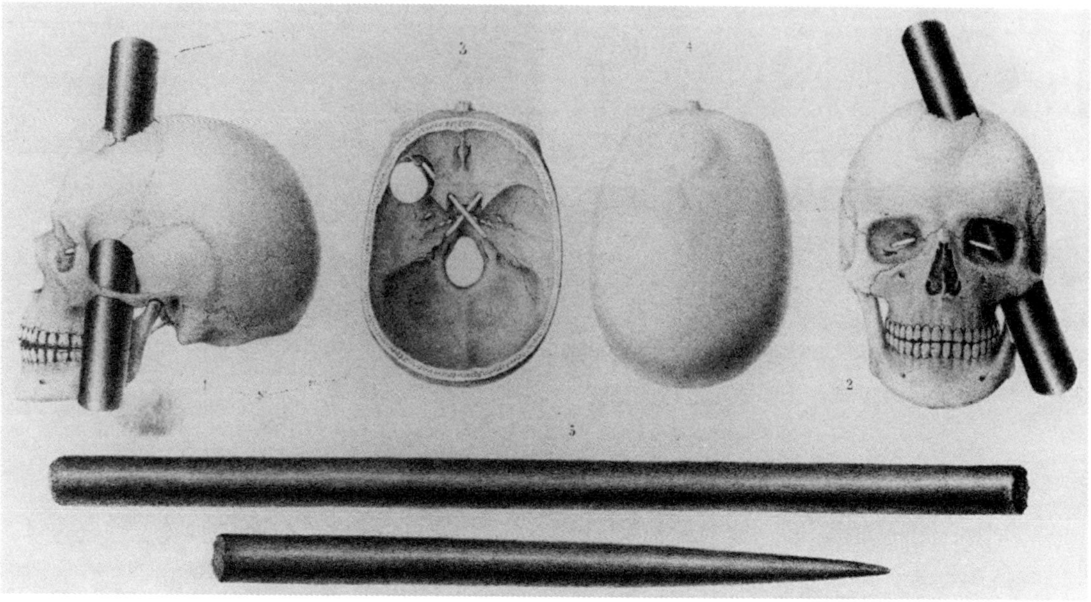

In 1848 an explosion drove a 3-foot iron rod through Phineas P. Gage's head. Though he miraculously survived the accident, the resultant brain damage changed his personality. (Reproduced from *American Journal of Medical Science* 39 (1850):13.) I am grateful to *Ministry* Magazine May 1986, Galen Bosley's personal help, and the gracious assistance of Ella Rydzewski.)[15]

fanity (which was not previously his custom), manifesting little deference for his fellows. He's impatient of restraint or advice, when it conflicts with his desires at times . . . obstinate, yet capricious and vacillating . . . A child in his intellectual capacity and manifestations, he has the animal passions of a strong man . . . His mind was so radically changed . . . that his friends and acquaintances said he was no longer Gage."

With far more subtlety, alcohol affects the frontal lobes of the brain and so changes a drinker's character. In both animal and human studies, alcohol, more than any other drug, has been linked with violence and aggression. Recent studies have related either acute or chronic alcohol use with suicides, murders, and sexual assaults. All these anti-social actions are directed by the pickled frontal part of the brain, the part first affected by alcohol.

15. Ministry Magazine, May 1986.

"Twenty to forty percent of patients treated in hospitals are there because of misuse of alcohol."[16]

Lost brain cells are not replaceable. Damage to brain cells leads to mental deterioration with memory loss. There are no tracers for lost brain cells.

The brain orders the liver to rid the body of alcohol. The liver works hard at the task, so hard that in one case out of twelve alcoholics, it self destructs by overwork and we have cirrhosis of the liver.

CIRRHOSIS OF THE LIVER

As few as three drinks a day can cause liver cirrhosis.[17] Alcoholics are twelve times more likely than non-alcoholics to die of cirrhosis of the liver.

The U.S. National Center for Health Services has traced the deaths in the U.S. due to cirrhosis. The following chart, based on its data, bears out the

16. Sullivan 1990.
17. Sixth Report to Congress.

Deaths (Per 100,000) From Cirrhosis in the United States[18]

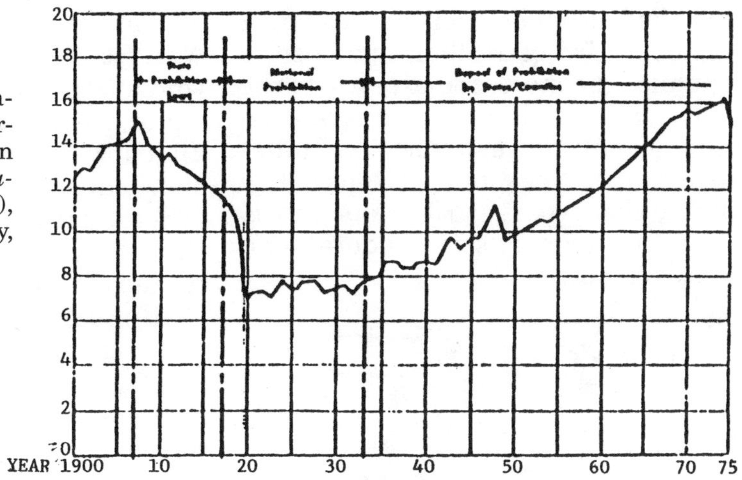

Prohibition

18. From the U.S. National Center for Health Services. Chart and information from Ross McLennan, *Propaganda Vs. Facts* (1978), SANE Press, Oklahoma City, OK 73105.

fact that national prohibition (1917 to 1933) brought about a tremendous decline in deaths due to cirrhosis. When prohibition ended, the increase in alcoholic consumption corresponded closely to the increase of early deaths from cirrhosis.

Small amounts of alcohol cause fatty deposits in the liver. The liver works hard to get rid of the poison of alcohol. Overtaxing it results in cirrhosis, which can lead to death. Many alcoholics die before the age of 50.

COST TO ADDICTS AND TO SOCIETY

Economic

"Alcohol's cost to society in 1983 was $117 billion" (Research Triangle Institution, 1989).

"The economic cost to society of alcoholism, and alcohol abuse, are estimated at nearly $117 billion a year, including $18 billion from premature deaths" (Campbell, "Alcohol's Cost to Society," U.S. News and World Report, 6/1992).

Longevity Affected

As volatile poisonous alcohol is circulated in the bloodstream, every organ is affected. This often results in changed blood pressure, disturbance of sleep patterns, and ulcers.

"Alcoholics are twice as likely to die of cancer, three times as apt to die of auto accidents, and six times as likely to commit suicide."[19]

"Alcohol is the third leading cause of death in America, right behind heart disease and cancer. It is estimated that 86,000 people die annually for reasons related to drinking. The life span of alcoholic persons is twelve years shorter than others."[20]

Alcohol should especially be avoided by those with gastritis, by depressed persons, and diabetics. It can cause convulsions in epileptics.

(A person who would die for a drink probably will.)

Alcohol's Public Expense

Besides the preventable death crashes, alcohol drinking causes much

19. Miller 1990.
20. Miller, Seventh Report to Congress, 1990.

more expense to the public. We all pay. Manning and his associates have computed that alcoholic excise taxes cover about one-third of alcohol's expense to the public. The increased expense to the public is in our collectively financed disability, group life insurance, criminal justice courts, fines, and prisons. They estimate these costs at $0.48 per ounce, or twice the average state, federal, and sales taxes now paid.[21]

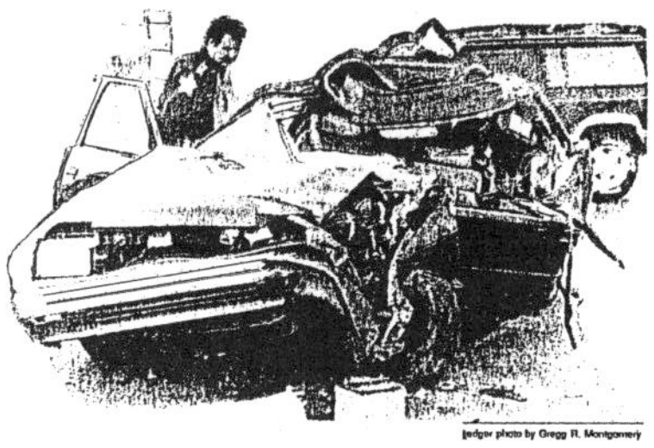

Alcohol a Factor in Broken Homes and Crime

Loss of inhibition has been a factor in many homes broken by alcohol. "According to one survey, one third of Americans regard alcohol as the single greatest threat to family life."[22] Also, alcohol is involved (along with other drugs) in most robberies, rapes and murders.

DRINKING MOTHERS

Pregnant Women Must Not Drink

The American Medical Association and the U.S. Surgeon General agree that there is no safe amount of alcohol that might be consumed by a pregnant woman. Fetal Alcohol Syndrome (FAS) results in a damaged fetus.

Even the moderate drinking mother, according to researcher Dr. Kenneth Lyons Jones, has unfortunate birth results. Possibly as many as 10% of the babies born to moderate drinkers have alcohol related problems! A University of Washington study, by psychologist Ann Streissguth, found that women who averaged one or two drinks a day while pregnant bore children who had difficulty in paying attention and were slow learners.

Some states are trying to do something about the bearing of these retarded children. New York passed a law that liquor dealers should put up signs warning pregnant women of the dangers of alcohol. In doing so they have had to fight the FEMINISTS. This opposition to the warning signs was led by Molly Yard, of the National Organization of Women (N.O.W.).*

N.O.W., with its basis in the atheistic humanist manifesto, should not be confused with the Christian organization of Concerned Women for America, led by Beverly LaHaye, or Christian activist attorney Phyllis Schlafly.

Sarah was warned in the 13th chapter of *Judges* not to drink alcoholic wine while pregnant. Greek and Roman women of child bearing age were not allowed to drink alcoholic liquids. With a large part of Christian society approving of alcohol, we are more liberal. (For more on this subject, see notes in *Judges* chapter 13.)

Since women had been so successful with the WCTU, many temperance people worked hard for women's suffrage, expecting that would help the temperance cause; it did not. It worked in reverse.

Before the 18th amendment, women were scarcely ever seen in a saloon. Some saloons had a side entrance for women. But in the abandonment following the victory over the Germans in 1918, women started to go to the "speak-

21. Manning 1989.
22. Schiller 12/1985.

* (Give 'em a Yard, they'll take the neighborhood.)

MADD®
Mothers Against Drunk Driving

There's a drinking driver in their memories

Milo Kirk,
National MADD
president

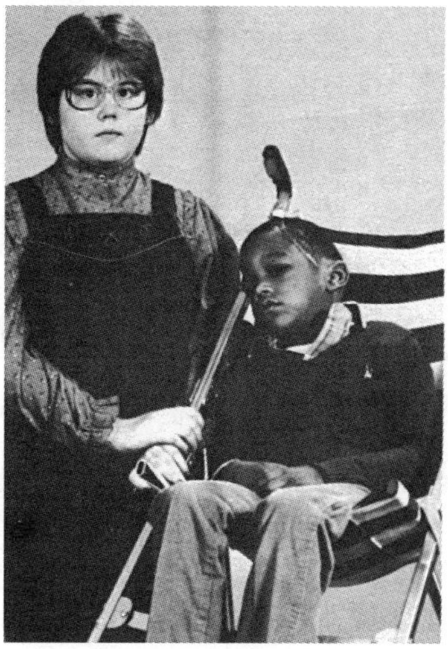

easies." After the repeal of the Eighteenth Amendment, saloons were called taverns and frequented by women as well as men. It was then the flapper and the jazz age. Temperanoe workers got discouraged.

Courts—A Problem

Unfortunately, those who are concerned about not having a large part of our country behave like idiots have had to fight the courts. Some of these courts are more concerned about the right of women to indulge than about the welfare of our country. The Michigan Court of Appeals ruled that 24-year-old drug addict Kimberly Hardy should not have been tried for child abuse charges, because the statute did not actually mention fetuses.[23] Even the Supreme Court voted against a mandatory Wisconsin fetal protection policy. But prostitute Lee Ann Moore has been required to spend her last month of pregnancy in a drug treatment center in Rockford, IL.

DRUNK DRIVERS

Fifty percent of all highway deaths are caused by drunk drivers, who kill the innocent as well as themselves.

23. *Newsweek* 4/29/1991.

Drinking any amount of alcohol impairs the ability to drive. Drivers with .10 percent blood alcohol concentration are fifteen times more likely to have a fatal accident than non-drinking drivers. This makes it unsafe for all of us on highways.

In a survey of uniformed policemen in the province of Ontario, the arrest, per officer, for drunk driving, was only ten persons a year. Yet an evening roadside checkpoint by the Interministerial Committee on Drinking Driving revealed the shocking information that 6.6 percent of the drivers stopped were over the legal percentage allowed. But the police felt that they had more important things to do.[24]

A new *Catechism for the Catholic Church* was released in November of 1992. "New, is the condemnation of drunken driving and drug abuse."[25]

Alcoholic Highway Slaughter

Keeping drunk drivers off the road is at the top of the list for many safety officials. Autopsies show that more than 50% of drivers killed in accidents were legally drunk at the time. In the past 10

24. Vingilis 1985.
25. Kenneth Woodward, *Newsweek* 11/20/1992 p. 71.

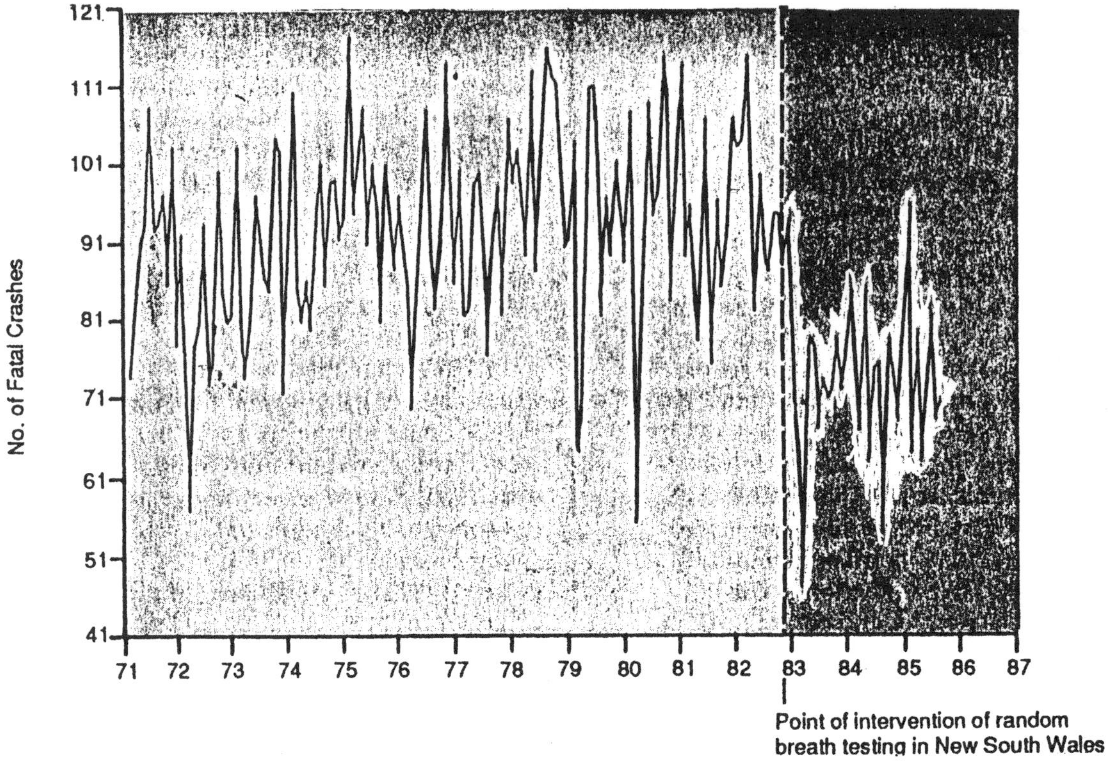

Monthly fatal crashes in New South Wales, January, 1971 to July, 1985. Source: Hormel, 1986.

years, more than 250,000 have died in crashes involving intoxicated drivers.[26]

The brain remains numb, after the blood count evidence disappears. This results in continued bad driving.[27]

(Headline: "Police stops drunk driver. This gives him a license to live".)

Under a Michigan law, if a motorist fails a breath test or refuses to take one, police may on the spot confiscate and destroy his driver license.

In Stockton, California, blitzes were made for three months a year, October through December. Arrests were tripled during these blitzes. A three-year review showed a 43% reduction in drivers with a blood alcohol content (BAC) of 10% or more. This resulted in 10% less accidents during week nights, and 15% less accidents on weekends.

A Mexico license revocation law reduced alcohol crash deaths by 10%, simply by "increased actual swiftness of punishment." This was achieved despite police resistance, less arrests, and little help from the media.[28]

For speedy punishment, an Ontario law that has been getting results, is a 12-hour revocation law. There is no arrest, no trial. The officers make random stops. If the BAC is above .05, the license is taken on the spot for 12 hours.

The American Civil Liberties Union (ACLU) would probably squawk (it seems, in my opinion, ACLU means Anti Civil Liberties Union). They'd rather have license than highway safety.

26. *U.S. News and World Report* Sept. 10, 1981.

27. Tufts University.

28. Ross 1985.

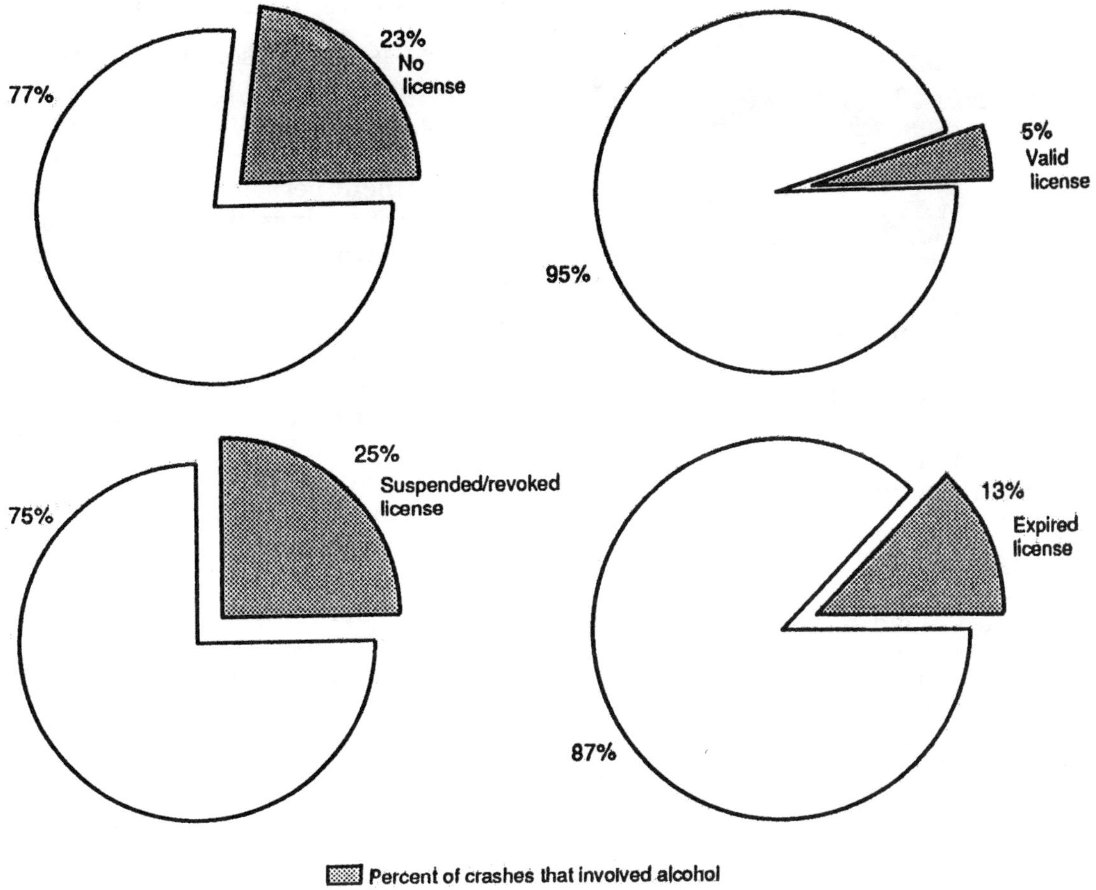

Alcohol involved crashes as a function of license status, 1986.
Source: Adapted from NHTSA 1988b.

One program in New South Wales, Australia, has had fantastic results. With effective police "blitzes" in its first year, one in every three licensed drivers was stopped and tested for Alcoholic content. The timing and duration of testing periods were carefully planned in order to be most effective. Different from most programs, which depend on free media promotion, there was a substantial expenditure to publicize the program.

The result was a twenty-three percent reduction in highway deaths after 32 months.

One fourth of all crashes were caused by drivers who had their license suspended. These people were five times more likely to have been drinking.

Drivers with expired license were three times likelier to have been drinking than drivers with a valid license. Those not using seat belts were three time likelier to have been drinking than drivers using seat belts (NHTSA 1988b) (National Highway Traffic Safety Administration).

While half of the accidents are caused by alcoholics, we must not forget that many accidents are caused by those who have indulged in a single bout of drinking.

Media Cooperation Saves Lives

A study of Maine's increased penalties for drunk driving, along with media promotion in 1981, showed a sharp

Eleanor Mill
Mill News Art Syndicate
Hartford, CT

decline in the number of people being killed in fatal auto crashes.[29]

Research findings definitely show that publicity increases the results of law enforcement.[30]

From the Associated Press "In Boston, a trolley car rammed into another that was unloading passengers at an underground station injuring 33 passengers . . . The driver of the moving trolley tested positive for alcohol in his blood" (AP 12/20/1990).

In an airplane crash at about the same time, the pilot's blood showed alcohol from a binge of the previous night. Five crew members and 87 passengers were killed.

Extra aqua police have been put on Geist Reservoir in Indiana because of accidents caused by drinkers with speed boats.

On land, sea, or air, are we safe anywhere?

Mike Brake of the Oklahoma Department of Education says, "We make people learn how to drive. Why don't we require a license to drink?" (Newsweek, 3/14/94, p.11.)

One for the road may lead to a dead end.

Make your next drink for the road a *nixed* one.

Should drunk drivers who kill innocents be given a face lift? A rope around the neck?

29. Kingston 1987.
30. Ross 1985.

Abstinence Vs. Drunk Driving

Blessed is the person whose church and parents teach abstinence, the drinking of non-alcoholic wine—grape juice—but never alcoholic beverages.

No abstinent person has ever become a drunk driver. It is the use of alcohol that causes trouble, not the abuse of alcohol.

We will see in chapter four the churches that believe in abstinence. Unfortunately, there is now very little teaching and preaching about alcohol and drugs.

The prohibition years were preceded by strenuous teaching against alcohol in our schools. Sunday schools had a temperance lesson in every quarter of the year. There was fiery preaching against alcohol use.

Sadly, most of this was dropped when prohibition was achieved. After repeal, drunk driving increased like a sky rocket.

MEDICAL USES OF ALCOHOL

Pure alcohol is a colorless, poisonous liquid with a bitter taste. Ethyl alcohol (ethanol), the kind used in beverages, is less toxic but still poisonous.

Medically, it is used to cleanse and harden the skin, and to cool the skin during a rubdown. Decreasingly, it serves as a solvent in medicine, as a tranquilizer, and as an antiseptic. It hardens and preserves cadavers.

Since alcohol burns, it must not be used by those with stomach ulcers.

Methanol alcohol also serves at times to cool the skin, and as an antiseptic. If swallowed, it can cause blindness and death.

Isopropyl alcohol is used to a lesser extent as a rubbing alcohol. But, due to the fact that it is both extremely volatile and poisonous, it can go right through the skin, causing intoxication, convulsions, and even death to children. Veterinarians warn against putting alcohol on pets' skin, as it can kill them.

Alcohol has many calories, but not the vitamins, minerals, and necessary nutrients, so fat results—the beer belly.[31]

(Refuse alcohol, avoid hazardous waists.)

B. SOLUTION ATTEMPTS

MINIMUM AGE LAWS

"Drunk driving is the leading cause of death for the 15 to 24 age group."[32]

In 1984, Congress set a minimum drinking age of 21. If states did not comply, their highway funds were to be cut off. By 1988 all states and the District of Columbia, were in compliance.

Most states set the blood alcohol content limit at 0.10. Maine, one of the driest states set the limit at 0.08. That limit has also been set by Utah, Oregon and California. (The National Safety Council, Ithica, Illinois.) Some states are now experimenting with a 0.05 limit.

The National Highway Traffic Safety Administration (NHTSA) showed there had been a big decrease, even up to 30%, in fatal accidents from among those states that previously had no such law. Many states are now reducing the drinking age to 18.

The U.S. General Accounting Office (GAO) combined 14 studies. Reductions in traffic crashes were found in most states affected by the minimum drinking age limit (Seventh Report to Congress p. 16).

The minimum age law reduced deaths caused by drunk drivers, according to a conservative study by Decker and his Associates, in 1985.[33]

The American Medical Association is hoping to get the average 10% legal limit lowered. Some states use the impairment definition of .05%. Tests show a wide range of response to alcohol for people of the same age and weight. For some persons one drink may be too much to be able to drive.

The chart on next page was prepared by the National Highway Safety Administration. Younger people's driving is impaired earlier. A small 4 oz. glass of wine, a 12 oz. can of beer or a 1.2 oz. of 80 proof whiskey each have the same amount of alcohol and the same effect.

"Permitted only under police control."[34]

(A person who's too young to drink is too young to die).

Partially Legal Alcohol

"There is no inherent right in a citizen to sell intoxicating liquors . . . it is a privilege of the state or as a citizen of the United States . . . By general concurrence of opinion of every civilized and Christian community, there are few sources of crime and misery to society equal to the dram shop . . ." (United States Supreme Court, 137 US 86 & 137 US 83). (Since then, my opinion is to agree with the one who said that we now have too many heathens on the Supreme Court.)

"The liquor trade may be permitted only under police control."[35]

There is no inherent right to use alcohol. From the United States Supreme Court: "The right to hold intoxicating li-

31. U.S. Department of Agriculture.
32. Mothers Against Drunk Drivers (MADD).
33. In Seventh Report to Congress, p. 235.
34. Maine State vs. Lafleur 4/1/1952.
35. Maine State vs. Lafleur 4/1/1952.

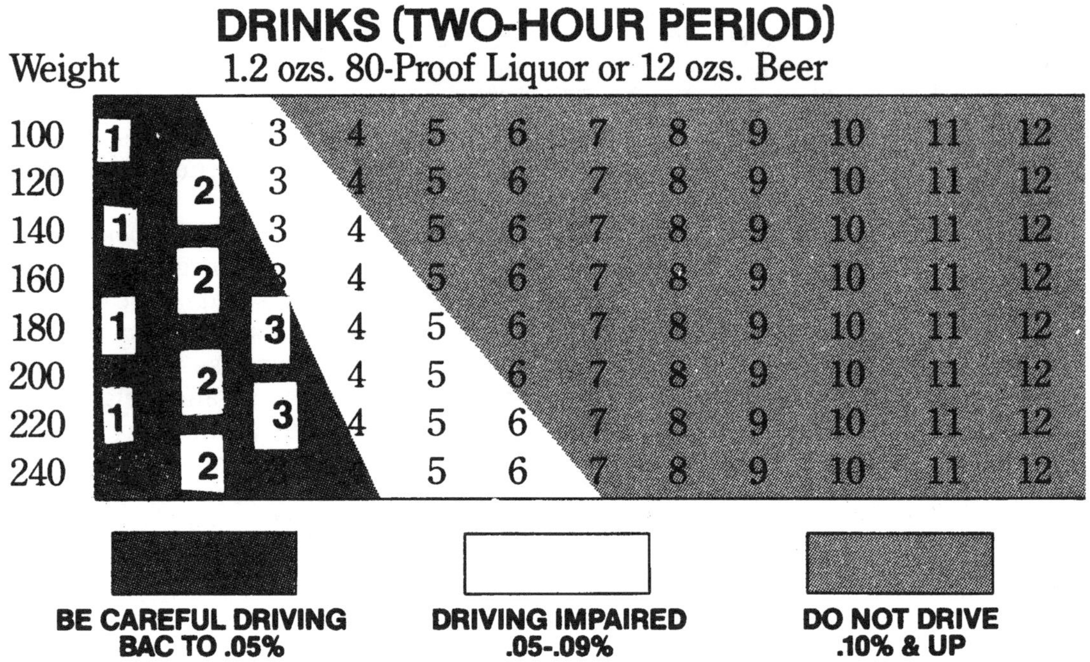

Source: NHTSA

quors for personal use is not one of those fundamental privileges of a citizen." (Green vs. Campbell, United States Supreme Court).

Since the use of alcohol as a beverage has caused more problems than illegal drugs, its legal use has often been questioned.

If we had not inherited alcohol beverage in our society, and if it had been just recently discovered, no doubt it would be declared illegal. The Moslem countries have made it illegal.

RELIGION

There is practically no alcoholism among Mormons, Moslems, Evangelical Quakers, Fundamentalist Christians, some Baptists, Seventh Day Adventists, and others who promote abstinence, holiness, and a "separated life." "Religion, environment, and education can make a huge difference."[36]

According to a study by Strauss and Bacon, forty million Americans belong to church groups that believe drunkenness is wrong and abstinence the only answer.[37]

Dr. Seigle says, "The drive to intoxication is irrepressible, unstoppable. It functions almost like hunger and sex."[38] Ordinarily this is possibly true, but religious training can make a big difference. I consider myself average, with normal appetites, but I have never had an unstoppable appetite for intoxication. Perhaps it was because my parents and my church taught me that the use of illicit drugs, alcoholic beverages, and tobacco was wrong. I never tried any of these.

But even with the best of nurturing, there are slips. When one realizes the need for help, the pastor is usually the first contact. But pastors are trained to preach and to moralize. Generally, they

36. Driver and Swan, Report to Congress, 1987.

37. Yale Press 1953.

38. Seigle 1989.

have had no alcohol and drug training and know less of drugs than the kid on the street. Drug facts must be known to be taught.

The best treatment is counseling. Sociopsychological and physical factors are involved. One needs special training in counseling. The best course of action to take with an alcoholic is to be sympathetic, refer them to Alcoholics Anonymous, and be willing to give prolonged cooperation and help.

TAXES

Tax on Alcohol is a Joke

Alcohol is government controlled, therefore taxed. But the amount of tax revenue does not come any where near meeting the expenses caused by alcohol. It should.

Below are shocking facts regarding alcohol and drug abuse, that have been presented to Congress in the Seventh Special Report from the Secretary of the U.S. Department of Health and Human Services, January 1990, regarding Drug and Alcohol Abuse.

Alcohol Taxes Saves Lives

Here Congress should definitely help. Econometric studies compared the relationship between alcohol use and alcohol-related automobile crashes, in the period between 1975 and 1988. Grossman and his associates came to the shocking conclusion that a $1.50 increase per case of beer (24 unit case of 12 ounce cans) would: reduce highway mortality among

15-20-year-old drivers by 18%,
18-21-year-old drivers by 27%,
24-year-old drivers by 19.1%[39]

Phelps—adding to Grossman's data, combined with the 1984 autopsy data, projected that a 35% increase in the price of beer would halve the fatalities among 16 to 21 year-old drivers. A 50% tax would eliminate 75% of drunk driver deaths.[40]

Therefore, the higher the tax on alcohol, the more lives are saved. Grossman and Phelps studies show millions of lives could be saved by higher alcohol taxes. However, are you ready for this? *"FEDERAL TAXES ON BEER AND WINE HAVE NOT BEEN RAISED SINCE 1951."* A very small change has now been made in 1991. President Bush did push for a small raise in the sin taxes, tobacco and alcohol.

Restoring federal alcohol taxes to their 1993 real values would require a fourfold increase in the taxes on beer, wine, and liquor—to $1.27, $.74, and $46.00 per gallon, respectively. By our estimate, this "inflation-catch-up" increase in taxes would raise about $11 billion in revenues and reduce the social costs of alcohol abuse by $7.6 billion.[41]

39. Grossman 1987.
40. Phelps 1987.
41. Pogue and Sgontz (January 1989).

That means through inflation, prices on other commodities have skyrocketed, but the real cost of alcoholic beverages has declined. Alcohol taxes ought at least to be kept up with inflation; they have not.

The failure of Congress to at least ensure,—taxes keep pace with inflation has cost the lives of thousands of innocent law-abiding highway users. Saffer and Grossman, after examining the variables, the taxes in different states, along with the alcohol-related death fatalities, have estimated, deaths could have been decreased by 54%.[42]

Question: Do campaign funds have to do with not raising alcohol taxes?

Campaigning congressman after voting for alcohol tax increase: "You might not be here without me."

WITHDRAWAL

I have found that it is useless to attempt to be of help, to try to give treatment to alcoholics without their request.

Alcoholics at first seldom realize they are addicts. In the beginning they may act quite normally. It is for others to recognize the situation. The signs are: drinking frequently and excessively, drinking alone, making excuses for drinking, nausea, nervousness, diarrhea, chronic gastritis, and tremor of hands, especially if they have been without a drink for some time. There then comes an emotional instability and a mental slowdown.

Usually, it is difficult to get the addict to admit to being an alcoholic.

But there can be no hope of a cure until he or she does admit to their addiction, and is willing to ask for divine help. The alcoholic is often good at covering up. (There is the story of the wife who didn't realize her husband had a problem until he came home sober one night.) But when the problem is identified, the addict must be confronted.

A bee tried to get out of the house. He futilely banged and banged against the window. Finally exhausted, he fell to the sill and walked out the crack of the partly opened window. The crack was there all the time. When a person gives up, he will find God is there all the time.

For an acute bash, contrary to popular opinion, coffee does not help. The drunk should certainly not be allowed to drive. They should be put to bed and given plenty of liquid and time—six to twelve hours—to allow the liver and kidneys to get rid of the alcohol.

Withdrawing from alcohol use is far worse than withdrawing from heroin.[43] Joining Alcoholics Anonymous has helped thousands. Previously predominantly male and middle class, A.A. has recently experienced an influx of female and low income members. Those in the same boat can give an understanding and sympathetic approach.

In extreme cases, a psychiatric physician is needed, both to relieve pain and the "shakes," and to counsel the withdrawing. Still some may die in withdrawal attempts.

Alcoholics Anonymous

A call to A.A. can ring a bell for a new life with the Twelve Steps. Here are Alcoholics Anonymous' suggestions:

1. We admit we are powerless over alcohol—that our livers have become unmanageable.
2. We have come to believe that a Power greater than ourselves can restore us to sanity.
3. We have made a decision to turn our will and our lives over to the care of God as we understand Him.

42. Saffer and Grossman 1987.

43. Fort 1973.

4. We have made a searching and fearless moral inventory of ourselves.
5. We have admitted to God, to ourselves, and to another human being the exact nature of our wrongs.
6. We are entirely ready to have God remove all these defects of character.
7. We humbly ask Him to remove our shortcomings.
8. We have made a list of all persons that we have harmed, and have become willing to make amends to them all.
9. We have made direct amends to such people wherever possible, except when to do so would injure them or others.
10. We have continued to take personal inventory and when we are wrong, personally admit it.
11. We have sought through prayer and meditation to improve our conscious contact with God as we understand Him, praying only for knowledge of His will for us and the power to carry that out.
12. Having had a spiritual relationship as a result of these steps, we have tried to carry this message to other alcoholics and to practice these principles in all our affairs.

Contact with A.A. can usually be made by checking a phone listing in most large U.S. cities, or by checking health or welfare agencies.

It will quickly be seen how the principle of faith in God, turning lives over to Him, and contacting Him through prayer and meditation, and making restitution, are all part and parcel of the Christian procedure. I have been happy to be invited to speak as a minister of the gospel to Alcoholics Anonymous.

AL-ANONS are groups of family members who band together to give support to each other, and to help their alcoholic spouses.

ALATEENS are teenage children of alcoholics who meet together to gain understanding, and learn how they can help speed parental recovery. ALATEENS also believe in relying on a higher power.

Since the principles of A.A. are similar to those of the Christian faith, alcoholics can assist each other. Our church in Minneapolis worked with the city mission. One mission convert became a very dear friend. He surprised us with his education, ability, and contribution to society. Churches can and should help.

But there are times when short-term use of barbiturates — administered by a qualified physician — is necessary. Christian psychiatric help is often required, at times possibly with the use of hypnotism. With hard core alcoholics, about 5% die in sudden withdrawal attempts.

CHAPTER FOUR

MILESTONES TO TEMPERANCE

"Greatly Needed, Enjoyable Fascinating Reading."

George Ormesby, S.E.
Former International President,
International Order of
Good Templars, IOGT,
Vice President, National
Temperance Committee for
Prevention of Drug Abuse

CHAPTER FOUR MILESTONES TO TEMPERANCE

A. DRUGS, SPIRITS AND THE SUPERNATURAL

Even Today We Call Alcoholic Drinks Spirits

How did getting drunk help one get to Heaven? Coexisting with the ancients' craving for intoxicants was a desire for an immortal relationship with a higher power outside themselves.

A visit to the awesome Egyptian pyramids deeply impresses a person regarding the tremendous desire of the ancients for spiritual immortality. The pyramids are made of as many as two million large blocks of rocks averaging 2 1/2 tons each. Some of these blocks are as heavy as 30 tons and came from as far away as 700 miles. Blocks were lifted over 480 feet high on the great Khufu Pyramid. Parts of them are fitted so precisely, without mortar, that in places one cannot penetrate a knife blade.

Make the arduous climb to the top. There you will find a large room originally fitted with all the furniture, vessels of food, miniature servants and companions, all the necessary needs for a comfortable afterlife.

All is protected by solid rock, but now one observes a small hole to the outside. This is the place for the return of the Life Giving Spirit.

Drugs Became Gods

Recognizing the mind altering and behavior changing ability of drugs, the ancients considered them supernatural spirits and worshiped them as such. Even today, alcoholic products are named spirits. These spirits became deified with personalities and names. The Vedic religion of India as far back as 2000 B.C. centered on oblation to the intoxicating liquid soma. The Zoroastrians sacrificed to their sacred liquid *haoma*.

Centuries before Christ, in Egypt, there is evidence of the use of wine and beer in worshiping the believed creator Osiris.

Of the polytheistic gods, for the Greeks Dionysus-the-divine, the adopted son of Zeus, was god of wine and fertility. Although very liberal in most things, he was very strict in requiring participation in his worship. Worship of Dionysus consisted in his spirit taking over the mind with the debauches of wine. It was assumed that one would get drunk. Bacchus was god of wine and fertility for the Romans as Dionysus was for the Greeks. Only the name was changed. Bacchus, god of wine and fertility, had the same demand of intoxication in worship.

Back in the earliest times, the use of alcoholic worship bothered some thinking, conscientious men. There is evidence of temperance concerns in early Egyptian history.

Plato for Temperance

Plato dutifully attended religious ceremonies, but that was about the only time that he would drink. For him, a thinking man was not a drinking man. He was placed in the same uncomfortable situation as Aristotle, taking alcoholic communion. Both Plato and Aristotle otherwise advocated prohibition. Especially would they have abstinence for judges, soldiers, women, those under thirty, men planning children, and slaves.

Christians Influenced by Bacchus Sacramental Wine

The early Hebrews were constantly influenced by the profligate Baal animism, that had some similarities with Bacchus. Likewise, early Christians were influenced by their surroundings. It was quite natural for Gentile converts to associate the observance of the Lord's Supper with the use of Bacchus' sacramental wine. Alcohol became legalized for Christendom, when the Roman church allowed some churches to put alcoholic wine in the mass. Today some Christian churches cannot have communion without the mind altering alcohol.[1]

Baal

Dr. D. James Kennedy, writes in *Christendom Vs. Christianity,* 1994, relative to the crusades: "The necessity of distinguishing between Christendom and Christianity. Christianity is composed of those who have repented of their sins and truly believe in Jesus Christ as their Savior and their Lord. . . . Today Christendom is comprised of true Christians and professing Christians who have never experienced the saving grace of Christ."[2]

Constantine Legitimizes Christianity

Accentuated by the benevolent Roman Emperor, Constantine the Great, Christianity was watered down from the Biblical position on wine in the early fourth century.

During Constantine's campaign against Maxentius, he saw a flaming cross beneath the sun bearing the inscription, "In this sign you will conquer." With the defeat and drowning of Maxentius, Constantine declared his conversion to Christianity.*

At once, Christianity became the *de facto* religion of the Roman Empire. Persecution of Christians stopped. Confiscated property was returned to the Christians, and they became eligible for public office.

Constantine's Obligation to Promote Wine

Constantine did not become baptized until shortly before his death. Instead, he continued to hold the traditional office of *pontifex maxiumus* as the high priest of the official pagan worship. Under his leadership, modified emperor-worship was encouraged. This included also the continued devotion to Bacchus, the god of wine. Devotion to Bacchus required festivals in which his spirit was allowed to influence by intoxication. If one wanted a good afterlife, that person had better satisfy Bacchus.

The pagan influence persisted after Constantine until today. Some Christians use alcoholic wine in their liturgy. The result is the acceptance of alcohol by the Roman church, as well as in much of Protestantism. Bacchus and Christ are worshiped together by using Bacchus' help, in some wine-using churches.

Constantine Influences Eastern Orthodoxy

We are primarily interested in western Christianity, and of Constantine's duty as emperor to support the Roman established pagan religion, also his choice to defend Christianity. But Constantine changed the seat of Roman

1. The Catholic Encyclopedia 1967.
2. Kennedy 1994, p. 209.

* A legend has Constantine marching his army into the river for a mass baptism. I have not found original documentation for this.

government to Constantinople (city of Constantine) in the Greek Byzantine area. Because of Constantine's dispute with the Arian Christians at Nicaea in 325 A.D., he probably has had a large influence on today's orthodoxy. The Eastern Orthodox Church has been affected by Constantinople's relation to Bacchus, as has the western church been affected by Rome's Bacchus wine.

Both are probably greatly affected by Constantine, the defender of Christianity, but also the supporter of Roman polytheism, including Bacchus, the god of wine.

Russian orthodox church dedicated to Mary the Magdalene on Mount of Olives.

In Dark Ages the Church Supported Wine

"During the Dark Ages, it was the Church that was largely responsible for the survival of most of the skills of civilization, not least that of wine making, and many of the great vineyards of Europe owe their existence to the church."[3]

("Dark Ages, you couldn't see in the dark wine cellars.")

Later, when the Church had a campaign against coffee drinking, the Mohammedans, as an alternative to wine, were encouraging coffee drinkers to help in the prohibition of alcohol.

Southern Churches Did Not Need Spirits of Alcohol

The churches that were geographically furthest from the influence of Rome used the juice from raisins in the Eucharist. These included St. John's Church of Bassorah, Iraq, the Church of St. Thomas in India, the Abyssinian Church of Jerusalem, and the Nestorian Church.

Perhaps this is one reason that the abstinent Moslems, so firmly against alcohol, were easier on the Nestorian Christians than on the Western Roman Christians. (As a ship landed on the shores of Moslem Zanzibar, a passenger asked if it were possible to get a drink there. He was told that he could, if he were able to show that he was a Christian.) The Moslem word at the time was "Drunken Christians."

Alcoholic Spirits Survived the Reformation

Alcohol became strongly imbedded in the western churches. The Reformation, which tried to rid the church of pagan influence, did not affect the main body of Christianity regarding Bacchus alcohol. To this day, in many western Christian Churches, the rite of communion often contains alcohol, and practically all Bibles translate grape juice as wine. The Roman Church has had a tremendous influence on Western Christianity and civilization.

Bob Thayer in Frank and Ernest—mixture of wine and holy water is, "Amazing Grapes."

Pietist in Seventeenth Century

There were always some within the Roman and Protestant churches who decried the use of alcohol. But it was

3. The Illustrated Science and Invention Cyclopedia 1983.

not until fifteen hundred years after Christ, the Pietists began conscientiously to take the Bible seriously regarding its teaching on alcohol. The Pietists included the Baptists, and later the Quakers, Methodists, Wesleyans, Fundamentalists, the Holiness Movement, the Adventists, and others.

Cromwell's Puritanism

In the middle of the 17th century, Puritanism took over in England. Oliver Cromwell's cavalry was composed entirely of *men of religion.* They did not drink or swear. They advanced their charge with the singing of psalms. They were never defeated in battle. In 1648 Cromwell's army took over England's Parliament.

George Fox
Founder of
Quakers

Cromwell's Puritanism had a tremendous but short lived effect on England. However, soon after his death, England returned to classical Christianity and restored the monarchy, episcopacy, the Prayer Book, and allowed the drug alcohol in worship.

Revivals Bring Temperance

Oliver Cromwell
Portrait by
Chinn

Drug abuse, though ever present, rises and falls with a rhythmic trend. Trends are influenced by powerful religious leaders. Temperance crested with Cromwell. In the 18th century, John Wesley, with powerful preaching, stirred the English speaking world toward spiritual revival and temperance. It has been said that he influenced England's drinking habits for 100 years.

John Wesley

John Wesley's orders to his Methodist Societies were, "Take no spirituous liquor, no dram of any kind, unless prescribed by a physician," and, "Touch no dram, it is sure poison. It saps the very springs of life."[4]

Francis Willard used to tell of one who asked, "How is it I can't find a drink in this wretched place?" An old man answered, "Over a hundred years ago John Wesley came to these parts."

Many liquor places were closed, and many stopped drinking also during The American Finney Revival, 1824-1860. Many Temperance organizations sprang up. In 1881 The Baltimore Temperance Society employed Dr. John Marsh, a Congregational minister, to campaign in Washington, D.C. In 1851, the abstinent International Order of Good Templars was founded. It presently promotes abstinence.

Prohibition Came Slowly

It did not come over night. There would be evangelistic spurts of enthusiasm. States would go dry, then interest would cool and enforcement would wane. The first to go dry and stay dry was Maine in 1851 followed in order by:

Kansas	1880
North Dakota	1889
Georgia	1907
West Virginia	1912
Virginia	1914
Oregon	1914
Washington	1914
Colorado	1914
Arizona	1914
Alabama	1915

4. John Wesley 1703-1791.

Arkansas	1915
Iowa	1915
New Mexico	1917
Texas	1918
Ohio	1918
Wyoming	1918
Oklahoma	1907
Mississippi	1908
North Carolina	1908
Tennessee	1909
Idaho	1915
South Carolina	1915
Montana	1916
South Dakota	1916
Michigan	1916
Nebraska	1916
Indiana	1917
Utah	1917
New Hampshire	1917
Florida	1918
Nevada	1918
Kentucky	1919

By the time of the ratification of the 18th Amendment all 46 states had prohibition, only Connecticut and Rhode Island did not have state prohibition.

Women's Christian Temperance Union

During and following the Civil War, 1861-1865, interest in temperance waned, but in 1874, Francis E. Willard founded the Women's Christian Temperance Union (WCTU). Their work resulted in a wave of state prohibition legislation, beginning with Kansas. Soon scientific temperance instruction was placed in every state in the union. In this period, Carrie Nation took her hatchet and started chopping the illegal Kansas saloons into pieces. But she did not stay in the dry state of Kansas: she went on a national spree. This pioneer *ax assessor* was arrested 30 times. She kept going by raising money selling souvenir hatchets to pay her fines.

Again the interest in temperance waned and by 1905 only three of the 18 states that had gone dry were vigorous in enforcement. The Anti-Saloon League (formed in 1893) was becoming very powerful. It coordinated the efforts of churches and all existing temperance agencies. The League engaged in educational and political work by investigating the records, and ascertaining the attitudes of candidates for office.

In 1913 the Webb-Keaven Act was passed by Congress. This prohibited the shipment of alcoholic beverages from a wet state to a dry one.

Billy Sunday—B. 1862

Then Billy Sunday came on the scene. Along with the efforts of the WCTU, the Anti-Saloon League, and Billy Sunday, things began to happen.

Billy Sunday's meetings had much the same effect as Finney's revival. Sunday's evangelistic campaigns were not only known for winning converts, but also for contributing to the temperance cause. This resulted in much less alcohol used and crimes greatly diminished.

Billy Sunday's preaching antics, as I observed them in his campaign against booze in Cleveland, Ohio.

Billy Sunday
Eller Introduction 1914

In the winter of 1908, Sunday conducted a five-week revival meeting in Bloomington, Illinois. A few days later there was another series of meetings in Decatur, Illinois. After the spring election it was found, "Fifteen hundred saloons had been knocked out in one day, and much of this was directly the result of Sunday's efforts. Many counties became dry. Towns and cities that had been considered hopelessly wet, were listed in the dry columns."[5]

When the *drys* were trying to win over the state of West Virginia, Sunday chartered a train and spoke at several places every day. It is believed that the overwhelming dry victory was largely due to his strenuous labors there.

I have not heard of any of today's evangelistic meetings closing public drinking places. Rev. Billy Graham said, "I do not believe that the Bible teaches teetotalism, Jesus drank wine, that wasn't grape juice as some try to claim . . ." according to an interview published in the Miami Herald (December 26, 1976).

Graham's statement so aroused the ire of his knowledgeable abstinent supporters that he quickly made a retraction with an article, *Graham on Drink, Don't.* In *Christianity Today* he wrote, "Since alcohol is a devastating problem in America Today . . . it is better for Christians to be teetotalers" (2/4/77, p. 63).

Saloon keepers took dust baths in the dust that gathered on their bars.

5. Brown 1914.

World War One Brought Temperance

When the World War came in 1914, people were frightened that Kaiser Bill and the Germans would take over the world. It was a time for serious thought. Churches were filled. Austerity, temperance, rationing, and victory gardens were in evidence. The grain, used for alcohol, was needed for the war effort.

Kaiser Williams II
Proud and humorless.

First the sale of liquors to sailors and soldiers was prohibited. Next the president was empowered to prohibit the use of grains, fruits, etc., in manufacturing liquors for beverage purposes. It was a favorable climate for the temperance workers, who for years had worked hard for prohibition. The wartime Prohibition Act, prohibiting the sale of intoxicating beverages, except export, was passed on November 21, 1918. Forty-six states became dry, clearing the way for the 18th Constitutional Prohibition Amendment. National Prohibition began January 16, 1920.

Some Ritualistic Churches and Alcohol

Some ritualistic churches that used alcoholic wine in their worship were not generally defenders of prohibition. The government allowed wine for their communion. They were generally not abstinence-minded. For some, if alcohol was all right in worship, it must be right otherwise.

("Prohibition didn't bother some, since they could drink in Church on Sundays.")

We have to say there always have been temperance people from highly ritualistic churches. Some priests, and other pastors refused to use alcohol in worship, and I have personally known many Catholic teetotalers. Some work for me. Capuchin Father Theobald Matthew sparked a strong temperance movement in Great Britain and Ireland. He got hundreds of thousands to sign abstinent pledges. In Cork, along with Quaker governor William Martin, they started The Total Abstinence Society in 1839. This resulted in the Pioneers, the largest group of Roman Catholic abstainers in the world today.

Many prominent Catholics were active in the American Temperance movement. Speaking to American Catholics in 1887, Pope Leo XIII said:

"We have rejoiced to learn with what energy and zeal, by means of various excellent associations and especially through the *Catholic Total Abstinence Union,* you combat the destructive vice of intemperance. For it is well known to us how ruinous, how deplorable, is the injury both to faith and to morals, that is to be feared from intemperance in drink . . . Let pastors, therefore, do their best to drive the plague of intemperance from the fold of Christ by assiduous preaching and exhortation, and to shine before all as models of abstinence."[6]

The distinguished Catholic Cardinal Henry Edward Manning declared in 1875:

"The chief bar to the working of the Holy Spirit of God in the souls of men and women, is intoxicating drink. I know of no antagonist to the Holy Spirit more direct, more subtle, more ubiquitous. The drink trade is our shame, scandal and sin, and unless brought under by the will of the people it will be our downfall."[7]

Archbishop Ireland unequivocally expressed himself:

"We have seen there is no hope for improving in any way or form the liquor traffic: there is nothing now to be done but to wipe it out completely. The state alone can save us. Would God place in my hand a wand with which to dispel the evil of intemperance, I would strike the door of every saloon, of every distillery, of every brewery, until the accursed traffic should be wiped from the face of the earth."[8]

Roman Catholic priest, Father J. J. Curan served as vice president of the Anti-Saloon League for twenty-five years.[9] The Anti-Saloon League united all temperance groups, including the Catholic Clergy Prohibition League, into a powerful temperance force. It was largely influential for the Eighteenth Amendment.

Bishop Leniham of Montana said, Prohibition would contribute to the "spiritual progress of the Catholic Church."[10]

B. THE SUCCESS OF PROHIBITION

I have trained parrots to give short Bible verses. When I ask for a verse, they do not ask the reason why, but in a mode of do or die, they give it with the exact words that I taught them. Ask some people about prohibition. They will parrot, without knowledge, the exact words that the alcoholic propagandist taught them: "prohibition was a failure."

We will show you the facts, prohibition was successful.

Not many people today are aware of the success of prohibition. Few living now have seen, as I have witnessed first hand, the improvements that were made during prohibition. Before prohibition, I saw drunks kicked out of a sa-

6. Calvin 1926.
7. Willebrandt 1929.
8. Willebrandt 1929.
9. Curan 1930.
10. Clark 1933.

loon. They were left to lie on the sidewalk. I didn't see that during prohibition.

The period of prohibition was also a period of developing interest in the science of statistics. The religious periodical of the day was *The Christian Herald.* This magazine gave continually statistics from police records showing reduced arrest for crimes, including fewer wife beatings.

Contrary to Wet propaganda: Checks of savings accounts in the banks showed sharp increases. Physicians noted decreases in health problems especially related to the liver. We will again show the chart:

Mortality Rate Deaths (Per 100,000)
From Cirrhosis in the United States

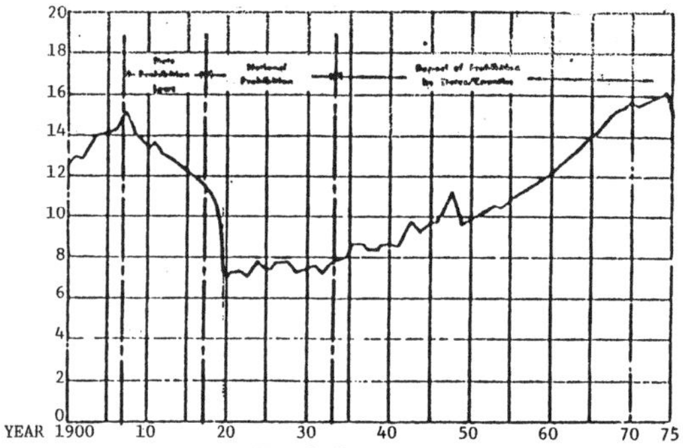

Prohibition

Seeing the success of prohibition in North America, other countries experimented with prohibition legislation, including England, Iceland, Finland, Russia, Norway and Australia.

Are we more prone to believe the Wets' propaganda?

Dobyns Documents Prohibition Success

Fletcher Dobyns was Assistant Attorney General during prohibition. In his book, *The Amazing Story of Repeal,* he lists the successes of prohibition. He writes: "Ross McClennan, in his *Propaganda Vs. Facts* shows by chart and year listings, the tremendous drop in beer production during prohibition." The beer that was allowed and produced was *Near Beer,* which contained one half of one percent alcohol.

Professor Fisher was not originally in favor of prohibition. However, after a thorough study he writes during prohibition: "It is evident that the total consumption of alcohol today in beverage form is less than 16 percent of pre-prohibition consumption, and probably less than 10 percent."[11]

11. Fisher 1932.

Per Capita Consumption of Beer 1900-1975 (in Gallons)

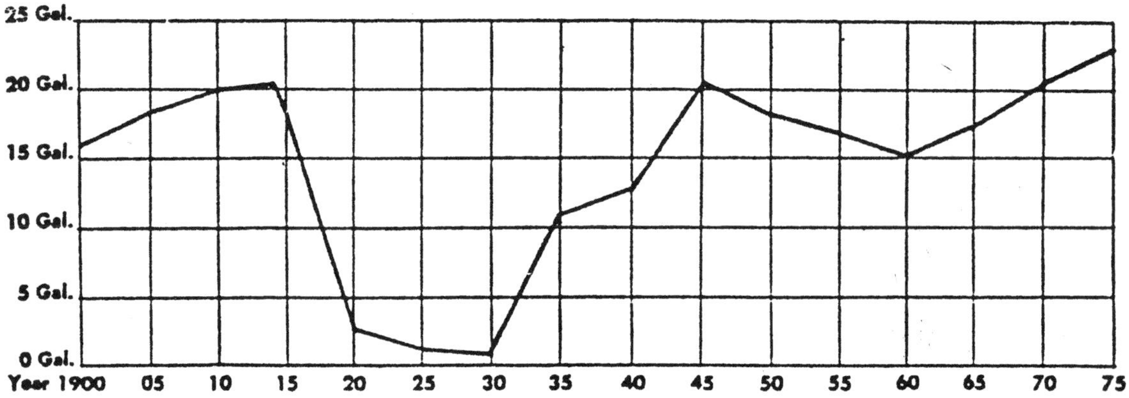

Prohibition Years

U.S. Department of Commerce

Samuel Crowther made an exhaustive and impartial study, and came to the conclusion in his book, "The amount paid for a volume of liquor certainly cannot exceed 20 percent of that sold in the pre-war trade."[12]

Herman Feldman spent nine months interviewing and corresponding with men from every part of the country, who were in a position to know the facts. He wrote, "It appears to us most likely that the great mass of the people, however, are spending much less on drink today than in pre-prohibition days."[13]

Whitney Williams, an investigative reporter, disguised himself as a laborer in 1919 and again during prohibition in 1930. He wrote, "All the speak-easies of Homestead are not handling in a whole average day of 1930 as much of either alcohol or money as crossed a single average saloon bar in Homestead during a single morning of 1919 .... The fact is plain that the saloon is not only dead but its soul is not marching on in the speak-easies."[14]

Feldman also reports that the National Federation of Settlements made a nation wide survey. He quotes: "Employers everywhere are agreed that the law is a great benefit to the working man and a great aid to efficient operation in industry. They are for it."

Also he states, "During the pre-Volstead days, a large number of our employees would get all their pay checks cashed at a saloon. Today the endorsers of these checks are the groceries [stores], the meat markets, and the dry-goods stores . . ."[15]

Samuel Blythe, distinguished author and journalist of his day, wrote in an article for the Saturday Evening Post, "A new and gigantic purchasing power has developed in this country since we have had prohibition, that accounts for the prosperity of our railroads, our manufactures, our trade in all directions." (July 19, 1927).

At the annual 1926 meeting of the American Economic Association, everyone favored prohibition on economic grounds.

During one period, the government profited from prohibition's enforcement, according to Dr. J. M. Doran, prohibition commissioner:

From fines, penalties, seized property and incidentals	$460,502,792.76
Cost to Coast Guard and customs enforcement	141,179,485.00
Government profit, June 15, 1929	$319,323,307.76[16]

Decrease in State Hospitals, Drunkenness and Disorderly Conduct Arrests

Admission to state mental hospitals declined during prohibition from 10.1 per 100,000 in 1919 to 4.7 in 1928. Arrest for drunkenness and disorderly conduct dropped 50 percent from 1916 to 1922. These are the amazing facts researched for the *New York Times* by Mark Moore.[17]

Ross J. McLennan former Vice President of Taylor University is the Director of Sooner Alcoholic—Narcotics Education since 1959. He is one of the most active temperance workers today. He initiated several state laws that prohibit alcohol advertising, liquor by the drink, and anti-gambling laws. His book *Propaganda Vs Facts** embodies much of his research and life long gathering of prohibition Facts. Documenting the success of prohibition, he shows

12. Crowther 1930.
13. Feldman 1927.
14. Williams 1931.
15. Feldman 1927.

16. Doran 1940.
17. The Statesman 1990.
*Propaganda Vs. Fact is available from Sane Press, 101 N.E. 23rd St., Oklahoma City, OK 13105.

how the liquor traffic has, in his words, "*bamboozled* people to believe otherwise." We will list some of these facts:*

PROHIBITION RESULTS IN:

1. All people benefited.

Andrea Siegfried, former opponent of prohibition had to admit, "The great mass of people are undoubtedly benefiting, in health, standard of living, working efficiently, and in increased wages." (Andrea Siegfried, *America Comes of Age,* p. 89)

2. Automobile Business Improved in Detroit. "Favorable effects of prohibition are apparent even to a blind man. This is despite the fact that we are just across the river from wet Canada. Prohibition, is good for City Motor Company." (Henry M. Leland, President, Lincoln Motors)

"Am glad to advise you prohibition has done wonders in our city." (H. B. Smith, Secretary and Treasurer, McInnes Steel Co. Ltd. Carry, PA)

3. Business Conditions Greatly Improved

From a former Anti-prohibitionist:

"In my own business, conditions have greatly improved since our employees no longer have unlimited use of liquor; and from conversations I have had with hundreds of retail merchants throughout the country . . . benefited. Prohibition has been a proven fact."[18]

4. Increased Deposits and Savings Accounts

In 1922 compared to 1917:

- 30 more savings banks and trust companies
- 431 more building and loan associations
- 40,917 more depositors in savings books

(Annals of the American Academy of Political and Social Sciences, September, 1923).

5. Increased General Well Being

"Less lost time, less accidents, less incompetence, less carelessness and inefficiency, better work, better houses, more thrift, happier families, and sober and safer . . . now find out what it means really to live where they formerly merely existed."[19]

6. Good Results Produced Fast

"It would be difficult to find in all of the history of social legislation a case where the effects of a law can be traced so quickly and so accurately.

We see that prohibition has produced just the kind of effect that was desired."[20]

7. Improvement in Home Life

"I find a marked improvement in the number of men who are saving their money and who own their houses or are buying their houses, and I find a decided improvements in the home life of the workers due to the fact that the women and children have more food, more clothing, and better care in every way. Back of all that the worker takes his family to the picture show or to the park now, where he formerly spent his evenings in the saloon drinking and spending his money."[21]

8. Income and Wages to Workers Increased

"The real rise of real wages was particularly marked during the years of 1919-1923 when the enforcement of the

18. Edward Freschi, Pres. Holeproof Hosiery Co., Milwaukee, WI.

19. George M. Verity, President, American Rolling Mill Co., Middleton, Ohio.

20. Prof. Henry Farnam of Yale University, quoted in Ross J. McLennan Files, *Propaganda Vs. Facts.*

21. W. S. Stone, Ground Chief, Brotherhood of Locomotive Engineers, Cleveland, OH.

prohibitory amendment was probably more effective . . ."[22]

9. Mortality of Drunk Driving Suppressed

"The suppression of the drunk traffic is an expression of the highest *mortality* upon which we are entering."[23]

10. Psychosis Hospital Admissions Down According to Dr. Howard of Columbia University:

"The evidence is very definite that in 1919, 1920, and in 1921, a lower level was reached than had ever occurred before."[24]

11. Youth Being Saved

From Arthur Brisbane, editor of the Hearst Newspapers—Originally opposed Prohibition. "Three hundred thousand traps have been closed, into which a considerable portion of the country fell every year."[25]

McLennan says that he has hundreds of similar quotes from leaders in American society.

Dr. Jack Van Impe and Roger F. Campbell in their book, *Alcohol: The Beloved Enemy,* have a chapter entitled, "Prohibition, What Really Happened". They give a general statement: "Deaths from Brights' disease, pneumonia, and tuberculosis, dropped dramatically during prohibition, and admissions to mental hospitals for alcoholic psychosis fell to their lowest point in history."[26]

Documentation is then given:

Alcoholic Psychosis

"With the advent of prohibition the alcoholic psychosis as far as this country is concerned have become little more than historical interest. The admission rate in New York state hospitals for 1920 was only 1.9 percent as compared with 10 percent in 1909-1912, "For many years articles on alcoholism literally disappeared from American medical literature."[27]

Jack and Rexella Van Impe

Drunkenness Prohibition Miracle

Connecticut along with Rhode Island was one of the only two states that did not become dry until they were forced to by the Eighteenth Amendment.

Prisoners in Connecticut jails charged with drunkenness fell from 7,314 in 1917 to 943 in 1920!

Accidental Deaths in 1917 were 10.7 per 10,000; in 1920 it was 7.3. Automobile Death Rate fell by 40%.

Death from pneumonia, (alcoholics are particularly liable) dropped from 15.3 per 10,000 in 9.6 in 1921[28]

Deliver Us From Evil

"Common Sense is that a substantial number of people wanted to stop, both their own and other people's drinking, and that the saloons where most people had done their drinking were closed . . . There is every reason to suppose that most Americans outside the larger cities

22. H. F. Miller 1930 (RM).
23. Brisbane, In McLennon, 1978.
24. December *Survey Graphic,* Art. The Prohibition Question.
25. A. Carlson Brisbane in McLennon, 1978.
26. Van Impe 1980.
27. Van Impe, 1980.
28. Farnam.

never knew a bootlegger, . . . Would not have known where to look for one."[29]

Less Crime During Prohibition

There was less crime during prohibition. Referring back to Professor Farnam, "Arrest for assault and breach of peace declined to less than one third."[30] What were all the headlines on gangland crimes? They were just that. As usual, gangsters were fighting and killing each other. The public was not involved. One bootlegger said, "It just don't make no sense to rough up our customers."[31] (Prohibition) "Elimited the chief cause of crime, poverty, and misery among our people" (Charles W. Elliot, President of Harvard, speaking to the Massachusetts Legislature in 1922, quoted by Burgess, 1973).[32]

Prosperity Under Prohibition

America enjoyed it highest period of prosperity under prohibition. In 1928 the people voted for dry congressmen by a huge majority. But a world wide depression helped precipitate the crash of our stock market resulting in depression.

Those against prohibition took advantage of the confusion to blame the depression on prohibition, which had absolutely nothing to do with prohibition. In reality the results of the depression would have been much worse if the people had not accumulated as a result of prohibition.

But people bought the idea because of the millions that the industrialists spent in propaganda, believing tax on liquor would keep them from having to pay income taxes. People believed because of the huge amount spent in the scam by the brewers. The news media, hungry for alcohol advertising, *bamboozled* the public as Ross McLennan said. The factual benefits that Prohibition brought went down the drain with repeal.

Following are the judgmental facts of success as opposed to the propaganda put out by the *Wets,* brewers, taverns, etc.

C. THE RAPE OF PROHIBITION—REPEAL

Dobyns tells of the mammoth lying propaganda that overthrew the 18th amendment; still today its deception makes the public believe, both then and now, that prohibition was a failure.

Pierre DuPont, in his factory's management, was dry. If any one came to work with an alcoholic breath, he was fired on the spot. He made a big switch. Here's the story of why:[33]

Before Kaiser Bill and the First World War, income taxes were comparatively inconsequential. But, with the fear that the Germans were trying to take over the world, income taxes began to climb.

"To pay for the higher taxes, factory owners hit on the idea that taxes on liquor would eliminate income taxes. In a Washington lobby hearing a copy of a letter of October 26, 1926 was produced: Irenee DuPont said that one of his companies would save $10 million a year in corporation tax if we had a similar tax to the British tax on beer."[34]

Thomas W. Phillips Jr., President of T.W. Phillips Gas and Oil Company, wrote a letter to Pierre S. DuPont, including:

". . . that if it were not for the expense connected with enforcing prohibition, and the loss of revenue occasioned by the Eighteenth Amendment, the income taxes could be eliminated entirely or greatly reduced . . ."[35]

29. Clark 1976.
30. Farnam.
31. Burgess 1973.
32. Ibid, p.152.
33. Dobyns 1940.
34. Dobyns 1940.
35. Dobyns 1940.

The Association Against the Prohibition Amendment was formed. This association had a big task ahead of it. The public favored prohibition. President Herbert Hoover, the Quaker dry, received a plurality of 6,300,000 votes. Congress was dry 90 to 16 in the Senate and 328 to 106 in the House. But millions upon millions of dollars were spent in propaganda. The industrialist wanted to get rid of income taxes. They believed the millions spent in propaganda would justify the income tax elimination.

The first casualty was Andrew Volstead, the father of the national Volstead Prohibition Acts. Lies upon lies were perpetrated on the public. Media went along, because they were told of the millions that the brewers wanted to spend in advertising. They would tell the farmers of the big market for grain. The public was told that most of their taxes would be eliminated. It was also implied that criminal groups would be done away with. This propaganda has been compared to that of Hitler and the Communist dictators. Tell a lie often enough and people will believe it. In spite of the increase in taxes and crime, the propaganda brainwashing still makes people think prohibition was a failure.

After Repeal—Bacchus Wins Again

Herbert Hoover, was a dry president. But when Franklin D. Roosevelt took over the presidency from Hoover, there came the 21st amendment to repeal prohibition, February 29, 1933.

In a Hindu area or a Moslem country such as Saudi Arabia, Prohibition has endured, but not in a Western Christian culture.

After Repeal—Dobyns List the Results

After the repeal of the eighteenth amendment, saloons were called taverns and frequented by women as well as men. Pagan deity Bacchus had won again. Crime and drugs are now rampant. Temperance workers have become discouraged.

Some of Dobyn's findings:

The brewers, Tammany Hall politics, and the unscrupulous elements of big business, got the results that were foreseen by intelligent people. Everything was thrown open.

Our ports were opened wide to the wineries, brewers and distillers of the world, with great quantities of alcohol pitched to on the market.

The country was again filled with saloons, taverns, night clubs, and road houses.

Ban on liquor advertising was removed, and high powered salesmanship was used to induce people to drink.

Traffic accidents were greatly increasing.

The *Wets* propaganda quickly undid the work of generations as to the horrible effects of alcohol.

The debauchery of youth by alcohol, once confined to wealthy classes, now spread to all levels of society.

Repeal Brought Under Age Drinking

The Los Angeles Times of February 12, 1934, reported from the Division of Attendance of the superintendent of schools. Thirty percent of purchases of beer and wine are made by those under age. Cliff Hellyer, former police officer for the investigators, said, "the young people are drinking heavily."

From the *Chicago Herald Examiner* of March 6, 1934: "A blond child of about 16 is dancing for the crowd at the bar. Her skirts are up to her hips. She is drunk . . . They're raffling off a pint of bonded whiskey for a dime a chance . . . a 16 year old girl screams with pleasure when she wins it."

Dr. Alice Phillips Aldrich, superintendent of the Illinois Vigilance Association, declared:

"The ancient and blood stained commerce in the agonized souls of girls has been revived, since the return of the tavern and promiscuous dancing."

In the *Country Home* for April 1938, Paul T. Sturges tells of an investigation he made in liquor conditions in six farming states:

"Drinking among the younger crowd, is worse than it was during prohibition, and gambling and vice, I found, are traveling in its wake. I have talked with parents, business men, ministers, teachers, even bootleggers. All agree that highway hot spots which are not decently operated are so damaging to the morals of rural youth that continuation of abuses will lead to another prohibition movement. I like my glass of beer as well as the next man. However, after investigating these places, I feel like a crusader, ready to fight against this widespread invasion of the countryside by the lowest sort of city vice."

Women Did Not Enter Saloons Before Repeal

Addressing the Senate on May 2, 1934, Senator Borah read from reports of the Chicago investigation:

"One of the great arguments in the campaign against the Eighteenth Amendment was that the bootlegger and the speak-easy were to be done away with . . . Much worse than the saloon has returned. It is worse. It is a legalized dive, a protected rendezvous of crime."

From the *New York Times,* January 2, 1936:

"Cardinal Daugherty, speaking to his Catholic diocesan societies, criticized women who drink intoxicants, and mothers who encourage it as a means of enhancing their daughters chances in society. No wonder broken marriages, divorce, and shameful scandal abound."

He urged the immediate establishment of total abstinence societies in all parishes under his jurisdiction "where they do not now exist".

From Bishop Edgar Blake of Detroit in *The Zion's Herald,* October 1936, "Never have we witnessed such drunkenness and debauchery . . . as we have witnessed today . . . Never has our American womanhood fallen so low as since repeal.

"Thirty Detroit high school children, 14 to 17 years of age, were *laid out* dead drunk at a beer party. The girls were so intoxicated it required three hours to get them sober enough to go home . . . According to the police records of Detroit, in the first five months of repeal, *traffic accidents attributed to liquor increased 164 percent."*

As a Result of Repeal, Society Degenerated

In a sermon preached in May of 1936, Dr. Harry Emerson Fosdick said: "The repeal of Prohibition did not solve our problems. It simply plunged us back to the *status quo ante,* plunged us once more into the intolerable situation which our fathers faced two generations ago when they rose up in indignation against the liquor traffic . . . As surely as history repeats itself, a revolt is due, a change of public attitude born out of disgust with, and fear of the intolerable estate we are now in."

Repeal Brought Economic Problems, Crime and Girls Drinking

On May 14, 1936, the General Conference of the Methodist Episcopal Church adopted a resolution:

"Repeal has been a more ghastly failure, in less than three years, this *ignoble experiment* stands indicted and convicted before the bar of public opinion. No promise upon which repeal was secured has been kept . . . Repeal has added to the economic disaster. Crime and liquor violations have increased. Thousands of young girls are yielding to the advice to 'learn early how much liquor they can stand'. Often to be brought home lifeless or virtue-less, and sometimes both.

"Another tragedy of this hour is that funds from the liquor traffic are being turned into public school treasuries, that thus may be stilled the voices of educational leaders that should be raised in an aggressive campaign to acquaint our youth with the facts concerning this habit forming drug. *We protest the use in this way of money so acquired.*"

Media Perverts the Truth

In the *Christian Century* for November 25, 1936, Dr. John Haynes Holmes, one of the outstanding religious and civic leaders of America, had an article entitled "The Third Year of Repeal," in which he said:

"The record of this year, as told from . . . newspaper, is worse than ever . . . The wet press, fattening on its ravages of alcohol . . . If the liquor news were handled today the way the liquor news was handled yesterday, this nation would get a shock that would carry us back to Prohibition in a year.

"We have given repeal three years to prove itself, and it has failed, just as every sane and instructed mind knew it would fail."

Repeal Brought Increase in Robberies and Traffic Manslaughter

The judge in Cuyahoga County, Ohio, ordered the grand jury to make an exhaustive investigation of conditions in Cleveland since repeal. They reported to the court April 21, 1937:

"An overwhelming body of evidence was submitted to us in robbery cases indicating that beer parlors occupy an importance out of all relationships to their numbers as the places in which robberies originate . . ."

"In every one of the distressing cases of death caused by a motor vehicle, . . . liquor was an important element, if not the chief factor, leading to the accident."[36]

Salute to Fletcher Dobyns, Thank You!

Space does not let us record all of the facts of the deterioration caused by repeal of the eighteenth amendment as gathered by assistant federal prosecutor Fletcher Dobyns.

Since Repeal to 1994

1930—We were under Prohibition
1933—Beer was legalized in April
Total Repeal on December 5
1934—First full year after repeal

The statistical report from the Distilled Spirits Council of the U.S. Inc. report on wine consumption.

The report shows how the people had gotten out of the habit of drinking in 1933 during Prohibition. In 1934 the consumption was about half of what it became in 1935. From then on alcoholic consumption speedily increased. Except there is a small decrease in drinking since 1980. Headline in *Readers' Digest,* "Why Americans Are Drinking Less" (January 1985, p.48).

Another strong argument for government control will be seen in comparison of licensed states and control states.

Consumption in control states is about a third of what it is in licensed states.

Look at 1934:
Consumption in licensed states
46,892,000 use 79.2%
Consumption in controlled states
12,073,000 use 20.8%

36. Dobyns 1940.

Apparent Consumption of Liquor in the United States, License and Control States, 1934 – 1988

Year	License States\a Wine Gallons (000)	License States\a Percentage of Total Consumption	Control States Wine Gallons (000)	Control States Percentage of Total Consumption	Total Wine Gallons (000)	Percentage Change	Resident Population (000)	Adult Population (21 & Older) (000)	Per Capita Consumption (Resident) (gal/person)	Per Capita Consumption (21+) (gal/adult)	Number of States
1934	45,892	79.2	12,073	20.8	57,966	—	126,374	77,919	0.46	0.75	28
1935	66,219	72.7	24,482	27.3	89,670	54.7	127,250	78,761	0.70	1.14	41
1936	87,107	71.3	35,011	28.7	122,118	36.2	128,053	79,825	0.95	1.53	43
1937	94,691	69.9	40,692	30.1	135,383	10.9	128,825	80,867	1.05	1.67	44
1938	88,447	69.7	38,446	30.3	126,893	-6.3	129,825	81,978	0.98	1.55	45
1939	94,522	70.2	40,131	29.8	134,654	6.1	130,880	83,104	1.03	1.62	46
1940	101,736	70.2	43,256	29.8	144,992	7.7	131,954	84,311	1.10	1.72	46
1941	111,224	70.3	46,933	29.7	158,157	9.1	133,121	85,563	1.19	1.85	46
1942	133,831	70.3	56,417	29.7	190,248	20.3	133,920	86,390	1.42	2.20	46
1943	106,879	72.8	39,690	27.2	146,529	-23.0	134,245	86,634	1.08	1.69	46
1944	124,414	74.6	42,266	25.4	166,680	14.8	132,885	86,899	1.26	1.95	46
1945	142,220	74.8	47,911	25.2	190,131	14.1	132,481	88,200	1.44	2.23	46
1946	175,029	75.8	55,962	24.2	230,992	21.5	140,054	91,996	1.65	2.51	46
1947	130,128	71.6	51,520	28.4	181,648	-21.4	143,446	93,600	1.27	1.94	46
1948	118,637	69.4	52,364	30.6	171,021	-5.8	146,093	94,913	1.17	1.80	46
1949	120,471	71.1	48,074	28.9	168,545	-0.9	148,665	96,364	1.14	1.75	47
1950	138,996	73.1	51,053	26.9	190,020	12.1	151,868	96,060	1.25	1.94	47
1951	139,765	72.1	54,002	27.9	193,767	2.0	153,982	98,914	1.26	1.96	47
1952	131,409	71.5	52,278	28.5	183,687	-5.2	156,393	99,862	1.17	1.84	47
1953	140,390	72.1	54,283	27.9	194,693	6.0	158,956	100,796	1.22	1.93	47
1954	136,955	72.3	52,516	27.7	189,471	-2.7	161,884	101,810	1.17	1.86	47
1955	145,422	72.9	54,148	27.1	199,571	5.3	165,069	103,179	1.21	1.93	47
1956	164,518	73.7	58,707	26.3	216,225	7.8	168,088	104,307	1.28	2.06	47
1957	154,590	72.9	57,514	27.1	212,073	-1.5	171,187	105,340	1.24	2.01	47
1958	159,257	73.9	56,209	26.1	215,466	1.6	174,149	106,243	1.24	2.03	47
1959	167,364	74.2	58,090	25.8	225,453	4.6	177,135	107,299	1.27	2.10	48
1960	175,573	74.8	59,141	25.2	234,715	4.1	179,979	109,346	1.30	2.17	49
1961	182,707	75.7	58,742	24.3	241,449	2.9	182,992	109,418	1.32	2.21	49
1962	192,693	76.0	61,008	24.0	253,701	5.1	185,771	110,498	1.37	2.30	49
1963	196,780	76.0	62,200	24.0	258,979	2.1	189,483	111,909	1.37	2.32	49
1964	209,721	76.0	66,141	24.0	275,862	6.5	191,141	113,261	1.44	2.44	49
1965	223,889	76.1	70,355	23.9	294,244	6.7	193,526	114,506	1.52	2.57	50
1966\b	233,071	75.4	75,846	24.6	308,917	5.0	195,576	115,761	1.58	2.67	51
1967	244,368	75.3	80,094	24.7	324,462	5.0	197,457	116,940	1.64	2.77	51
1968	261,514	75.5	84,730	24.5	346,244	6.7	199,399	119,126	1.74	2.91	51
1969	272,534	75.3	89,240	24.7	361,774	4.5	201,385	121,036	1.80	2.99	51
1970	279,534	75.4	91,039	24.6	370,574	2.4	203,984	123,321	1.82	3.00	51
1971	288,368	75.4	94,156	24.6	382,523	3.2	206,827	125,868	1.85	3.04	51
1972	296,281	75.2	97,555	24.8	393,836	3.0	209,284	128,188	1.88	3.07	51
1973	306,727	75.4	100,332	24.6	407,059	3.4	211,357	130,623	1.93	3.12	51
1974	314,476	75.4	102,841	24.6	417,317	2.5	213,342	133,110	1.96	3.14	51
1975	318,697	75.3	104,735	24.7	423,432	1.5	215,465	135,748	1.97	3.12	51
1976	320,086	75.1	106,307	24.9	426,394	0.7	217,563	138,514	1.96	3.08	51
1977	323,813	75.0	107,740	25.0	431,553	1.2	219,760	141,335	1.96	3.05	51
1978	332,925	75.1	110,536	24.9	443,461	2.8	222,095	144,340	2.00	3.07	51
1979	335,419	75.0	112,078	25.0	447,497	0.9	224,567	147,398	1.99	3.04	51
1980	337,631	75.1	111,786	24.9	449,417	0.4	227,255	150,480	1.98	2.99	51
1981	339,177	75.5	110,276	24.5	449,453	0.0	229,637	153,369	1.96	2.93	51
1982	330,677	75.6	106,982	24.4	437,659	-2.6	231,996	156,269	1.89	2.80	51
1983	327,055	75.8	104,331	24.2	431,386	-1.4	234,284	159,014	1.84	2.71	51
1984	324,240	76.0	102,512	24.0	426,752	-1.1	236,477	161,661	1.80	2.64	51
1985	317,681	76.0	100,237	24.0	417,918	-2.1	238,736	164,205	1.75	2.55	51
1986	297,649	75.4	96,898	24.6	394,547	-5.6	241,107	166,647	1.64	2.37	51
1987	293,920	75.7	94,305	24.3	388,225	-1.6	243,419	168,805	1.59	2.30	51
1988	286,755	75.8	91,542	24.2	378,297	-2.6	245,807	170,823	1.54	2.21	51

NOTE: Because of rounding, detail may not add to total. Excludes Hawaii, 1934–64. Population data includes all states for all years except Hawaii & Alaska from 1934–1949.

a\ Includes District of Columbia.

b\ Includes Mississippi gallonage from July through December 1966.

SOURCES: Distilled Spirits Council of the United States, Inc.; Bureau of Census, U.S. Department of Commerce.

DISTILLED SPIRITS COUNCIL OF THE U.S., INC. - JANUARY 1990

Drunkenness charged

1932—180,026—Under Prohibition
1933—308,829—Partial Prohibition
1934—455,616—Repeal
1935—533,609—Repeal

As the restraints of Prohibition wore off, driving while drunk rapidly increased. Figures obtained by Sam Morris.

Economics and Statistics Administration

Drunkenness—Public

1932— 180,026—Under Prohibition
1935— 533,609—Repeal
1940— 655,774—Repeal
1943— 756,370—Repeal
1970—1,391,000—Repeal U.S. Dept. Commerce/Census Bureau

Bureau of the Census

Who said Prohibition was a failure? After Prohibition, one was three times more likely to be killed by a drunk driver, and three times as apt to suffer loss of life and property from the intoxicated.

Three years after repeal, there were three times as many arrested for public drunkenness as there were under Prohibition. These are terrific figures. It is amazing, as to know some will say Prohibition was a failure.

Prohibition did not stop all drinking. It was not designed to do so. Prohibition was a plan to stop the manufacture and sale of alcoholic beverages, except *near beer,* one half of one percent alcohol. Alcoholics (we don't have drunks anymore, far too crude) will do almost anything under the moon to gratify their addiction.

Persons Arrested—Drug Use

In comparison, there were practically no arrests under prohibition.

Note the amazing drop after age 44. By that age people have gained more sense, more experience in the futility of drug use, and are drinking less.

No. 302. Persons Arrested, by Charge, Sex, and Age: 1990

[Represents arrests (not charges) reported by 10,206 agencies (reporting 12 months) with a total 1990 population of 194 million as estimated by FBI]

CHARGE	Total (1,000)	PERCENT DISTRIBUTION							
		Male	Under 15 years	Under 18 years	18-24 years	25-44 years	45-54 years	55-64 years	65 yr. and over
Total arrests	**11,250**	**81.6**	**5.3**	**15.6**	**30.1**	**47.0**	**4.9**	**1.8**	**0.7**

Driving While Intoxicated—Prohibition Compared to Today

As the restraints of prohibition wore off, driving while drunk rapidly increased.

The following figures from the U.S. Department of Commerce show the numbers of people arrested for drunk driving:

1932—14,238—Under prohibition
1933—19,150—Partial prohibition
1934—23,399—Repeal
1935—28,875—Repeal
1940—42,274—Repeal
1943—43,763—Repeal

The number of people arrested and charged with drunk driving after two years of repeal was twice as high as three years earlier in 1932 under prohibition.

Beer Consumption Before, During and After Prohibition

Constitutional prohibition began in 1920. Repeal was in 1933.

The following figures show the per capita beer consumption from 1900 to 1975. Charted by Ross McLennan, they are taken from the U.S. Department of Commerce and the Bureau of Census, which gathers data every five years. Note in 1930 beer consumption dropped close to, "being on the wagon" (Water Wagon).

Year	Population of U.S.	Gallons of Beer	Gallons per Capita
1900	76,094,000	1,224,500,000	16.09
1905	84,090,000	1,534,500,000	18.24
1910	92,407,000	1,844,500,000	19.96
1914	98,918,000	2,052,200,000	20.74
1915	100,546,000	1,853,800,000	18.43
	Prohibition Years		
1920	106,461,000	285,200,000	2.67
1925	115,829,000	158,100,000	1.36
1930	123,077,000	114,111,000	0.92
	Repeal		
1934	126,415,000	1,168,018,000	9.23
1935	127,250,000	1,402,099,000	11.01
1940	131,954,000	1,701,652,000	12.89
1945	132,481,000	2,684,724,000	20.26
1950	151,235,000	2,753,017,000	18.20
1955	164,308,000	2,783,521,000	16.94
1960	179,979,000	2,930,988,000	16.28
1965	193,526,000	3,348,465,000	17.30
1970	203,810,000	4,174,274,000	20.48
1975	213,100,000	4,893,970,000	22.96

Near beer (half of 1 percent alcohol) was allowed to be brewed and sold during prohibition.

U.S. Department of Commerce

Drinking Percent Per Person

U. S. Government figures on drinking before prohibition

1914—22.80 Gallons per capita

One year immediately after prohibition

1934—8.96 Gallons per capita

Conclusion: During prohibition people lost their desire to drink.[37]

The Consumer Data Bank of the *Chicago Sun Times/Daily News* in 1968 published the following chart on men beer drinkers in the Windy City.

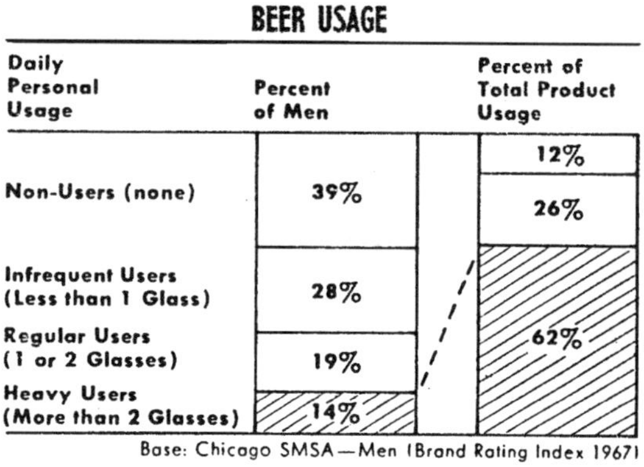

D. TEACHINGS OF PRESENT DAY DENOMINATIONS—1993

The basics to fight Bacchus are still in the evangelical churches. Abstinent churches generally do not use fermented wine in the sacrament.

Many evangelical churches claim their only creed is the Bible. They have no written creed, but many theologians will say that often the unwritten beliefs are the most vigorously defended.

There is variation between churches regarding temperance teaching. Most churches have conventions, where common beliefs are discussed and recorded; or they have quotations from auxiliary writings.

Moderation churches are largely concerned with the care of alcoholics. This is natural because 10% of moderate drinkers become alcoholics. Abstinent groups are interested in stopping the sale, advertising, and use of alcohol.

Not all members follow the teaching of their church. The teaching of some churches about whether abstinence or moderation follows. Note the sparse

37. Van Impe and Campbell.

mention of the Bible's opposition to alcohol use.

Apostolic—Abstinent

"We don't use it. We don't have a written discipline. We go only by the Bible. The Bible says that it is a mocker." These are the words of Robert Jordan, who says that he is the representative for the apostolic churches of the Indianapolis area.

Assemblies of God—Abstinent

"The General Council of the Assemblies of God has historically opposed the consumption of alcohol in any form. Early documents of the church declare, without reservation or compromise, a position of total abstinence."[38]

"A studied review of the Scriptures affirms a stern warning against intoxicating drink and a call to separation from this evil for the purpose of better service to God and mankind."[39]

"We call upon every member and adherent in our Fellowship, including both the ministry and the laity, to teach by word and example a life style that abstains totally from the consumption of alcoholic beverages."[40]

Baptist, American—Moderate

Nowhere is there "Thou shalt not". The primary concern is with dependency and its resultant problems, and how to help those who succumb.

"Resolution on Alcoholism and Other Dependencies":

"Stewardship includes responsible use of the gifts of the body, mind, and spirit, as well as the gifts of grapes, grain and chemicals.

"At least 10% of the adult population is dependent on alcohol or other drugs. One out of four families is suffering from the effects of alcoholism and other drug related problems. This dependency is the leading cause of death in the United States and a major factor in accidental death and violent crimes.

"Persons who come from families where alcoholism or other chemical dependency is a problem for a parent or grandparent, are particularly susceptible to being themselves addicted. Or they marry persons who are chemically addicted. When children from such homes show symptoms of inappropriate behavior, that behavior is often diagnosed as an individual problem rather than a family illness."

The General Board of the American Baptist Churches

1. Become familiar with the problems related to alcoholism and other chemical dependencies and the ministry that can be given to chemically dependent persons and their families through local church fellowships;
2. Create an environment in their churches in which caring, sharing and learning about alcoholism and other chemical dependencies can occur;
3. Enable persons to make responsible decisions about alcohol and other chemical use;

The General Board of the American Baptist Churches urges American Baptist seminaries and others to:

1. Equip ministers with an understanding of the nature of alcoholism and other chemical dependency.

Governmental action: The General Board of the American Baptist Churches will support efforts to:

1. Designate income from taxes on liquor and liquor substances to fund treatment of alcoholism and other chemical dependencies;

38. Assemblies of God, 1985.
39. Ibid, p.1.
40. Ibid, p.1.

2. Restrict advertising which encourages the use of chemicals that can result in addiction;
3. Mobilize our church bodies to assist teenagers in resisting the peer pressure that seeks to draw them into the use of alcohol and other addictive drugs.

American Baptists urge local congregations and regional organizations to:

1. Study the experience of communities* which have put into effect the requirement that persons arrested for driving while intoxicated attend "Driving While Intoxicated" schools.
2. Encourage and support the inclusion of information on the adverse effect of alcohol and other drugs on driving ability in driver education courses.

Baptist, Southern—Abstinent

The oldest strongly evangelical denominations are the Baptists. We have to use the plural because there are so many kinds.

That which claims to be the largest group is The Southern Baptist Convention. The Southern Baptists are in line with those who teach abstinence.

"Whereas, beverage alcohol consumption is responsible for untold thousands of accidents, deaths, illness, and dysfunctional families:

"Be it therefore RESOLVED, that the messengers to the Southern Baptist Convention . . . express our total opposition to the advertising, manufacturing, distribution and sale and consumption of alcoholic beverages and "Be it further RESOLVED that we support stringent laws which will both deter drinking and driving and also ensure swift prosecution of those who are accused of such."[41]

Church of the Brethren—Mildly Abstinent

Another denomination with roots in the long past is the *Church of the Brethren.* They state their present stand in a report from a 1976 annual conference.

"Moderation in all things: abstinence from harmful things."[42]

The Annual Conference 1781 statement against distilling of alcohol beverages is repeated, as is the 1948 statement against the advertising of alcoholic beverages. There is a request to other denominations to cooperate, and a repetition of the 1952 formal statement, calling alcohol "one of America's greatest problems". However, a survey revealed, 13.3% of their pastors use alcohol.[43]

Catholic Conference of Indiana—No Position

Archbishop Daniel Buechlein of Indianapolis says, "We have no written position regarding alcohol."

The present Pope John Paul II advocates temperance in his travels. New to the last catechism is a statement against alcohol use (Woodward).

The Catholic Pioneers have been called the largest abstinent group.

"Alter wine may be made from dried grapes or raisins." Vol. 14, p.959 *New Catholic Encyclopedia.* (unfermented)

The Christian Church—Disciples of Christ—Mildly Abstinent

"THEREFORE BE IT RESOLVED that the General Assembly of the Chris-

* Consult with: American Council on Alcohol Problems, 119 Constitution Avenue, N.E., Washington, D.C.

41. Resolution, No. 9 on Alcohol, Discipline, 1988.
42. 1 Corinthians 3:16-19, Romans 2:12 and 6:12.
43. Church of Brethren, 1976.

tian Church (Disciples of Christ) commend the following guidelines to local, state and province, and national governments:

"That scientific classification of drugs, especially fatal addictive narcotics need to be considered in establishing regulations and penalties. This is especially true with the dangerous drugs of heroin, marijuana and alcohol.

"Congregations are urged to relate to agencies and programs that provide care and rehabilitations for addicts and drug abusers and to provide training to clergy and laity that enables them to minister in these programs."[44]

The emphasis on abstinence varies with the location, such as in the Bible belt. I know of no Disciple Church where alcohol is allowed in communion; not in the church in Iowa City, IA, where I was a supply pastor.

Church of Christ—Abstinent

A Christian Tract, *Keep Your Body,* discusses: Broken Homes, Crime, and Tobacco, but mostly alcohol. After assigning several paragraphs to alcohol problems of health, drunk driving, addiction, and to Bible verses against alcohol, the conclusion is reached: "The Christian does not drink."[45]

Church of God, Anderson, Indiana—Abstinent

The church does not have a discipline, and very little in printed rules. However, the general understanding is abstinence. Its sense of biblical teaching on alcohol can be gathered by its opposition to the repeal of the Eighteenth Amendment.

"The 1928 General Ministerial Assembly spoke clearly.

WHEREAS we regard this propaganda as a challenge to the mortality and public welfare, therefore be it

RESOLVED, That we urge a strict enforcement of the present prohibition laws, and be it further

RESOLVED, That we put ourselves upon record as favoring no candidate or political party that favors modification of the present prohibition law."[46]

Church of the Nazarene—Abstinent

"34.5. [The *discipline* forbids] The use of intoxicating liquors as a beverage, or trafficking therein; giving influence to, or voting for, the licensing of places for the sale of the same; using illicit drugs or trafficking therein; using of tobacco in any of its forms, or trafficking therein.

"Holy Scriptures and human experience together justify the condemnation of the use of intoxicating drinks as a beverage. The manufacture and sale of liquors for such purposes are a sin against God and the human race. Total abstinence from all intoxicants should be the Christian rule for the individual, and total prohibition of the traffic in intoxicants the duty of civil government [903.1, 904.4]. [Proverbs 20:1; 23:29-24:2; Habakkuk 2:5; 1 Corinthians 6:9-12, 19-20; Galatians 5:21; Ephesians 5:18]

"[Only unfermented wine and unleavened bread[47] should be used in the sacrament of the Lord's Supper] [403.7, 404.2, 405, 423.10, 802].

"34.6 [The discipline forbids] The unprescribed use of hallucinogenics, stimulants, and depressants, and the misuse and abuse of regularly pre-

44. Disciples of Christ, 1971.
45. Barnett.
46. Callen.
47. Church of Nazarene.

scribed medicines. Only on competent medical advice and under medical supervision should such drugs be used.

"[Matthew 22:37-39, 27:34; Romans 12:1-2; 1 Corinthians 6:19-20; 9:24-27]"

Episcopal Diocese, North District—Moderate

I contacted Bishop Francis Gray in South Bend, Indiana, and was referred to Deacon Frank McKee. Frank is a reformed alcoholic and has initiated a crusade to help other alcoholics. He has been elevated to "Deaconate" because of his efforts. He ministers to various churches using Dr. Jellinek's Chart of 29 Manifestations. Also, he works with "Hazelton".

Friends, Society of (Quakers)—Abstinent

George Fox and Cromwell were opposed to the liberal alcohol stand of the Established Church of England. This was a century before John Wesley and the Methodists. They thought that many conscientious anabaptists (probably the first abstainer group) were too liberal. Fox formed the *Society of Friends (called Quakers).*

From the *Faith and Practice of the Western Yearly Meeting of Friends, Book of Discipline:* "Friends advocate total abstinence because any use of intoxicants is harmful, and because occasional indulgence frequently leads to excess which results in loss of self-control and enslavement to appetite . . . Friends for many years have been opposed to the entire liquor traffic."[48]

The Western Yearly Meeting extends west from Indianapolis through Illinois. Other Yearly Meetings may be different.

48. Friends Church, 1974.

Lutheran, Evangelical of North America—Moderate and Abstinent

The A Center — **Think Before You Drink!**

This is included in the packet sent out by national headquarters, part of a gentle suggestion of abstinence.

Lutheran King of Glory Church

"This church, largely of Scandinavian roots, in general preaches against anything that is harmful to the body. Some members are abstinent except for wine in the sacrament." Evelyn Ryan, Sec.

However, also included in the packet is a statement from the Lutheran Brotherhood, "Drinking should not be an activity for its own sake, but an adjunct to other activities. The value of social events results from the camaraderie, friendship and support" (Winter 1990—*Bond Magazine*).

Also, included in the packet is a warning from Hazelden, "Alcoholism may begin with a single glass of sherry or a double shot."[49]

While in Denmark, I talked with my relatives' pastor, who preached abstinence, but another *prest* was proud of his large collection of beautiful beer mugs.

Lutheran, Missouri Synod—Moderate

Christ Lutheran

"We have no rule forbidding alcohol use. The Bible teaches moderation in all things; this is our position. Our church has her roots in Germany. You are probably aware of the Germans' love of beer." Judy Ladage, Sec. New York.

From a phone call to Ann and Harold Kuhn, missionaries to Germany, I was

49. King of Glory Church.

informed there has been a five-year campaign in Germany to cut down on alcohol consumption. When they first went to Germany, it was almost impossible to get a meal without beer or wine. Now, milk is served and is also available in grocery stores.

Methodist-United—Abstinent

The results of John Wesley's spiritual and temperance revival are still endemic in the Methodist and Wesleyan rooted Churches.

So the *Book of Discipline of the United Methodist Church* accepts the Biblical standard: "We affirm our long-standing support of abstinence from alcohol, as a faithful witness to Gods' liberating and redeeming love for persons."[50] This is also especially stressed in the old Methodist hymnal.

(From Wesley's roots follow others, such as the Free Methodist, the Church of the Nazarene, and the Wesleyan Church.) From the Methodists' *Church Discipline:* "To abstain from using or trafficking in substances known to be destructive of physical and mental well being, such as alcoholic beverages and tobacco, and from using drugs for other than medical purposes." (1992, sec.(8)). Rev Michael Biggs

Methodist, Free—Abstinent

"*Christian Conduct:* alcohol, a legalized drug, is damaging to individuals, families and society. It is unpredictably addictive and its destructive effects cannot be fully measured. Where it is used, it leaves a trail of broken marriages, family violence, crime, industrial loss, ill health, injury, and death. As concerned Christians, our people practice abstinence for the sake of healthy family and neighbors."[51]

Mormons—Abstinent

WORD OF WISDOM

Word of Wisdom is the common title for a revelation that counsels Latter-day Saints on maintaining good health, and is published as Doctrine and Covenants: section 89. The practice of abstaining from all forms of alcohol, tobacco, coffee, and tea, which may outwardly distinguish active Latter-day Saints more than any other practice, derives from this revelation.

"A revelation given to the first prophet of this dispersion, Joseph Smith, in 1833" (Letter to the author from a President Michael W. Ellis, July 2, 1943).

Pentecostal—Abstention

Rev. David Totman of Lighthouse Tabernacle, Indianapolis.

"Pentecostalism is a movement rather than a church denomination. We preach abstinence from alcohol because that is the Bible's teaching.

However, we do not make a big issue of it when a contrary opinion might discourage participation in our group."

Presbyterian, Reformed—Abstinent

An example of the dilution is the change of stand of the Reformed Presbyterian Church.

The former declaration was:

"The followers of Christ should totally abstain from the manufacture, sale and use of intoxicants as a beverage."

This was made a bit easier in 1980: "It is altogether wise and proper that Christians refrain from the use, sale and manufacture of alcoholic beverages." Chapter 26.

---

50. p.96.

51. A336, p.48.

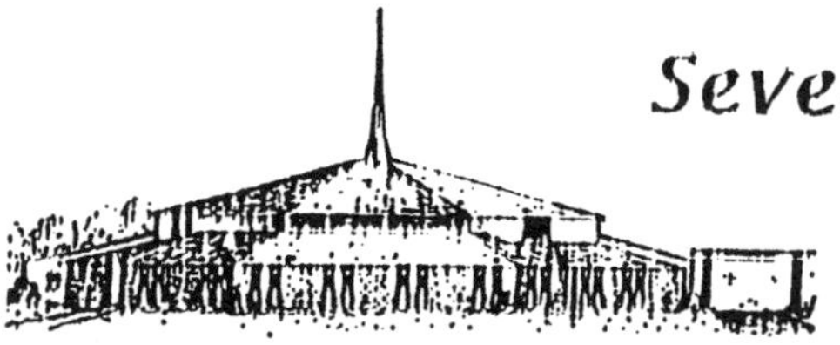

Seventh-day Adventist Church

24445 State Road 19, P.O. Box 558
Cicero, Indiana 46034

Seventh-day Adventists Believe . . .

We are called to be a godly people who think, feel, and act in harmony with the principles of heaven. For the Spirit to recreate in us the character of our Lord we involve ourselves only in those things which will produce Christlike purity, health, and joy in our lives. This means that our amusement and entertainment should meet the highest standards of Christian taste and beauty. While recognizing cultural differences, our dress is to be simple, modest, and neat, befitting those whose true beauty does not consist of outward adornment but in the imperishable ornament of a gentle and quiet spirit. It also means because our bodies are the temples of the Holy Spirit, we are to care for them intelligently. Along with adequate exercise and rest, we are to adopt the most healthful diet possible and abstain from the unclean foods identified in the Scriptures. Since alcoholic beverages, tobacco, and the irresponsible use of drugs and narcotics are harmful to our bodies, we are to abstain from them as well. Instead, we are to engage in whatever brings our thoughts and bodies into the discipline of Christ, who desires our wholesomeness, joy, and goodness.

—Fundamental Beliefs, 21.

(Courtesy Pastor Lyle Davis)

Presbyterian U.S.A.—Moderation

I was unable to get a definitive answer from national leaders. From some members, I was told that it is moderation.

If we may dip into the past, in promoting the 18th amendment of Prohibition, the General Assembly of the Presbyterian Church said: "The Assembly would hail with acclamations of joy and Thanksgiving the utter extermination of the traffic in intoxicating liquor as a beverage."[52]

Rev. William H. Hudnut was a leading Presbyterian pastor in Indianapolis and the Protestant spokesman on a regular TV all faiths program. He was also four time mayor of Indianapolis. A news story in the *Indianapolis Star* for July 28, 1993, headlines him as a counsultant to selling beer from the Monarch Beverage Company promoting non-alcoholic beers.

Wesleyan Church—Abstinent

This church has her roots in John Wesley's abstinent Methodism. It faithfully follows Wesley's teaching of abstinence—"To abstain from using or trafficking in substances known to be destructive of physical and mental well-being, such as alcoholic beverages and tobacco and for using drugs for other than proper medical purposes."[53]

"The Wesleyan Church is opposed to the production, sale, purchase and use of alcoholic beverages, tobacco, narcotics and other harmful drugs, unless for mechanical, chemical or medicinal purposes."[54]

52. Fletcher Dobyns, 1972.

Bacchus Wins Too Often Vs. Christ and the Prophets

It is sad that some of western Christianity assimilated the pagan religion of the alcohol god Bacchus, so contrary to its Scriptures. Wherever Western Christian culture has gone, so has fermentation, distillation of alcohol and drunkenness. This was given to the American Indians, to the Aztecs, Hindus, to converted Moslems who never tasted it, and now to the moon, with a bottle of thanksgiving wine.

But we have God's Word, "The truth shall make us free."

E. UPDATE

Current Rebound

With Repeal all drinking restraints were taken away, and we have seen how the drinking problem has ballooned, immorality is rampant.

As former Dodgers top star, Steve Hoivey, said after his career was ru-

53. The Discipline, 1992.
54. The Discipline, 1992.

THE BORN LOSER® by Art Sansom

ined by drugs, "Booze and drugs are real patient. They sit there and wait."

Since temperance people lost Prohibition, the *Fermentist* Brethren have had a field day teaching the non-biblical theory of moderation. Nowhere is moderation taught in the Bible in relation to alcohol. Sunday School lessons no longer have a quarterly lesson on temperance. We have not been hearing many sermons on arousing the genuine spiritual dimension as the answer to temperance living. Therefore, we need a spiritual temperance revival.

Update FBI Arrest Figures

These figures show the tremendous increase after repeal of driving while intoxicated. There were only 14,238 drunk driving arrests in 1932 during Prohibition, compared to 1,391,000 arrests for DWI in 1990 after repeal (Statistical Abstract Table 302, p. 187). In comparison, there were practically no arrests for DWI during Prohibition.

This is far more than the relative increase in population. All the shackles of Prohibition have been thrown off. Over 50 percent of the highway deaths are now caused by drinking drivers. "23,500 are killed annually in alcohol related accidents and 700,000 more are injured." *Readers Digest Special Gallop Report*, (September 1985, p.51). "25,000 people in our country die every year in alcohol-related crashes. That is one death every 23 minutes, 68 every day." (Radio Advertising Bureau). In any two years period over 50,000 die in alcohol related accidents (Burgess p.31) "Drunk driving is a national crises." (President George Bush, December, 11, 1989).

Notice the amazing drop in drug use and drinking alcohol after the age of 44. At that age people are getting more experience, and more are seeing the futility of drug use. They are using alcohol and drugs less often.

Three people killed.

The Cost of Bacchus' Alcohol

Figures Available 1944

1. Number of Alcoholics

The National Council on Alcohol and Drug Abuse, NCAAD has compiled this data:

10.5 million alcoholics
7.2 additional persons have impaired health and social functioning due to heavy drinking.

2. Financial cost to Nation

85.8 billion in 1988.[55]
12.2 billion brought in by laws 4-a Statistical Abstract
73.6 loss to nation. But President Bill Clinton says taxes on beer should not be raised. It is the poor man's beverage. (February 1994).

3. Crime, alcohol used just before crime.[56]

68% convicted on manslaughter
62% on assault
49% murder or attempted murder
52% rape or other sexual assault

4. Family Problems

One fourth of all family related problems are related to alcohol.[57]

55. D. P. Rice, et al.
56. Sixth Report to Congress.
57. The Gallup Pole 1987.

5. Deaths—Alcohol Related, 1987

300 Deaths daily related to alcohol; total of 105,095 yearly. Each victim lost 25.9 years of life on the average.[58]

6. Birth Defects

Fetal alcoholic syndrome is one of the top three known causes of mental retardation caused by mothers drinking during pregnancy.[59]

7. Suicide

21% of suicide victims are alcohol dependent.[60]

8. Health Care

A quarter of all hospitalized patients have alcohol related problems.[61]

9. High School Seniors

35% of high school seniors have had 5 or more drinks in a row at least once prior to a nation survey.[62]

10. Alcohol Consumption

Two thirds of the population drink, but 10% drink half of the alcohol used.[63]

Update—Number of Alcoholics

I have read all sorts of estimated figures on the number of present day alcoholics. So I went to the people who are really supposed to know, The National Council on Alcohol and Drug Dependency, 12 W. 21st. St., New York.

I was given the astounding 1992 figures of 10,500,000 alcoholics. In addition 7.2 million show persistent heavy drinking associated with impaired health and/or social functioning.

Alcoholics

1932	During prohibition	80,026
1992	Under repeal	10,500,000

Did some one say Prohibition was not successful?

1988 N.C.A.D.D.

Alcohols cost to the nation .... 85.8 billion
Other addictive drug cost .... 61.0 billion

I heard a lawyer say, "You can't legislate morals." As a lawyer, he should have known better. Except for regulatory laws (driving on the right side, stopping at stop signs, landlords required to have smoke alarms in buildings, and such) all laws are moral laws. Murder—thou shalt not kill. Burglary, robbery, fraud—thou shalt not steal. Perjury—thou shalt not bear false witness, etc. About all laws are prohibitions.

Is the glamour of alcohol losing its luster? Are prohibitions needed? Apparently the feeling is yes.

Now merchants are prohibited from selling alcohol to anyone under 21. Liquor establishments are prohibited from selling alcohol near churches and schools. Many states prohibit containers in the front seat of cars. Hosts are prohibited from allowing a guest to get drunk. The New Jersey Supreme Court hold a host liable for damage by a drunken guest. A Minnesota employer was made responsible for the damage done in an accident caused by a driver having had drinks at the company's party. Increasingly, pregnant women are being prohibited from using drugs and alcohol. Tax payers are rebelling against paying for constant support of idiots born to drinking mothers, etc.

58. Centers for Disease Control.
59. NIAA Seventh Report to Congress.
60. D. Flavin, et al.
61. N.I.A.A.A.—Seventh Report to Congress.
62. N.I.D.A. 1975-1988.
63. N.I.A.A.A.—Seventh Report to Congress.

The free ride is over, and Americans are drinking less. Many are switching to beer without alcohol. Will we get prohibition again?

Here is a chart showing the difference between consumption of wine between license states and control states. Check the bottom line. People drink three times as much in licensed, as in control states.

January 1990—License and Control States

Control States

Year	Wine/gallons (000)	Percentage of total consumption
1985	100,237	24.0
1986	96,896	24.6
1987	94,305	24.3
1988	91,542	24.2

License States

Year	Wine/gallons (000)	Percentage of total consumption
1985	317,681	76.0
1986	297,649	75.4
1987	293,920	75.7
1988	286,755	75.8

(Sources: Distilled Spirits Council of the United States, Inc.; Bureau of Census, U.S. Dept.)

WHY AMERICANS ARE DRINKING LESS

PULSE OF A NATION
A Reader's Digest/Gallup Survey

112th Edition
Statistical Abstract of the United States 1992
U.S. Department of Commerce
Barbara Hackman Franklin, Secretary
Rockwell A. Schnabel, Deputy Secretary
Economics and Statistics Administration
J. Antonio Villamil, Under Secretary for Economic Affairs
Bureau of the Census
Barbara Everitt Bryant, Director
BERNAN PRESS
Lanham, Maryland

This is a January 1985 headline regarding a *Reader's Digest*-Gallup Survey. *This should be an encouragement to temperance workers and to all Americans in general.

Around 1980 there started a decrease in Americans drinking, which had been until then steadily climbing.

Coffee and tea use remained fairly constant, but soft drink use doubled.

In 10 years consumption of alcohol jumped up from 35.7 to 42.8 in 1980. But from the 1980's 42.8 consumption steadily dropped to 39.5 in 1990.

We see the immediate acceleration of drunken driving after Repeal. Now let us bring the figures to date.

* *Reader's Digest* does not advertise alcoholic beverages or tobacco. It is said to be America's most popular magazine.

No. 207. Per Capita Consumption of Selected Beverages, by Type: 1970 to 1990

[In gallons. See headnote, table 205]

COMMODITY	1970	1975	1980	1983	1984	1985	1986	1987	1988	1989	1990
Nonalcoholic [1]	95.8	95.8	101.7	100.4	101.1	102.1	102.5	104.5	105.1	106.6	105.8
Milk (plain and flavored)	31.2	29.5	27.6	26.3	26.4	26.7	26.5	26.3	25.8	26	25.7
Whole	25.4	21.0	17.0	15.1	14.7	14.3	13.5	13.0	12.3	11.3	10.5
Lowfat	4.5	7.1	9.2	9.9	10.3	10.9	11.5	11.7	11.7	12.4	12.6
Skim	1.3	1.3	1.3	1.2	1.3	1.5	1.6	1.6	1.9	2.3	2.7
Tea	6.8	7.5	7.3	7.0	7.1	7.1	7.1	7.0	7.1	7.1	6.9
Coffee	33.4	31.4	26.7	26.3	26.8	27.4	27.5	26.7	25.7	26.9	26.7
Soft drinks	20.8	22.2	35.0	35.2	36.0	35.7	35.8	39.2	41.1	41.8	42.5
Citrus juice	3.6	5.2	5.1	5.6	4.8	5.2	5.6	5.3	5.4	4.8	4.0
Alcoholic (adult population)	35.7	39.7	42.8	41.7	41.1	40.5	40.6	40.0	39.5	38.9	39.5
Beer	30.6	33.9	36.6	35.6	35.0	34.4	34.7	34.4	34.1	33.7	34.4
Wine	2.2	2.7	3.2	3.3	3.4	3.5	3.5	3.3	3.2	3.0	2.9
Distilled spirits	3.0	3.1	3.0	2.7	2.6	2.5	2.4	2.3	2.2	2.1	2.2

[1] Excludes vegetable juices, noncitrus fruit juices and drinks, canned concentrated citrus juices, and chilled-fresh citrus juices produced for local sale. Includes chilled citrus juices produced commercially from fresh fruit in Florida.

Source: U.S. Dept. of Agriculture, Economic Research Service, *Food Consumption, Prices, and Expenditures*, annual; and unpublished data.

(These are in thousands so we need to add 3 zeros)

Alcohol and Road Safety Laws

No. 1012. State Legislation—Alcohol and Road Safety Laws: Various Years

STATE	ALCOHOL LEGISLATION			MANDATORY BELT USE LAW			Child safety seat law date [5]	Motor-cycle helmet law [6]	65 SPEED LIMIT	
	21 year drinking age since [1]	Open con-tainer law [2]	BAC limit [3]	Effec-tive date	Enforce-ment [4]	Seating posi-tions			Effec-tive date [7]	Applic-able vehicles
Northeast:										
N.E:										
ME	1985	no	0.08	none	(X)	(X)	9/83	[8,9]15	6/87	all
NH	1985	no	0.10	none	(X)	(X)	(1)	18	4/87	all
VT	1986	no	0.10	none	(X)	(X)	7/84	yes	4/87	all
MA	1985	no	0.10	repealed	(X)	(X)	1/82	yes	none	(X)
RI	1984	no	[10]0.10	none	(X)	(X)	7/87	(11)	none	(X)
CT	1985	no	0.10	1/86	1	front	1982	18	none	(X)
M.A:										
NY	1990	no	(NA)	12/84	1	front	4/82	yes	none	(X)
NJ	1982	no	0.10	3/85	2	front	4/83	yes	none	(X)
PA	1935	no	0.10	11/87	2	front	11/83	yes	none	(X)
Midwest:										
E.N.C:										
OH	1987	yes	[10]0.10	5/86	2	front	6/83	[8]18	7/87	some
IN	1935	no	0.10	7/87	2	front	1/84	18	6/87	some
IL	1980	yes	0.10	7/85	2	front	7/83	no	4/87	some
MI	1978	yes	(NA)	7/85	2	front	3/82	yes	12/87	some
WI	1986	yes	[10]0.10	12/87	2	front	4/84	[8]18	6/87	all
W.N.C:										
MN	1986	yes	0.10	8/86	2	front	8/83	[8]18	6/87	all
IA	1986	yes	0.10	7/86	1	front	1/85	no	5/87	all
MO	1945	no	0.10	9/85	2	front	1/84	yes	4/87	some
ND	1936	yes	0.10	none	(X)	(X)	1/84	18	4/87	all
SD	1987	yes	0.10	none	(X)	(X)	7/84	18	4/87	all
NE	1985	no	0.10	repealed	(X)	(X)	8/83	yes	4/87	all
KS	1985	yes	0.10	7/86	2	front	7/81	18	5/87	some
South:										
S.A:										
DE	1983	yes	0.10	none	(X)	(X)	6/82	[8,12]19	none	(X)
MD	1982	no	0.10	7/86	2	[13]front	1/84	18	none	(X)
DC	1986	no	0.10	12/85	2	[13]front	7/83	yes	none	(X)
VA	1986	yes	0.10	1/88	2	front	1/83	yes	7/88	some
WV	1986	yes	0.10	none	(X)	(X)	7/81	yes	5/87	all
NC	1986	yes	0.10	10/85	1	front	7/85	yes	4/87	all
SC	1986	yes	0.10	7/89	2	front	1/89	21	7/87	all
GA	1986	no	0.12	9/88	2	front	7/84	yes	2/88	all
FL	1985	yes	0.10	7/86	2	front	7/83	yes	4/87	all
E.S.C:										
KY	1938	no	0.10	none	(X)	(X)	7/82	yes	6/87	all
TN	1984	no	0.10	4/86	2	front	1/78	yes	5/87	all
AL	1985	no	0.10	none	(X)	(X)	1982	yes	1987	all
MS	1986	no	0.10	3/90	1	front	7/83	yes	4/87	all
W.S.C:										
AR	1957	no	0.10	none	(X)	(X)	8/83	yes	4/87	all
LA	1987	no	0.10	7/86	2	front	1/85	yes	4/87	all
OK	1983	yes	0.10	2/87	2	front	11/83	18	4/87	all
TX	1985	no	0.10	9/85	1	front	1/85	yes	5/87	some
West:										
Mt:										
MT	1987	no	(NA)	10/87	2	all	10/83	18	4/87	all
ID	1987	[14]Yes	0.10	7/86	2	front	1/85	18	5/87	all
WY	1988	no	0.10	6/89	2	front	4/85	18	5/87	all
CO	1987	no	0.10	7/87	2	front	1/84	no	4/87	all
NM	1934	yes	0.10	1/86	1	front	5/83	18	4/87	all
AZ	1984	no	0.10	1/91	2	front	1984	18	4/87	all
UT	1935	yes	0.08	4/86	2	front	4/83	18	5/87	all
NV	1933	no	0.10	7/87	2	all	7/83	yes	4/87	all
Pac:										
WA	1934	yes	0.10	6/86	2	all	1/84	yes	4/87	some
OR	1935	yes	[10]0.08	12/90	1	all	1/84	yes	10/87	some
CA	1933	yes	0.08	1/86	2	all	1/83	15.5	5/87	some
AK	1983	yes	0.10	9/90	2	all	7/85	19	none	(X)
HI	1986	Yes	0.10	12/85	1	front	1983	18	none	(X)

X Not applicable. [1] Year in which original law became effective, not when grandfather causes expired. [2] Law prohibiting open liquor containers in motor vehicles. [3] Percent blood alcohol concentration (BAC) which constitutes the threshold of legal intoxication. [4] "1" indicates primary enforcement (law can be enforced on its own). "2" indicates secondary enforcement (Law enforced only if vehicle stopped for a separate offense). [5] Effective data of original law, not of subsequent revisions. [6] Presence of law or age below which riders are required to wear helmet. [7] Includes administrative action as well as legislation. [8] Plus instruction permit holders. [9] Plus novice license holders. [10] Different legal limit for minors. [11] Passengers only. [12] Possession of helmet required by all. [13] Excluding front center seat. [14] Does not include beer.

Source: National Safety Council, Itasca, IL, *Accident Facts*, annual.

Courts a Problem

United States Transportation Secretary Samuel Skinner said, "I'm totally committed to a drug-free transportation system." One of his projects was to have drug testing for 200,000 mass transit workers. But he had to stop when an appeals court ruled the Transportation Administration exceeded its authority when it issued anti-drug regulations. So we continue to have people killed in accidents that have operators with high alcoholic blood count. Thank you, your honor, appeals court.

Prohibition did not stop all drinking. Laws against murder do not stop all murders, laws against theft do not stop all thefts. Except for a minute group of anarchists I have not heard of anyone advocating doing away with laws because they are not 100% effective.

Drive to Ban Alcohol

From all the figures and opinions prohibition did as much and probably more good than other laws. Now again people are drinking less.

Persons Arrested—Drug Use

No. 302. Persons Arrested, by Charge, Sex, and Age: 1990

[Represents arrests (not charges) reported by 10,206 agencies (reporting 12 months) with a total 1990 population of 194 million as estimated by FBI]

CHARGE	Total (1,000)	PERCENT DISTRIBUTION							
		Male	Under 15 years	Under 18 years	18-24 years	25-44 years	45-54 years	55-64 years	65 yr. and over
Total arrests	**11,250**	**81.6**	**5.3**	**15.6**	**30.1**	**47.0**	**4.9**	**1.8**	**0.7**
Driving while intoxicated	1,391	87.2	(Z)	1.1	25.0	61.1	8.3	3.3	1.2
Liquor laws	552	81.3	1.9	22.1	55.2	18.6	2.6	1.1	0.4
Drunkeness	717	90.0	0.3	2.7	24.0	58.3	9.3	4.1	1.6

Source: U.S. Federal Bureau of Investigation, *Crime in the United States*, annual.

The same horrible conditions that prompted Prohibition are showing up, along with the realization that restrains are needed. Temperance people became discouraged after repeal, but are now starting to get reinvigorated.

DRIVE TO BAN ALCOHOL, this was the headline of an article in the Noblesville Ledger January 8, 1994. The article was about The Women's Christian Temperance Union, WCTU, and its "battling booze." That such an article was highlighted indicates that the climate is now right for a realization that restraint is necessary.

One effective restraint is alcohol tax.

University Professors Concerned

Professor Peter Nathan, vice-president for academic affairs at the University of Iowa, is a nationally known researcher on alcohol. Sitting in his office, decorated with Norwegian temperance posters, he said, "People are more concerned about their habits as they affect their longevity and quality of life."

Another University Professor admits genes make up a predisposition but says, "Genes and cells don't make decisions: people make decisions" (Harold Muford). He adds, "Half of the alcohol is consumed by approximately 10% of the population, but the individual health risks of heavy drinking are getting more attention.

Neoprohibition

Is Dr. Marshall right, have we entered a period of "Neoprohibition?" Will we have Prohibition again?

Office of Strategic & Policy Analysis
Distilled Spirits Council of the U.S., Inc.
January 1990

License and Control States

	License States a/		Control States		Total
Year	Wine Gallons (000)	Percentage of Total Consumption	Wine Gallons (000)	Percentage of Total Consumption	Wine Gallons (000)
1971	288,368	75.4	94,156	24.6	382,523
1972	296,281	75.2	97,555	24.8	393,836
1973	306,727	75.4	100,332	24.6	407,059
1974	314,476	75.4	102,841	24.6	417,317
1975	318,697	75.3	104,735	24.7	423,432
1976	320,086	75.1	106,307	24.9	426,394
1977	323,813	75.0	107,740	25.0	431,553
1978	332,926	75.1	110,536	24.9	443,461
1979	335,416	75.0	112,078	25.0	447,497
1980	337,631	75.1	111,786	24.9	449,417
1981	339,177	75.5	110,276	24.5	449,453
1982	330,677	75.6	106,982	24.4	437,659
1983	327,065	75.8	104,331	24.2	431,386
1984	324,240	76.0	102,512	24.0	426,752
1985	317,681	76.0	100,237	24.0	417,918
1986	297,649	75.4	96,898	24.6	394,547
1987	293,920	75.7	94,306	24.3	388,225
1988	286,755	75.8	91,542	24.2	378,297

NOTE: Because of rounding, detail may not add to total. Excludes Hawaii, 1934–64.

a\ Includes District of Columbia.
b\ Includes Mississippi gallonage from July through December 1966.

SOURCES: *Distilled Spirits Council of the United States, Inc.; Bureau of Census, U.S. Dept.*

DISTILLED SPIRITS COUNCIL OF THE U.S., INC. – JANUARY 1990

No. 196. Alcoholism and Drug Abuse Treatment Facilities and Clients, by Facility Location and Ownership: 1989

[As of September 30. Based on the National Drug and Alcoholism Treatment Unit Survey (NDATUS), a census of all known drug abuse and alcoholism treatment facilities in the U.S. Data collected in cooperation with State agencies which defined what constitutes a facility for reporting purposes]

FACILITY LOCATION AND OWNERSHIP	TOTAL			ALCOHOLISM TREATMENT			DRUG ABUSE TREATMENT		
	Units reporting [1] [2]	Clients in treatment [2]	Budgeted capacity	Units reporting [2]	Clients in treatment [2]	Budgeted capacity	Units reporting [2]	Clients in treatment [2]	Budgeted capacity
Total	7,642	718,968	903,250	6,374	374,437	469,603	6,170	344,529	433,647
Community mental health center	956	107,613	123,145	883	60,627	75,665	848	38,989	47,480
Hospital [3]	1,353	88,921	127,397	1,244	45,637	64,291	1,150	43,284	63,106
Correctional facility	113	13,753	21,480	82	3,657	6,020	104	10,096	15,460
Halfway house	745	19,293	23,455	705	11,933	14,851	451	6,360	8,604
Other residential facility	1,049	50,009	69,215	789	20,506	28,959	663	29,503	37,206
Outpatient facility	2,977	366,934	459,993	2,347	187,153	248,603	2,389	169,601	210,390
Other location	449	73,463	81,545	324	20,924	30,214	305	40,539	51,331
Private for profit	1,258	91,632	145,110	1,129	53,167	81,013	1,047	38,465	64,097
Private nonprofit	4,950	431,576	529,576	4,132	221,242	272,044	4,025	210,334	257,532
State and local government	1,235	171,907	199,105	942	84,691	97,657	997	87,210	101,440
Federal government	199	23,851	29,159	171	15,337	18,900	131	8,514	10,570

[1] Unduplicated count. [2] Excludes data from 117 units which did not report budgeted capacity. With these data included, total number of clients in treatment was 734,955 (383,525 alcoholism clients and 351,430 drug abuse clients). [3] Includes general hospitals, alcoholism hospitals, mental/psychiatric hospitals, and other specialized hospitals.

Source: U.S. National Institute on Drug Abuse and U.S. National Institute on Alcohol Abuse and Alcoholism, *1989 National Drug and Alcoholism Treatment Unit Survey: Final Report.*

No. 197. Drug Use, by Type of Drug and Age Group: 1974 to 1991

[In percent. Current users are those who used drugs at least once within month prior to this study. Based on national samples of respondents residing in households. Subject to sampling variability; see source]

AGE AND TYPE OF DRUG	EVER USED						CURRENT USER					
	1974	1979	1982	1985	1988	1991	1974	1979	1982	1985	1988	1991
12 TO 17 YEARS OLD												
Marihuana	23.0	30.9	26.7	23.6	17.4	13.0	12.0	16.7	11.5	12.0	6.4	4.3
Cocaine	3.6	5.4	6.5	4.9	3.4	2.4	1.0	1.4	1.6	1.5	1.1	0.4
Inhalants	8.5	9.8	(NA)	9.2	8.8	7.0	0.7	2.0	(NA)	3.4	2.0	1.8
Hallucinogens	6.0	7.1	5.2	3.3	3.5	3.4	1.3	2.2	1.4	1.2	0.6	0.8
Heroin	1.0	0.5	(NA)	(NA)	0.6	0.3	(NA)	(NA)	(NA)	(NA)	(NA)	0.1
Stimulants [1]	5.0	3.4	6.7	5.6	4.2	3.0	1.0	1.2	2.6	1.6	1.2	0.5
Sedatives [1]	5.0	3.2	5.8	4.1	2.4	2.4	1.0	1.1	1.3	1.0	0.6	0.5
Tranquilizers [1]	3.0	4.1	4.9	4.8	0.2	2.1	1.0	0.6	0.9	0.0	0.2	0.3
Analgesics [1]	(NA)	3.2	4.2	5.8	4.2	4.1	(NA)	0.6	0.7	1.6	0.9	1.1
Alcohol	54.0	70.3	65.2	55.5	50.2	46.4	34.0	37.2	30.2	31.0	25.2	20.3
Cigarettes	52.0	54.1	49.5	45.2	42.3	37.9	25.0	12.1	14.7	16.3	11.8	10.8
18 TO 25 YEARS OLD												
Marihuana	52.7	68.2	64.1	60.3	56.4	50.5	25.2	35.4	27.4	21.8	15.5	13.0
Cocaine	12.7	27.5	28.3	25.2	19.7	17.9	3.1	9.3	6.8	7.6	4.5	2.0
Inhalants	9.2	16.5	(NA)	12.4	12.5	10.9	(NA)	1.2	(NA)	0.8	1.7	1.5
Hallucinogens	16.6	25.1	21.1	11.3	13.9	13.2	2.5	4.4	1.7	1.9	1.9	1.2
Heroin	4.5	3.5	1.2	1.2	0.4	0.8	(NA)	(NA)	(NA)	(NA)	(NA)	0.1
Stimulants [1]	17.0	18.2	18.0	17.1	11.3	9.4	3.7	3.5	4.7	3.7	2.4	0.6
Sedatives [1]	15.0	17.0	18.7	11.0	5.5	4.3	1.6	2.8	2.6	1.0	0.9	0.6
Tranquilizers [1]	10.0	15.8	15.1	12.0	7.6	7.5	1.2	2.1	1.6	1.6	1.0	0.6
Analgesics [1]	(NA)	11.8	12.1	11.3	9.4	10.2	(NA)	1.0	1.0	1.8	1.5	1.5
Alcohol	81.6	95.3	94.6	92.6	90.3	90.2	69.3	75.9	70.9	71.4	65.3	63.6
Cigarettes	68.8	82.8	76.9	75.6	75.0	71.2	48.8	42.6	39.5	36.8	35.2	32.2
26 YEARS OLD AND OVER												
Marihuana	9.9	19.6	23.0	27.2	30.7	32.9	2.0	6.0	6.6	6.1	3.9	3.3
Cocaine	0.9	4.3	8.5	9.5	9.9	11.0	(NA)	0.9	1.2	2.0	0.9	0.8
Inhalants	1.2	3.9	(NA)	5.0	3.9	4.4	(NA)	0.5	(NA)	0.5	0.2	0.3
Hallucinogens	1.3	4.5	6.4	6.2	6.6	8.0	(NA)	(NA)	(NA)	(NA)	(NA)	0.1
Heroin	0.5	1.0	1.1	1.1	1.1	1.7	(NA)	(NA)	(NA)	(NA)	(NA)	(NA)
Stimulants [1]	3.0	5.8	6.2	7.9	6.6	7.1	(NA)	0.5	0.6	0.7	0.5	0.2
Sedatives [1]	2.0	3.5	4.8	5.2	3.3	4.5	(NA)	(NA)	(NA)	0.0	0.3	0.3
Tranquilizers [1]	2.0	3.1	3.6	7.2	4.6	5.7	(NA)	(NA)	(NA)	1.0	0.9	0.1
Analgesics [1]	(NA)	2.7	3.2	5.9	4.5	5.5	(NA)	(NA)	(NA)	0.8	0.1	0.5
Alcohol	73.2	91.5	88.2	89.4	88.6	88.7	54.5	61.3	60.6	60.6	54.8	52.5
Cigarettes	65.4	83.0	76.7	80.5	79.6	77.0	39.1	36.9	34.0	32.0	29.8	26.6

NA Not available. [1] Nonmedical use.

Source: U.S. National Institute on Drug Abuse, *National Household Survey on Drug Abuse: 1991.*

"Neoprohibitionism" has already entered our society according to Keith Marshall an anthropology professor at the University of Iowa. (My major graduate studies alma mater.) But he is increasingly worried about alcohol as being a legal substance.

Existing Laws of Neoprohibition

Merchants are prohibited to sell alcohol to minors.

Drivers are prohibited from driving with an alcohol control of .10.

Drivers are prohibited from drinking alcohol while driving.

Drivers and passengers are prohibited from riding without seat belts.

From a TV broadcast: "My father was a blue collar manager, who would stop to drink at the tavern on his way home from work. He was very proud of the fact that he was the head usher on the first Sunday of each month at our church.

I started drugs and alcohol in high school, and changed to the sloppy way of the addicts. Later, I took amphetamines in the daytime to keep me going on my job, and alcohol to relax in the evening. When I woke up one morning with a stranger in my bed, I knew my alcoholism had gone too far. I tried to quit alcohol but could not. Life became so unbearable that I made plans to commit suicide. While in this degraded state, a stranger, a church janitor said to me, "The Lord loves you just as you are." This was the first time anyone talked to me like that. I looked him up in the church basement. He said immediately, 'Let's pray and ask the Lord to forgive you and save you now.' I prayed and mentioned every sin until the janitor became goggle eyed. But I found a peace and joy that I never knew existed. I went out shouting to everyone that I was saved. I joined the Campus Crusade for Christ. A fellow worker one day said, 'Let's get married,'; and we did. We never kissed, never dated, but got married immediately. It is now a wonderful life in the Lord's work."

August 19, 1991, WHMB
The Million Watt Christian TV station that my friends and I built on our farm.

Israel vineyard 11/12/94.

1994. Israel vinepress. Dark raining. Garden of Gethsemane. To my knowledge, the only current published vinepress picture. Jerusalem Museum does not have one. The slab, 2 fifths above, slants down for the grape juice to run into a receptacle, as the grapes are trod. The white at the lower left is a stone walk way.

CHAPTER FIVE

THE TWO WINES

"I still believe the scriptures are totally reliable, infallible, inerrant . . . But I have long since discovered that translators, and lexicographers, are not."

"Dr. Hansen, If there are substantial errors in your writing, I have failed to find them. I still think your approach to history and your handling of the Greek is scholarly and sound . . . I agree with the point in your chapter and the chapter heading The Two Wines". Wilbur Dayton, January 19, 1990, in personal letter to the author.**

**Among other schools Dr. Dayton has served as professor of Theology and Greek, at Asbury Theological Seminary, Wesley Biblical Seminary where he was Vice President, and Union Biblical Seminary, Yeotmal, India.

CHAPTER FIVE
THE TWO WINES

A. THE PROBLEM OF THE ONE WINE THEORY

James (not his real name) was a husky, congenial fellow. The rough life of the streets prepared him well for starring on the high school football team. Maybe his grades were not the best, but an alcoholic mother didn't help. Later he married.

Construction work beckoned and he had the brawn for it. Together, he and his wife lived the *good life.* A good job, a comfortable chair, a bottle of wine and TV shorts.

But with the recession, construction work plummeted. Jim was soon out of a job. The only thing that increased in that little home was the amount of liquor consumed. Finally, Jim's wife kicked him out. He worked for a time, clearing tables and cleaning up. Sometimes he worked without sleep. Without an alarm clock he missed work and was fired.

Courtesy U.S. News, 3/8/82, p. 61
Photo by Darryl Heikes,

Cold winter winds whistled. Jim hunted for a grate for warmth. When the heat quit, he shuffled on. A dumpster provided a bit of shelter. He pulled a bottle from his pocket. Only a scurrying rat heard his voice, as he mumbled to himself. "I wasn't stuck with this stuff until it got so cold. I'd freeze without it. And they call me a wino." Drunk and stumbling, he headed for a subway bench and fell asleep. Wham! A night policeman's stick jarred him awake; he was told to move on. *(TIME* February 2, 1987:26).

Shivering, he made his way around a corner and saw bright lights. Music enticed him toward the light. He was met by a friendly smile. He noticed that first. Someone handed him a blanket and showed him a spot on the floor where he could sleep. This seemed like Heaven. He was given breakfast. Chapel followed; at least it would be a warm place to pass some hours. He heard an unusual story of someone who loved him as he was. He heard about a God who could turn his life around. He had never heard that. The speaker invited anyone to come and ask God for help. He was propelled down the aisle. Later he felt as if the world had been made anew.

God was there to help, and he was living without liquor. His friend Monty, helped him find a job. His wife gave him a second chance. He found a church. What a change!

But as Jim smelled the Communion wine, he hesitated a moment. He gulped it. He decided to stay for the second service.

Jim didn't go home that night . . .

The problem—an alcoholic is never cured. He can never drink again without losing control. Restrictive brain cells have been killed by alcohol.

The Two Wines

Today *wine* by dictionary definition and current usage means fermented grape juice. The present fashion is for some Bible Scholars to take this present use and apply it to Biblical times. *They say, wine* has one meaning—alcoholic beverage, but at that time the word wine had two meanings.

Let us look up *must* in a current Webster's Dictionary. "Must: new wine; the juice pressed from grapes or other fruit before it has fermented. New wine." (By the way *must* has 2 meanings; it usually means an obligation.) *MUST* is always a must.

It is really very simple. Fresh fruit juice is new unfermented wine. (Nonalcoholic) "Wine making is a complex and difficult art. " (Johnson's Universal Cyclopedia Vol. VIII New York, 1896). Alcoholic wine is man made. After it ferments it becomes an alcoholic wine. Alcohol: yeast excrement, manure.

"Is this wine or WINE?"

Before fermentation, it is purely nonalcoholic, new wine. After fermentation, it becomes alcoholic wine with completely different chemical formula. That is the basis for the two wines, with current dictionary definitions and sanction. We shall see later that it is possible to keep the fresh juice in its nonalcoholic state for years, possibly permanently. Just as we keep grape juice fresh in our homes. Your Welch's grape juice will not ferment, no matter how many years you keep it. This was true of the ancients of Bible times. They preferred unfermented wine and knew how to keep it that way.

Wine, A Blessing And A Curse

The two meanings are further evident when we consider that God uses wine as a blessing in some cases, but as a curse in other places. Seminary professor Dr. Robert P. Teachout explains this in his book *The Use of Wine in the Old Testament*:

"The problem, then, of God's apparently contradictory evaluation of wine . . . as both, on the one hand, the epitome of His blessing and, on the other, a product which has so corrupted man and is thus condemned . . . is in essence a lexical rather than a theological one. When it is recognized that the same word may legitimately refer to two distinctly different beverages, it becomes clear that God always approves of grape juice and never approves (in any amount) of wine."[1]

"Light begins to break through. The Bible speaks of two kinds of wine: good wine and bad wine, unfermented and fermented wine."[2]

Gods View Must Be Consistent

With the 'one meaning theory', we have the problem of consistency of God's Word.

Usually Christians believe God reveals Himself to man through his conscience, as in Romans 2:13,14; through the Holy Spirit, John 16:13; and Revelation—the Bible (11 Timothy3:16).

1. Teachout, 1980, Preface.
2. Dr. Jack Van Impe with Roger F. Campbell, 1980. *The Beloved Enemy*.

The *Bible*, as God's Word, must be clear, direct, and without contradictions. We believe that the same Holy Spirit that inspired the Scriptural writings also inspired the selection of noncontradictory books. The reformers did not include books of the apocrypha, partly because they felt that they had contradictions. There can be no contradiction with God. God cannot both commend and condemn alcoholic use.

Moderation Has No Biblical Basis

The problem of moderation (the result of the one meaning theory) is that there is no basis for it in the Bible.

Apologetic scholars have realized that the *Bible's* strong condemnation of drunkenness leads to death and exclusion from the kingdom of God. To overcome this contradiction they have come up with a very strange explanation which has absolutely no scriptural basis. They say, God approves of *moderate* alcoholic use, moderately drunk but not to the point of total drunkenness. *Moderate* alcohol use is not in the *Bible*. Any amount of alcohol intoxicates, that is why usually it is drunk.*

1. Moderation is mentioned only once in the KJV, Philippians 4:5 and was translated from the Greek word *Epieikes*, which means 'gentleness primarily, but also mild, fair, and kind': The New King James says, "Let your gentleness be known to all." Similarly do most modern versions translate. The other four times that *epieikes* is in the Greek, King James translates it as gentleness three times and once as patience. It is never used in relation to alcohol.

2. At least it becomes clear it has nothing to do with alcoholic wine.

3. As related to alcohol, moderation is intrinsically wrong. Alcohol is bitter tasting; it is not drunk for taste. People drink intoxicants for one purpose, to get intoxicated. To get a sense of freedom from worry and care, to feel good, to loosen their brain, tongue, inhibitions, control, and judgment. Possibly more than any other consumed product volatile alcohol is likely to join with any substance. From the first sip it enters the blood stream and the brain. Getting rid of judgment is a pleasant sensation.

4. This sense of relief brings a desire for more, so alcohol is strongly addictive. The more one drinks the more one wants to drink, the more one loses judgment. For many this is close to making moderation a farce. With temporary enjoyment and with judgment gone, how can a drinker desire and judge to be moderate? To a large extent, moderationalism is intrinsically wrong. For at least 10% it does not work, there are disastrous results.

Problems of the one meaning theory are—unscientific and historically false.

Ten percent (10%) of all moderate drinkers become alcoholics; does God commend something that dangerous? Alcohol is involved in a large part of violent crimes, home breakups, and suicides. Does God give His approval? Should the Christian Church? The obvious answer, given by history, is completely overlooked by some scholars. May God let them see the truth.

Copy Cat Scholars

The original publication of *The King James Version,* was almost 400 years ago. Some who have followed with so called modern translations seem to have taken the easy way out. They basically copied the word *wine* in the same way that it was used in the KJV. In that respect, their translations are not modern. As Christian brothers and sisters we love them, but we feel they do much harm in indiscriminately calling grape juice wine.

*There may be cases where alcoholic drinks are used, when there is germ infested water.

Baseless—One Wine Theory

The problem is assuming all Bible wine is alcoholic. That is baseless.

Some have translated grape juice as wine, with its alcoholic connotation, when the context clearly means grape juice. The one wine theory that wine (*yayin*), *oinos* and other Hebrew and Greek words always mean alcoholic has no factual basis. There is no Biblical basis for the moderation theory.

Even fresh juice in a cluster of grapes is sometimes called wine in modern translations. When the juice comes straight from the presses, with no time to ferment, it is erroneously translated wine. Time and the controlled fermentation process are required for producing alcoholic wine. Today we use the term cider or punch for both fresh and fermented juice. Likewise, the Hebrews, Greeks, and Romans used the word *wine* for both fresh and fermented grape juice. These meanings we shall document. Most modern translators seem unaware of, or are oblivious to this fact.

Laws Limiting the Word Wine to Fermented Grape Juice

We keep fresh grape juice in our homes, so did the ancients, as we shall show. However, Croesus and Bacchus have made an alliance and are winning, since there is more money made in selling alcoholic wine than in selling grape juice. So France passed a law in 1905 stating that the word *wine* could be used only for a drink "exclusively produced from the fermentation of fresh grapes or from the juice of fresh grapes." An Italian law of 1925 defined *wine* as "The product of fermentation of the juice of grapes." The Germans passed a similar law in 1930. And so by the fiat of government law, the meaning of the word was restricted! No longer could *wine* mean sweet grape juice. By law, the word *wine* could be *fermented juice* only.[3]

(Money is the *loot* of all evil.)

Wine Today Means Alcoholic

Now the English word *wine* normally means only an intoxicating grape beverage. But the word also has meant unfermented grape juice.

The fact that most people assume Bible wine refers only to a fermented beverage has brought great confusion to the study of God's word today. For example, note how Solomon refers to wine in two very distinct and different ways. Solomon tells us to drink wine abundantly (Song 5:1). But Solomon also says don't even look at it (Proverbs 23:31). It bites like a serpent. (Proverbs 23).

Bites like a serpent.

B. THE SOLUTION—RESEARCH THE FACTS

Wine In the Past Had Two Meanings

The solution will begin here.

The confusion regarding the usage of the word *wine* in the Bible is based on its originally having two distinct definitions: alcoholic fermented wine, or non-alcoholic grape juice. The word juice does not appear in the New Testament, and only once in the Old Testament. So

3. Wechsberg 1963.

all grape juice was called *wine*. With any growing, developing language, definitions change and become narrowed or expanded. The nonalcoholic definition of wine has faded into the background in this century, thus leaving the alcoholic definition of wine as the present one. Some theological scholars, contrary to all historical and linguistic facts, still claim there is only one meaning for the word wine in the *Bible*. To them, since Noah drank wine and got drunk, all Bible wine is intoxicating. Therefore, "The guests have had too much to drink; but you have saved the best till now" (NIV John 2:10). Jesus made 120 gallons more of booze so they could really get stoned. Therefore, by the example of our Lord it is all right to drink intoxicating liquor. Therefore, it is right for churches to serve alcohol at communion, contrary to Proverbs 23:31 (don't even look at it. It is a mocker) (Proverbs 20:1).

Approval of a chemical drug by part of the church, which is supposed to be the mentor of morals, has helped pave the way for our drug problems. Lay it at the feet of sincere but misguided *wet* scholars. "I believe the scriptures are totally reliable, infallible and inerrant. I have long ago discovered that translators and lexicographers are not" (Dr. Wilbur Dayton Wesleyan Biblical Seminary, 1/19/1990).

"Scripture and historical facts prove there were two kinds of wine. One was intoxicating, the other was not" (Dave Wilkerson in *Sipping Saints,* 1978, p.30).

1. WORDS AND THEIR DEFINITIONS CHANGE WITH TIME

The Authorized Version was authorized to be read in churches, and remains the most popular version today. Exhaustive concordances and other scholarly works are based on the KJV, making it easier to use in this research. Modern versions have updated some words, as replacing *charity* with *love.* Charity now means benevolent help. However, most versions have not updated the word wine to differentiate clearly between alcoholic or nonalcoholic beverages.

Before the meaning of the word wine changed to mean only an alcoholic beverage, it clearly meant either alcoholic or nonalcoholic wines. Other words have double meanings. Our word *cider* today means either fermented or unfermented apple juice. Punch to many Christians means fruit juice and possibly carbonation, but the dictionary also says "fruit juice with alcohol." Living languages do change. They pulse with life, but can result in confusion of terminology. The good word *gay* has just recently gone bad. In the King James Version of James 2:3 *lampros* is translated *gay* clothing. New translations render fine clothing. Today gay clothing indicates clothing of homosexuals (Webster 1988). Modern translators change charity to love, when the context indicates love. Why can they not change wine to fruit juice where the context indicates fruit juice?

Historical Use of Unfermented Wine

Following are some references from ancient classical literature in which wine is indicated as nonalcoholic or unfermented.

The Greeks B.C.

800 B.C., Homer, the poet of the Odyssey said, "Sweet black wine is a divine drink, . . . imperishable."[4] Eight hundred years before Christ, sweet grape juice was called wine.

4. Odyssey book *ix* p.44.

600 B.C., Ancreon, the poet who sang of love and wine, alluded to "the wine imprisoned in the fruit of the stem."[5]

525 B.C., Aeschylus, the writer of tragedies, describes Zeus as creating wine, *oinos,* within the green grape.[6]

400 B.C., Hippocrates, the physician, called the Father of Medicine, said, "Sweet kinds of wine do not make the head heavy."[7]

Hippocrates was the first to reject the superstition that disease was caused by the pagan gods. He made medicine a scientific study with emphasis on diet, fresh air, medicinal waters and abstinence from alcohol. He was known for his morals as well as for his medicine. He favored prohibition of alcoholic beverages and promoted sweet wine, with which there is "no hangover."

385 B.C., Aristotle and Plato were sober philosophers. Aristotle said of the sweet wine (*gluekos*) of his day, that it did not intoxicate (Ode, 48). He favored prohibition of alcoholic beverages, as did Plato, especially total abstinence for a soldier in a military campaign; for rulers in office; for judges deciding cases; for anyone needing to make an important decision; and for couples desiring pregnancy.[8] He was concerned for the terrible deformed and retarded babies because of drinking parents (see Chapter 8, Judges 13:4, 7, 14.)

Aristotle
Ewing Gallery

200 B.C., Cato, the Elder, known for his strict virtue, gave instructions for making various kinds of wines, including sweet wine.[9]

5. Plato Laws 2.674 a-b, Teachout 1980.
6. Nott, *Lectures on Temperance*, 1863.
7. Nott 1863.
8. Field 1892.
9. Patton 1871.

200 B.C., Nicander of Colophone, physician and poet stated. "And Aeneus, having squeezed the juice into hollow cups, called it wine" (*Oinos*) (Field 299).

See the birdie?

Found in Creton tomb.
Origin before Classical Greek history.

The Romans B.C.

205 B.C., Polybius, the renowned Greek historian stated, "Among the Romans, the women were allowed to drink a wine which is called "*passum,* made from raisins which drink very much resembled Aegusthenian and Cretan *glucos,* sweet wine, and which men used for the purpose of allaying excessive thirst."[10]

200 B.C., Plautus, the Roman playwright wrote, "Even mustum signified both wine and sweet wine."[11]

70 B.C., Virgil the poet, was to Rome what Homer was to the Greeks. He commented on the boiled wine allowed to women, and that the use of this inspissated (condensed) juice became general.[12] (Boiling evaporates the alcohol away).

65 B.C., Quintus Horace, Roman poet wrote: '*Hic innocentis Pocula Lesbil, Duces sub umbra.*"[13] 'Here shall you drink under the shade, cups of unintoxicating wine.'

The Greeks A.D.

200 A.D., Athenaeus, the Greek grammarian and mathematician said, "The

10. Patton 1871.
11. Patton 1871.
12. Patton 1871. Boiling evaporates the alcohol away.
13. Patton.

sweet wine (*gleukos*) which among the Sicilians is called *Pollian*, may be the same as the Biblinos *oinos* . . . good for the stomach."[14]

412 A.D., Proclus, the deeply religious Neo-Platonic philosopher, in annotating *The Works and Days of Hesiod,* in his comments on line 611, explains the process of treading out grapes and treading out the wine.[15]

Freshly trodden must is, of course, nonalcoholic but is here called wine (Nott 1870).

The Romans A.D.

23 A.D., Pliny the Elder stated, "The most useful wine has all its force or strength broken by the filter. These were the best wines." Delfin adds that these wines were filtered as clear juice without the enzyme contained in the pulp, without which there can be no fermentation.[16]

45 A.D., Columella, Lucius Juneius, a contemporary of the Apostles, gave a recipe for grape wine that was "sweet, firm or durable and healthy to the body."[17]

His recipe for grape juice called wine: "Gather the grapes and expose them to the sun for three days. On the 4th day at midday, tread them. Take the mustum that is the flowing juice, before you use the press and when it has settled, add one ounce of powdered iris, strain the wine and pour it into a vessel."[18]

75 A.D., Papius of the Apostle era, said, "Each grape when pressed shall yield five and twenty measure of wine (*oinos*)."[19] The freshly pressed juice, unfermented, was called wine.

So, from the classical Ancients themselves, from 800 B.C. to 75 A.D., we see categorically these were unfermented wines, called wines, were sweet, durable, delicious and would not spoil. They would not intoxicate for they had no alcohol.

14. Lees p.374.
15. Prochus, Field.
16. Rackham 1871.
17. Lees & Burns 1868.
18. Ibid.
19. Rackman 1960, Patton 1871.

2. WORDS HAVE MULTIPLE MEANINGS

It is amazing how some will say that the word wine has only one meaning. James A. Wesley suggests a study of the word spirit.[20] Let us try the Greek word (*pneuma*) and see if it has only one meaning:

God is spirit (*pneuma*) but those who worship Him must worship in spirit (*pneuma*) and truth John 4:24.

Is God (*pneuma*)? Is man's worship (*pneuma*)?

Let's try another meaning for this one word

The wind (*pneuma*) blows where it wishes, . . . so is everyone who is born of the spirit (*pneuma*) John 3:8. Is the wind (*pneuma*)?

Or is man's born again (*pneuma*)?

Let's try another meaning of (*pneuma*).

[Paul] said to the spirit (*pneuma*), "I command you in the name of Jesus Christ to come out of her." Is the demon (*pneuma*)?

Yes (*pneuma*) is all of these, it has many meanings. And so do *oinos* and *yayin* have more than one meaning. The one meaning theory of *yayin* and *oinos* does not stand up. *Oinos* and *yayin* can *mean either nonalcoholic or alcoholic.

Our English language, like many others, seems lacking in the number of words needed to express shades of meaning. This problem exists with Greek and Hebrew as well. However, both Greek and Hebrew are richer in some words with more specific meanings than in English.

20. Wesley 1983.

The Greek language has three words for the one English word *love* each with a specific meaning.

1. *Philia*—affection expressed as friendly brotherly love.
2. *Agape*—God's giving love, as in I Corinthians 13.
3. *Eros*—sexual attraction; basis for erotic love. *Eros* is not in the New Testament

Close to twenty different words in Hebrew and Greek are translated into just one English word: *wine*. Whether alcoholic or not, we use the one word *wine* in English. The result is confusion, not only to laity but to ministers and Bible scholars as well.

Some of our English words have contradictory meanings. The word fast has nine different meanings. It can be defined as swift, but there is also an opposite meaning, to be anchored solidly. It can mean to go without food or, contrariwise, to eat quickly, as in restaurants noted for quick service or fast food. It can also refer to women of loose character. The Bible tells us to love our neighbor, but if I would tell my wife I was over loving our beautiful widow neighbor . . .

Early Dictionaries

The definition of wine as alcoholic or nonalcoholic remained in our dictionaries until recent years. It is not surprising the KJV, 380 years ago, simply spoke of *wine* when the context in some instances indicated unfermented and in others, fermented wine.

My father's 1913 *Funk and Wagnall's Dictionary* is time worn. Its front cover and first pages are missing. But it is still a functional book. Page 2718 defines wine as:

1. **Wine . . . in loose usage, the juice of the grape, whether fermented or not.**
2. By extension, the expressed fresh or fermented juice of some fruit other than the grape.

The Century Dictionary, 1899, in my library has this to say: "Wine 2 The juice, fermented or unfermented, of certain fruits or plants . . ."[21]

On the changes of word meanings through time, John Stewart Mills writes in his *System of Logic*:

> "A generic term is always liable to become limited to a single species, if people have occasion to think and speak of that species oftener than anything else contained in the genus. The tide of custom first drifts the word to the shore of a particular meaning, then retires and leaves it there."[22]

James A. Wesley, in his book, *Was Jesus The Lil' Ole' Winemaker*[23] refers to John 1:1—"In the beginning was the Word, and the Word was with God and the Word was God."

According to the one meaning theory, the word wine in the Bible has only one meaning, fermented. We would have problems, with the 'one wine theory,' referring to the word. Does the word mean Christ only, or does word have two meanings? If it is admitted that it does, why cannot the word wine have two meanings, alcoholic or nonalcoholic? The 'one meaning of a word theory' falls and splatters all over.

Let me cite an illustration of this type of multiplicity of meanings and the contextual use.

Once after presenting our Bible Birds program, we were invited to the pastor's home for dinner. The pastor's wife asked if I would like cider. I answered "Yes, please," She did not need to

21. Century Dictionary, 1899.
22. Patton 1871.
23. James A. Wesley, *Was Jesus the Lil' Ole Winemaker?* pp 17-19.

specify, soft or hard cider. Knowing each other, we both knew what kind of cider was meant. It had to be fresh cider only.

And I, knowing Christ, believe firmly that He made New Wine, a nonalcoholic wine, for the wedding feast in Cana. I believe His wine was sweet and nutritious, really sweet grape juice, as opposed to poisonous, intoxicating, alcoholic wine. He changes water into grape juice every year.

3. WORD DEFINED BY CONTEXT

Almost anything can be proved from the Bible by taking words out of context. Stealing is accepted in the *Bible*, if Proverbs 9:17 is used out of context. It says, "Stolen waters are sweet, and bread eaten in secret is pleasant." But including verse 13 gives a different view of the word. "A foolish woman is clamorous: she is simple, and knoweth nothing." Taken in context, Proverbs 9:12-18 does not indicate that stealing is acceptable. Rather, the idea comes from a foolish woman.

Also, Job's wife said to him, "Dost thou still retain thine integrity? curse God and die" Job2:9.* The context shows these are the words of Job's wife, not God's words, though they come from the Bible. The Hebrew *barach,* as here, means to curse. It also has two meanings, the other is the opposite, to *bless*.

Even in Isaiah 65:8 "New wine is found in the cluster" is still retained in some modern versions. The word wine in a bunch of grapes is completely out of context, to make wine takes care and above all a period of time. It should be grapes juice in the cluster.

The word moderation, appears only once in the Bible. When used for permission to drink alcoholic beverage, it is taken completely out of context. Phil. 4:5

Mustum designates a pure and unfermented beverage made from the grape. It is used by all the Roman rustic writers, Cato, Columella, Vorro, and Pliny.[24]

* *Curse* is the way *barach* is always translated in this verse. However Dr. Charles Butler reminds us that *barach* also in other places has a diametrically opposed meaning. Usually in other places it is translated as *bless*. Many words have two meanings, as did wine,—meaning to be determined by context.

C. OUR REMEDY—GET THE FACTS KNOWN

Wine Even Now Means Nonalcoholic

There still is a residual meaning for wine to mean nonalcoholic. In spite of the change in some modern dictionaries and common usage, there are those who use the word *wine* as nonalcoholic grape juice.

From *The Ritual* of the United Methodist Church: "At the time of Holy Communion, the Lord's Table shall have upon it a fair white linen cloth. The elements of bread and wine shall be placed thereon. The pure unfermented juice of the grape shall be used" (Board of Publication, 1964, 1966).

We also find this dual meaning in the *Discipline of the Wesleyan Church*. Under "Distribution of Bread and Wine," directions are given for distribution of the elements (Discipline 1988, p. 404). But under the heading of "The Lord's Supper": "Only unfermented grape juice shall be used in observing the Lord's Supper" (Discipline 1683).

The Church of the Nazarene calls wine unfermented juice: "Only unfermented wine and unleavened bread should be used in the sacrament of the Lord's Supper 403.7, 402.2, 405, 423.10, 802."

24. Field 1892.

These samples show the word *wine* is presently used with its former meaning—unfermented grape juice.

But all of this seems strange, for in no place in the New Testament is the word *wine* used in relation to the Last Supper. Jesus said, "Fruit of the vine." Paul said, "The cup."

Baptist Seminary Professor, Robert P. Teachout, has a Masters and Doctorate from Dallas Theological Seminary. His doctoral thesis, "*The Use of Wine in the Old Testament*", substantiated the two meanings for the word wine. He had this to say in his later book, "sufficient evidence has already been presented from extra-biblical sources to confirm that the Hebrew word *yayin*, the Greek word *oinos*, Latin *vimum* and English word wine can refer to any grape beverage, whether as fresh juice or as fermented wine." *WINE, The Biblical Imperative: Total Abstinence*, Teachout, 1983, 1986, p.30, Taylor MI 48180.

Department Head Jerry D. Hull, of Northwest Nazarene College says, "Many biblical references to "wine" refer to nonintoxicating juices. . . The most often used word for wine in the Bible is *yayin*. It is a generic term referring to both intoxicating and non-intoxicating wine." *No! The Positive Response to Alcohol* 1989, p.41.

Educator Ross J. McLennan, "The only reasonable explanation of this inconsistency is that the word yayin is a general term used for all kinds of beverages produced from the vine, whether fermented or unfermented." Post graduate Garrett Theological Seminary, Vice President Taylor University, (Where I also taught). He authored *Propaganda Vs. Facts* 1978, p.66.

The English translator of the whole Bible, Ferrar Fenton M.R.A.S., M.C.A.A., writes "(*Yayin*) was not confined to a fermented intoxicating wine but more frequently referred to a thick syrup or jam produced by boiling the grape juice" (Boiling destroys the alcohol) Charles Wesley Ewing, *The Bible and its Wines* 1967, p.5.

TV evangelist Dr. Jack Van Impe, along with Roger F. Campbell, in *Alcohol: The Beloved Enemy,* writes "The Bible speaks of two kinds of wine: good wine and bad wine, unfermented wine and fermented wine, wine that does not intoxicate and wine that does intoxicate" (1980, p.111).

Italian Professor and author, Dr. Samuele Bacchiocchi, given a scholarship gold medal by Pope Paul VI, writes "Wine in English, *vinum* in Latin, *oinos* in Greek, and *yayin* in Hebrew . . . these linguistically related words have been used historically to refer to the juice of the grape, whether fermented or unfermented" (Bacchiocchi, *Wine in the Bible*, 1989, p.73).

It must be understood that the NIV is just that, a *New 'International' Version.* On the committee were translators from European countries, where wine drinking is much more prevalent than in the American states. (A past study showed that in France deaths from heart trouble and cirrhosis of the liver are "five times higher than they are in America").[25]

Stephen M. Reynolds, Ph.D. from Princeton University, a member of the NIV committee, was so disappointed with the outcome of the NIV translation that he wrote the book, *Alcohol and The Bible*. He states specifically, "Moderation is not the answer" (p.10). Reynolds says further: "It will be demonstrated in a separate place that *yayin* is in Biblical Hebrew the appropriate word for the unfermented juice of the grape . . . The dual use of the same word is similar to that of the double use of the English word *cider*, (either non-alcoholic or alcoholic)."[26]

25. Bauer, 1965.
26. p.13. (Founder, *Lorine M. Reynold Foundation for Bible Translation*)

Dr. Reynolds continues, "I do not make adverse criticism of the committee on which I worked, but my experience on this project, herein called the NIV, is that at least some human error entered into the final results."[27]

"All readers of the Bible in translation must be made aware that not all readings in their favorite Bible translation are necessarily certain. A ruling elder in a Presbyterian Church said that alcoholic drinks are permitted by the Bible because the New International Version in Deuteronomy 14:26 translates *shekar* as the fermented drink."* (p.15, Reynolds 1983).

Dr. Ralph Earle of Nazarene Theological Seminary was part time chairman of the NIV committee, as his teaching work allowed. He was the first scholar to show me that *oinos* had two meanings, alcoholic and nonalcoholic. When I pointed out to him some of the wine inconsistencies in the NIV he answered me in a letter:

"I plan to take up the matter with the committee on Bible Translation for the NIV. I think the CBT [Committee on Bible Translation] plans to incorporate some revisions . . . perhaps A.D. 2000" (Earle 1990).

27. p.16.

*Reynolds, *Alcohol and the Bible* is available from the Challenge Press, Little Rock, AR 72205.

Allen B. Kraft, educator and author, wrote in the book, *The Wedding Feast*:

"The Greek word '*oinos*', translated '*wine*' in our story, means the juice of the wine press. It is similar to our word '*cider*,' which means the juice of the cider press. In both cases, the juice left setting for a period of time will ferment; then, if enough is consumed, it will make one drunk. Let us also remember when it is consumed fresh from the press it is healthful, beneficial, and good; but if consumed when fermented it could bring sorrow, heartaches, and even death" (Kraft, 1965, p.14).

"It may at once be conceded that the Hebrew term "wine" refers occasionally to an unfermented liquor" (The International Standard Encyclopedia, p.1010). From page 1016 "There is no positive proof that the liquid used by our Lord in instituting the sacred communion was alcoholic."

Wesleyan seminary professor and administrator, Dr. Wilbur Dayton firmly believes in the two meanings of the word wine. He says for fifty years he has encouraged students to be checking up on the results of those who interpret otherwise.

A start is being made to purify the Bible from mistakes regarding the translation of wine. Contact the Rev. Dr. Charles J. Butler, 1674 Dyre Street, Philadelphia, PA 19124, for information on the Lorine L. Reynolds Foundation's position on alcohol and other ethical drug problems. Dr. Wendell Hansen is a trustee of this translation foundation. Dr. Stephen M. Reynolds is the Settler.

Boiled, I can't get it to ferment.

Fresh, strained. I can't get it to ferment.

CHAPTER SIX

PREVENTING FERMENTATION
THE ANCIENTS' MAIN EIGHT WAYS

Dear Dr. Hansen:

You have done the indepth research to bring out the facts. You have made the case well, and I am certain you are correct about the changing meaning of the word wine. It is interesting also to read about how the ancients prevented fermentation. You have said what needed to be said.

Bryan Aubrey, Ph.D.
Professor of Literature
Marharishi University

CHAPTER SIX
PREVENTING FERMENTATION

A. ANCIENT ALCOHOLIC WINE OFTEN SPOILED

Properly Processed Sweet Grape Juice Did Not Spoil

Contrary to popular modern belief, it was harder for the ancients to keep fermented wine from spoiling than it was to keep grape juice fresh and sweet.

Pliny (26 A.D.) lays out the problem, "It is a peculiarity of wine among liquids to go moldy or else to turn into vinegar; and whole volumes of instructions on how to remedy this have been published."[1] One of his suggestions was to boil the wine. It would then keep but it would be nonalcoholic wine or just plain boiled grape juice.

Contrast that with:

"If there is plenty of wood, it is better to boil the must and clear off all the scum with the dregs; if this is done, a tenth part will be lost, but the rest keeps good forever."[2] ('Must' = pure, clean, sweet grape juice without the pulp or contaminants. Natural droppings before being trod.)

For fermentation, the juice was left open so the yeast spores from the air could get into the liquid. But in allowing the yeast to get in, many other forms of bacteria also got absorbed. This contamination eventually caused acidity and moldiness. This remained fermentation trouble until the time of Pasteur. This problem prompted the wine merchants to request Pasteur to do his pasteurization experiments.

As early as the second century before Christ, Marcus Cato The Elder speaks of this in his *De Agricultura* as it relates to the difficulty for the "sale of wine in jars."[3] Strangely, one remedy that he suggests was using "must boiled down from untrod grapes,"[4] sometimes using, besides must, marble dust, resin

1. Pliny 14, 26.
2. Columella, 50 A.D. 12:20-8.

Egyptian Wine-press, from Wilkinson

The drain on the upper right is for the must that flows naturally from untrod broken grapes. It will not ferment. To get all the juice, it is trod. It will contain pulp which contains the enzymes that causes fermentation. This juice will have to be heated to kill the enzymes, if it is desired to keep it from fermenting.

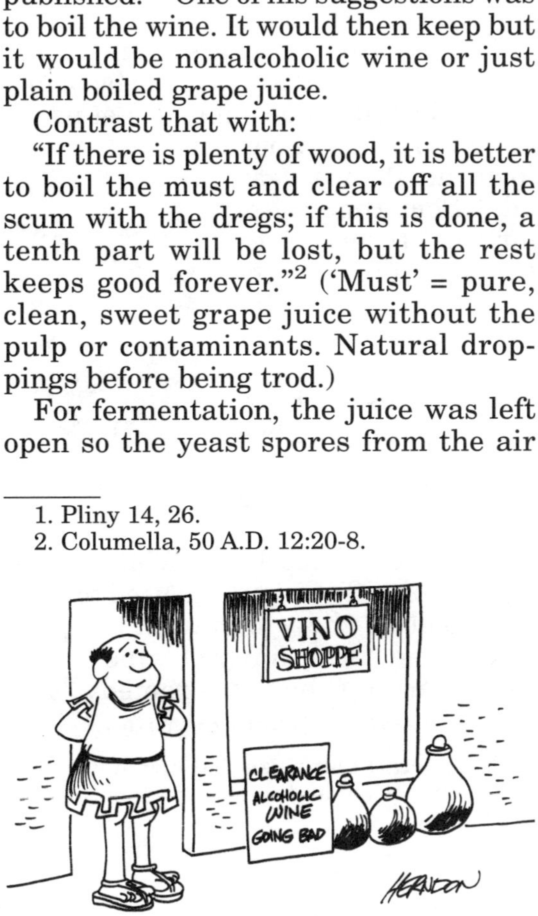

Clearance Alcoholic Wine

3. Cato, 191 B.C.
4. Cato.

and crushed iris. The early run off of pure must from untrod grapes did not contain the enzymes that are in the skin and seed pulp. The enzymes are necessary for fermentation. Pure grape juice without the pulp that contains the enzymes will not ferment.

Bad odor in Alcoholic Wines

To sweeten bad odor, Cato suggests, "Make four pounds of flour from vetch, and mix from *iyathi* of wine with boiled down must: make into small bricks and let them soak for a night and a day; then dissolve with wine in the jar, and seal sixty days later."[5] Note the use of boiled down, nonalcoholic must to try to save alcoholic wine from developing bad odor.

If this did not cure bad odor, Cato gives another remedy: "Heat a thick clear piece of roofing tile thoroughly in the fire. When it is hot, coat it with pitch, attach a string, lower it gently to

"Heat a thick clear piece of roofing tile—
let's see now—
how do you say that in Latin?"

the bottom of the jar. Leave the jar sealed for two days. If the bad odor is removed the first time that will be best; if not, repeat until the bad odor is removed."[6]

Cato shares other means for preventing odor in alcoholic wine: "If necessary, add the fortieth pound of must boiled down from untrod grapes . . . If you use marble dust, add one pound to *celleus;* mix with must in a vessel, and then pour into the jar. If you use resin, pulverize it thoroughly, three pounds to the *celoms* of must, place it in a basket, and suspend it in a jar of must; shake the basket often so that the resin may dissolve. When you use boiled must or marble dust or resin, stir frequently for twenty days and press down daily."[7]

A couple of centuries later, during Jesus' lifetime, Columella, the Roman agriculturist, gave directions on preserving fermented wine. It can be seen from his studies how much more simple and inexpensive it is to stay with the sweet wine, must. (Nor did it give the headaches that fermented wine gave.)

Columella wrote at great length on how to preserve alcoholic wine by using primarily boiled down must: "Let us be careful to preserve our wine with boiled down must of a year old."[8] Sometimes also, various preservatives were added: myrrh, turpentine resin, pitch, balsam and cinnamon. The mixture had to be just right or the preservatives would ruin the flavor and "drive away the purchaser."[9]

Writes Bacchiocchi in *Wine of the Bible*, "The different means used to prevent spoiling the wine reveal the perplexity and uncertainty of wine growers regarding how to remedy the deterioration of fermented wine."[10]

(Customer: "I didn't like that myrrh, turpentine, pitch, balsam and cinnamon wine. I prefer grape juice.")

5. Cato.
6. Cato.
7. Cato.
8. Columella, 12.20.1.
9. Columella, 12.20.6.
10. Bacchiocchi, 1989.

B. AVAILABILITY OF FRESH GRAPE JUICE, FRUIT AND VEGETABLES THE YEAR ROUND

Contrary to popular misconception, grape juice, as well as fruits and vegetables, were available all the year round. Some came from southern climes; some were available because of means of preservation.

The ancients could not only preserve grapes, but all sorts of fruits and vegetables. Josephus lived during the first century A.D., in the later part of the Jewish nation. Historians depend on this Hebrew army general, Greek and Hebrew scholar, and historian.

"Got a nice '92 fresh wine?
I mean 1892, of course."

Fresh Fruit Kept Nearly 100 Years

Josephus wrote: "Here was laid up corn in vast quantities, and such as would subsist for a long time; here was also wine and oil in abundance, with all kinds of pulse and dates heaped up together; . . . These fruits were also fresh and full ripe, and no way inferior to such fruits newly laid in, although they were little short of 100 years from the laying in these provisions . . . they found them not corrupted all that while."[11]

This does seem exaggerated, however; we have no documentation as to when the produce was put in storage. (See "Eggs good after 2,000 years, under moisture excluded," this chapter.)

(Warranted, fruit stays fresh 100 years or your money back.)

Patton had access to a copy of Josephus that gave a footnote by the translator William Whiston: "Pliny and others confirm this strange paradox, that provisions thus laid up against sieges will continue good a hundred years, as Spanheim notes upon this place" (Patton, p.23). This note is also in the T. Nelson edition of 1871, 9.776 (Butler). There are many verifications of this knowledge of keeping fruits fresh.*

Recipes to Preserve Fruit in Christ's Time

Let us lay down a couple of scientific facts that I have personally verified by experiments. Pure grape juice without the pulp will not ferment, even when yeast is added.

Enzymes are necessary for fermentation. Enzymes are contained in the pulp that clings to the insides of the skins, as well as in the pulp that surrounds the seeds. Strain out the juice from the pulp, or make the enzymes inactive by heat or fumigation, and there will be no fermentation. Pure juice was obtained in early days by catching the runoff juice before the grapes were crushed. Or the juice was obtained by being strained through cloth. No enzymes remained in the juice.

Columella in his *De Agricultura* gives us some of the methods used to preserve vegetables and fruit. Boiled down grape juice was boiled to a thick syrup and had the same preserving qualities as the heavy sugar syrup used today in the canning of fruits. (Ham is preserved

11. Josephus, 91 A.D.

* Josephus is discredited by Jewish historians since he wrote of Jesus, "He is the Christ . . ." (p.548).

ANTIQUITIES OF THE JEWS.

872 [Book VII.

vance) easily get to the end of it; and after such a manner was the citadel fortified, both by nature and by the hands of men, in order to frustrate the attacks of enemies.

As for the furniture that was within this fortress, it was still more wonderful on account of its splendour and long continuance; for here was laid up corn in large quantities, and such as would subsist men for a long time; here was also wine and oil in abundance, with all kinds of pulse and dates heaped up together; all which Eleazer found there when he and his Sicarii got possession of the fortress by treachery. These fruits were also fresh and full ripe, and noway inferior to such fruits newly laid in, although they were little short of 100 years from the laying in these provisions [by Herod], till the place was taken by the Romans; nay, indeed, when the Romans got possession of those fruits that were left, they found them not corrupted all that while: nor should we be mistaken, if we supposed that the air was here the cause of their enduring so long, this fortress being so high, and so free from the mixture of all terrene and muddy particles of matter. There was also found here a large quantity of all sorts of weapons of war, which had been treasured up by that king, and were sufficient for 10,000 men: there was cast iron, and brass and tin, which show that he had taken much pains to have all things here ready for the greatest occasions; for the report goes how Herod thus prepared this

THE WORKS

FLAVIUS JOSEPHUS

CONTAINING THE

ANTIQUITIES OF THE JEWS

A HISTORY OF THE JEWISH WARS;

AND

LIFE OF FLAVIUS JOSEPHUS, WRITTEN BY HIMSELF.

TRANSLATED FROM THE ORIGINAL GREEK,

BY WILLIAM WHISTON, A. M.,

PROFESSOR OF MATHEMATICS IN THE UNIVERSITY OF CAMBRIDGE.

TOGETHER WITH NUMEROUS EXPLANATORY NOTES,

AND

Three Dissertations,

CONCERNING

JESUS CHRIST, JOHN THE BAPTIST, JAMES THE JUST GOD'S COMMAND TO ABRAHAM, ETC.

WARS OF THE JEWS.

548 (Book XVIII.)

Now, there was about this time Jesus, a wise man, if it be lawful to call him a man, for he was a doer of wonderful works,—a teacher of such men as receive the truth with pleasure. He drew over to him both many of the Jews and many of the Gentiles. He was [the] Christ; and when Pilate, at the suggestion of the principal men among us, had condemned him to the cross,* those that loved him at the first did not forsake him, for he appeared to them alive again the third day,† as the divine prophets had foretold these and ten thousand other wonderful things concerning him; and the tribe of Christians, so named from him, are not extinct at this day.

by sugar.) Our word for cane sugar had its origin in the early sugary use of grape syrup and syrup from trees (see chapter 7).

Columella gives this recipe for keeping fruit "Wild plums and onyx-colored plums should be picked while they are still hard and not very ripe; they must not, however, be too unripe. They should then be dried for a day in the shade; then vinegar and must, boiled down to half or one third of its original volume, should be mixed and poured in (the vessel containing the berries or plums). It will be necessary to add some salt, so that no worms or other forms of animal life can be engendered in them."[12]

Ice Cellars 1000 Years B.C.

As revealed by the poet Shim Ching, there were ice cellars in China 1000 years before Christ. The Greeks and Romans stored compressed snow in cellars insulated with grass, manure and earth. Strangely, the Egyptians and Indians produced ice by "placing water in porous clay vessels which were left overnight in holes in the ground; freezing resulted because of radiation of heat and vaporation of some of the water."[13]

Preserving Fruit in Sawdust

It was many years after my birth that the modern refrigerator came into general use. But no matter how hot the summer, the ice man delivered ice to our ice box. The ice was taken from the lake and stored in an old wood shack insulated with sawdust. A contemporary of Christ, Columella tells how fruit was kept fresh in a barrel between layers of sawdust then sealed with clay.[14] Similar to sawdust, dry chaff was also used.

(Waitress: 'Grape syrup, or palm syrup?")

12. Columella, 12.10.3.
13. Oakley, Americana, 1969.
14. Columella 12.46.6.

Many Ancient Preserving Methods

Columella tells of giving fruit a thick covering of clay, and hanging it in a cool place. When it was desired to use this fruit, "Dissolve the clay in water. The fruit will be as fresh as when first picked."[15]

Columella gives several more complex recipes for keeping grapes at least a year:

It helped to acquire the grapes on long branches and then seal the cut by dipping in boiling pitch. When using chaff for covering and insulation, there was a sifting to get rid of dust. Another hygienic precaution was to use a new container. This was also necessary for no possible contact with fermentation.

"Place the fruit in layers between either barley bran or boiled down must. The lids should be sealed and stored in a dry cool place."[16]

Another covering was dry flour of gypsum. "Make sure the grapes are slightly on the green side, not too ripe, and be careful to cut away defective grapes."

Preserving Fruit Through Winter Just By Hanging

If all of this is too much work, simply hang the grapes in a granary over a bin of wheat. But in this case they will lose moisture and tend to become more like raisins (Columella, 12.44.4).

Pliny also suggests the method of hanging "for lasting all through the winter". He also adds another method: "Others will keep merely in their own natural vigor by being stood in earthenware jars with casks put over them."[17]

"As to the subsequent treatment of the wine, we have little information. Sometimes it was "preserved" in its unfermented state, and drunk as must

15. Columella 12.46.5.
16. Columella 12.44.3.
17. Pliny, 14.3.16.

. . . ."[18] Note: unfermented juice is called wine.

Preserving Fruit With Honey

Writes Bacchiocchi, "The submersion of fruit in liquid honey was viewed as one of the safest methods of preservation because as Columella remarks, 'such is the nature of honey that it checks any corruption and does not allow it to spread' ".[19]

Palestine was part of this land of milk and honey, and blessed with the soil and weather that produced the best grapes: "And cut down from thence a branch with one cluster of grapes and they bare it between two upon a staff" (Numbers 13:24).

They knew how to keep grapes fresh the year round, and preferred to drink the fresh grape juice.

Freshly Squeezed Grape Juice Preferred

The ancients' preference for a nonalcoholic drink may be inferred from their words and actions. The Pharaohs had juice squeezed directly from the fruit into the cup. Dr. Ebers discovered a picture on the walls of the temple of Edfu of a king standing with a cup in his hand. The inscription read: "They press grapes into the hand and the king drinks."[20] An ancient picture exhumed at Pompeii shows Bacchus squeezing grape clusters into a wine cup.[21] Note also the phrase, "pressed into Pharaoh's Cup" (Genesis 40:11).

We have shown in the words of the ancient scholars that fruit was actually kept fresh the year round. Fruit of the vine at Jesus' Last Supper could have been juice squeezed directly from grapes.

C. KEEPING GRAPE JUICE SWEET: THE ANCIENTS' MAIN EIGHT WAYS

1. AIR EXCLUDED

The results of Pasteur and Hallier's research have established that the spore or fungi of yeast are introduced by ordinary air into fermentable fluid.[22]

"Perfectly pure grape juice does not ferment, unless the process has been started by at least temporary contact with ordinary air. This cardinal fact was discovered by Gay-Lussac. He caused clean grapes to ascend through the mercury into the Torricellian vacuum, where he crushed them by means of a mercurial column. The juice remained unchanged; but the addition to it of ever so small an air bell induced fermentation, which when once started was always found to take care of itself."[23]

Schwann heated putrefied flesh and other putrefied objects, and sealed them hermetically. There was no sign of life. But when exposed to the air they soon swarmed with living organisms.[24] The Ancients knew this, even if they did not understand the theory.

Greeks and Romans used an earthen amphora.[25]

This container was sealed air tight with pitch, then filled with fresh juice, sealed, and placed either under water or buried in the earth. These directions are found in works by five authors:

18. Pliny.
19. Bacchiocchi, 1989.
20. Ebers, 1872, p.480.
21. Biblicothea Review, 1881.

22. Appleton 1963.
23. *Britannica* 1894.
24. *Britannica* 1894.
25. Amphora.

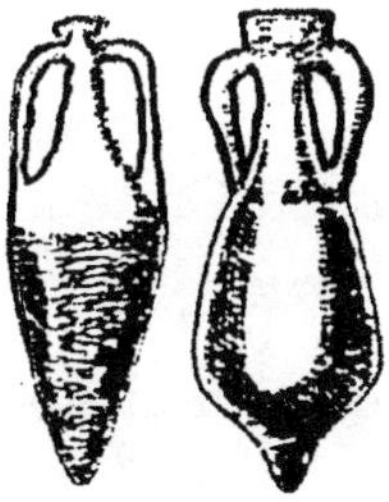

Amphoras
Pointed for placing in cool earth.

Cato,[26] Pliny,[27] Plutarch,[28] Geopnica,[29] and Columella.[30]

"That your must may always be as sweet as when it is new, thus proceed: Before you apply the press to the fruit, take the newest must from the lake (pool of juice), put it into a new amphora, bung it up and cover it very carefully with pitch, lest any water should enter; then immerse it in a cistern or pond of pure cold water, and allow no part of the amphora to remain above the surface."[31] A new amphora was stipulated, without any residue of fermentation.

As says Professor Donovan, "Grape juice will not ferment when the air is completely excluded."[32]

Baron Tieberg records, "If a flask be filled with grape juice and made air tight, then kept for a few hours in boiling water, the wine does not now ferment"[33]. "The Romans, real corkers, invented the screw press and the cork stopper, which kept the air out longer than did the old clay plugs."[34]

2. BOILING

Boiling grape juice is a simple method of preventing fermentation. Grape juice will not boil until 212°F (100°C), but alcohol boils at 172°F (78°C); so boiling can easily expel any alcohol in grape juice. Enzymes are the organic catalyst. Without the enzymes, there is no fermentation. Enzymes are destroyed at 110°F (43°C).

The 8th century B.C. Lacedaemonians, who were the forerunners of the Spartans, boiled their wines "upon the fire till the fifth part was consumed; then after four years were expired, began to drink them."[35] It appears that the boiling of grape juice to prevent fermentation was by that early time already an ancient custom.

Homer, also from the 8th century B.C., related that Ulysses took with him a goat skin of black wine, given him by Marion, the priest of Apollo. He said, "It was sweet as honey, imperishable, and would keep forever." Prepared as a beverage, it was diluted with twenty parts of water, and "from it a sweet and divine odor exhaled."[36]

Strictly a boiled grape juice called wine! The alcohol in alcoholic wine boils away.

Another ancient authority on wines was Aristotle, born in 384 B.C. He was so concerned about the effect of fermented wines on people that he advocated prohibition. He said the boiled wine of Acadia would not intoxicate. It

26. Field 1882.
27. Ibid 14:9.
28. 2 N-26 Ibid.
29. 6:16.
30. Anti Bacchus.
31. Columella liber XII.
32. Lardners 1849.
33. Bible Commentary 1871.
34. Amerine 1963.

35. Potter, 1674.
36. Nott, 1868.

"Why don't you relax and read the paper, dear? I just started boiling the wine."

was so thick it was necessary to scrape it from the "skin" bottles in which it was contained, and to dissolve the scrapings in water.[37]

An alternate method of making wine unfermentable called for water to be added to the juice and then boiled back to its usual consistency. The opposite option was to boil the juice to a thick syrup, then dilute to its usual consistency.[38]

Virgil, born 70 B.C., pictured the housewife boiling the moisture of the sweet wine away by fire, an early Georgian method of condensing a product.[39]

Later, Pliny, born in 23 A.D., records that grape juice was still drinkable when boiled down to one third of its volume.

Also recorded by Pliny is the fact that some Roman wines were as thick as honey.[40] Though called wines, they could not be alcoholic; alcohol boils away. The noun *syrup* is derived from an Oriental term for wine. This type of wine is called "honey" in the east. "It is by the prophet (referencing Isaiah 7:22) approximately connected with milk, as a thing to be eaten."[41] It appears that the boiling of grape juice was not only for the purpose of keeping grape juice sweet for drinking, but also for eating when boiled down thick.

(Today's special: Wine chips)

In order to make grape juice keep, the must was boiled down to one half, after which it was called 'defrutum'.[42]

The Mishna states that the Jews were in the habit of using boiled wine.[43] With the alcohol boiled out, it was no longer wine, in todays meaning of wine.

37. Nott, 1868.
38. Harris, 1944.
39. Georgi.
40. Patton, 1871.
41. Fellows 1909.
42. Adams 1791.
43. Kittos 1845.

Water Mixed With Grape Syrup—Mingled Wine

Leiber, the chemist, visited Crete in 1817. He wrote that great quantities of wine, which had been made by boiling in large coppers, were produced at Retino and Candida. He himself had observed this.[44] Boiling removed the alcohol, but it was called mingled wine when diluted with water.

According to Homer, Pramnian, Meronian, and Hippocrates, wines required twenty parts of water to one of wine.[45] This fact is also stated in the *Dictionary of Classical Literature and Antiquities from the German*, "Wines of ancient Greece were mixed with twenty parts water."[46] If this were alcoholic wine so diluted, there would be little left of the flavor or anything else. It is only reasonable to understand that these drinks were usually grape juices boiled down to a syrup, called dibbe or grape molasses.

"The ancients mixed their **wine** with water; **not because they were strong with alcohol** as to require dilution, but because being rich syrups, they needed water "prepare them for drinking,"[47] (emphases are mine).

(Customer: "A slice of wine and 20 cups of water, please").

Nonintoxicating Esteemed The Best

Captain Treat, in 1845, wrote, "When on the south coast of Italy, last Christmas, I inquired particularly about the wines in common use, and found that those esteemed to be the best were sweet and un-intoxicating. The boiled

44. Patton 1871.
45. Lees.
46. Glaisher 1882.
47. Patton 1871.

juice of the grape is in common use in Sicily."[48]

Robert Alsop, a minister of the Society of Friends, wrote to Dr. Frederick R. Lees in 1861, "The syrup of grape juice is an article of domestic manufacture in most every house in the vine districts of the south of France. It is simply the juice of the grape boiled down to the consistency of treacle."[49] Treacle is British for sugar molasses.

Athenaus, second century, wrote, "Let him take sweet wine *glukus,* either mixed with water or warmed . . . as being very good for the stomach."[50]

In Syria, the general custom of the country was to reduce the must (freshly extracted grape juice) to two-thirds of its quantity.[51]

"It is observable that when sweet juices are boiled down to a thick consistency, they not only do not ferment in that state, but can not be brought into fermentation when diluted with as much water as they had lost in the evaporation, or even with the very individual water that was exhaled from them."[52] This is because all enzymes are destroyed by heat.

Boiling became one of the most widely used methods of preparing grape juice as a beverage and sometimes as food. Grapes grew in abundance in that climate. Boiling proved to be a method of preservation, which one could later dilute and use as a drink. It is believed this dilution is meant in Proverbs 9:2, "She mingled her wine," grape and/or other syrups, mingled with water. Presently boiled nonalcoholic dinner wines are still used in Europe. In France they are known as *VIN Cuit.* I didn't know that years ago. I paid for drinking water there, with my meals, when I could have received the nonalcoholic wine free. These boiled wines are called *nardink* in Syria, *dibs* in Arabia, and *Vino Cotto* in Italy. So says Dr. Samuele Bacchiocchi, the native Italian scholar who received a gold academic medal from Pope Paul VI (1989:17)[53].*

Dr. Samuele Bacchiocchi
Andrews University
Professor

3. COOLING

Another means of preventing fermentation is by prolonged cooling. Horace stated of grape pulp, or gluten, "The gluten will settle to the bottom by its own weight, if the mass can be kept under 40° (4°C) from fermenting."[54]

Gluten contains the enzymes that allow fermentation. If these enzymes are killed by reducing the temperature below 40°F, fermentation will be stopped. If the juice is deprived of the gluten or pulp, it will not ferment.

Columella, a contemporary of Christ, said, "Gather the grapes and expose them for three days to the sun; on the fourth, at midday, tread them, take the must, that is, the juice which flows before you use the press, and when it has settled, add one ounce of powdered iris; strain the wine from the settlings, and pour it into a vessel. This wine will keep sweet, firm or durable, and healthy to

48. Lees 1868.
49. Lees 1861.
50. Nott.
51. Volney 1788.
52. Nott 1863.

53. * (see Endnote 53 for details of his *Wine in the Bible* book, 1989 $12.95 post paid.)
54. Horace, 65 B.C.

the body."[55] (Sweet juice is here called wine.)

Patton deciphers three means of preventing fermentation involved in the cooling-subsiding method.[56]

1. Must flows spontaneously before being pressed.
2. Gluten allowed to subside.
3. Powdered iris put in.

Again from Columella, "That your must may always be as sweet as when it is new, thus proceed: Before you apply the press to the fruit, take the newest must from the lake, put it into a new amphora, bung it up, and cover it carefully with pitch, lest any water should enter; then immerse it in a cistern or pond of pure cold water, and allow no part of the amphora to remain above the surface. After 40 days take it out, and it will remain sweet for a year."[57]

Kittos stated, "The must or new wine was refined with the egg yolks of pigeon eggs, which occasioned the subsidence of the albumen or ferment. But on the new wine being allowed to stand, this principle would subside by natural gravity; hence, the Ancients poured off the upper and luscious portion of the grape juice into another vessel. Repeating the process as often as necessary, until they procured a clear, sweet wine that would *keep*.[58] *Notice that the ancients called the non*alcoholic processed juice wine.

4. DRYING AS RAISINS

Preventing Fermentation by Drying Grapes as Raisins

Besides drinking grape juice fresh and keeping it from fermenting, the ancients had another way of using the fruit of the vine and preserving it in a nonalcoholic form. That method was by drying the grapes as raisins and later soaking them to make a sweet grape drink.

"No, no, I didn't say you're well preserved. I was talking about the wine."

According to Polybius, 205 B.C., the Roman women were allowed to drink *passum,* a nonalcoholic drink, made simply by soaking raisins. These, having the bulk of the water dried from the grapes, would not spoil and were available all year round.

This *passim* "very much resembled the Cretin *glucose* or natural sweet juice and which men use for allaying excessive thirst."[59]

The word 'flagons' of the KJV of the Old Testament is *ashiyshah* in the Hebrew and should mean a measure of liquid. It is often incorrectly translated as a cake of raisins. It probably means the juice from raisins, as in the Song of Solomon 2:5, "Stay me with raisin drink."

Baron Tavernier (1652) said the Christians of St. John at Bassorah used juice from soaked raisins for the Eucharist. The Christians of St. Thomas celebrated the Lord's Supper with juice from raisins soaked overnight.[60] In the administration of the Lord's Supper, the Nestorians used raisin water.[61] The Abyssinian Church of Jerusalem stated, "The wine is the juice of dried grapes

55. Nott, 1863.
56. Nott, 1863.
57. Patton 1871.
58. Kitto Cyclopedia 1843.
59. Nott 1863.
60. Lees 1868.
61. Lees 1868.

with water."[62] Noah, a leading Jew of New York, informed Delevan that the use of wine prepared from steeped raisins was general among American Jews. Some raisins are steeped in water for a few days before the Passover. Dr. Cunningham, the learned Hebraist, said, "What is now chiefly used by the Jews at the Passover for wine is a drink made of an infusion of raisins in water which is either boiled at once or simmered in water."[63]

Grapes on the vine do not ferment. They dry up as raisins. I know. I raise grapes.

This bunch of grapes hung in our kitchen for two years. They did not spoil or ferment but became delicious raisins.

(Old grapes never die, they just fade away as raisins.)

5. FILTERING OUT THE PULP

Grape juice contains two major ingredients besides water; sugar and pulp. Sugar is composed of three elements: Carbon, hydrogen and oxygen. Pulp contains four elements: carbon, hydrogen, oxygen, and nitrogen. Nitrogen, in all its compounds, is an unstable element because it disengages itself from one union to another. With this pulp instability, the decay of vital organisms is hastened and new substances tend to form. Subsequently, these new substances afford a favorable condition for the reception and growth of yeast fungi in the pulp.

Yeast are micro-organisms which are floating freely in the air. If the grape juice is not protected from the infiltration of yeast spores, and if such spores get into the pulp, the sugar and carbohydrate substances will be gradually converted into alcohol and carbonic acid.

Enzymes form a catalyst for ingestion. Each substance must have a specific enzyme in order to result in a substrate action as a catalyst. For natural fermentation, the grape enzyme catalyzes the protein-like inner pulp lining of the skin and seed covering, and starts fermentation of the juice.

The ancients knew that if they were careful to get only the must juice without the pulp, they would have grape juice that remained sweet. They devised ways of filtering out all the pulp.

Columella, during the time of the Apostles, gave a recipe for keeping grape juice fresh. He directed that the grape's juice be kept free of everything that had come through the press.[64]

Pliny, also of the Apostolic age, said in describing the filtering process, "They gently crush and press the clusters."[65]

The juice obtained from this careful pressure could be preserved for drinking in its unfermented state.[66]

"Such juice . . . may be rendered perfectly limpid and transparent by filtration through bibulous paper. Grape juice where left to itself, after having been thus clarified, may remain unchanged for a definite time; but when mixed with ever so little unfiltered juice, it is sure sooner or later to undergo a change."[67] This method of filtering grape juice was discovered pictured on the walls of the tomb of Egyptian Beni-Hassan.

The most simple method of filtering consisted merely of a bag in which the grapes were placed, and squeezed by fastening the cloth sack to a pole and

62. Lees 1868.
63. Lees 1868.

64. Columella 1882.
65. Pliny 1882.
66. Geopon VI.
67. *Encyclopedia Britannica* 1894.

turning in a contrary direction. A container was placed below to receive the falling juice.[68]

Latin writers also refer to the straining while pressing.[69] Cloth sacks, according to Virgil, were a regular accompaniment of the wine press.[70]

(Special today, grape juice filters—
3 denier)

Nonalcoholic Wine Preferred

Pliny said, "The most useful wine for everybody is that whose strength is destroyed by the filter. There is a juice which by the fermenting has made itself strong."[71] According to Pliny, the strained juice was the norm, but the fermented wine was less desirable.

In Delphin's notes on Horace is this statement: "Filter your wines, for of a truth the Ancients were in the habit of straining the must repeatedly through a filter before it could ferment."[72]

Getting out pure grape juice by filtering through cloth. If pure grape juice comes through without any pulp, this juice will never ferment.

It is certain that the wines were filtered to prevent their being intoxicating. Plutarch, late Apostolic period, said, "The strength being thus withdrawn, the wine neither inflames the head Pliny, of the Apostolic times, said, "That we may drink the more wine, we destroy its strength by the filter"[73] nor infests the mind."[74]

From Horace, "Be careful to prepare for yourself wine percolated and defecated by the filter, and thus render sweet and more in accordance with nature and a female taste."[75]

6. FUMIGATION

In spite of the preventive methods used, any carelessness could still result in fermentation beginning. When this happened, there was still a method of arresting the fermentation. This method was called fumigation.

"The way to preserve new wine in the state of must was to put it up in very strong but small casks, firmly closed on all sides, by which it was to be kept from fermenting, But if it should happen to begin to ferment, the only way to stop it was by the fumes of sulphur."[76]

Adams, gathering his information from Pliny and others, said that the Romans fumigated their wines with sulphur. They also mixed it with mustum, the yolks of eggs, and other items containing sulphur.[77]

Cyprus Reading said that the object of sulphur is to impact to wine both clearness and the principle of preservation.[78]

The sulphur operation consists partly in absorbing oxygen, thus eliminating both yeast and moisture. T. S. Carr said, "The application of the fusarium of the mellowing of wines was borrowed from the Asiatics, and that the exhalation would go on until the wine was reduced to the state of syrup."[79]

"Such preparations," said Barry, "are made by the modern Turks, which they

68. Wilkinson 1882.
69. Virgil 70 B.C.
70. Virgil 70 B.C.
71. Pliny 70 A.D.
72. Delphin Notes.
73. Pliny 70 A.D.
74. *Lees Bible Commentary* 1861.
75. Horace Car lib i ode ii.
76. Gardener's Dictionary.
77. *Roman Antiquities*.
78. Nott 1863.
79. Carr 1863.

frequently carry with them on long journeys and occasionally as a strengthening and reviving cordial."[80]

Count Dandalo wrote, "The last process in wine making is sulphurization; its object is to secure the preservation of all wines even the common sort."[81]

One early method of getting sulphur to stop fermentation was by using egg yolks or pigeon eggs.

80. Kitto.

81. Dandalo 1812.

Study Notes

7. SALT

Salt will preserve most things, including the freshness of grape juice. To preserve and prevent forbidden leaven in the offering to God, it is written in Leviticus 2:13, "With all thy offerings thou shalt offer salt." The wide use of salt is described in the *Encyclopedia Americana* this way: "Salt has been used by man as far back as there are historical records. . . Salt is produced in quantities exceeding most if not all other commercial chemicals . . . Commercial salt finds many uses . . . the preservation of food is probably the most familiar."[82]

We also find that salt was used by the Greeks to preserve vintage drinks.[83]

The salt used now in the new wines is actually 'Cream of Tartar', since this salt is less soluble at lower temperatures.[84]

No writer seems to be certain that this saline brine was the favorite 'Pause that Refreshed', but it did meet the Biblical requirement of providing salt with the libation, preventing fermentation. Exodus 12:19 says, "there shall be no leaven found in your houses" during the Passover feast; the penalty resulted "in being cut off from Israel."

8. WATER EXCLUDED

"Experience shows that no fermentical chemical will ferment except in the presence of water."[85]

Two ways in which the removal of water is effected: by evaporation, or by the addition of sugar from without. After this process, the grape juice that remains does not ferment when the ratio of water to sugar falls below a corollary limit.[86]

82. *Encyclopedia Americana* 1963.
83. Dictionary of *Ancient Greek Civilization*.
84. *Encyclopedia Americana* 1963.
85. Fermentation 1894.
86. Encyclopedia Britannica 1894.

Organic materials deteriorate because of bacteria; germs or fungi are carried partly by water and in the air. Without moisture as carriers, foods and liquids will not spoil.

Excavations at Herculaneum, near Pompeii, have unearthed dry eggs that were perfectly good, though nearly 2000 years old. Pompeii was destroyed by the eruption of Vesuvius in 79 A.D. We have all heard of the flesh of animals found in the Arctic climates, thousands of years old, where bacteria action has been prevented by the intense cold. In the same way, keeping bacteria and spore-laden water from grape juice will prevent fermentation.

Again we use this quote from Columella, "Cover it carefully with pitch, lest any water should enter; then immerse it in a cistern or pond of pure cold water, and allow no part of the amphora to remain above the surface. After 40 days take it out, and it will remain sweet for a year."[87]

D. WINE FOR THOUGHT

Freshly squeezed juice was available from grapes, which were preserved and available largely year round, or from the subtropics.

An account from Florence, Italy, showed that Signor Pippinini, one of the largest grape juice processors, "had for the use of his table, until the next vintage, a quantity of grapes sufficient to make one hundred gallons of wine; that grapes could be had, at any time of the year, to make any desired quantity and that there was nothing in the way of obtaining the fruit of the vine free from fermentation in wine countries at any period. He sent a large basket of grapes to my lodging, which were delicious and looked as fresh as if recently

87. Columella 50 A.D.

taken from the vines, though they had been picked for months."[88]

Moses made no regulation providing for the fruit of the vine. But whenever introduced, it fell under the law prohibiting the use and the presence of ferment during Passover week. This was from the 14th to the 21st of the month *Nisan*.

The *Encyclopedia Britannica* states, "The rabbis would seem to have interpreted the command respecting ferment as extending to the wine as well as to the bread of the Passover. The modern Jews, accordingly, generally use raisin wine."[89] Note that the above statements are from the 19th century.

The Passover

The *Bible* connects the use of 'fruit of the vine' with the Passover preparation. Since there could be no ferment of any kind in the Passover period, it is assumed that the Jews and Jesus used one of the means of obtaining sweet grape juice for the Passover celebration. Jesus never called it *oinos*, which could be wine, but He called it 'fruit of the vine'. We now know there were many means of having sweet nonfermented grape juice at the Last Supper.

88. Nott, 1868, and Lees, 1869.
89. Kerr, 1885.

Did someone say that only alcoholic juice was available at the time of the Passover?

From history, we know the word WINE, as made and used by the Greeks and Romans, included an unfermented wine similar to our present day simple fresh grape drink. From this perspective we shall now look at *Bible* wines in the next chapters. Remember that the *Bible* uses generic words that can mean either sweet or alcoholic wine depending on the context or circumstances.

Christians who are redeemed need to follow Christ. We have northern Christians in Ireland fighting Catholic Christians. In our own country we had Southern Christians and Northern Christians killing each other over slavery. All of this is completely opposite of Christ's teaching of "Love your enemies." Nor should Christians rationalize the use of a poisonous chemical substance to anesthesia the brain.

We are discussing the eight ways of preventing fermentation. There are also other ways. (For instance yeast will not work under 50°F or above 90, or in the sun, depending on height above sea level.)

Dare we say our drug problem is partly due to Christianity's certain scholars' approval of so-called recreational drugs?

Study Notes

ספרא די מתאלף למלכות שמיא דָמֵא לגברא
מר ביתא די מפיק מבית גנזוהי חדתָן ועתיקָן

A "man of letters instructed in the kingdom of heaven" - "is as a householder which brings forth from out of his treasure things new and old".

Matthew 13:52

CHAPTER SEVEN

A COMMENTARY ON

EACH USE OF THE WORD WINE IN THE

OLD TESTAMENT

PENTATEUCH

Dr. Wendell Hansen Has Done

A Tremendous Job In His Book.

After discussing the words for "wine" in the Old and New Testaments, and noting their different meanings as given by ancient writers as well as modern scholars, he treats every occurrence in both Testaments. It is by far the most thorough treatment I have ever seen. He shows when it obviously means 'grape juice', and when it indicates an intoxicating beverage.

With its high scholarship, this is a book that demands attention. I would hope that it would be read carefully by pastors and laymen everywhere. It is "the last word" on this important subject.

Ralph Earle, M.A., B.D., Th.D.
Professor Emeritus, Nazarene
Theological Seminary
Evangelist
Foreign Missionary
Part Time Director Translation
New International Version of
the Bible, NIV
Author of over 50 books,
including *Word Meanings*

CHAPTER SEVEN
A COMMENTARY OF EACH USE OF THE WORD WINE— THE PENTATEUCH

THE UNTOLD STORY

I attended many schools and received several degrees. Finally I received a Ph.D., and still wondered why Christ would make wine. It really bothered me. I asked my former class mate Dr. Ralph Earle. He would know—he did. He told me what should have been obvious. There were two meanings for the word wine, alcoholic and nonalcoholic, just as cider and punch have two meanings. Two Nazarene ministers, Keith Sparkman and Leslie Waltz gave me a copy of Dr. William Patton's Bible Verses, 1871. From that seventeen years ago, I earnestly started my in-depth research. I studied in city libraries, seminary libraries, the Library of Congress in Washington, and the Hebrew University in Jerusalem.

I soon discovered that there were many other honest and highly educated scholars that were advocates of abstinence. We are in a minority, but all reforms were started by a sincere minority; this included the campaign against slavery, and even the establishment of Christianity. We know eventually the truth will prevail.

One probable use of this study is as a reference for those interested in particular verses. So, there will be repetition. Wine in the King James Version is translated from *Yayin* 141 times in the Old Testament. *Yayin,* the Hebrew word used three-fourths of the time, will not be indicated. When another of the thirteen Hebrew and Greek words are translated as wine, they will be introduced.

Heb. יַיִן, *yah'yin* (Gr. *οἶνος*, wine),

From the Popular and Critical Bible Encyclopedia:—

"Yah'yin, in Bible use, is a very general term, including every kind of wine made from grapes.

a. (grapes) to be sucked, gathered or eaten.
b. the blood of the grape, freshly expressed.
c. boiled wine or syrup.
d. a wine made strong and inebriating by the introduction of drugs.
e. fermented grape wine, a general term for all such."

The Bible Encyclopedia puts the first three meanings as unfermented types of yah'yin wine. (1909. pp. 1724-1725.)

(Twelve other beverage words in the Bible will be designated. As a reference book for particular verses there will be repetition.)

CHAPTER SIX REVIEW

Keeping Grape from Fermenting

Chapter six is devoted to the ways that the ancients were able to keep grape juice from fermenting.

Briefly, pure grape juice will not ferment.

For fermentation, there must be pulp that lines the inner skin and the seeds. The pulp contains the enzymes that are necessary for fermentation. Carefully squeezing the juice from the pulp, and keeping it from other fermented material, one would have grape juice that never would ferment even if leaven (yeast), were added.

Yeast and enzymes will not act in very cold or very hot temperatures, or in bright light. On the vine, grapes dry and become raisins.

Leaven (yeast) alcohol was not allowed in meat and grain sacrifices to God. (Lev. 2:11)

Drunkenness could be punishable by death. (Deut. 21:20)

Our purpose here is to determine, if possible, whether the word wine means alcoholic or nonalcoholic, from the context, exegesis, and consistent with the Bible's teaching.

Old Testament Commentaries

New Testament Commentaries:

THE PENTATEUCH—THE LAW

GENESIS

Genesis 9:20-21 (Intoxicating):

Heb. יַיִן, *yah'yin* (Gr. *οἶνος*, wine)

> And Noah began to be an husbandman, and he planted a vineyard: And he drank of the wine, and was drunken; and he was uncovered within his tent.

It is noticeable that the first mention of alcoholic beverage in the Bible is connected with drunkenness; from then to now it has been so. Drunkenness is condemned in the Bible, to the point of death. (Deuteronomy 21:20). Noah became a vine grower. The inference might be that as a shipbuilder he was not aware of what the consequences of fermentation might be. Some suggest the flood might have made climate changes that affected fruit in a way that was not understood[1]. Is it possible Noah was ignorant of the fermentation process?

Or he might have gotten stewed on purpose. Men of faith are not necessarily perfect. David was mentioned in the faith chapter as a man after God's own heart (Acts 13:22), yet he was an adulterer and a premeditated murderer. There was only one Perfect Man.

A good man was the first victim of this alcoholic spell. He made a practical discovery of its danger. A lesson posterity could have learned from this beginning. After his intoxication, Noah cursed a member of his family.

Genesis 9:24-25 (Alcoholic):

> And Noah awoke from his wine, and knew what his younger son had done unto him. And he said, Cursed *be* Canaan; a servant of servants shall he be unto his brethren.

In Chapter LXX of the Septuagint, Noah became sober from the wine.

Noah's son, Ham, told his brothers of their father's nakedness. Noah prophesied that Ham's evil would result in suffering for his generations to come. Was this the first case of homosexuality after the flood? This long-range result of sinfulness is further indicated in Deuteronomy 5:9:

> . . . I the Lord thy God am a jealous God, visiting the iniquity of the fathers upon the children unto the third and fourth generation of them that hate me.

Children suffer from parents' alcoholism for they are susceptible to becoming alcoholics themselves.

Fabricus relates a Jewish legend concerning Noah planting the vine. He killed a sheep, a lion, an ape, and a sow. He mingled their blood on the roots of the vine. As a result, the fermented blood of the grape has ever produced the stupidity of the sheep, the fierce-

1. Butler.

ness of the lion, the senseless chatter of the ape, and the love to wallow in the dirt and mire of the sow[2].

If Noah had been really wise, he would have swatted those two flies.

Genesis 14:18-19 (Nonalcoholic):

> And Melchizedek king of Salem brought forth bread and wine: (grape juice) and he *was* the priest of the most high God. And he blessed him, and said, Blessed *be* Abram of the most high God, possessor of heaven and earth:

"Brought out bread and grape juice,"[3] "Unfermented,[4]

Verse 20 states, "And he gave him tithe of all."

Melchizedek's present was given as a refreshment for Abram and his men after their battle and long journey. Sweet grape juice refreshes, as does bread. Alcohol stupefies the body. (See Hebrews 7:2 notes and following verses.)

It is assumed that the wine referred to in this instance is nonalcoholic for refreshment, possibly simple grapes. Formerly the phrase *bread and grapes* referred to food in general. Dr. Kitto, in his encyclopedia, mentions *bread and wine* in reference to all kinds of food in the Scriptures, much as we used the terms *meat and drink* in our early culture.

To assume that the reference here is to fermented grapes would be a groundless conjecture.

The first two references to *yayin*, nonalcoholic and alcoholic, in Genesis illustrate how the word was used for both alcoholic and nonalcoholic beverages. This is much as we use the word *cider* for either alcoholic or nonalcoholic drinks. In English, the statement "Let's get a drink" can have two very different meanings.

Says Dr. Ralph Earle, Professor Emeritus of Nazarene Theological Seminary, "The important thing to note is that *oinos* is used in the Septuagint for both fermented and unfermented grape juice. Since it can mean either one, it is valid to insist that in some cases it may simply mean grape juice and not fermented wine" (Ralph Earle, 1987, M.A., B.D. Th.D).

Writes Dr. Wilbur Dayton, Vice President Wesley Biblical Seminary and former president of Houghton College: "I agree with your Greek scholarship, there are two meanings to the word wine in the Bible, and it does teach abstinence." (Wilbur Dayton, B.D., MRE, MA, Th.D.)

The Hebrew word *yayin,* that is uniformly rendered as *wine* throughout Old Testament Scripture can mean either unfermented fresh grape juice, or fermented intoxicating wine. Here it meant fresh juice as in Jeremiah 40:10 "Gather ye wine and summer fruits." Or gather grapes and other summer fruits.

Dr. Jerry Hull of Northwest Nazarene College writes, "First, many biblical references to *wine* refer to nonintoxicating juices or products from the field . . . *Yayin* is used to refer clearly to

2. Lees 1868.
3. Teachout 1980.
4. Impe and Campbell 1980.

intoxicating wine only about 20 times out of 138 references"[5].

Genesis 19:32-33 (Alcoholic):

> Come, let us make our father drink wine, and we will lie with him, that we may preserve seed of our father. And they made their father drink wine that night: and the firstborn went in, and lay with her father; . . .

Lot's drinking of wine led to immorality.

The Vulgate is strong, "Let us inebriate him." They did entrap him.

Due to intoxication, Lot impregnated his own daughters. His daughters knew that intoxication caused people to do things or to behave in ways of which they were unaware. Here was the only righteous man in all of Sodom, and yet alcohol caused him to commit incest. Alcohol first hits the brain and inhibits normal thinking recesses, then inflames the passions.

Peter called Lot just (II Peter 2:7). Could there have been drugs unknown to Lot in unfermented wine? Lees points out that in the fourth book of Homer's *Odyssey*, "Helen pours into the wine for Talemachus, a drug (*pharmakon*) to assuage grief, allay anger and cause oblivion to all ills."

Moses said of Sodom: "Their vine is the vine of Sodom, . . . Their wine is the poison of dragons, . . ." (Deuteronomy 32:32, 33).

"He perceived not when she lay down, nor when she arose" (Deuteronomy 32:33). Being really drunk, he did not know who it was that had lain with him.

Genesis 27:25

> . . . Bring it near to me, and I will eat of my son's venison,
> . . . and he brought him wine, and he drank.

This involves Jacob deceiving his own father, Isaac. Ferrar Fenton designates this reference as unfermented. This also is indicated in the book *Alcohol: The Beloved Enemy.*[6] I feel that if Jacob and his mother were trying to confuse his father, they would try to befuddle his mind with alcoholic drink, unless he was a total abstainer, which was probable.

Genesis 27:28 (Nonalcoholic) *Tirosh:*

> Therefore God give thee of the dew of heaven, and the fatness of the earth, and plenty of corn and wine (*Tirosh*) (grapes):

"*Tirosh,* new wine, sweet wine" Young's Analytical Concordance, Index Lexicon to the Old Testament, 1910, p.50.

Tirosh, "In the Old Testament, every where when used for the Hebrew '*tirosh*' is new wine." Strong's Exhaustin Concordance, Comparative Concordance 1800, p.251. "Teeroshe—'vintage fruit.' The Popular and Critical Encyclopedia, 1909, p.1726.

New wine, "Must, before it has fermented, new wine." Webster, 1991.

New wine, "Must, unfermented juice, new wine." Funk and Wagnall's Standard Desk Dictionary, 1969.

Tirosh is never connected with intoxication.

Fenton translates, "Plenty of corn and fruit."

Corn and grapes are solid products of the soil, as "fatness of the earth." Alcohol is not fatness of the earth, but it is processed by aging, controlling temperature, omitting light, adding other substances, and putrefying it through fermentation.

This reference is to Isaac blessing Jacob.

Tirosh, when used to describe a beverage, means grapes, fresh grape juice, or stored grape juice. *Tirosh* is never related to leaven. The blessing in-

5. NO! The Positive Response to Alcohol 1989.

6. Impe and Campbell 1980.

cluded family possessions or an inheritance, especially stored grapes or a vineyard. Occasionally *tirosh* was used as an inclusive term to mean a beverage (nonalcoholic), and stored boiled grapes along with other possessions.

The *Targum of Jonathan* tells of the narrative which indicates that in the Chaldee version the word (*Khamar*) in this verse is applied to the unfermented grape juice. He says, "An angel brought wine from Heaven to Jacob, and he gave it to his father." This assumes there are no intoxicants in Heaven.

Most versions translated *Tirosh* as *new wine*, (new, before fermentation). But to a modern reader, *new wine* means an alcoholic substance.

Dahgan Ve-tirosh, solid produce as grapes, are particularly related to the harvest not corn made into bread nor grapes made into wine but the dew of heaven, corn and grapes.

Today, wine means an alcoholic drink; but when the King James version was written wine also meant unfermented grape juice.

A Webster definition of a scholar is one who learns from a teacher. As a result many scholars have not kept up with current thought.

Three centuries before King James, Chaucer wrote in the Pardoner's Tale:

> "Lo how the dronken loth, unkydely, lay by his daughters two, unwilynty: so drank he was, he myste what he wrought Herodes, who-so wel stories soght when he of wyn was replete at his feste."[7]

So languages do change, as a result of common usage, not necessarily by the philological statements of scholars. Each year dictionaries add many words that people start using. A short while ago if a school child referred to another as a *kid*, he would have been corrected and told that kid was a young goat. But now *kid* is in the dictionary as "*small child*". Yesterday's dictionary is as outdated as yesterday's newspaper.

Around two hundred years ago, wine by a dictionary definition meant grape juice, fermented or unfermented.* Today, wine to the average person, and by dictionary definition, means an alcoholic drink.

Copycat Scholars

Many Bible scholars have not caught up. They still use the word *WINE* when formerly both fermented and unfermented were meant. We love our brothers in Christ, but feel they do much damage in translating grape juice as wine when nonalcoholic is meant. There is a big difference. If I had stayed home, my father would have given me a fruit farm, complete with a rural home. He did not say, "Wendell, if you will stay home with us, I will give you cherry juice and cider." However, that is the way the King James translators rendered this verse (Genesis 27:28). Though proper in its time, it is not appropriate today.

Copycat scholars have simply duplicated instead of translating into today's meaning. Let's look at it again. Isaac is turning over the control of his grain,

7. Chaucer 1395.

*See Early Dictionaries in Chapter 5.

land, and vineyards. "Therefore God give thee of the dew of heaven, and the fatness of the earth, and plenty of corn and wine" (Grapes). If it were to be translated *wine*, then to be consistent it should have said, "plenty of corn bread and wine".

As with the other occurrences of *tirosh*, God is usually promising a blessing of a good harvest, or threatening a poor one. There is a big difference between a harvest and a finished product, like wine.

When I was a kid I helped my uncle at threshing time. The wheat was threshed out, but the wheat had little to do with the big noontime meal of meat, potatoes, vegetables and homemade ice cream. We said we harvested wheat. We didn't say we harvested bread, rolls and cake. Nor does it make any sense to say that the Biblical workers harvested wine; at least not for our day. We did not harvest the finished product. We harvested wheat, not meat, potatoes, vegetables and ice cream.

There is no basis for its being translated as *wine*. Also, of all the verses condemning wine in the Old Testament, there is one verse that the moderationists use to try to prove that the Old Testament does not teach abstinence:

Hosea 4:11:

> Whoredom and wine (*yayin*) and new wine (*tirosh*) (grape juice) take away the heart.

The claim is that *tirosh*, translated new wine, takes away the understanding, just as wine, *yayin*, in this case, does. Since wine and whoredom take away the heart, it is said, wine causes drunkenness, so then new wine causes drunkenness. In other words, it is said, there is just one meaning for the word wine, an alcoholic beverage.

We use what we feel is the proper translation. We say *tirosh*, meaning grapes, possession of grapes or vineyards, as Isaac willed to Jacob, takes away the heart. Possessions can take away the heart, as in the case of the rich ruler (Luke 18:22-24).

There is nothing here to indicate that the word *tirosh* referred to an intoxicating drink. Does whoredom mean intoxicating, does whoredom literally make one drunk?

We will discuss this verse in detail in its chronological place, Hosea 4:11.

Grapes, with unbroken skins, will not ferment. In my experimentation I have never known perfect grapes to ferment on the vine.* They turned to raisins. I know; I grow grapes.

Tirosh is not wine, old or new.

There are two references where *tirosh* can be juice:

"Thy presses shall burst out with *tirosh*" Proverbs 3:10. This could refer to possession and storage of grape juice.

"The sons of the stranger shall not drink thy *tirosh*" (Isaiah 62:8). The stranger might drink the fresh *yayin*, but the son might drink the stored *tirosh*. *Tirosh* is not wine at all, but the fruit of the vineyard in its natural condition.[8]

There is a possible third reference. The fats shall overflow with *tirosh*, (Joel 2:24). This probably means *vats*, (as translated in the NIV and NASB), which are usually related to holding liquids. Funk and Wagnells' *Unabridged Dictionary* gives vats five meanings; here are four:

1. Especially for holding liquids.
2. A liquid or dry measure, used especially in Netherlands.
3. Metal for drying ore.
4. A chamber for drying tin or other metal.

---

* Grapes with *broken skins* may ferment if confined in a container in a dark warm place.

8. *Bible Commentary* 1871.

So vats can also be used for holding solids, as grapes.

In all 38 references to *tirosh*, new wine, there is no mention of an Israelite drinking *tirosh*, new wine, the reference is usually to grapes, definitely not alcoholic wine.

Says Dr. Bacchiocchi in his recent, *Wine in the Bible*, "It is evident that *wine (tirosh)* is either the grape or fresh grape juice, since it is harvested together with grain and oil."[9] Tirosh is not wine!

In Walton's Polyglot Latin translation *tirosh* is rendered *musti*—unfermented wine.

"*Tirosh* itself is never connected with intoxication."[10]

Ferrar Fenton, M.R.A.S., M.C.A.A., an Englishman, undertook to translate the whole Bible. Ferrar Fenton was one of the early scholars to realize wine was the wrong word in many places.

The task took him fifty years. He begins his book with this verse, which he felt so important to the Bible's real meaning of the word WINE: "*Tirosh* is never connected with intoxication." Professor Arnold wrote the same statement to me: "Tirosh itself is never connected with intoxication."[11]

TIROSH USUALLY MEANS GRAPES

We show some of Fentons work, where he pens it in his own words. He gives a history and meaning of *tirosh*.

(A single fact will often spoil an interesting argument, Cryptograms III).

9. Bacchiocchi 1989.

10. Arnold, Wesley Biblical Seminary, December 1, 1989.

11. Wesley Biblical Seminary, December 1, 1989.

REFERENCES IN THE PENTATEUCH.

Gen. xxvii. 37: "But Isaac replied and said to Esau: 'Since I have made him your master, and have given all his brothers to him for servants, and with *increase* and *possession* I have endowed him—where now my son is there anything I can do?"

We have the same vocables here again דגן, *Dagan*, Increase, and ותירוש *Thirosh*, Possession, whilst the whole import of the words of the narrative excludes any reference to fermented liquor, which the perversity and ignorance of former translators has fixed upon them.

> Num. xviii. 12: "All the melted fat, and the best of the *produce* (or vintage), and the first of the corn which they present to the EVER-LIVING are given to you."

Here again we have the word תירוש, Thirosh, the root of which is ירא, Ira, "to rise up," and undoubtedly means *produce* or *fruit* of the earth for food,

So may GOD give to you the dew from the skies, and the fatness of the earth, and increase and POSSESSION.'"

It is thus seen, and my authorities for the fact are the two eminent Hebraists, Drs. S. Lee and B. Davidson, that the word תירוש, Thirosh, translated "Wine" (in the sense of intoxicating liquor), means here actually "possession." That is, Isaac at once handed over to Jacob the control of his estate, and not merely the promise of it in the future. The root of the word ירש, Irsh, is to take *possession* of.

THE BIBLE AND WINE

by

Ferrar Fenton, M.R.A.S., M.C.A.A.

"So may God give to you the dew from the skies, and the fatness of the earth, and increase and 'POSSESSION.' "

"It is thus seen, and my authorities for the fact are the two eminent. Hebraists, Drs. S. Lee and B. Davidson, that the word

"Thirosh, translated "Wine" (in the sense of intoxicating liquor), means here actually "possession." That is, Isaac at once handed over to Jacob the control of his estate, and not merely the promise of it in the future.

"*Thirosh,* Possession, whilst the whole import of the words of the narrative excludes any reference to fermented liquor, which the perversity and ignorance of former translators has fixed upon them."

Of particular interest is that a century ago Fenton tried to set straight a translation where grapes are as a possession rather than wine.

The Moderationist was warning the alcoholic about the dangers that the abstainers present.

His sincerity could not be questioned with a cross on his lapel and flask on his lip.

So we come to the conclusion that *tirosh* is a word with the compound meaning of the blessing of *possession of grapes* and stored grape. There is no basis for translating *tirosh* as wine, old or new wine; for readers of our time think wine refers only to an alcoholic drink.

There is no reference to any Israelite drinking tirosh.

Grapes are eaten; alcoholic juice is drunk. In relation to eating there are three references.

1. Thou mayest not eat within thy gate, the tithe of thy corn, or of thy wine (*tirosh*) (grapes), . . . (Deuteronomy 12:17).
2. And thou shalt eat before the Lord, . . . the tithe of thy corn, of thy wine (*tirosh*) (grapes) (Deuteronomy 14:23).
3. And he shall eat the fruit . . . which also shall not leave thee either corn, wine (*tirosh*), (grapes), or oil, . . . (Deuteronomy 28:51).

In all times, those translators who rendered *Tirosh* as wine were, in today's meaning of the word, inexcusably wrong.

Genesis 27:37 (Nonalcoholic):

> And Isaac answered and said unto Esau, Behold, I have made him thy lord, and all his brethren have I given to him for servants; and with corn and wine (*tirosh*) (grapes) have I sustained him: and what shall I do now unto thee, my son?

With corn and wine I have established him, (Vulgate).

This refers to Isaac's former blessing of turning the corn and *tirosh*, grapes and vine yards, that is the possessions, over to Jacob. Therefore, Jacob is like the boss or supervisor and Esau is like a hired hand or employee. Isaac realized that he had been tricked, but still kept his word. It is possible the blessing was irretrievable.

To convert *Tirosh* into an intoxicating liquid is a serious misappropriation of God's blessing.

Genesis 40:11 (Nonalcoholic):

> . . . I took the grapes, and pressed them into Pharaoh's cup, and I gave the cup into Pharaoh's hand.

We insert the passage here because it does show that the mighty Pharaohs relished the fresh, sweet juice as beverage.

Eudoxus (4th century B.C.) is cited by Plutarch, as evidence that until the reign of Psammelichus (B.C. 640) the Egyptian kings drank no alcoholic wine. Well would they enjoy the freshly squeezed grape wine.

Ancient usage of squeezing the juice of grapes into a cup has been exhumed at Pompeii. It is that of Bacchus standing by a pedestal, and holding in both hands a large cluster of grapes, and squeezing the juice into a cup.

Genesis 49:11 (Nonalcoholic):

> . . . he washed his garments in wine (grape juice), . . .

He will wash his garments in grape juice,[11] (translates Dr. Teachout 1983 Detroit Baptist Seminary.

Extravagance shows prosperity.

Actually, this is a metaphorical use indicating God's blessing on his people. When wine is used as a blessing it is nonalcoholic. When wine is used as a curse, it is alcoholic.

Genesis 49:12 (Nonalcoholic):

His eyes *shall be* red with wine, . . .

His eyes shall be more beautiful than grape juice.[12] Vulgate, "More beautiful are his eyes . . ."

This is part of a blessing and prophecy of the eminence of Judah's descendants, and of the continuance of the tribe until the Messiah should come from that tribe. Grape juice is used prominently in the blessing of God upon Judah. As God's blessing, it should be related to purity as opposed to alcohol. For it should be consistent with the teaching against wine, the poison, the mocker, and the instruction not even to look at it.

The *red eyes* mentioned here are found as a peculiar expression. Commentators usually overlook it. The New King James version (copyright 1982) reads, His eyes are darker than wine, as does the *New International Version* or *NIV*, (copyright 1978). But wine is not necessarily dark. I prefer the translation that Teachout suggests, "His eyes shall be more beautiful than grape juice," which was long before suggested by Jerome, in the Vulgate, "More beautiful." This is a more suitable metaphor to show the beauty of a godly life.

This verse, like the preceding one, is part of the blessing, *blood of the grape*, that can mean only nonalcoholic. Alcoholic wine is not pure grape juice or blood of the grape.

Van Impe and Campbell translate as unfermented.

12. Teachout 1983.

EXODUS

Exodus 12:8

And they shall eat the flesh in that night, roast with fire, and unleavened bread; . . .

The directions against leaven in the Passover are taken very seriously. In the Old Testament, leaven or yeast, with its fermentation, was a symbol of sin, because of the corruption that it caused. In the Pentateuch, no beverage was arranged for consumption during the Passover. Leaven (fermented beverages have leaven) was not allowed in the house for seven days.

Exodus 12:19

Seven days shall there be no leaven found in your houses: for whosoever eateth that which is leavened, even that soul shall be cut off from the congregation of Israel, . . .

To be cut off from Israel would mean they would lose their first born, and be left behind in Egypt as slaves.

Fermentation of grape juice is caused by leaven.

There is scarcely any alcohol in leavened bread, since the baking destroys the leaven or yeast as well as the alcohol. Fermented grape juice would be a far greater transgression of "there shall be no leaven found in your home" (Exodus 13:7).

Exodus 29:40 (Nonalcoholic):

And with the one lamb a tenth deal of flour mingled with the fourth part of an hin of beaten oil; and the fourth part of an hin of wine for a drink offering.

A hin is about three quarts. The actual kind of wine referred to here can be deduced from three mandates:

1) Exodus 29:37: "Whatsoever toucheth the altar shall be holy." Exodus 34:25: "Thou shalt not offer the blood of my sacrifice with leaven; . . ." Leaven = yeast = fermentation = putrefaction. "Their wine *is* the poison of

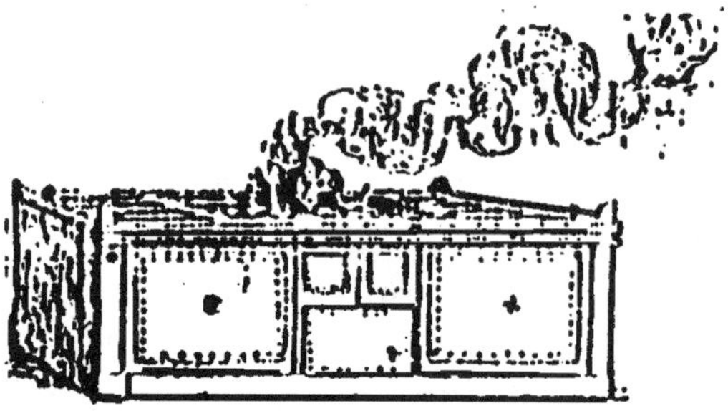

The Great Altar of Sacrifice

dragons," (Deuteronomy 32:33). All fermentation was considered unholy.

2) Exodus 12:8: "And they shall eat the flesh in that night, roast with fire, and unleavened bread; . . ." No corruption could be permitted.

3) Leviticus 10:9: "Do not drink wine nor strong drink, thou, nor thy sons with thee, when ye go into the tabernacle of the congregation, lest ye die . . . ."

In the time of the King James Version, wine could refer to either alcoholic or nonalcoholic drink. This was a dual meaning for hundreds of years. But today people think of wine only as an alcoholic drink. Yet even the New King James Version, copyright 1979, 1980, 1982, incorrectly, in my opinion, translates this verse a hin of wine. To attach a modern English meaning to Ancient Hebrew words which, at the time, meant something different would not be a very accurate method of translation. A straying word is lost in translation.

Exodus 34:25 (Nonalcoholic):

> Thou shalt not offer the blood of my sacrifice with leaven; (yeast) (alcohol) . . .

Therefore no leaven in worship, no alcoholic wine in worship sacrifice. "And their drink offerings, even an offering made by fire" Leviticus 23:18. Fire burns out the leaven and alcohol. No leaven equals no fermentation. Leaven and yeast are the same. Leaven was a symbol of corruption. One is not permitted to bring intoxicating liquor [into the temple], Rabbi Jose on worship in the Talmud Talmudic, p.412). Rabbi Genseniour said, Leaven applied as really to the wine as to the bread,[13]

This is seen positively in the presentation of *first fruits* and negatively in the eschewing of fertility rituals.[14]

Genesis 6:14: "Make thee an ark of gopher wood." God was very specific in kinds of material, measurements and directions of use, including no wine (alcoholic), or those who had recently drunk wine, in the tabernacle.

I Corinthians 5:6-8 describes leaven as a symbol of corruption. "Purge out therefore the old leaven, . . ." (5:7). Leaven in wine is worse than in bread. Baking kills the leaven. NIV—Do not offer the blood of a sacrifice to me along with anything containing yeast.

Certainly, no leaven or fermentation should be allowed in Christian worship.

THE BOOK OF LEVITICUS

Leviticus 2:11

> No meat offering, . . . shall be made with leaven: (alcohol) . . .

Leviticus 2:4-11, All leaven, i.e., fermentation, was excluded from the offer-

13. thus no fermentation (Thayer 1871).
14. Bruce 1986. *Bible Commentary.*

ings to God. Rabbi Dr. S. M. Isaac said, "The Jews do not in their feast for sacred purposes, including the marriage feast, ever use any kind of fermented drinks."[15]

Leviticus 2:13

. . . with all thine offerings thou shalt offer salt.

Salt was required. A sufficient amount prevented fermentation and other corruption.

Ferrar Fenton, 1872, translates the verse as follows:

"Every offering presented by you shall be salted with salt: and you shall not withhold the salt of the Covenant of your God from your presence, upon every offering you shall offer salt."

Dr. Fenton's translation is interesting for his choice of words.

Leviticus 10:8,9 (Alcoholic):

***Shāy!kawr'* (Heb. שֵׁכָר), 'sweet drink.**

And the Lord spake unto Aaron, saying, Do not drink wine nor strong drink (*shekar*), thou, nor thy sons with thee, when ye go into the tabernacle of the congregation, lest ye die: *it shall be* a statue for ever throughout your generations:

Ezekiel 44:21 includes *any priest*.

The next verse (Leviticus 10:10) says, That ye may put difference between holy and unholy.

This priestly requirement of abstinence was also a requirement of the Egyptian priests, 200 years before Christ. According to Jecolliot, in *The Bible in India*, the Hindu or Brahmin priests were also required to be abstainers. The same was true of the Zoroastrian religious leaders.

Mohammed also forbid the use of alcohol in The Koran.

15. Patton 1871.

From the Pentalogue of Buddha (560 B.C.), we read this: Thou shalt not drink any intoxicating liquor, (Quoted by Malcolm in *Travels in the Burman Empire*).

These statements indicate that even non-Christian religions have rules forbidding the drinking of alcoholic beverages. But none have the severe rules about it that the God of the Israelites gave. Rebellious drunkenness could result in the death penalty being imposed.

. . . our son *is* stubborn and rebellious, he will not obey our voice; *he is* a glutton, and a drunkard. . . . stone him with stones, that he die: . . .[16]

According to Dr. Teachout, "wine and strong drink" is a hendiadys.* When used with sweet wine, it is sweet cider. When used with leavened wine (alcoholic) it is hard cider. 1980, p. 244.

The Jews had no name for alcohol. Yeast leaven, in wine resulted in intoxication. So, no leaven in offerings to God. (Leviticus 2:11) "Eat it without leaven beside the altar" (Leviticus 10:12).

16. Deuteronomy 21:20,21.

*Hendiadys—for emphasis, two nouns are joined, instead of the usual noun and modifer.

SHEKAR MEANS SWEET

The Root of *Shekar, a generic noun, is sweet* according to Dictionaries.

When *shekar* is spelled with an *e* or an *a*; it refers to the sap or, fruit of trees. There are no written vowels in early Semitic languages. Later specific vowel sounds of dots and markers were added in the early Hebrew Bibles. Either *Shekar* or *Shaker* is correct, depending on use.

We shall now delve into the origin of the word *shekar*. The King James Version translates *shekar* as strong drink. But dictionaries define *sugar* as *shaker.* In Webster's *1965 New Twentieth Century Dictionary,* we find the definition for sugar, Per. *shakar,* in other words, *shakar* in Persian is sugar.

The New Testament states, Drunkards shall not inherit the kingdom of God. Yet many of our churches today actually use alcoholic wine for Holy Communion! which has caused some drunkeness of former alcoholics, including Catholic priests. It is even given to minors, contrary to laws forbidding minors to use alcohol. Holy Communion may give unholy permission.

Shekar according to Dr. Teachout "strong drink" is a word, translated as strong drink in the A.V. Bible, it is either sugar, sweet, syrup, or a fermented sweet. Let's try some other dictionaries. Funk and Wagnalls, *1960 New standard Dictionary: Sugar in Arabic is Sakker*; Persian—*skekar*.

Shekar Means Sweet

According to Funk and Wagnall's *1960 New Standard Dictionary, sugar* in Arabic is *sakker*; in Persian, *skekar*.

The New American Encyclopedia Dictionary includes in its entry for sugar: Arabic *sakker*; Persian *shakar*; Greek, *sachar*. All convey the same message. As we add Oxford New Dictionary on Historical Principles, it gives: *Shekar* is the basic for sugar and cider. Says Ewing, "These are all variants of the Hebrew words *sheker, shakar* and *sachar" (1937, p.36).*

Try to say sugar without an *sh* sound; you can't because sugar comes from *shekar*. You would be wrong if you said sugar without *sh* for the dictionary gives *shug* as the correct pronunciation.

It is sweet juices from trees (orchard fruit or sap) rather than vines.

Shekar as a Noun?

Stephen M. Reynolds; Ph.D., of Princeton, goes back to the Syria roots to find that, "The proto-semitic root *sh-k-r* may have been a drink made from the date palm or honey." Dr. Reynolds connects the *non-intoxicating and intoxicating* varieties, so *shekar,* in his opinion, is a generic word from the cognate beginning.[17] He probably means the date palm juice is sweet nonintoxicating when fresh. But like most sugary juices, without proper care it would ferment or spoil as hard or strong drink.

The International Standard Bible Encyclopedia also digs into the ancient Assyrian-Babylonian cuneiform tablets and comes up with, "Probably the most common sort of *shekar* used in Bible times was palm-date wine."[18]

According to these scholars, Bible translators should have more accurately translated *shekar* as date juice, palm juice, syrup, sugar, or as Fenton's orchard fruit. All of these are very far from *strong drink*. Here is another: *Sikera* Sweet drink[19] (often fermented). (Under the title *Strong Drink. Analytical Concordancce of the Bible*, 22nd edition).

Shekar is related to the word sugar in all the Indo-Germanic and Semitic languages, and is still applied in the East, from India to Abyssinia, to the palm

17. Reynolds 1983. *The Biblical Approach to Alcohol*

18. 1939.

19. Young.

"Pass the *shekar*, er, uh—sugar."

sap, the shaggery made from it.[20] So actually, the word *Shekar* means *sweet* or *sweet drink*.

Frederick Richard Lees and D. Burns published the *Temperance Bible Commentary* in London in 1868. They showed how the word wine and *shekar* each had two meanings.

Shekar Was Juice From Trees Boiled Down to a Syrup— Sometimes Boiled to a Solid as a Sugar

According to Fenton, "Some scholars believe that *shekar* (strong drink) was not only a sweet beverage but also a juice boiled down to a syrupy form, and then to a solid substance of food—which sugar is." From the *Popular and Critical Bible Encyclopedia: Shekar,* (1) sweet wine or syrup. Luscious, saccharine drink or sweet syrup, especially sugar or honey of dates, or of the palm tree . . . The palm syrup denoted by *shay-kawr* (she chu) was used both as a sweetmeat or article of food, and as a drink, like the Hebrew *sobhe* and the Roman *sapa* (boiled wine), diluted with water, as with modern grape and honey syrups or sherbets (Proverbs 9:2,5) she hath mingled her wine; . . . drink of the wine *which* I have mingled[21] (1909).

Following the Saracenic conquest south and east, the use of the word spread. The Arabic — *sakar*; Persia & Bengali — *shukker* (whence our word for sugar-candy), *shukurund* (rock candy, certainly a solid); common Indian —*jagree or zhaggery*; Moresque — *sekkoue*, Portuguese — *assucar* (molasses being *mel-de-asucar*), honey of sugar abbreviated.[22]

Fructose, from orchard fruit or sap, has a stronger sweetening power than the sucrose of cane sugar.

As we change directions from south to north, we find the same similarity between the sound of *shekar* and its meaning of sugar . . . embodied in the Grecian and Teutonic languages. Hence, Greek — *sakehar*, Latin — *saccharum*, Italian — *zuchero*, German — *zuker* and *juderig*, Dutch — *suuiker*, Russian — *sachar*, Danish— *supper*, . . . *Sukkard* is used by the writers of the Middle Ages in the sense of dainty, dessert or sweetmeats.[23] All solids.

According to Fenton: "In Arabic and Persian the word *shekar* . . . is spelled *suker*, and *shugar*, and radically means *sweetness* or sugar, or any fruit or drink, and also in a general sense anything pleasant metaphorically, the same as in English. The Assyrian form of the word is *Sikari*, . . . which refers to the palm tree and a drink made from its sweet juice. Palm tree sap preceded sugar from canes."[24]

Why do we spend so much time showing that *shekar* is a generic term? *Shekar* sometimes meant sweet. Killing the enzymes in the juice by boiling or otherwise would keep it sweet. So there are places where strong meant nonalcoholic. Sometimes this is very critical to a proper understanding of the text, as in Deuteronomy 14:26. Unprotected, *shekar* would ferment and be strong drink, as it usually is meant, but not always.

---

20. Lees 1868.
21. Bible Encyclopedia, 1909.
22. Ibid 1909.
23. Ibid 1909.
24. Fenton 1907.

Leviticus 10:10 (Alcoholic):

> And that ye may put difference between holy and unholy, and between unclean and clean;

This refers to the story of Nadab and Abihu who offered *strange* fire before the Lord and died at God's hand because of it. What was their sin? Was it a drunken prank? I thought of the waiter I saw burning off the alcohol from the meat entree at the next table. Could it be that Nadab and Abihu dared to burn alcohol, a symbol of corruption, before the Lord instead of the sacred fire? God could not permit such desecration of His Holy place.

(Customer: Coffee with cream
and *shekar*, please.)

Arnold D. Peiskers (1967) comments on their death in *The Wesleyan Bible Commentary* in these words: That God at this particular time forbade the use of intoxicants by the ministering priest in the Tabernacle may indicate that Nadab and Abihu had been drunk . . . This has a very personal application for all Christians, for we are a body of priests unto the Lord . . . We are . . . obligated to refrain from befuddling intoxicants.[25]

It is observed by Jewish writers and many modern commentators that Nadab and Abihu were executed for drinking alcoholic wine before going into the Temple.[26]

Perhaps God said something like this to Aaron, I'm deadly serious. For a transgression, I just burned your two sons, Nadab and Abihu, to death. Absolutely no leaven (no alcohol), in my Temple! How about alcoholic communion in church?

25. Peiskers 1967.
26. Drummelow 1936.

Leviticus 23:13 (Nonalcoholic):

> . . . and the drink offering thereof shall be of wine (grape juice), the fourth *part* of an hin.

This is a repetition of Exodus 29:40. Please refer to those notes.

THE BOOK OF NUMBERS

Numbers 6:2,3,4 (Nonalcoholic):

> . . . When either man or woman shall separate *themselves* to vow a vow of a Nazarite, . . . He shall separate *himself* from wine (grape juice) and strong drink (*shekar*), (orchard cider) and shall drink no vinegar of wine, or vinegar of strong drink, neither shall he drink any liquor of grapes, nor eat moist grapes, or dried. All the days of his separation shall he eat nothing that is made of the vine tree, from the kernels even to the husk.

'*Shekar*-sweet cider. (It could become strong drink if allowed to ferment). Vinegar is not alcoholic. Usually *Shekar* according to Dr. Teachout "wine and strong drink" *is* a hendiadys.* When strong is used with sweet wine, it is sweet cider. When used with leavened wine (alcoholic) it is hard cider. (Teachout 1980) The Jews had no name for alcohol. They did not need one. They understood "leaven", yeast in wine resulted in intoxication. So, no leaven in offerings to God (Leviticus 2:11). "Eat it without leaven beside the altar" (Leviticus 10:12). So, here, drink no wine or strong drink, but in Song of Solomon 5:1, I have drunk my wine with milk . . . "drink abundantly" the difference is leaven or no leaven.

The Nazarite was by self sacrifice peculiarly dedicated to the Lord with a holy life. Their life was to be pure, free from fermented alcohol.

Without refrigeration, it could be tricky to have absolutely pure grape juice without enzymes in the pulp and

*Hendiadys, for emphasis two similar nouns are joined together with *and* instead of the usual noun and modifier.

a trace of the despised leaven (yeast). To guard against this, the Nazarite was not to touch anything that related to the grape. This included other juices that ferment as strong drink (*shekar*), made from other fruit juices, as of trees, or tree sap.

Numbers 6:20 (Nonalcoholic):

> . . . and after that the Nazarite may drink wine, (grape juice).

When he was no longer under a Nazarite vow he could drink wine, (but presumably not the alcoholic strong drink or alcoholic wine which is prohibited in Proverbs 23:29-31.) He was not under obligation to drink any kind of wine, fruit juice.

Numbers 13:23

> . . . and cut down from thence a branch with one cluster of grapes, and they bare it between two upon a staff; . . .

Clusters weighing twenty pounds are still seen in Syria.

Numbers 15:5,7,10 (Nonalcoholic):

> And the fourth *part* of an hin of wine for a drink offering shalt thou prepare with the burnt offering . . .
>
> And for a drink offering thou shalt offer the third *part* of an hin of wine, (grape juice) *for* a sweet savour unto the LORD.
>
> And thou shalt bring for a drink offering half an hin of wine, (grape juice) *for* an offering made by fire, of a sweet savour unto the LORD.

Alcohol was not to be brought into the tabernacle or temple, so it had to be nonalcoholic.

I have a bird act in which a bird flies through fire. It was featured in *LIFE Magazine*. We use alcohol fuel. The alcohol quickly burns up with a smoke odor, not very pleasing. But when we heat grape juice, it gives a sweet fragance, 'unto the LORD.'

Numbers 18:12 (Nonalcoholic):

> All the best of the oil, and all the best of the wine, (grape juice) (*tirosh*) and of the wheat, the firstfruits of them which they shall offer unto the LORD, them have I given thee.

Fenton translates wine as Orchard fruit. *Tirosh* is always nonintoxicating. Webster: "Before it has fermented, new wine." See notes on Genesis 27:28.

The best fresh first fruits, nonalcoholic were to be given to the Levites, God's representatives. Oil and wheat are natural, non-processed foods, as is pure, non-fermented grape juice. According to Fenton this indicates orchard fruit as well as vine fruit (1953 p.2).

Numbers 28:7 (Nonalcoholic):

> . . . in the holy *place* shalt thou cause the strong wine (*shekar*) (sweet orchard juice) to be poured unto the LORD *for* a drink offering.

Ferrar Fenton translates, Cause the drink offering. *Shekar* means sweet. See Leviticus 10:9. In today's meaning: "Cause sweet orchard juice to be poured out."

Like *yayin, shekar* is a generic term including palm wine and other saccharine beverages says Kittos' *Cyclopedia of Biblical Literature*.

God burned the two sons of a priest to death for bringing strong (alcoholic) fire into the temple. Numbers 3:4 He therefore would not allow an alcoholic drink brought to Him as a worshipful drink offering. It had to be, and was, nonalcoholic.

So I vigorously disagree with *NIV's, fermented drink* for *shekar* in this verse. No matter how conscientious, to me, such reasoning seems downright inconceivable, and sacrilegious.

Shekar is here translated *strong wine*, but it possibly means a drink with a very strong orchard fruit flavor. Better translations are the New King James Version and The Living Bible, which render it *drink offering*. The AV's *strong drink* is not appropriate for today. Modern readers think of *strong drink* as distilled liquor, such as whiskey (which is not now advertised on American radio or TV). Distillation was unknown to the Hebrews during Bible days, and was not generally used until the 12th century A.D. Please see Leviticus 10:9 for more on *strong drink*.

The following verse, Numbers 28:8, describes the purpose of the drink offering as a *sweet savour* unto the Lord. I don't believe the Lord loves the stink of alcohol any more than I do.

Numbers 28:14 (Nonalcoholic):

> And their drink offerings shall be half an hin of wine (grape juice) unto a bullock, and the third *part* of an hin unto a ram, and a fourth *part* of an hin unto a lamb: this *is* the burnt offering of every month . . .

It should be *half an hin of grape juice*. *Half an hin*—God is very specific. If he had meant for man to drink alcohol moderately, he would have set limits. He did not. What is moderation? A degree of intoxication starts with the first drink. People drink intoxicants to get intoxicated. Moderate drinkers become alcoholics 10% of the time. Alcoholics know no limits. Five percent of alcoholics die in withdrawal or from the results of alcoholism. "No meat offering, . . . shall be made with leaven: . . ." (Leviticus 2:11). So this had to be nonalcoholic wine.

Burning altar

To drink alcoholic wine before going into the tabernacle could bring the death penalty. So God did not want alcoholic wine brought to Him as a drink offering.

It is obvious that the God of Israel did not drink libations as pagan deities are portrayed doing; Dr. Teachout quotes Heidel. In the Gilagamish Epic (Tablet XI, lines 155-61), "I poured out a libation on the peak of the mountain. The gods smelled the sweet savor. The gods gathered like flies over the sacrifices."[27] Also in the Ugaritic eptics: Oblation of the gods to eat and oblation to drink to the holy ones.[28]

In the Old Testament libations were merely poured out before Him. Considering God's emphasis on details it would seem that He would be concerned. There are implications: God despised intoxication (Proverbs 23:29-35). It is natural to assume that He did not approve of a beverage that could bring on that condition.

Let's give one more irrefutable proof that the word *wine* meant either fermented or unfermented. Says Columella, the Roman writer, who lived shortly after the time of Christ. From his treatise, on Agriculture:

The cauldron-room, in which boiled wine is made, should be neither narrow or too dark, so that the attendant

27. Heidel 1963.
28. Lambert 1960.

who is boiling down the must* may move around without inconvenience (p.75).

(Production of nonalcoholic wine is in lighted rooms.)
(Production of alcoholic wine is in darkened spaces.)

Boiled grape juice herein called wine is never alcoholic:

1. Boiling kills the enzymes, There is no fermentation without enzymes.
2. Boiling kills all yeast and evaporates alcohol.

Each of the products offered was natural—flour, not bread; sheep, goats, and bulls, not steaks or spare ribs. Therefore, the reference was to natural grape juice, not fermented wine.

Leviticus 2:11

No meat (grain offering) . . . shall be made with leaven).

DEUTERONOMY

Deuteronomy 7:12-13 (Nonalcoholic):

> . . . if ye . . . keep, and do them, that the LORD thy God shall keep unto thee the covenant and the mercy . . . he will love thee, and bless thee, . . . bless the fruit of thy womb, and the fruit of thy land, thy corn, and thy wine, (*tirosh*), (grapes) and thine oil, . . . and the flocks of thy sheep, . . .

Fenton translates as "grapes," Lee, "vine fruit".

Tirosh, "new wine, sweet wine. Young's Lexicon, p.50.

Tirosh is always nonalcoholic (NASB and NIV say new wine).

These are the direct unprocessed products of the land; therefore, sweet grapes. The New King James Version gives *new wine* as it often does for *Tirosh*. According to Webster, *must* ought to be translated *vine fruit*, which is always nonalcoholic. But, wine in the minds of people today is alcoholic whether new or old wine.

In the thirty-eight times *tirosh* is mentioned in the Bible, there is no indication of it ever being drunk by an Israelite. Most likely it was boiled to save space and to prevent fermentation. Later, out of season, it could be diluted and drunk, or used as syrup or as sugar.

Deuteronomy 11:14-15 (Nonalcoholic):

> That I will give *you* the rain of your land in his due season, . . . that thou mayest gather in thy corn, and thy wine (*tirosh*) (grapes), and thine oil. And I will send grass in thy fields . . . that thou mayest eat and be full.

Your grain and your grape juice.[29]

Tirosh is particularly related to the harvest of the vineyard, with no time to ferment. Wine is not harvested, it is processed. Grapes are harvested. During harvest "Tiros uniformly refers to fresh grape pure juice."[30] It is always nonalcoholic.

Fenton's translation is: You will harvest your corn and your fruits and your oil.[31]

See notes on Genesis 27:28 for notes on *tirosh*.

Deuteronomy 12:17 (Nonalcoholic):

> Thou mayest not eat within thy gates the tithe of thy corn, or of thy wine (*tirosh*), (grapes) . . .

Tirosh is always nonalcoholic. Dr. Stephen M. Reynolds disagrees.

---

*Must is unfermented fruit juice. There is no such thing as boiled alcoholic wine. Boiling takes away the alcohol. So Columella meant nonalcoholic fruit juice.

29. Teachout 1983.
30. Teachout 1979.
31. Fenton 1907.

Fenton rendered *thy wine* as *your fruit*.

The tithe went to the Levites, the priestly tribe, who in general were given no land of their own. We know of the warning to priests against alcoholic wine in the tabernacle upon pain of death (Leviticus 10:9). So Fenton's translation here of fruit instead of wine makes more sense, though wine would not have been incorrect since wine meant both fresh grape juice or fermented juice. But note the phrase, *mayest not eat*, not *mayest not drink*. Grapes are eaten; people drink alcoholic wine.

Deuteronomy 14:23 (Nonalcoholic):

> And thou shalt eat before the LORD thy God, . . . the tithe of thy corn, of thy wine (*tirosh*), (grapes) . .

Tirosh is always nonalcoholic. No exceptions. There was a first tithe that was given to the Levites, out of which they paid a tenth to the priest. Then of that which remained, they ate before the Lord.

Since the tithe given to the Levities was unfermented juice, as *tirosh* always is, then naturally, the tithe of the tithe was also unfermented juice.

Fenton's translation renders it thus: Your corn, your fruits and oil.[32]

Deuteronomy 14:26 (Nonalcoholic):

> And thou shalt bestow that money for whatsoever thy soul lusteth after, for oxen, or for sheep, or for wine (*yayin*), (grapes) or for strong drink, (orchard fruit) or for whatsoever thy soul desireth: and thou shalt eat there before the LORD.

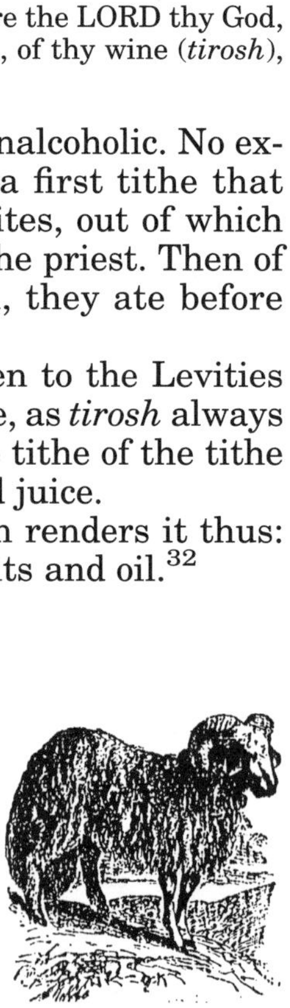
Broad-Tailed Sheep of the Orient

32. Fenton 1907.

Translating from the Septuagint, Fenton correctly gives *sugar* instead of *strong drink*. See Leviticus 10:9

This provision . . . unparalleled in the O.T.[33]

Common sense dictates that if Moses knew the possibility of addiction of his people to the use of alcohol he would not have recommended that they freely spend part of their tithe money on alcoholic *wine or strong drink*. Such a recommendation would represent not the *insight of an experienced and compassionate leader*."[34]

Fenton explains his reasoning in *The Bible and Wine:*

Yayin, "I think means, Fruit or Grapes in a fresh state. For the instruction is to *eat* it, not to *drink* it . . . ." Shekar evidently refers to sugar or other sweets [fruits], for that also is to be eaten, not drunk. They thus give strong support to my contention that the words indicating vegetable products were used to designate foods, and *Not Intoxicating Liquors*. In the present instance there is certainly no suggestion of their being enumerated or commanded to be used for the purpose of drunkenness or artificial excitement.[35]

The reference to *eat* is in the preceding verse 23 and in this verse 26.

And thou shalt eat before the LORD thy God, in the place which he shall choose to place his name there, . . .

It is so clear. People drink alcoholic wine. They eat grapes, and solidified grape products.

Dr. Frederick Lees, Editor of the *Temperance Bible Commentary,* 1870, had this to say of those who would put an intoxicating interpretation on this verse: page 54, (4).

33. Bruce 1986.
34. Bacchiocchi 1989.
35. Fenton 1907.

"The vulgar notion that this verse embodies a divine prescription to the Israelites to drink freely of intoxicating liquors, along with their households until their money was expended . . . No man of ordinary prudence would now issue such an unguarded order. Who can picture without a strong moral revulsion, fathers, mothers and children, of both sexes and all ages; rejoicing together over flagons of intoxicating fluids."

Strong drink (*shekar*) is a generic term that could mean sweet or fermented juice from trees.

God is changeless. He cannot approve of drinking an alcoholic beverage in one place while condemning it in another. The only sensible conclusion is that both wine and strong drink can have two meanings depending on the context. I cannot agree with the NIV here, or in other places, where the Levite, the priest, who is to put the difference between the holy and the unholy, (Leviticus 10:10) is advised by God to *buy wine or other fermented drink*. To me, this borders on the blasphemous and cannot originally come from the Holy Bible. The text can not be fulfilled, eating fermented drink before the LORD? May God grant wisdom and love.

Princeton's Dr. Stephen M. Reynolds, one of the *NIV* translating committee members makes an admission, "My experience on this project . . . is that at least some human error entered into the final result (p.16). A ruling elder in the Presbyterian Church said that alcoholic drinks are permitted by the Bible because the *New International Version* in Deuteronomy 14:26, translates *shechar* as other fermented drinks."[36]

Strong drink was used for medicinal purposes.[37]

36. Reynolds 1983.
37. Geisler 1982.

Deuteronomy 14:26 refers to an unfermented beverage,[38] Van Impe and Campbell also translate as unfermented, and also indicate *sheckar* means sweet. These scholars and reference sources agree: Patton, Prof. Moses Stuart, the *Oxford English Dictionary* (1933), *The New American Encyclopedia Dictionary* (1906), *A New English Dictionary on Historical Principles,* (1893), and many others.

The Targums Of Onkelos and Jonathan say, "Wine, new and old."

For more *Shekar,* strong drink, please see notes on Leviticus 10:9.

Deuteronomy 16:13 (Nonalcoholic):

Thou shalt observe the feast of tabernacles seven days, after that thou hast gathered in thy corn and thy wine (*yeqeb*): (grape juice)

Fenton rendered this verse as: Harvesting of your corn and vintage. Vulgate, "Gather thy fruits."

Yeqeb suggests storage, not really a word for wine.

Generally modern translations do not mention wine. The *Living Bible* paraphrases, After the grain is threshed and the grapes have been pressed.

The *NIV* says, After you have gathered the produce of your threshing floor and wine press . . . In that area the *Bruce Bible Commentary* (1986) mentions olives and grapes.

(Physician: I'll tell you when you are sick enough for another shot of medication.)

There is no reason to call grapes and olives, *wine*. Most class these as nonalcoholic, as do Dr. Jack Van Impe and Roger Campbell.

The *King James Version* was accurate for its day, 380 years ago. However, we must realize that these men were working under King James. It was

38. Dr. Bacchiocchi of Andrews University in *Wine in the Bible*, 1989.

known that he liked his wine. Where there were questions of translation, did the translators feel under pressure to please their employer? Beside wine then was a generic word, alcoholic or nonalcoholic.

For today it should be, "Gathered in your corn and stored your vintage." All males were commanded to attend and to bring their offerings before the LORD.

In Genesis 27:28, when Isaac gave his blessing of corn and wine, the word translated wine was *tirosh*, meaning fresh grape produce, a real blessing.

In Exodus 12:8 the emphasis was on *unleavened*. None of the corruption of leaven.

In Leviticus 10:9 priests were not to drink wine or strong drink before going into the temple, on pain of death.

In Leviticus 2:13, all offerings were to be made with salt, presumably partially to kill ferment.

In Numbers 6:2, 3, 4, Nazarites were not to touch any forms of the grape lest they become contaminated.

God wanted no part of alcoholic wine. To bring it as a part of worship would be an affront to God. It had to be nonalcoholic. God's religious feast took its needs from the stores of unfermented wine, or grapes.

Deuteronomy 18:4 (Nonalcoholic):

> The firstfruit *also* of thy corn, of thy wine (*tirosh*), (grape juice) . . . shalt thou give him.

Fenton omits "*Of thy wine*" and uses "Your fruit" instead. Lee translates: *vine fruit*, 1868.

Tirosh is generally translated as *new wine*, when it ought to be *grapes or vine produce*.

Fresh corn could be firstfruit, so could grapes. But alcoholic wine is not a firstfruit. Firstfruit mean *fresh*, the best, before being picked over, before fermentation. They were to be given to God's designated servants, the Levites, and the priests. It would be inconsistent for God to give the priest something which he forbad their using on the pain of death before entering the tabernacle. *Tirosh* always means nonalcoholic (please see notes on Genesis 27:28).

Deuteronomy 21:20 (Alcoholic):

> . . . *he is* a glutton, and a drunkard.

And all the men of his city shall stone him with stones, that he die: so shalt thou put away evil from among you; and all Israel shall hear and fear.

Gluttony is bad. (My friend Dr. C. S. Lovett has written a diet book titled: *Help, the Devil Wants Me Fat.*)

Drunkenness is sinful. If this dictum of God's Law were followed today and drunkenness were punishable by death, our drunk driving problems would probably be solved. We are not advising it.

Be not among winebibbers; among riotous eaters of flesh: For the drunkard and the glutton shall come to poverty: . . . (Proverbs 23:20-21.)

Compare the penalty for drunk driving in other countries:

Bulgaria—Execution for second offense

France—Three year loss of license; one year jail term, $1000 fine.

El Salvador—First offense is the last. Execution by firing squad. (PAPA 1986, p.5)

In early American history, colonists were hard on those who were heavy drinkers. According to Dr. Jack Van Impe and Roger Campbell in *Alcohol: The Beloved Enemy* (1980, p.5), the first offense would probably result in the stocks or the whipping stool. A man (note, a man) might be sentenced to wear a *D* around his neck for one year, so everyone would know he was a drunkard. It was not usually then heard of a woman to be drinking.

Deuteronomy 28:38

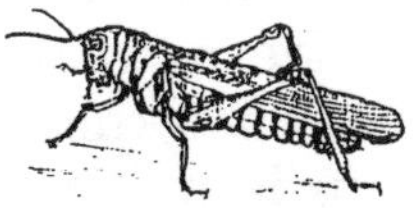

. . . the locust shall consume it.

(It is claimed many are killed by guns that were not loaded, and many by drivers that were . . .)

Deuteronomy 28:39 (Nonalcoholic):

Thou shalt plant vineyards, and dress *them*, but shalt neither drink of *the* wine (grape juice), nor gather *the grapes;* for the worms shall eat them.

Unfermented[39]

This is the curse of no grapes, prophesied for disobedience. Wine then was generic, alcoholic or not. Fermentation requires expressing the juice, keeping it at a proper temperature, with the right amount of water. Without a time period for fermentation there could be no alcoholic wine. That is quite different from drinking of *the wine*. Grapes on the vine do not ferment.

Deuteronomy 28:51 (Nonalcoholic):

And he shall eat the fruit of thy cattle, and the fruit of thy land, . . . which *also* shall not leave thee *either* corn, wine (*tirosh*) (grape juice), or oil, . . .

Your corn, your fruit and your oil.[40]

This is part of the continuance of the curse. In this case *tirosh* or fresh fruit is plunder, that the conqueror shall consume. *Tirosh* always refers to fresh juice or grape products that can be eaten. Raisins can be eaten. Alcohol can not be eaten. This is another indication that the word translated wine was actually nonalcoholic food. For further notes on *tirosh* see Genesis 27:28.

Deuteronomy 29:6 (Nonalcoholic):

Ye have not eaten bread, neither have ye drunk wine (yayin) (grape juice) or strong drink: . . . (*Shekar*) (sweet juice from trees). He hasn't let you settle down to grow grain for bread or grapes . . .[41]

Total desperation is forecast. There will be no time for fermentation of alcoholic wine.

Probably the most common use of *shekar* used in Bible times was palm-date wine.[42] Fermentation takes time, whether from grape juice or palm juice.

Deuteronomy 32:33 (Alcoholic):

Cobra
Critical and Popular Encyclopedia
1909, p. 170

Their wine *is* the poison of dragons, and the cruel venom of asps (cobras).

When alcoholic wine is used figuratively, it expresses a negative concept, not wine and roses. Here, used as the poison of a snake, it compares the evil deeds of Israel with the sins of Sodom and Gomorrah. To be bitten by an asp was usually immediately fatal. Wine is also poison. God says it. Science says it. As, a transient poison it effects every cell in the body, the brain first. It can poison to death. The liver tries hard to get rid of it.

Deuteronomy 32:38 (Probably Alcoholic):

Which did eat the fat of their sacrifices, *and* drank the wine of their drink offerings? let them rise up and help you, . . .

The heathen gods drank their drink offerings but where were they in Israel's hour of need? God is scolding Israel

39. Impe and Campbell 1980.
40. Fenton.
41. The Living Bible.
42. The International Standard Bible Encyclopedia.

for making drink offerings to heathen gods.

Deuteronomy 33:28 (Nonalcoholic):

> . . . the fountain of Jacob *shall be* upon a land of corn and wine (*Tirosh*) (grapes); . . .

Tirosh is always nonintoxicating.

Corn and grapes are solids, alcohol is not.

Fenton omits *wine* and uses the word *fruit* instead. As a symbol, corn and nonalcoholic wine refer to the best of the land. Alcoholic wine represents a curse.

Fountain is believed to be the blessings spreading out as the waters of a fountain.

Tirosh as a beverage always refers to fresh, storable pure grapes or juice. When stored, it is someones' possession, as here, a blessing of prosperity of grain and (*tirosh*) grapes.

Teachout translates this verse for modern Americans. Corn as we know it, was not known to the Hebrews; its origin is in America. So Teachout translates: A land of threshed grain and harvested grape juice.[43]

When we make changes from the King James Version we do not mean that the King James Version is incorrect. Its meaning is just not clear for our geographical area and times. Corn in England means wheat; in Scotland and Ireland it means oats. The term for our corn in Europe is generally maize.

When my father immigrated to America as a teenager from Denmark, he was asked what the cows were fed in Denmark. He replied, maize. He couldn't make his listeners believe him. With Danish pronunciation, maize sounded like mice.

---

43. Teachout 1983.

CHAPTER EIGHT

A Commentary of Each Use of the Word Wine in the Historical Books of the Old Testament

"If there has ever been a truth in God's Word which should have been settled and accepted long ago, it would be that God does not approve of the use of beverage alcohol by his saints in any age. The Old Testament and New Testament are clear on this matter.

"It is certainly true that the various available translations in the English language have helped to cause confusion. These translations have failed to take into account that the basic words in the original Hebrew and Greek and Latin texts which are translated by the English word "wine" actually refer to grape beverages which can be either fresh or fermented depending upon the context of the passage. Even the American dictionaries used to indicate that the word "wine" could refer either to fresh or to fermented grape drinks.

"This is the latest book to be published which makes this position clear. In it Dr. Hansen goes through the whole Bible and comments upon each verse which contains a reference to "wine", whether the word is used in the sense of fresh grape juice or in the sense of fermented wine. Because his commentary follows the biblical order, it is easy for the reader to immediately turn to whatever passage one would desire to have explained.

"The reader will especially appreciate Dr. Hansen's high view of God and his conviction that the Holy Scriptures are accurate and provide the only trustworthy guide for the practice of every serious believer."

Prof. Robert P. Teachout, S.T.M. Th.D
Dallas Theological Seminary
San Francisco Baptist Theological Seminary
Chairman, Old Testament Dept.
Detroit Baptist Theological Seminary
Chairman, O.T. Dept.
Pastor, Trinity Baptist Church, Taylor, Mich.
Author, *The Use of Wine in the Old Testament.*
WINE: The Biblical Imperative: Total Abstinence.

CHAPTER EIGHT THE HISTORICAL BOOKS OF THE OLD TESTAMENT

JOSHUA

Joshua 9:4,13 (Alcoholic):

> . . . and made as if they had been ambassadors, and took old sacks upon their asses, and wine bottles, old, and rent, and bound up;
> And these bottles of wine, which we filled, were new; and, behold, they be rent: and these our garments and our shoes are become old by reason of the very long journey.

The Gibeonites deceived the Israelites into making a treaty with them. It was quite possible that they brought the alcoholic wine that was so often used by heathen people.

Bottles here (*noad*) denote goat skins. They were stripped off without being cut up. They were tied where the legs and the lower parts and the tops were extracted. Such a goat skin would hold many of our bottles.[1]

JUDGES

Judges 9:13 (Nonalcoholic):

> And the vine said unto them, Should I leave my wine (grape juice) (*tirosh*), which cheereth God and man, and go to be promoted over the trees?

"Wine, in the Old Testament everywhere, when used for the Hebrew '*tirosh*' new wine." Strong's Exhaustive Concordance Comparative Concordance, p.151.

"*Tirosh*, new wine, sweet wine," Young's Analytical Concordance Index Lexicon, p. 50. "Tiros uniformily refers to fresh, pure grape juice." Teachout p.180.

Ferrar Fenton translates: "Should I leave my fruit which delights gods and men." Also, the Syriac and Arabian versions translate *tirosh* "my fruit." (L)

1. Butler 1994.

Some use this verse to defend drinking alcohol. But *tirosh* always means nonalcoholic. See notes on Genesis 27:28. So we dispense with the word wine here and use (*nonalcoholic*) fruit. It has nothing to do with drinking alcohol.

God can only be cheered or pleased with the fruit of the vine as the product of his own power, not man's work. Man is cheered when he sees the ripening clusters and when he partakes of it. It is obvious that God does not need alcohol to cheer Himself.

Judges 13:4,7,14 (Nonalcoholic):

> Now therefore beware, I pray thee, and drink not wine nor strong drink, and eat not any unclean *thing*:
> But he said unto me, Behold, thou shalt conceive, and bear a son; and now drink no wine nor strong drink, neither eat any unclean *thing*: for the child shall be a Nazarite to God from the womb to the day of his death.
> She may not eat of any *thing* that cometh of the vine, neither let her drink wine or strong drink, nor eat any unclean *thing*: all that I commanded her let her observe.

The Targumist renders *yayin* here, new wine, and we have seen before that *shekar* means sweet drink from trees. (L)

Lees renders this as: "Thou shalt not drink wine or sweet drink."[2] This was like a Nazarite command, not to have any thing to do with the fruit of the vine.

Women of Childbearing Age Shouldn't Drink

Mrs. Manoah, as Samson's mother, was to become the mother of the stron-

2. 1868.

gest man. Her Nazarite-like charge was only in relation to food and drink. As Samson's mother, she was to completely abstain from all alcoholic beverage or even the appearance of it.

Samson's mother refraining background, the Holy Spirit's strength, and his totally abstaining, all contributed to Samson becoming a man of terrific strength, who killed a thousand Philistines.

Abstinence for the sake of physical strength was practiced by the early Greek athletes. The famous Milo, six time champion of the Olympic Games in the sixth century B.C., was a total abstainer (Epictetus, Encheiridon Sec. 35).

As far back as 400 B.C., Plato, Aristotle, and later Plutarch and others, noticed the hereditary transmission of intemperate propensities.

Polybius, the Greek historian, 205 B.C., states, "Among the Romans the women were allowed to drink a wine which is called *passum*, made from raisins, which drink very much resembled . . . sweet wine and which men use for the purpose of allaying excessive thirst."[3] Juice from raisins will not ferment.

The Old Roman law of the twelve tables prohibited intoxicating wine to women, who by inference were permitted to drink any other drink (Lees 1868). The prohibition of intoxicating wines to women was enforced by the severest penalties.

Virgil, 70 B.C., in Georg, when referring to the boiled wine allowed to Roman women, stated, "The use of this inspissated juice became general." Boiling kills the enzymes, without enzymes, no fermentation for women to drink.

When I was a kid my father had a business place across the street from a tavern or saloon. I watched as drunks were kicked out and left to lie on the sidewalk, but not women. Ladies usually didn't go into saloons in those days. There was a saying "If a woman smokes, she'll drink. If she'll drink, she'll do anything."

With the repeal of Prohibition, we have the old dirty saloon, but also the dirty family booze tavern for men and women. Repeal was not progression, but regression, strictly evil, of the devil.

"Not only does alcohol kill the brain cells of pregnant women, but one drink penetrates the placenta and destroys brain cells in the fetus. Much of this results in a great percentage of mentally retarded children for society to support."[4]

Our country has become more enlightened and compassionate. Woman should have the same rights as men. Though women give birth to a batch of idiots, so what? Don't we have institutions to care for them?

Now society has tended to approve of moderate drinking for expectant mothers, despite warnings from older civilizations. It wasn't until the 1970's that the old warning was rediscovered by a University of Washington team.

In the survey, "The results were striking." Children from the drinking mothers had shorter noses, flatter midface areas, and smaller heads, indicating smaller brains. The average IQ ranged from 60 to 70; some were as low as 30.

While children from heavy drinkers were the worst, there were bad results from women who had no more than two drinks a day."[5]

What can happen to the fetus of a moderate drinking mother? Maisel's scientific report in the *Reader's Digest* states that a moderate drinker ". . . may

3. Polybius B. 205 B.C.

4. Lees 1868.

5. Impe 1980.

incur some loss of irreplaceable brain cells every time he drinks." So it only takes one drink to do brain damage. This becomes of greater concern to the fetus. A federal study shows "Women appear to be less resistant to illnesses caused by alcohol consumption . . . a more rapid and severe onset . . . then men."[6]

Many women who do drink believe they'll stop as soon as they become pregnant. "I'll quit when I get pregnant," seems to be a common belief. However, "Many women don't know when they get pregnant . . . don't know it for weeks. By the time they realize it, the alcohol could have already caused irreversible damage to the fetus."[7]

Sam Rhine says, "Fifty percent of birth defects could be prevented. Alcohol harms more babies than all other drugs combined." He cited statistics which say in Indiana, one baby born every two days is retarded because of alcohol abuse.

"Alcohol is the second leading cause of mental retardation in the United States."[8]

Infants born to alcoholic fathers are generally smaller than those born to fathers who do not use alcohol. The same applies to babies born to mothers who use alcohol even before becoming pregnant.

"Some babies smell like powder, some like cheap wine,"[9]

Unfortunately, there are now also babies born addicted to cocaine (crack), babies shaking like a leaf, and crying for help. Every drug affects the unborn child. They are born with smaller heads. They are tomorrow's candidates for a welfare life.

6. Centers for Disease Control 2/13/1987.

7. Sam Rhine, Geneticist at Noble Centers and the Generic Ed Center.

8. Rhine 1986.

9. Charles Turham with Elizabeth Schaffer in *Newsweek* 7/31/1989.

Judges 19:19 (Nonalcoholic):

> . . . and there is bread and wine (grape juice) also for me . . .

With all the main eight ways the Ancients had of keeping wine from fermenting, travelers could keep their wine sweet. Travelers would be more likely to carry nourishing beverage to go with the bread.

I & II SAMUEL

I Samuel 1:14-15 (Alcoholic and Nonalcoholic):

> And Eli said unto her, How long wilt thou be drunken? put away thy wine from thee. And Hannah answered and said, No, my lord, I *am* a woman of a sorrowful spirit: I have drunk neither wine nor strong drink, but have poured out my soul before the LORD.

When Hannah prayed silently with her lips moving, Eli mistakenly thought that she was drunk. Hannah protested that she had not been drinking.

Perhaps one reason God chose Hannah as Samuel's mother was because she did not drink alcoholic beverages. (Regarding women and alcohol, see notes on Judges 13:4,7,14.)

I Samuel 1:24 (Nonalcoholic):

> And when she had weaned him, she took him up with her, with three bullocks, and one ephah of flour, and a bottle of wine (grape juice), and brought him unto the house of the LORD in Shiloh: and the child *was* young.

Nebel

Hannah had orders to put away wine, even though she was innocent.

Bottles of wine were really goat skins. A bottle here *nebel* of wine a substantial earthen vesell. Reynolds

Remember, wine meant either fresh grape juice or fermented, like our word *punch* can be alcoholic or nonalcoholic. Their bottles for fluids in general were made out of the skins of goats, stripped off without being cut up. In the places where the legs were extracted, the lower part and the tops were tied. Such a goat skin would hold many of our bottles.

Wine (with leaven) was not to be brought to the house of the Lord (Leviticus 2:11).

To exclude airborne yeast, the skins were lined and sealed with pitch. The consecration offering was constituted of three elements: bullocks, juice, and flour. God condemned alcoholic beverages ("Look not thou upon the wine . . ." Proverbs 23:31), and the priests were forbidden to use it in the tabernacle ("Thou mayest not eat within thy gates . . . thy wine," Deuteronorny 12:17); therefore, this reference appears to be a nonalcoholic drink.

I Samuel 10:3 (Nonalcoholic):

> Then shalt thou go on forward from thence, and thou shalt come to the plain of Tabor, and there shall meet thee three men going up to God to Bethel, one carrying three kids, and another carrying three loaves of bread, and another carrying a bottle (nebel) of wine (grape juice) (wine skin):

The LXX says wine skin.

Versions vary here, The Vulgate translates *flagon of wine*, as raisin cake, certainly different from a bottle of wine. We feel it should be a measure of grape juice.

Possibly this referred to the thanksgiving offering. See also Leviticus 2:11 which describes an offering to God, forbidden to be used in the temple.

I Samuel 16:20 (Nonalcoholic):

> And Jesse took an ass *laden* with bread, and a bottle (wine skin) of wine, and a kid, and sent *them* by David his son unto Saul.

Kings were not to cloud their judgment with alcohol, so the wine was nonalcoholic (Proverbs 31:4). Alcohol would weaken judgment.

I Samuel 25:18 (Nonalcoholic):

> Then Abigail made haste, and took two hundred loaves, and two bottles of wine (grape juice), and five sheep . . . and . . . laid *them* on asses.

Abigail no doubt realized David and his soldiers needed nourishment, such as sweet grape juice would be. Her peace offering worked. David cooled down, he eventually married the *gal*. (See I Samuel 16:20, previous reference, regarding another peace offering.)

I Samuel 25:37 (Alcoholic):

> But . . . when the wine was gone out of Nabal, and his wife had told him these things, that his heart died within him, and he became *as* a stone.

This incident followed a drunken feast. Heavy drinking had not led him to generosity, or justice, or to health. His nervous system and heart were too enfeebled to recover from the shock.

II Samuel 6:19 (Nonalcoholic):

***Ash-ee-shaw'* (Heb. אֲשִׁישָׁה).**

> And he dealt among all the people, . . . to every one a cake of bread, and a good piece of *flesh*, and a flagon (cake) of wine *(ashishah)* (raisins) (2 pints).

Flagon is a measure, *ashishah* is raisin.

In the King James Version the word translated *wine* in this verse refers to raisin cake, as it also is rendered in many new versions. *NASB, NIV,* and *NKJV* do not mention wine here. They translate the word, a cake of raisins.

See also the Song of Solomon 2:5, and Hosea 3:1 for raisin cakes.

The raisin cakes were nutritive delicacies given to weary travelers.

II Samuel 13:28 (Alcoholic):

> . . . Mark ye now when Amnon's heart is merry with wine, . . . kill him, . . .

Becoming drunk is often the way for an individual to place his life in jeopardy; a good reason for abstinence, especially when driving a car. Half of all highway fatalities are related to alcohol and innocent people are often killed because of it.

II Samuel 16:1 (Nonalcoholic):

> And when David . . . Ziba . . . met him, with . . . a bottle (skin) of wine (grape juice).

Ziba's gift of food and drink was presented for travel nourishment for David and his men in the desolate wilderness. All the items offered were provisions which would foster health. To have given [alcoholic] wine at such a time would show lack of wisdom and might have been subversively interpreted by David.

The faint and weary needed refreshment of the kind grape juice could give, rather than a stupefying drink.

KINGS

II Kings 18:32 (Nonalcoholic):

> Until I come and take you away to a land like your own land, a land of corn and wine (*tirosh*) (grapes), . . .

F. R. Lees translates, "vine fruit."

Tirosh, or fresh grape juice, was a term used by God in telling Israel that He would bless them. It represented God's blessings. *Tirosh* always means unfermented. (Please see Genesis 27:28.)

CHRONICLES

I Chronicles 9:29 (Nonalcoholic):

> *Some* of them also *were* appointed to oversee the vessels, and all the instruments of the sanctuary, and the fine flour, and the wine (grapes), and the oil, and the frankincense, and the spices.

The priests were not to use alcoholic wine before going into the sanctuary, on pain of death (Leviticus 10:9). Yet they were to bring wine to the LORD as a drink offering (Exodus 29:40). What if a priest took some alcoholic wine, either without thinking, or by temptation? And why would God want a wine that He so vehemently condemned? For me to think of all Bible wine as alcoholic is contradictory, and incompatible with the Bible's teaching against alcoholic wine.

All of the above are solids, we presume, grape juice boiled down to a solid is meant here. Alcohol boils away. Boiled down juice would be nonalcoholic. Alcoholic wine is not food for sober thought.

I Chronicles 12:40 (Nonalcoholic):

> [And they brought David] . . . meat, meal, cakes of figs, and bunches of raisins, and wine (grape juice), and oil, . . .

In Psalms 60:3 and 75:8 David characterizes alcoholic wine as a punishment for evil. Here it is a food, so nonalcoholic.

I Chronicles 16:3 (Nonalcoholic):

> And he dealt to every one . . . and a good piece of flesh, and a flagon of *wine* (*ashishah*) (raisin cakes).

Fenton translates "The best of the corn and fruit."

We would drop flagon of wine and use raisin cakes as others do.

In modern versions, wine is not mentioned here. *Ashishah* should be translated as raisin cake or raisin drink, as in *The Living Bible, NASB, NIV,* etc. Raisins and raisin drink are nonalcoholic.

I Chronicles 27:27 (Nonalcoholic):

> . . . over the increase of the vineyards for the wine (grape juice) cellars *was* Zabdi the Shiphmite:

Sacrificial wine was necessary the year round, so it had to be stored. The penalty was death for the priest to bring alcoholic wine into the temple or tabernacle. It should be safe to assume this verse refers to nonalcoholic wine (Leviticus 10:9 and Ezekiel 44:21). "Grape juice, which is sealed to keep all air out and which is kept in a cool, dry cellar will not ferment if it is first properly treated (Malone Greek Professor Dr. Byron Osborne, my early Greek professor).

II Chronicles 2:10, 15 (Nonalcoholic):

> And, behold, I will give to thy servants, . . . twenty thousand baths of wine (grape juice) . . .
> . . . and the barley, the oil, and the wine (grapes), which my lord hath spoken of, . . .

A bath was equal to seven gallons and four pints. No employer wants his help inebriated. Laws have made employers responsible for illegal acts committed while under the influence of alcohol provided by employers at parties.

II Chronicles 11:11 (Nonalcoholic):

> And he fortified the strong holds, and put captains in them, and store of victual, and of oil and wine (grape juice).

Food and drink were stored so that the people would have the necessities of living in case of Judah involved in a war against Israel. Grape juice provides nourishment. Alcohol is not a necessary or nourishing beverage.

II Chronicles 31:5 (Nonalcoholic):

> And as soon as the commandment came abroad, the children of Israel brought in abundance the firstfruits of corn, wine (grapes) (*Tirosh*), and oil, and honey, and of all the increase of the field; and the tithe of all *things* brought they in abundantly.

Lees translates, "corn, vine fruit, instead of wine."

Firstfruit is nonalcoholic fresh fruit. The Lord deserves the best, the firstfruits, the new wine which is the uncontaminated grape without spot or blemish. *Tirosh*, translated new wine in later translations, refers to nonalcoholic drinks (See Genesis 27:28).

II Chronicles 32:28 (Nonalcoholic):

> Storehouses also for the increase of corn, and wine (*Tirosh*) (grape harvest), and oil; . . .

Lees again translates as "corn, vine fruit, instead of wine" (1868).

It is *new wine* in the *NIV*. *Tirosh* is always nonalcoholic.

Grapes were nutritious; it was not necessary to store alcohol.

For the nonalcoholic meaning of *Tirosh* see Genesis 27:28. For eight ways grape juice could be kept fresh, see Chapter 6.

EZRA

Ezra 6:9 (Nonalcoholic):

Chaldee term *Cheh'mar*

> And that which they have need of, both young bullocks, and rams, and lambs, for the burnt offerings of the God of heaven, wheat, salt, wine (grape juice), and oil, according to the appointment of the priests which *are* at Jerusalem, let it be given them day by day without fail:

(*Chamar*) or (*Hamar*) is wrongly translated wine here.

Hamar is a genaric Arabic Chaldean word used for preserved grape juice or wine, here it is grape juice.

Grape juice was necessary and nutritious; alcohol was not needed for food, or for offerings to God. Offerings with leaven are not to be made (Exodus 23:18 also Leviticus 2:11). (See the following verses Ezra 7:21-22 for description of *Chamar*).

Ezra 7:21-22 (Nonalcoholic):

> And I, *even* I Artaxerxes the king, do make a decree . . . that whatsoever Ezra the priest . . . shall require of you, it be done speedily, Unto an hundred talents of silver, and to an hundred measures of wheat, and . . . wine (grapes) (*Chamar*), and . . . oil, and salt . . .

Chamar or *chemer* is descriptive of the foaming appearance of the juice of the grape newly expressed. It is *pure* juice in its fresh, foaming condition. "The compilers of the Talmud considered *khamra* as a 'sweet wine.' "[10]

Liebig, the German chemist, says, "Vegetable juice, in general, becomes turbid when in contact with the air before fermentation commences."[11]

The Bible Commentary says, "Thus it appears foam or turbidness, what the Hebrews called *KHEMER*, and applied to the foaming *blood* of the vine is no proof of alcohol being present."[12]

Apparently we have another generic word here. Teachout writes, "Although the Aramaic *hamar* can refer to wine as an intoxicant, it can also denote grape juice as well. Twice the word is used in the Book of Ezra." Since the required libation was grape juice, it is obvious that the word *hamar* here does not refer to wine." pp.165,166.

What is meant in this verse is sweet grape juice. Its use here was for sacrificial worship to God who is opposed to wine as an alcoholic beverage in offerings (Leviticus 2:11).

10. The Critical and Popular Encyclopedia 1909.

11. Liebig, Chemistry, 3d Ed.

12. Lees 1868, Premlin footnote p.XX.

NEHEMIAH

Nehemiah 2:1 (Alcoholic or Nonalcoholic, uncertain):

> And it came to pass in the month of Nisan, in the twentieth year of Artaxerxes the king, *that* wine *was* before him: and I took up the wine, and gave *it* unto the king . . .

Some heathen kings were known for their love of alcoholic drinks, where it was allowed for them. Possibly this was alcoholic. Possibly not.

Nehemiah 5:11 (Nonalcoholic):

> Restore, I pray you, to them, even this day, their lands, their vineyards, their oliveyards, and their houses, also the hundredth *part* of the money, and of the corn, the wine (*tirosh*) (grapes), and the oil, that ye exact of them.

Lees translates, "The vine fruit," [not wine] and the olive and orchard fruit."

Tirosh is always nonalcoholic. The *NIV* and *NASB* translate it *new wine*.

The Arabic uses *etzer*, which is always expressed as juice or fresh juice. It is doubtful that the virtuous Nehemiah would request restoration of the poisoned kind.

Nehemiah 5:15 (Nonalcoholic):

> But the former governors that *had been* before me . . . had taken . . . bread and wine (grape juice), beside forty shekels of silver; . . .

When linked with bread, wine usually meant unfermented, or food, as we use the expression *food and drink*.

Nehemiah 5:18 (Nonalcoholic):

> Now *that* which was prepared *for me* daily was one ox and . . . sheep; also fowls . . . and . . . all sorts of wine (grape juice) . . .

Because of the evident ethics of Nehemiah and the divine prohibition against alcohol in worship and, especially for rulers, and for all Hebrews in Proverbs 23:29-31, this wine should have been nonalcoholic.

Nehemiah 10:37 (Nonalcoholic):

> And *that* we should bring the firstfruits of our dough, and our offerings, and the fruit of all manner of trees, of wine (*tirosh*) (grape juice) and of oil, . . .

The Vulgate does not use wine here but, "of vintage fruit also and of oil." Grapes are a first fruit. Alcohol wine is not.

F. R. Lees "vine fruit and olive and orchard fruit" Notice how the kings men preferred the word wine.

Wine, here is *tirosh* and is fresh, always unfermented.

Fenton said the firstfruits amounted to one percent of the money, of the corn, and fruits.

When reference is made to dough or ground meal, the verse is certainly speaking of fresh, natural, unprocessed food, as *tirosh* always is.

Nehemiah 10:39 (Nonalcoholic):

> . . . shall bring the offering of the corn, of the new wine (*tirosh*), (sweet grape) . . .

Note "new wine", as in so many translations of *tirosh*. It is strange that Jerome after translating as *vintage fruit* in verse 37 should slip back to *vindemiae* here.

Tirosh is always unfermented. New wine without time to ferment is always fresh and sweet.

Nehemiah 13:5 (Nonalcoholic):

> And he had prepared for him a great chamber, where aforetime they laid the meat offerings, the frankincense, and the vessels, and the tithes of the corn, the new wine (*Tirosh*) (grape juice), and the oil, which was commanded *to be given* to the Levites, . . .

New wine, follows *mustrum* of Continental versions.

Tirosh has never been connected with drunkenness.

Nehemiah 13:12 (Nonalcoholic):

> Then brought all Judah the tithe of the corn and the new wine (*Tirosh*) (grapes) and the oil unto the treasuries.

In both references (Nehemiah 13:5 and 13:12), Fenton translates *tirosh* as fruit, rather than the new wine. *Tirosh* is always nonalcoholic.

Nehemiah 13:15 (Nonalcoholic):

Wine Press. Heb. גַּת, *gath*, an upper vat

> In those days saw I in Judah *some* treading wine (*gath*) presses on the sabbath, and bringing in sheaves, and lading asses; as also wine (grape juice), grapes, and figs, and all *manner* of burdens, . . . and I testified *against them* in the day wherein they sold victuals.

The technical Hebrew word for "grape press" is *gat*.

In the immediate demand and competition, it is probable here that the freshly pressed grape juice from the vine presses was sold as fresh juice without time for fermentation.

To be alcoholic wine would take "ten to fourteen days for fermentations," Easley's Winery, Indianapolis, Indiana.

ESTHER

Esther 1:7 (Alcoholic):

> And they gave *them* drink in vessels of gold, . . . and royal wine in abundance, . . . (See below in Esther 1:10)

We have labeled this alcoholic as have Van Impe and Campbell. (The Targumist tells a strange story of how the vessels from Jerusalem turned the kings vessels to lead, and turned the kings wine into fresh grape juice.)

Esther 1:10-11 (Alcoholic):

> On the seventh day, when the heart of the king was merry with wine, he commanded . . . the . . . chamberlains . . . To bring Vashti the queen . . .

The Vulgate, "More jovial."

It takes the *Living Bible* (1971) to state it succinctly in today's English. "On the final day when the king was feeling high, half drunk from wine, he told the . . . aides . . . to bring Queen Vashti . . ."[13]

Alcohol definitely numbs the brain!

Esther 5:6 (Alcoholic):

> And the king said unto Esther at the banquet of wine, What *is* thy petition? and it shall be granted thee: . . . even to the half of the kingdom it shall be performed. (See Esther 7:2 below)

Esther 7:2 (Alcoholic):

> And the king said again unto Esther on the second day at the banquet of wine, What *is* thy petition, queen Esther? . . . and it shall be performed, *even* to the half of the kingdom.

The king must have been *half drunk* at each of these times for him to be so rash as to give away half his kingdom!

Esther 7:7-8 (Alcoholic):

> And the king arising from the banquet of wine in his wrath *went* into the palace garden: . . . Then the king returned out of the palace garden into the place of the banquet of wine; . . .

Unfermented wine was used primarily with food to quench thirst and to give nourishment. The banquet of wine was prepared to make one feel good, to get rid of worries and inhibitions.

These references are to alcoholic wine.

(See Judges 13:4,7,14)

13. The Living Bible, 1971.

CHAPTER NINE

A COMMENTARY ON
EACH USE OF THE WORD WINE IN
THE POETRY BOOKS
Old Testament

I have made some notes on your Chapter 9, which by the way, I like very much and pray that it will do much good. You make many excellent points for the cause. I feel confident that your efforts will be rewarded by our Heavenly Father.

May God richly bless you in your labors for biblically based total abstinence from alcoholic beverages, and in your presentation of the Gospel through one of the most marvelous of God's created works, the birds.

Prof. Stephen M. Reynolds, M.A. Ph.D
Princeton University
Lincoln University
Faith Theological Seminary
Crozer Theological Seminary
Gordon Conwell Theological Seminary.
NIV, New International Version, Staff
Author
The Biblical Approach to Alcohol
Alcohol and The Bible
Contributor
The Journal of Biblical Literature
Zeitschrift fur die neutestamentliche Wessenschaft

CHAPTER NINE
THE POETRY BOOKS OF THE OLD TESTAMENT

JOB

Job 1:13 and 1:18 (Nonalcoholic):

> And there was a day when his sons and his daughters *were* eating and drinking wine (grape juice) in their eldest brother's house:

Some question the validity of the word wine here. Teachout writes: "There is no need to interpret the word [*yayin*] as wine."[1]

The Syrian omits all mention of wine in verses 13 and 18. Also the LXX has just *pinonton*, drinking. Accordingly the *Living Bible*, paraphrased, "Sons and Daughters were feasting in their older brother's house."

Eating and drinking in this case as in others, probably means food and drink taken for nourishment, not alcoholic beverages which have few nourishing qualities. There is no condemnation or sad results in this instance, as there often was with the sad results of alcoholic wine, such as Noah's drunkenness, and Lot's sexual aberration.

Job 1:13 and 1:18 (Nonalcoholic):

> . . . Thy sons and thy daughters were eating and drinking wine (grape juice) in their eldest brother's house:

(This is the same as Job 1:13 above.)

The tremendous pressure of carbon dioxide ($C0_2$) resulting from fermentation would break any wine skin, new or old.

Jesus himself stated this fact in Matthew 9:17, where he said, "Neither do men put new wine into old bottles: else the bottles break, and the wine runneth out, and the bottles perish: but they put new wine into new bottles, and both are preserved." New wine is *oinos neos*, must, clear fresh droppings without any pulp from around the skin or the seeds. The pulp contains the enzymes that make fermentation possible. If the new wine does not contain any pulp, it will never ferment, like the Welch's grape juice in your refrigerator will never ferment. It can not. New bottles have no residue of fermentation. Elihu, here, is contradicting the *popular view* of Matthew 9:17, that new wine should be put in new bottles to allow for expansion. Without a vent, as Elihu said, it would burst, as would any wineskin, new or used, if fermenting liquid were sealed in. (See Matthew 9:17, chap. 11)

To keep new wine (grape juice) from breaking the wineskin, it had to be put in a new *clean* one, to be sure there was no fermenting or enzyme particles in it. This would contaminate the fresh juice and could cause fermentating to begin, causing expansion of the wineskin, and ultimate breakage. The juice had to be filtered to get out all bulk which contained the enzymes, without which there could be no fermentation.

Elihu was saying that he would burst if not allowed to say, or let out, what he so strongly felt he must say.

1. p. 292.

Study Notes

PSALMS

Psalms 4:7 (Nonalcoholic):

> Thou hast put gladness in my heart, more than in the time *that* their corn and their wine (grapes) (*tirosh*) increased.

"Their wine," *tirosh*: Young's Index Lexicon: "new wine, sweet wine." p.50 Must, "New wine": Webster: "grape or other juice before it has fermented." Funk and Wagnall's Unabridged Dictionary: yr. 1913 "Fermented or unfermented juice of the grape or other fruit" p.2718.

Lee translates, "Corn and their vine fruit abounded."

Tirosh is never connected with intoxication. Scholars agree on this, but usually call it *new wine*, which is why versions such as the *NASB* and the *NIV* read "new wine". *The Living Bible* says, "bountiful crops". Even better, Fenton translates, "When our corn and fruits increase."

The wine in this case refers to actual fruit produce, such as corn and grapes. See Isaiah 65:8: "The new wine found in the cluster." Grapes, not wine, are found in the cluster.

Psalms 60:3 (Alcoholic):

> Thou hast shewed thy people hard things: thou hast made us to drink the wine of astonishment.

Fermented wine here is a symbol of God's punishment. One commentary states that in this instance "the people were broken and reeling like a drunken man", and had gathered in the temple for a ceremony of national lamentation.

Psalms 75:8 (Alcoholic):

> For in the hand of the LORD there is a cup, and the wine is red; it is full of mixture; and he poureth out of the same: but the dregs thereof, all the wicked of the earth shall wring them out, and drink them.

Usually, alcoholic wine is a symbol of God's punishment. Contrast that with the nonalcoliolic wine in Psalms 4:7, wherein God puts gladness in the hearts of his people.

The BDB's Lexicon renders the verb "is red" by ferment, boil or foam up. The Arabic root meaning of ferment is leaven. God is more interested in fermentation than in color. (See the notes on Proverbs 23:31.)

Psalms 78:65 (Nonalcoholic):

> Then the Lord awaked as one out of sleep, and like a mighty man that shouteth by reason of wine.

Shouteth (*ranan*):, BDB reads, "give a ringing cry in joy, adulation especially in praise to Yahweh" (p. 943). "A warrior refreshed by sleep and invigorated by refreshing grape juice" (Dr. Charles J. Butler, 4/15/94).

Psalms 104:15 (Nonalcoholic):

> And wine (grape juice) that maketh glad the heart of man . . .

Fenton renders this: "Fruit to gladden man's heart" (1903).

Unadulterated wine, nonalcoholic, exhilarates and invigorates, it makes him cheerful, and provides for the continuance of that cheerfulness by strengthening the muscles, and bracing the nerves."[2]

Such is the difference between bad and good wine, the alcoholic and the nonalcoholic.

Baptist Seminary Professor Teachout states, "If in some contexts, such as Psalms 104:15 and Deuteronomy 14:26, Yahweh specifically approves of wine for man's consumption, while in others (many cited already), He vehemently condemns it, then an obvious logical resolution would be that wine can refer

2. Clarke 1823.

to two beverages distinctly different in nature and effect: grape juice and wine."[3]

From the *International Bible Commentary:* "Home of beast, bird, and man: vineyard, olive grove and corn field are pledges of His caring and proofs of His wish for man to be healthy, happy and high in morale."[4]

Healthy: Grape juice is healthy, but alcohol, as poison, deteriorates and brings death.

Happy: Grape juice gives lasting happiness. Alcohol brings sorrow.

Morale: The abstainer has high morale. Alcohol does nothing to improve morale.

PROVERBS

Proverbs 3:10 (Nonalcoholic):

> . . . and thy presses shall burst out with new wine (grape juice) (*tirosh*).

Alcoholic wine does not come out of the presses. "It takes 10 to 14 days for grape juice to be fermented", (Easleys Winery, Indianapolis, Indiana.) This is one of the rare cases where *tirosh* means juice, usually it means either fresh grapes or a dehydrated form for storage.

Newer versions usually translate *tirosh* as *new wine*.

Naturally, just coming out of the presses, it would be fresh, unfermented, and ready to drink in that state. Properly cared for, it could remain nonalcoholic.

Wine Press

But, coming out of the presses it could be subject to fermentation if the air could get to it with yeast spores, and if the temperature were somewhere between 45°F and 75°F, depending on the proximity to sea level. For, coming out of presses without straining, some of the pulp with its enzymes would be with the juice. Some means would have to be used to keep it fresh. When it was desired to keep the *must* fresh without pulp, squeezing through a strainer was often done by hand. The pure juice, without the pulp, does not ferment.

New wine here is the translation from *tirosh*, as in the translation in ten other places in the Authorized Version. Twenty-six times it is translated in the *AV* as *wine,* and once as *sweet wine* (Micah 6:15). It is *sweet wine, Young's Lexicon*, p.50, nonalcoholic *Funk and Wagnalls.* Often it is boiled, thick and sweet.

Proverbs 4:17 (Alcoholic):

> For they . . . drink the wine of violence.

Alcoholic wine is a cause of violence and woe. This is the conclusion of a wicked man's lifestyle. We used to talk about sinning, now we talk about lifestyles. But however we try to excuse it, alcohol is responsible for half of the highway deaths, and is involved in most violent crimes.

Proverbs 9:1,2,5 (Nonalcoholic):

> WISDOM hath builded her house, . . . she hath mingled her wine (juice); she hath also furnished her table. Come, eat of my bread, and drink of the wine (grape juice) *which* I have mingled.

This is a blessing to which friends are invited by the woman whose name is Wisdom. Often, grape juice was boiled down to preserve it from fermenting and to need less space for storage. Later the syrup had to be mingled (mixed) with water for drinking. Also, aromatic spices may have been mixed in to gratify the taste with

3. Teachout 1979.
4. Bruce 1986.

delicate flavor, but not to fire the blood with alcohol. (Henry, Vol. 3 p.849) According to Homer, Pramnian and Hippocrates, wines required twenty parts of water to one of wine. (Lees 1882) See "Boiling" in Chapter 6.

Wisdom is consistent with God's holy character. In verses 4, 5 and 6 of this chapter is found:

> . . . for him that wanteth understanding, she saith to him, Come, eat of my bread, and drink of the wine . . .; go in the way of understanding.

Taste of the true pleasures that are to be found in the knowledge and fear of God.

Proverbs 20:1 (Alcoholic):

> Wine is a mocker, strong drink is raging: and whosoever is deceived thereby is not wise.

The American Revised Version translates, "strong drink is a brawler."

Wisdom says to be not deceived by alcoholic beverages. The lack of wisdom causes one to become enticed by alcoholic beverages, which ensures that everything done or said while under its influence is folly.

"Wine is a mocker." The Scripture outrightly condemns its use, not its abuse.

Dr. R. Laird Harris of St. Louis', Covenant Theological Seminary points out to me that most ancient alcoholic wines, without distillation, were only 4 to 7% alcohol. In a letter to the author, he remarks, "The Jews cut this wine with two or three parts of water . . . which would hardly make an intoxicating product." Certainly this bears no relation to the high alcoholic content of today's potent wines.

"Some table wines used in foreign countries are either nonalcoholic or so low in alcohol it is hard to detect that they have any". (Robert Bruce) "The modern Italian table *vino cotto* (boiled) has been found by chemical analysis not to contain a particle of alcohol."[5] Alcohol boils away easily at 78.4°C (172°F), well before water, which boils at 100 C (212°F) at sea level.

Proverbs 21:17 (Alcoholic):

> He that loveth pleasure shall be a poor man: he that loveth wine and oil shall not be rich.

Let us look at the context. The preceding verse (21:16) states, 'The man that wandereth out of the way of understanding shall remain in the congregation of the dead.'

The following verse (21:18) is: "The wicked shall be a ransom for the righteous, and the transgressor for the upright." All three verses describe one who does not follow the straight and narrow, so in the context, it refers to an alcoholic wino.

Money spent for alcohol is wasted; heavy drinking leads to poverty.

Proverbs 23:20-21 (Alcoholic):

> Be not among wine-bibbers; . . . For the drunkard and the glutton shall come to poverty: . . .

Cost of Alcohol

This is so universally true; we have all seen it happen. The cost is so large that we cannot properly conceive of it. *Forty-three billion a year*, according to the National Council on Alcoholism. We all pay for it in our taxes for welfare, for the police and other related ways. Can a value be put upon the thousand of innocent victims of drunk drivers? On the application for a driver's license in Michigan, one question asks, "How many drinks are necessary before a drivers judgement is distorted?" The

5. Field.

answer is ONE DRINK. I have not heard of any heavy drinker of grape juice coming to poverty. Paul indicates in I Corinthians 6:10 the greatest poverty of all: "Nor . . . drunkards, . . . shall inherit the kingdom of God." I Corinthians 6:10.

Proverbs 23:29-30 (Alcoholic):

Meh'sek (Heb. מֶסֶךְ), once translated 'mixture.

> Who hath woe? who hath sorrow? who hath contentions? who hath babbling? who hath wounds without cause? who hath redness of eyes? They that tarry long at the wine; they that go to seek mixed wine (*mimsak*).

Sorrow and woe exists for those who tarry over wine. It is acknowledged that drunkenness brings sorrows and woe, but Solomon says that mixed wine can also cause sorrow and woe. Two opposite reasons existed for mixing wine. They were:

1. To prevent fermentation, juices were boiled into a highly condensed or concentrated form, often thick enough to eat with a spoon. When needed as beverage, this was diluted with water, sometimes as much 20 parts water to one part concentrate. There was no more fermentation after boiling. (Boiling kills yeast and enzymes. Enzymes do not return.)
2. Or, as here, to create a most palatable drink, spices and herbs were added and no caution to prevent fermentation. This enticed people to tarry long over it and become drunk, as is evident in this alcoholic reference.

Ancients cup found in a tomb in Laconia in 1889

If alcoholic wine is a mocker and drinking it is sinful, then drinking even in moderation is wrong as well. There is no Biblical reference as to how much alcohol is allowed.

Proverbs 23:31 (Alcoholic):

> Look not thou upon the wine when it is red, when it giveth his colour in the cup, *when* it. moveth itself aright.

"Look," according to Webster, "Is to direct one's attention mentally on something"; "To direct one's eyes on." According to *Funk and Wagnells*, it means "To consider," "regard," "expect," "pay attention to." "To search; seek," "anticipation." English man *Adam Clarke of Clarkes Commentaries* writes "Let neither the color, the odor . . . entice thee to drink."

Commentator Matthew Henry: "Looks so well it even says 'Come and drink me' " "Covet not that which pleases the eye."

Van Impe

LOOK NOT. Dr. Jack Van Impe writes in *Alcohol: The Beloved Enemy*. "The word 'look' as Solomon used it means 'to lust for' or 'desire'. He is simply saying that we are to have nothing to do with wine after it has fermented."[6]

According to Reynolds, Look not is an *absolute command*. It will not be taken

6. 1980.

any lighter than in Genesis 19:17, where Lot's wife was turned to a pillar of salt for disobeying, "don't look." The Biblical Approach to Alcohol.

Red Is Not Important

We notice that the word red is not in this verse in the *Latin Vulgate of Jerome,* the Septuagint or in the *Judeo—Spanish or Ladino.*

Princeton Ph.D. Stephen M. Reynolds calls attention to the fact that God is not interested in color. "Does only red wine bite like a serpent?" He believes somewhere along the line, the words *it is* and *red* have been inserted. The Hebrew stem of the verb is reflexive. He then would translate, "Look not on the grape juice *when it 'makes itself'* (leavened). ". . . therefore, the rather difficult term *yithaddam* must mean (the grape juice) makes itself [leavened] or alcoholic and not it makes itself red." "Just ask yourself which command is fitting for our wise God to give. 'Don't look at red wine,' or 'Don't look at grape juice when it makes itself alcoholic.' "[7]

Proverbs 23:32 (Alcoholic):

> At the last it biteth like a serpent, and stingeth like an adder.

Egyptian Adder

As a mocker, (Proverbs 20:1) wine ridicules God's highest creation. Wine lures one into drink by promising celebration, but the ridicule comes when the drinker realizes he has been duped. There is then no celebration; only remorse. This verse carries the analogy even further, to that of snakes and adders. The adder snakes of North America are harmless, and valuable as rodent killers. But in the Holy Land, and in Africa, the adder is a very poisonous deadly viper. Jeremiah 8:17 prophesied of the hostile snakes;

> For, behold, I will send serpents, cockatrices, among you, which *will* not *be* charmed, and they shall bite you, saith the LORD."

According to Williams Smith's *Dictionary of the Bible*, a deadly type of snake, hidden in the grass and weeds, would snatch at the heels of horses, resulting in disaster. Deuteronomy 32:33 refers to alcohol in drinks as poison, and it is so here addressed as well. Snakes can entice, for many of them are beautiful, but their venom can be deadly. Alcohol deceives in the same manner.

AT THE LAST. The ultimate end of drinking fermented wine can be disastrous and ruinous to those whom God created to honor, worship and glorify Him.

Proverbs 23:33 (Alcoholic):

> Thine eyes shall behold strange women, and thine heart shall utter perverse things.

Wine, women and song. Who hasn't heard that statement in reference to *wild living*? Lust and perversion are companions of wine. Someone has said, "Wine makes a man see double, but feel single."*

Herbert's poems—The Church Porch

> "He that is drunken may his mother kill; but with his sister, he hath lost the reins; is outlawed by himself. All kinds of ill did with his liquor, slide down his veins. The drunkard forfeits man; and doth divest all worldly right, save what he hath by beast."[8]

Liquor causes people to lust and commit adultery.

---

7. Alcohol And The Bible, Reynolds, 1983.

*Gentlemen, I came to register twins.
Why do you say gentlemen when I'm the only one here?
Oh, oh, I better go back and count.

8. Clarke 1842 v.3.

Proverbs 23:34 (Alcoholic)

Yea, thou shalt be as he that lieth down in the midst of the sea, or as he that lieth upon the top of a mast.

The drunk seems to utterly disregard life. This verse illustrates this carelessness with the idea of one who ascends the supporting ropes up to the masthead and there falls asleep.

Perhaps there is a reason for referring to those ropes as *shrouds*! For if one falls asleep in such a place, he will fall either onto the ship's floor far below, and possibly be killed, or will fall into the ocean and could be drowned.

Proverbs 31:4,5 (Alcoholic):

It is not for kings, O Lemuel, *it is* not for kings to drink wine; nor for princes strong drink: Lest they drink, and forget the law, and pervert the judgment of any of the afflicted.

This is advice to Lemuel, an unknown king. Notice the emphasis by repetition. In other words, *Don't touch it!* Individual rulers often made decisions alone witliout any advisors. Decisions were considered so important that such rulers were forbidden to use fermented wine. Thus was prohibition strictly enforced on the early pharaohs and others. But most of all it would apply to Jesus, the King of Kings. He could not drink alcoholic beverage.

Don't bring me anything but grape juice.

The New Scientist Magazine of February 26, 1981, after stating the well known fact that alcohol kills brain cells, reports that the holes left by those dead cells are just that—holes or *blank* spaces left in the brain. The writer further states that the brains of chronic alcoholics are less dense than those of non-drinkers.

Proverbs 31:6 (Alcoholic):

Give strong drink unto him that is ready to perish, and wine unto those that be of heavy hearts.

Alcohol numbs the brain, much as modern anesthetics do. Alcohol had one positive benefit, it was used to relieve the suffering of the dying or condemned criminals. It was offered to Christ on the cross, but He refused it. (Mark 15:23). "We now have drugs that are more effective anesthetics than alcohol could ever have been," says my retired physician anesthetist, Dr. Alton H. Ridgeway.

Alcohol is so violative that as soon as it gets into the mouth, it is being absorbed into the bloodstream, it goes immediately to the brain. It does not have to get into the digestive system to start coagulating the blood and numbing the brain.

Morphine now is a far better analgesic. It was not known during the period that Proverbs was written.

(The best way to break a bad habit is to drop it.)

ECCLESIASTES

Ecclesiastes 2:3 (Alcoholic):

I sought in mine heart to give myself unto wine, yet acquainting mine heart with wisdom; and to lay hold on folly, till I might see what *was* that good for the sons of men, which they should do under the heaven all the days of their life.

The first part of the book of Ecclesiastes deals with "all is vanity." In the conclusion, the book shows the way to true happiness and worth that comes from a religious and virtuous life. By this way, a man in the lowest of circumstances may be happy. So Jesus said, "Life consisteth not in the abundance of the things which he possesseth."[9]

According to this verse, the writer tried "to give myself unto wine". "Yet I acquainted my heart with wisdom." In verse 11, following, he concluded "and behold all was vanity". True joy is a true spiritual relationship with God, without the *spirits* of alcohol. Abstinence makes the heart grow stronger. All else is vanity.

Ecclesiastes 9:7 (Nonalcoholic):

> Go thy way, eat thy bread with joy, and drink thy wine (grape juice) with a merry heart; for God now accepteth thy works.

The subtitle for Ecclesiastes is *The Preacher*. By chapter nine, the preacher has come to the realization that happiness does not come from alcoholic wine or anything else, but only from seeking God. Now that he has learned that lesson, he will try to find satisfaction not through the *spirits* of wine, but from the Spirit of the Lord. He may now enjoy the blessing of pure, unfermented wine which he is, in fact, encouraged to do, as opposed to laying hold of folly, as is indicated in Ecclesiastes 2:3. The last two wine verses clearly show the two kinds of wine. God never encourages the drinking of alcoholic wine, he forbids it. (Proverbs 31:4,5)

Ecclesiastes 10:19 (Nonalcoholic):

> A feast is made for laughter, and wine (grape juice) maketh merry: but money answereth all *things*.

Fenton translates in his book, *The Bible and Wine*, "A feast is made for enjoyment, and fruit cheers the living." For that English scholar, the translation since *KJV* should be *fruit*.

It seems that Ecclesiastes, the preacher, has now passed the section about alcohol imbibing vanity, and proceeds to the nourishment of fruits available with money.

There is nothing here to indicate fermentation.

SONG OF SOLOMON

Song of Solomon 1:2 (Nonalcoholic):

> Let him kiss me with the kisses of his mouth: for thy love *is* better than wine (grape juice).

"Your love is better than grape juice." (translates Robert P. Teachout 1983).

Formerly, in Proverbs, Solomon condemned alcoholic wine, as a mocker, as a snake, and instructed his readers not even to look at it. In these seven verses in the Song of Solomon he tells of the other kind of good wine, and a reason for drinking it.

The love of a spouse (or of God) is far more satisfying than the pleasant effects of nonalcoholic wine. However, it is better to have fresh grape breath, than alcoholic breath! Continually wine is referred to as a blessing, as here, or a curse; therefore, the word is used for two kinds of wine, alcoholic or pure grape juice.

Song of Solomon 1:4 (Nonalcoholic):

> . . . we will remember thy love bore than wine (grape juice): . . .

"Remember your love more than grape juice."[10]

Wine is a blessing from God; unfermented wine, that is. Also, in I Corinthians 13:13, the superiority of love over wine or anything else is shown. As

9. Luke 12:15.

10. Teachout 1983.

in Henry Drummond's book, "Love is the greatest thing in the world."

Song of Solomon 4:10 (Nonalcoholic):

> . . . how much better is thy love than wine (grape juice)!

"How much better is your love than grape juice."[11]

Could it be that God makes poisonous intoxicating wine the emblem of those spiritual blessings which insure peace and prosperity in this life, and prepares for blessedness hereafter?

Would alcohol, with all its untold suffering, be made such a symbol of blessing by an omniscient all-wise God?

God's love is greater than delicious, nutritious grape juice or anything else. "Your love is better than life itself" (Butler).

Song of Solomon 5:1 (Nonalcoholic):

> . . . I have drunk my wine (grape juice) with my milk: eat, O friends; drink, yea, drink abundantly, O beloved.

Here God is advising heavy drinking, but certainly not getting drunk. When one drinks abundantly of intoxicating wine, one gets drunk. Is God advocating intoxication? Such an idea is contrary to God's real teaching, for a rebellious drunkard was to be stoned to death. (Deuteronomy 21:20-21). He is obviously speaking of unfermented grape juice. This is another place in which one of the 141 occurrences of the word *yayin* should have been translated *grape juice*. Both milk and grape juice are healthy even taken in abundance. "They drink copiously as if it were fresh grape juice."[12]

11. translates Teachout 1983.
12. Teachout.

Song of Solomon 7:9 (Nonalcoholic):

> And the roof of thy mouth like the best wine (grape juice) for my beloved, that goeth *down* sweetly, causing the lips of those that are asleep to speak.

The New International Version translated it thus:

". . . And your mouth like the best wine. May the wine go straight to my lover, flowing gently over lips and teeth." (Copyright 1978)

This is the Biblical comparison between two of God's gifts to man: pure, unadulterated grape juice or fruit juices and love between lovers. Many true love relationships have been broken as a result of intoxicating wine. Heartbreak, physical pain, and destitution have come to parents and children from alcoholism. This is the comparison God makes between sweet love and satanic alcohol. God is not in the business of making *winos*!

I believe the translation of the word *WINE* in the Scripture for today has caused misunderstanding, and is in large part responsible for tragedies caused by wine. Originally, the same word was used for alcoholic wine and grape juice. Alcoholic wine does not flow gently. As poison, it has a sting. Pure grape juice does go down gently. So sweet is this love, one is continually compelled to speak of God's goodness even in sleep and dreams.

Song of Solomon 8:2 (Nonalcoholic):

Aw-sees', Heb. עָסִיס, occurs in five texts only

> . . . I would cause thee to drink of spiced wine (*asis*) of the juice of my pomegranate.

Instead of *spiced* the Syrian and the Arabic have *sweetest.*

Asis, treaded out fresh sweet juice, in Greek, as *Gleukos,* nonalcoholic.

This is the one place where the word WINE in the AV refers to something other than the *fruit of the Vine*. Usually a beverage from the pomegranate would be called *strong drink*. While unfermented here, like grape juice, under certain conditions, it could ferment.

Pomegranate

In Biblical times it was customary for the bride and groom to drink from the same cup to symbolize sharing both the blessings and the problems of life together. For the same shared symbol today, brides and grooms feed each other a bite of their wedding cake and many share a goblet of their punch or even take communion as part of the ceremony.

This verse then implies that God wishes to share our joys and our sorrows. This is indicated in a promise made to Joshua in 1:5 where we read, ". . . as I was with Moses, so I will be with thee: I will not fail thee, nor forsake thee."

This reassuring idea of God's companionship and caring is well illustrated in the story titled "Footprint":

'But, Lord, I have noticed that during the most troublesome times in my life, there is only one set of footprints. I don't understand why when I needed you most, you would leave me.' The Lord replied, 'My precious, precious child, I love you and I would never leave you. During your times of trial and suffering, when you see only one set of footprints, it was then that I carried you.'

And the Lord said to Moses, "My presence shall go with thee, and I will give thee rest." (Exodus 33:14) His grace is sufficient. (II Corinthians 12:9) The Lord did *not* say, 'I'll give you some fermented pomegranate wine that will let you forget your troubles for a time, but after you sober up, your troubles will still be there, probably the worse for the imbibing.'

Wherever the use of wine is prohibited or discouraged it means fermented wine. Where it is encouraged and is spoken of as something for our good it means the unfermented. (Ewing 1967).

Asis occurs in five texts only: here in Song of Solomon 8:2; Isaiah 49:26; Joel 1:5; 3:18; Amos 9:13. The name is from au'sas, *to tread down*, and denotes the expressed juice of the grape or other fruit. By the Greeks it is called *gleukos*, sweet; by the Latins, *mustum*, from the Hebrew, *fresh, sweet, pure*.

CHAPTER TEN

A COMMENTARY ON
EACH USE OF THE WORD WINE IN
THE PROPHECY BOOKS
Old Testament

Dear Dr. Hansen:

My own denomination, the American Presbyterian Church, is a total abstinence body built on the Two Wine Theory and understanding the Bible to teach that we should not "look on the wine when it is alcoholic."

Your chapters show ability to make scholarly research clear and concise with a flair for making things interesting for the large body of non-scholars among the Lord's people.

Charles T. Butler, Philadelphia, PA

BD and STM, Faith Theological Seminary
MA (Religion), Temple University
MBA, St. Joseph's University
Ph.D, Temple University

CHAPTER TEN THE PROPHECY BOOKS OF THE OLD TESTAMENT

ISAIAH

Isaiah 1:21-22 (Nonalcoholic):

So'beh (Heb. סָבָא, to drink freely)

How is the faithful city become an harlot! it was full of judgment; righteousness lodged in it; but now murderers. Thy silver is become dross, thy wine (sobe, so'beh) (grape juice) mixed with water:

There are thirteen Hebrew and Greek words that refer to wine and grape juice in the Old and New Testament. Some have two meanings. *Sobe* (enticing beverage to be drunk freely) was used three times for beverage in the Old Testament. Twice as alcoholic, in Nahum 1:10 and Hosea 4:18. But in this case Isaiah laments that the good silver has now become dross. In line with other places where good wine is valuable, it is reasonable to believe Isaiah is lamenting that good wine (grape juice) is being diluted. Therefore we assume *sōbe* is generic and in this case means *nonalcoholic*.

Isaiah considers it a tragedy that the wine has to be mixed with water, as the silver has become tarnished and lost its luster. Could this be indicative of a deep depression? Their society went from righteousness to murder. Could their economy be so bad that their sweet juice could not be drunk without diluting it down to make it go farther?

We have seen how the grape juice was boiled so that it would not ferment. If boiled sufficiently, it became thick and jam-like, and could be eaten with a spoon. This was stored and later diluted with up to 20 parts water to create a nourishing, refreshing drink. However, this does not seem to be the case here.

After the period of the prophets ended, it is said the Jews sometimes watered down their wines to make them weaker, but there is no evidence that this was done during Biblical times. This passage does not indicate that they weakened it down for any reason, except, in their poverty, to make it go further.

If fermented beverages are inherently wrong for consumption, (their wine is the poison of serpents), then they are wrong regardless of the degree of alcohol they contain. Who would decide how much is acceptable? The Old Testament declares it to be wrong, but does not qualify as to when it might be right, except for relieving the misery of the dying. (Proverbs 31:6). Solomon did not say, "Too much wine is a mocker." There is no recipe giving quantities to be drunk. Could we say that murder in moderation is acceptable? Alcohol causes murder. In no place does the Bible say alcohol may be drunk in moderation. Isaiah believes it's a shame to have to dilute God's pure grape juice. It was an evil and poverty-stricken society.

Isaiah 5:11 (Alcoholic):

Woe unto them that rise up early in the morning, *that* they may follow strong drink (*shekar*); that continue until night, *till* wine inflame them!

Vulgate, "To pursue inebriation."

Dr. Joel Fort, who has helped hundreds of alcoholics, in his book, *Alcohol Our Biggest Drug Problem,* points out this salient fact: "In spite of our present extensive knowledge of alcohol and its effects, there is no way of picking out a pre-alcoholic personality; that is, predicting in advance who will become alcoholic as a result of using the drug. It should be assumed it can happen to any drinker."[1]

Winton Beaver writes in *Ministry*: "One of the most pervasive myths over the past thirty years has been the idea that alcoholics and social drinkers are two entirely distinct breeds with nothing in common . . . The challenge to the myth of social drinking began in 1968. An article by Jan de Lint and Wolfgang Schmidt, two Canadian researchers at the Addiction Research Foundation in Ontario, Canada, appeared in the *Quarterly Journal of Studies on Alcohol.*"[2]

Beaver in the same vein follows with the results of a French research team, Sully Lederman and Skog, Brunn Cartright and Popman. They concluded that when it comes to drinkers, "Drawing a line between 'nonalcoholic and alcoholic' consumption is difficult and ultimately arbitrary."[3] It is all too easy for drinkers to change from nonalcoholic to alcoholic classification. One who starts drinking doesn't think he will become an alcoholic.

WOE TO THEM

Without God's help it is difficult, sometimes even fatal, to try to stop, yet to continue in delirium tremens will bring certain deaths. "Withdrawal from alcoholic addiction is extremely hazardous. Even in the finest hospital with the best of care, about 5% of advanced alcoholics die either from alcoholism or during withdrawal. This is far worse than even heroin withdrawal," writes Dr. Fort (*Alcohol Our Biggest Problem,* 1973, p.100). Some take a drink to get the courage to stop.

1. Fort 1973.
2. Beaver 1983.
3. Durk 1981.

Isaiah 5:12 (Alcoholic):

> And the harp, and the viol, the tabret, and pipe, and wine, are in their feasts: but they regard not the work of the LORD, neither consider the operation of his hands.

In Proverbs 23:33, we mentioned "wine, women, and song" as related to womanizing. This verse gives the music. Wild living does not go with a God-centered, sensible life.

Isaiah 5:22 (Alcoholic):

> Woe unto *them that are* mighty to drink wine, and men of strength to mingle strong drink:

The *NIV*: "Woe to those who are heroes at drinking wine and champions at mixing drinks." (Copyright 1978).

"A force like fire wine used when it enters into strongest men." (Athenaeums 300 B.C.).

Isaiah 16:10 (Nonalcoholic):

> . . . the treaders shall tread out no wine (grape juice) in *their* presses; I have made *their vintage* shouting to cease.

"Grape juice" Young's Analytical Concordance, p.1058.

The Talmud says, "Newly pressed wine, prior to fermentation, was known as *yayin mi-gat*"— *Wine from the press, prior to fermentation, yet called wine,—therefore two meanings for wine. Fermentation takes time: "Ten to fourteen days." Easley's Winery, Indianapolis, Ind.

Teachout translates, "Shall tread out no grape juice."

Writes Dr. Reynolds in *Alcohol and The Bible*, 1983: "To assume *yayin* is always alcoholic, is a mistake that has led

*Sanhedrian 70-a.

too much confusion and too much intoxication which might easily have been avoided. Isaiah 16:10 says: 'No treader shall tread out *yayin* in the presses,'... Fermentation is a time process.

Therefore alcohol is excluded from this passage."[4]

> Woe—no blue ribbons to wine drinkers.

A good harvest was celebrated with harvest festivals, with shouts of joy, encouragement, and possibly rhythm among the treaders of fresh grape juice. But with the punishment of the once proud Moabites, there was no grape harvest and no treading, no shouting. Light treading brought out the fresh unfermented juice while the presses squeezed out the pulp. It was impossible for the fresh juice being treaded out to be alcoholic. It should not be called wine in today's translations.

Isaiah 19:14 (Alcoholic):

> The LORD hath mingled a perverse spirit in the midst thereof: and they have caused Egypt to err in every work thereof, as a drunken man staggereth in his vomit.

What a picture expressing the result of drinking, which is supposed to be so lovely, and such a pleasure. That last line shows a true picture of sickness and disgust. Alcoholic advertising never shows the possible result of crime, sickness and death.

Isaiah 22:13 (Alcoholic):

> ... eating flesh, and drinking wine: let us eat and drink; for to morrow we shall die.

This is the philosophy of those who seek their fulfillment in the present, regardless of the future which may result from their chosen actions.

4. Reynolds 1983.

Isaiah 24:7 (Nonalcoholic):

> The new wine (*tirosh*) (grapes) mourneth, the vine languisheth, all the merryhearted do sigh.

Funk and Wagnalls: "must, unfermented juice, new wine."

Webster: "Must, new wine, before it has fermented."

Ferrar Fenton translates this verse as: " 'Grapes' mourn: the vine stock faints."

See Genesis 27:28 for notes on *tirosh*. This is a clear case where *tirosh* means "grape". Here, wine, *tirosh*, mourns while its vine languishes. Grapes are never alcoholic on the vine. As this is being written, today's radio news broadcasts, that due to present heat and drought, grapes on the vines are turning to raisins. Because now the word *wine* denotes an alcoholic drink, *tirosh* here should never be translated as *wine* for today's readers. *Tirosh* is never related to alcohol.

This verse predicts drought, as if it had already occurred. There is a serious fallacy in those Bible dictionaries which define wine as fermented juice. This fallacy also applies to some translations which are supposedly prepared in easy to understand English for today's readers. At least the *AV* translates it as *new wine* which is easily understood as fresh, different from the old fermented wine. While *yayin* is a generic word like our word *cider*, or punch, *tirosh* always denotes grapes, sweet juice, or the harvest to be stored, and ought to be so translated. There is no mention of an Israelite drinking *tirosh*.

Isaiah 24:9 (Alcoholic):

> They shall not drink wine with a song; strong drink (*shekar*) shall be bitter to them that drink it.

This constitutes Isaiah's prophecy to those that transgress.

Bishop Loweth translates it as: "With songs they shall no more drink wine." That is, from grapes. Palm wine shall be bitter to them. Real punishment.

Isaiah 24:11 (Uncertain):

There is a crying for wine in the streets; all joy is darkened, the mirth of the land is gone.

Are they crying for the nutritious grapes? Or, are they crying for the narcotic effect of wine to relieve the pain and desperation? In any case, there is none of either kind, alcoholic or nonalcoholic. There is only the punishment for Tyre's deserting God.

Isaiah 25:6 (Nonalcoholic):

Sheh-maw-reem' (Heb. שְׁמָרִים), 'preserves'

And in this mountain shall the LORD of hosts make unto all people a feast of fat things, a feast of wines (*shemarim*) (grape juice) on the lees, of fat things full of marrow, of wines (juice) on the lees well refined.

"*Shemar* to preserve, so preserves or jellies." Popular and Critical Bible Encyclopedia, 1909, p.1726. This fits in with aged as used by TLB, NASB, and NIV instead of "wine on the lees."

The poetic "*Shemarim* can either refer to the sediment or dregs of a beverage, or it can designate grape juice which has been preserved for a long period of time" (Teachout 1986 p.381). Ferrar Fenton, " 'Grape juice' well thickened by age." Thickened or syrupy grape juice will not ferment. (See chapter 4, Boiling.)

The lees are the settlings, the dregs. 'Well refined' is that which has had the dregs strained out. Dr. Lees said, "Well refined as 'well filtered' from the lees, so it would not ferment" (1868, p.251). In this, Lees concurs with Zodhiates' Lexicon.* When the pulp which forms the lees and includes the yeast and enzymes is strained out there can be no fermentation. Luther translates, "Wine in which there is no yeast." In this verse in Hebrew, wine is not mentioned.

TLB, NASB and NIV, leave out 'wine on the lees' and use the word aged. Before Pasteur, hundreds of years before, there was more difficulty in keeping fermented wines than pure grape juice. Writes Pliny, "It is a peculiarity of wine among liquids to go moldy or else to turn into vinegar." (Natural History, 14:26). But *Vins cuits*, boiled wine, without alcohol could be kept for years and according to some, improved with age. Covered and sealed, "No harm will befall it" (Columella 12:26). *Shemarim*, aged grape juice, "Does not mean aged in itself. No scholar thinks it does." (Reynolds, Biblical Approach to Alcohol p.15).

Isaiah 27:2 (Nonalcoholic):

Kheh'mer Heb. חֶמֶר.

In that day sing ye unto her, A vineyard of red wine. (Khemer) (fruitful vineyard).

Khemer—"Fruitful vineyard." *NIV* and also *Popular and Critical Cyclopedia*, 1907, p. 1725.

Jack Van Impe and Roger F. Campbell, and Robert P. Teachout: label this as unfermented.

Dr. Teachout thinks in this case the King James' men incorrectly read the Hebrew. Modern translations do not usually mention red. The *New American Standard Bible (NASB)* translates, "a vineyard of wine". *The Living Bible* says, "Let this anthem be their song." So, no concern about red wine. No concern about wine, this is about vineyard. Lees translates, "A vineyard of foaming juice." Pliny said, "That we may take

* "Preserved *ie* the settings," 8105, "to strain", 2212.

** Loel Classical Library Book XXVIII

the more wine, we break its strength by the filter."[5]

Apparently this is a case of the ancient custom of a divided song. Alternately, Jehovah and the vineyard sing to each other. Would some writers have God singing, tantamount to a beer drinking song, or join the singing of an inebriated wino?

Isaiah 28:1 (Alcoholic):

> WOE to the crown of pride, to the drunkards of Ephraim, whose glorious beauty *is* a fading flower, which *are* on the head of the fat valleys of them that are overcome with wine!

Ephraim had plenty to be proud of, but her use of intoxicating wine could cut her down.

While at the University of Minnesota, I worked part time as a social caseworker. I was impressed with how often alcohol was involved with poverty. Devout Christians were scarcely ever in the caseload. Another year, my field work with the University involved being a probation officer in Minneapolis. The reports showed that most crimes involved alcohol.

Isaiah 28:7&8 (Alcoholic):

> But they also have erred through wine, and through strong drink (*shekar*) are out of the way; the priest and the prophet have erred through strong drink, they are swallowed up of wine, they are out of the way through strong drink; they err in vision, they stumble in judgment. For all tables are full with vomit *and* filthness . . .

Shekar means sweet, or sweet juice from trees. Without protection sweet juice does ferment and does indeed become strong drink. When it is classed with fresh grape juice, it is sweet. When classed with alcoholic wine, we do not object to its being called strong drink.

Verse one of this chapter refers to Ephraim, or Israel, the ten tribes. But now Judah also erred through wine. The priests were commanded to abstain while in divine service upon pain of death, but now were guilty of sacrilege: The prophets, who are thought to have been trained as like Nazarites, became great backsliders from their early temperance life.

When the brain is swallowed up with wine, error and stumbling in judgment are the natural result.

Galen Bosley writes in *Ministry*; (May, 1986 p.24):

"Of particular interest is the effect that alcohol has on the specific area of the brain concerned with moral discernment. This is located in the frontal lobes of the brain, directly behind the bones of the forehead. In 1955, Courville found that the size of this area of the alcoholic brain was significantly decreased in proportion to the size of the rest of the brain. In other words, the frontal lobes, the center for moral judgment, were found to be atrophied or shrunken."

Bosley continues to tell of Phineas Gage, who, in an accident, had a shaft blown through the front part of his head. Later he recovered. Before the accident he was a temperate man of good character. But after the accident, he was fitful, irreverent, obstinate, capricious, and vacillating, to such a point that his friends and acquaintances said he was not the same Gage they formerly knew.

Intoxication will have the same effect on the frontal part of the brain; some of the effects are permanent. Well did God say through Isaiah, "They stumble in judgment." I wonder about some of our judges who are so easy on alcohol-guilty criminals, who are guilty of manslaughter.

5. Bible Commentary 1868.

Isaiah 29:9 (Alcoholic):

> . . . cry ye out, and cry: they are drunken, but not with wine; they stagger, but not with strong drink (*shekar*).

Through sin, Judah has become unsteady and helpless. As alcohol affects the brain, staggering is a natural result. Ariel, Jerusalem, has great problems.

Isaiah 36:17 (Nonalcoholic):

> Until I come and take you away to a land like your own land, a land of corn and wine (*tirosh*) (grapes), a land of bread and vineyards.

Young's Lexicon, "Tirosh, new wine, sweet wine." *Funk and Wagnall's Dictionary*, "Unfermented juice of the grape, new wine."

F. R. Lees, *"Tirosh"*, vine fruit.

These are the words of Rabshakeh, Assyrian King Sennacherib's general. The general held out as bait, fresh grape juice, one of the most desirable.

Fenton translates this as: "A land of corn and 'fruit,' a land of bread and orchards." *Tirosh* is never related to alcohol. See Genesis 27:28, Which is why the NIV and the NASB translate as "new wine." New wine, "must not yet fermented, new wine." Webster, 1991.

See notes on II Kings 18, 31, 32 for same words.

Isaiah 49:26 (Nonalcoholic):

Aw-sees', Heb. עָסִיס, *awsas,* 'to tread down'

> And I will feed them that oppress thee with their own flesh; and they shall be drunken with their own blood, as with sweet wine: (*asis*) (grape juice).

The Hebrew word here is *asis*. In 1611 A.D. sweet wine meant nonalcoholic. Today it means a sugary alcoholic wine. *Asis* is always used biblically with reference to freshly pressed juice having no time for fermentation. A more legitimate translation would be ". . . and they shall drink copiously of their own blood as if it were fresh juice." (Teachout p. 160)

Do people get drunk (*asis*) drinking their own blood? Have you ever heard of that? Of course not. This is not to be taken literally. So leave drunken out. It therefore means: They shall be made to drink copiously of a bitter pill. They shall be made to drink it as fast as if they were enjoying fresh grape juice.

As alcoholic wine causes drunkenness, so does affliction cause complete disorientation.

Isaiah 55:1 (Nonalcoholic):

> Ho, every one that thirsteth, come ye to the waters, and he that hath no money; come ye, buy, and eat; yea, come, buy wine (grapes) and milk without money and without price.

"Grape juice" Young's Analytical Concordance, p.1058.

Patton, in *Bible Wines,* has this to say regarding this verse:

> "How incongruous to say, Buy milk, and drink abundantly of it, for it is innocent and nutritious, and will do you good; and then to say, Come, buy wine (*yayin*), and intoxicating beverage, which, if you drink habitually and liberally, will begat the drunkard's appetite, and shut you out of heaven! (No drunkard "shall inherit the kingdom of God" I Corinthians 6:10).[6]

Five to ten percent of even moderate drinkers become alcoholics, that is, some drink more than they want to, many become drunkards. They don't want to. They just do.

That the wine referred to here is nutritious grape juice is evident from the next verse, "Wherefore do ye spend your money for that which is not bread? and your labour for that which satisfieth not?" Alcohol is not bread, nor a nourishing food, and not satisfying.

---

6. Patton 1871.

Isaiah 56:12 (Alcoholic):

> Come ye, say they, I will fetch wine, and we will fill ourselves with strong drink; and to morrow shall be as this day, and much more abundant.

To fill ourselves with alcoholic wine and strong drink would most surely lead to drunkenness.

Adam Clarke, in his Commentary, says, "The spirit of this epicurean sentiment is this: 'Let us indulge ourselves in the present time to the utmost, and instead of any gloomy forebodings of the future, let us expect nothing but increasing hilarity for every day we shall live.' Thus, 'Counting on long years of pleasure here, are quite unfurnished for the world to come.' "

Isaiah 62:8 (Nonalcoholic):

> . . . and the sons of the stranger shall not drink thy wine (*tirosh*) (grape juice), for the which thou hast laboured:

Lee, "Shall not drink thy vine-fruit."

Fenton translates this as, "Nor foreigners feast on the 'fruits' that you cultured."

Tirosh is the collective name for the natural harvested, preserved fresh and stored produce of the vine.

"New Wine, grape juice before it has fermented." Webster.

Tirosh occurs 38 times; this is one of the three occasions it is connected with not drinking by others. Never is there a mention of an Israelite drinking *tirosh*. Gensenius explains *qah-botz* reference as signifying to collect things as grapes. Usually it means harvested and preserved grapes for possessed storage. We may assume Isaiah is speaking figuratively.

Isaiah 65:8 (Nonalcoholic):

> Thus saith the LORD, As the new wine (*tirosh*) (grape juice) is found in the cluster, and *one* saith, Destroy it not; for a blessing *is* in it: 'so will I do for my servants' sakes, that I may not destroy them all.

"*Tirosh*—new wine, sweet wine," Young's Lexicon, p.50.

Tirosh is never connected to alcohol. (See Genesis 27:28).

Lee, "Vine Codex A of the LXX, "a blessing of the Lord is in it." Fruit in a cluster (or on a vine-stalk).

Israel is compared to a cluster of grapes. There are righteous people in it, so God will not destroy them all; the juice is valuable. The righteous will not be purged away.

This verse is one of the best examples of the use of the generic word *wine*. The following points are noted:

1. When they used the generic term *new wine*, the King James' translators meant unfermented grape juice that is why they wrote *new wine*. New wine, "Must, unfermented juice . . . new wine." Funk and Wagnall's Dictionary.

There is absolutely no fermentation in a cluster of grapes hanging on the vine. The skin of the grape protects from the entrance of yeast fungi. With time, they dry up as raisins, or rot if the skin is broken. The juice must be stored in an open container where the yeast in the air can get to the pulp's enzymes, or have yeast added to it. It must be kept warm, and above all, there must be a period of time for the yeast to putrefy.

Please little cluster, I need some intoxication.

2. Some new versions supposedly written to be more easily understood by English speaking people in this day are simply inadequate on the subject of the word *wine*, whether or not the adjective "new" is used with the word. As dictionaries define it today, people in general think "alcoholic beverage" whenever they see the word *wine. The American Standard Bible (NASB)* (1973), still uses *new wine*, as does the

New King James Version (NKJV) (1982). These translations give people the wrong meaning. People today think of any wine as alcoholic. More accurate here is *The New International Version (NIV)* (1978-88), this verse is rendered correctly when 'juice' is still found in a cluster of grapes and men say 'Don't destroy it, there is yet some good in it.' " In another instance, the NIV translates *tirosh* properly as crushed grapes, (Micah 6:15). Present day translators often translate the same word four different ways. Why call it 'wine' in 36 references; cluster of grapes in one place and crushed grapes in still another? Is *Tirosh* considered a generic term? It is never alcoholic. Do they translate it according to context, as we do with *Yayin*?

We are consistent in translating *Tirosh* as harvested fresh grape, or juice, usually compressed for storage, a good nonalcoholic grape substance.

Fenton translates this verse as: "As one finds in a cluster, ripe juice."

The Living Bible (1971), does well in paraphrasing, and giving the whole meaning. Dr. Taylor translates this verse as follows: "But I will not destroy them all, says the Lord for just as good grapes are found among a cluster of bad ones (and someone will say, 'Don't throw them all away—there are some good grapes there') so I will not destroy all Israel, for I have true servants there."[7]

It soon becomes clear that there is no consistent reason for calling *tirosh,* wine. It is definitely fresh grape juice or stored grape juice. It should be so rendered, to give today's English speaking people the right understanding. *Tirosh* should be translated as grapes, "grape juice" or formerly as "vine fruit."

7. Taylor 1971.

JEREMIAH

Jeremiah 13:12,13 (Alcoholic):

> Therefore thou shalt speak unto them this word; Thus saith the LORD God of Israel, Every bottle shall be filled with wine: . . .
> Then shalt thou say unto them, Thus saith the LORD, Behold, I will fill all the inhabitants of this land, even the kings that sit upon David's throne, and the priests, and the prophets, and all the inhabitants of Jerusalem, with drunkenness.

The LXX, "A skin-bag of wine."

It is a symbol. The user is the loser. You and your kings, and priests, and prophets, are represented by these bottles. The wine is God's wrath against you.

The ancient adage is here fulfilled:—

> "Quos Deus vult perdere, prius dementat."
> "Those whom God determined to destroy, he first renders foolish."

(The wrath of grapes.)

Jeremiah 23:9 (Alcoholic):

> Mine heart within me is broken because of the prophets; all my bones shake; I am like a drunken man, and like a man whom wine hath overcome, because of the LORD, and because of the words of his holiness.

Jeremiah was shocked out of his senses by the profanity of the other prophets, as contrasted to the holiness of God, so shocked he became as silly as a wine drinker.

Even strong men, like some of the other prophets, could succumb to alcohol. None are safe when the enemy is admitted through the lip gates; by excluding it, the weakest are secure.

Jeremiah 25:15 (Alcoholic):

> For thus saith the LORD God of Israel unto me; Take the wine cup of this fury at my hand, and cause all the nations, to whom I send thee, to drink it.

This is not the fresh grape juice of God's blessing. A cup of fermented wine can well be a symbol of a cup of fury. It contains the seed of that which debauches, and in the nature of things causes destruction. It often leads to crime, poverty and broken homes.

Jeremiah 31:12 (Nonalcoholic):

> Therefore they shall come and sing in the height of Zion, and shall flow together to the goodness of the LORD, for wheat, and for wine, (*tirosh*), (grape juice) and for oil, and for the young of the flock . . .

"Corn and fruit and oil" (Fenton's translation).

"With olive-and-orchard-fruit" (Lee's translation).

TIROSH. Unfermented, a food always used as a blessing, never a curse. "The fact that the Old Testament usage normally differentiates in its vocabulary between the stored harvested juice and the table beverage, *yayin,* is simply an easily documented phenomenon."[8]

Tirosh also refers to clear clean juice, without the pulp, as must before storage. This meaning is in addition to its being stored as a syrupy possession.

Jeremiah 35:2 (Uncertain):

> Go unto the house of the Rechabites, and speak unto them, and bring them into the house of the LORD, into one of the chambers, and give them wine to drink.

Lee, "The house = family of the Rechabites."

The references in this chapter to Rechabites are the only references to them in the Old Testament. The tribal father, Rechab, is mentioned 13 other times, starting with II Samuel 4:2. Rechab was not a descendant of Jacob, but probably a descendant of Jethro, the father-in-law of Moses. As such he would not be bound by the Mosaic law. They were very devout in their worship of Jehovah, and even practiced circumcision. They were forbidden to drink wine, to plant or have vineyards and were to keep to themselves with a distinct tribal life, living in tents. Rechab feared the possibilities of being contaminated with other peoples if they should settle in cities, or even on farms. Rechab was right in regard to cities. Cities always have been centers of wine drinking, immorality, and crime, citadels of temptation. From the amount of alcohol tax collected, the federal government deduces from each state the amount of alcohol consumed per person. Except for Chicago, Illinois, Detroit, and Michigan, the central and south states show the smallest amount per person. The eastern states with their big cities, and California, show the highest percent of alcohol per person consumed. One is safest in a small town where only the lights go out at night. I was told at a hotel in Washington, D.C., "You are now in the city. Do not go out in the streets at night." In St. Louis I was told, "Use the dead bolt and chain. Use the peep hole before letting anyone in." In contrast I have relatives in rural Indiana that have no operating locks on the doors of their homes.

Jeremiah 35:5 (Uncertain):

> And I set before the sons of the house of the Rechabites pots full of wine, and cups, and I said unto them, Drink ye wine.

Vulgate, "Gablets filled with wine, and cups."

Dr. Teachout thinks it would be a greater temptation for them to take grape juice than the condemned alcoholic wine.

Jeremiah 35:6

> But they said, We will drink no wine: for Jonadab the son of Rechab our father com-

8. Teachout 1980.

manded us, saying, Ye shall drink no wine, neither ye, nor your sons for ever:

Lo nishteh yayin, "We do not drink wine."

Jonadab, signifies "Whom the Lord impels."

Rechab, 'a horseman' probably a family name.

Jeremiah 35:8

Thus have we obeyed the voice of Jonadab the son of Rechab our father in all that he hath charged us, to drink no wine all our days, we, our wives, our sons, nor our daughters;

Did wine here mean only fermented? Were grapes included as in the Nazarite vow? We know so little of the Rechabites.

Some earlier commentators say that Peter and Jesus' brothers had a strong sympathy with the Nazarites, the Rechabites, and the Essenes, all of whom were strict abstainers. The Bible commended them for not using, not for not abusing. The term "abusing wine" is not found in the Bible. It never commends the use of alcoholic beverage.

Eusebius, called the representative of the era of Constantine, quotes Hegesippus as saying, "St. James, the Lord's brother, did not drink wine." Traces of this may be perceptible in I Peter 1:13, 4:3,7,8; and in II Peter 1:6.

Alcohol has one good use, to preserve organs in the laboratory. "If you want to keep a dead man, put him in whiskey. If you want to kill a living man, put the whiskey in him"[9]

Jeremiah 35:14 (Nonalcoholic):

The words of Jonadab the son of Rechab, that he commanded his sons not to drink wine (grape juice), are performed; for unto this day they drink none, but obey their father's commandment: notwithstanding I have spoken unto you, rising early and speaking; but ye hearkened not unto me.

9. Thayer 1869.

"Grape juice" Young's Lexicon p.1058.

God says He rises early to try to get people to obey Him. He asked for obedience in reasonable areas, like the Rechabites who obeyed their father.

The Lord praises the sons of Rechab, as opposed to those of Judah, for not drinking wine. God ends this section with verse 19, in which He blesses the Rechabites, "Jonadab, the son of Rechab, in which He blesses the Rechabites, "Jonadab, the son of Rechab shall not want a man to stand before me forever." Adam Clarke feels that the Essenes were descendants of the Rechabites, and became the first converts to the Gospel. The separate abstinent Rechabites seemed to be one of God's favorites because of their abstinence.

Jeremiah 40:12 (Nonalcoholic):

Even all the Jews returned out of all places whither they were driven, and came to the land of Judah, to Gedaliah, unto Mizpah, and gathered wine and summer fruits very much.

Collect ye vintage fruit." (Vulgate).

Laborers in a Vineyard.

Returned Jews were to put themselves under Gedaliah, who had been appointed by the king of Babylon, to supervise them, to gather their crops, and to live peacefully. They were to gather wine (grapes) and summer fruits. One does not gather alcoholic wine with summer fruits, but gathering of grapes go with gathering of summer fruits. In Jeremiah's mind such a gathering of fresh produce was nonalcoholic and preserved. Former references by Jeremiah showed alcoholic wine as a curse, Jeremiah 13:13; 23:9; 25:15 from God, and nonalcoholic as a blessing of God. Jeremiah 31:12, 35:11

Summer fruits, "Use for grapes, or for 'wine in the cluster' "—(The Popular and Critical Encyclopedia, 1909, p.1725). Grapes or wine in the cluster cannot possibly be other than nonalcoholic. Ferrar Fenton translated this as "fruit."

"Gathered the 'fruit' and harvested the crops," (Ferrar Fenton's translation 1907).

"Gathered 'grape clusters' and 'summer fruits.' " (Fellows, 1909).

"No one, we suppose, can carry prejudice so far as to impose upon himself the belief that fermented and bottled wine was thus taken from the fields."[10]

Fermented juice is not gathered with fresh fruits. This is another case where fresh juice is incorrectly labeled wine.

Grapes or vine fruit, are summer fruits that are nonalcoholic.

Jeremiah 48:33 (Nonalcoholic):

> And joy and gladness is taken from the plentiful field, and from the land of Moab; and I have caused wine to (grape juice) fail from the winepresses: none shall tread with shouting; *their* shouting *shall* be no shouting.

"Grape juice." Young p.1058.

Vulgate, "I have removed wine from thy presses."

How could these Moabites be treading fermented wine directly from the wine presses? Fermentation takes a period of time. This is a case where *wine* meant fresh juice, nonalcoholic.

The joy and the shouting were related to fresh juice coming out of the wine press. But in this case, the treaders were to be unemployed. There were no grapes to harvest because of the Moabites' treatment of the Israelites.

10. Bible Commentary.

Grape, vine fruit and nonalcoholic juice, should not be translated as wine because wine today means fermented.

Jeremiah 51:7 (Alcoholic):

> Babylon *hath been* a golden cup in the LORD's hand, that made all the earth drunken: the nations have drunken of her wine; therefore the nations are mad.

Here wine is not a blessing, but represents God's punishment poured out.

Can "out of the same mouth proceed blessing and cursing?

My brethren, these things ought not to be" (James 3:10). Nor will they be, if the word *Yayin* is correctly translated. It means two kinds of wine, just as we have two kinds of cider, or punch, alcoholic or nonalcoholic, with the meaning determined by the context.

LAMENTATIONS

Lamentation 2:12 (Nonalcoholic):

> They say to their mothers, Where *is* corn and wine (grape juice)? when they swooned as the wounded in the streets of the city, when their soul was poured out into their mothers' bosom.

"Grape juice." Young p.1058.

"Where is grain and grape juice?"[11]

The Nebuchadnezzar calamities were brought on the daughter of Zion by Divine anger, because of disobedience charged largely to false prophets. She chose not to believe the truth. Rather, she listened to the false prophets who spoke words more to her liking. But eventually, the day of reckoning came. Now where were the blessings, the necessities of food and drink? Would the starving children of the mothers' bosom be crying for alcoholic wine? Or nutrition? How inconsistent can some translators get? We do credit *The Living Bible*, here for it paraphrases

11. Teachout 1986.

" 'Mamma, Mamma, we want food,' they cry."

"Congruity and probability are alike shocked by supposing that little children would cry to their mothers for *intoxicating drink* because of want of food and water."[12]

EZEKIEL

Ezekiel 27:18 (Nonalcoholic and Alcoholic):

> Damascus *was* thy merchant in the multitude of the wares of thy making, for the multitude of all riches; in the wine of Helbon, and white wool.

Fenton translates, "Rich grapes of Helbon." Damascus in Syria was known then, as well as now, for its fine grapes. The climate and the soil make the finest grapes. So, grapes and grape products played an important part in their economy. That's the reason there are 234 references to wine and grape juice in the Old Testament, besides the many references to grapes and vineyards. Their productivity is noted in Numbers 13:23. "And cut down . . . one cluster of grapes, and they bare it between two upon a staff."

So, the prophet in this chapter tells of the prosperity that Damascus once had in its trading of wine and wool. But he also tells the tragedy of its downfall as well.

The Greeks and Romans enjoyed those grape products, which were probably boiled down to a syrup for transportation.

Ezekiel 44:21 (Alcoholic):

> Neither shall any priest drink wine, when they enter into the inner court.

Jesus was the priest of priest, the eternal priest.

The same as Leviticus, where the penalty was death. As both priest and prophet, Ezekiel was vitally concerned with the ethical teachings of Leviticus. Contrast with some Christians that use wine in worship. (See notes on Leviticus 10:9 and 10:10). Alcohol destroys respect and reverence for people, things, and God.

12. The Temperance Bible Commentary 1868.

DANIEL

Daniel 1:5 (Possibly Alcoholic):

> And the king appointed them a daily provision of the king's meat, and of the wine which he drank: so nourishing them three years, that at the end thereof they might stand before the king.

Verse three used the words ". . . and of the king's seed." These would have been children of nobility—the best educated, the best able to teach others, and probably healthier than the others. In short they would have been best able to teach other Israelites, the Chaldean language and culture. The king instructed that they were to have the same nutrition as contained in the foods he consumed. He thought this would maintain their good health, and they would become better able to teach.

Daniel 1:8 (Possibly Alcoholic):

> But Daniel purposed in his heart that he would not defile himself with the portion of the king's meat, nor with the wine which he drank: therefore he requested of the prince of the eunuchs that he might not defile himself.

Daniel felt he could not eat the food that did not conform to Yahweh's food laws and standards of nutrition. Nor did he think he could drink wine offered to idols that could possibly be intoxicating.

There is no evidence that Daniel ever drank alcoholic wine. We do not believe that he did.

The Hanging Gardens of Babylon

Daniel 1:16 (Probably Alcoholic):

> Thus Melzar took away the portion of their meat, and the wine that they should drink; and gave them pulse.

Daniel followed God's directives regarding food consumed, and he refrained from eating anything that had been strangled. Along with that, he also refrained from eating the flesh of unclean animals, and that which had been dedicated to idols. "Pulse" was a vegetarian diet of grain and vegetables.

They became good salad citizens.

Fermented or alcoholic wine was also removed from his diet. The result of this kind of diet is found in verse 1:20, where the king . . . "found them ten times better than all the magicians and astrologers that were in his realm". Notice this especially implies mental capacity and capability. The consumption of alcoholic beverages destroys brain cells as well as causes the body to deteriorate. According to Daniel 10:3, Daniel did drink nonalcoholic wine or grape juice.

To say that drinking alcoholic beverages is unhealthful seems almost superfluous. Alas, many think that drinking in moderation is not harmful. Refer to Maisel's article, *One Drink Kills Irreplaceable Brain Cells*, under notes of Proverbs 31:4-5. Also, on brain damage, see Bosley in Isaiah 28:7 notes.

Besides, alcohol destroys liver cells. During Prohibition in this country, the number of deaths from cirrhosis of the liver dropped sharply. After repeal the number of such deaths again rebounded.

The U.S. National Center for Health Services

Mortality Rate Deaths (Per 100,000)
From Cirrhosis in the United States

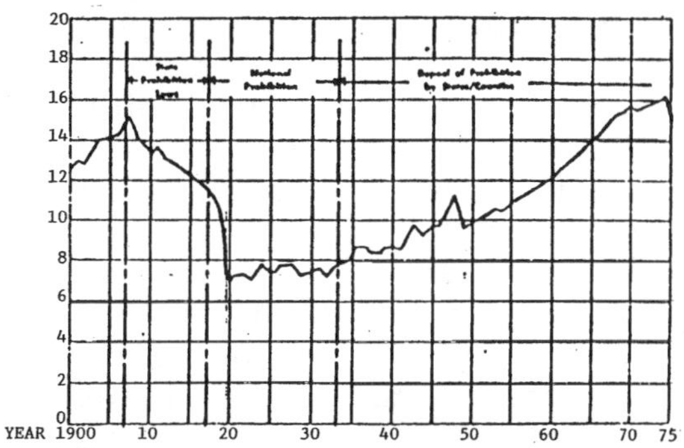

Lowest deaths during Prohibition years

Chart and information supplied by Propaganda VS Facts Copyright 1978 by Ross J. McLennon used by permission. Sane Press Oklahoma city, OK 73105

Daniel 5:1,2,3,4 (Alcoholic):

> Belshazzar the king made a great feast to a thousand of his lords, and drank wine before the thousand. Belshazzar, whiles he tasted the wine, commanded to bring the golden and silver vessels which his father Nebuchadnezzar had taken out of the temple which was in Jerusalem; that the king, and his princes, his wives, and his concubines, might drink therein. Then they brought the golden vessels that were taken out of the temple of the house of God which was at Jerusalem; and the king, and his princes, his wives, and his concubines, drank in them. They drank wine, and praised the gods of gold, and of silver, of brass, of iron, of wood, and of stone.

Some interpret this reference to "a thousand of his lords" as referring to a "lord" or "satrap" who was in charge of a troop or platoon of 1000 soldiers. Otherwise, it might have been difficult to get a thousand people into a hall for a feast and drinking party. Whatever the logistics were, it was quite a bash.

The word *wine* is the translation of the *Aramaic* word *Chamar*, which refers either to alcoholic or intoxicating wine. Alcoholism, or at least intoxication, is sin. No drunkard shall inherit the kingdom of God. (I Corinthians 6:10).

Commentator Adam Clark says of verse two: "He tasted the wine and as the wine got fully in, wit went fully out; and in consequence he acted the profane part." The profane part, of course, was desecrating the consecrated vessels from the Temple at Jerusalem. Perhaps without the intoxicating wine, his better judgment would have prevailed and he would have been spared God's judgment. Alcoholic wine curbs inhibitions and allows one to do all sorts of bizarre activities, from immorality to criminality, and irreverence. God will allow such debauchery to go only so far.

Daniel 5:23 (Alcoholic):

> But hast lifted up thyself against the Lord of heaven; and they have brought the vessels of his house before thee, and thou, and thy lords, thy wives, and thy concubines, have drunk wine in them; and thou hast praised the gods of silver, and gold, of brass, iron, wood, and stone, which see not, nor hear, nor know: and the God in whose hand thy breath *is*, and whose are all thy ways, hast thou not glorified:

Leviticus 10:9 stated that drunkenness for a priest in the tabernacle was punishable by death. Also in Deuteronomy 21:21, drunkenness was punishable by death. This severe sentence was necessary that the Jewish people might see clearly the difference between the holy and the unholy, the clean and the unclean. Leviticus 10:10 states God's Temple vessels were holy. To blaspheme by using them for fermented drinks, a symbol of evil and sin, was the height of willful transgression.

Belshazzar called for the vessels from the Temple and drank from them in honor of Bel, god of idols. This was extreme blasphemy and God could not tolerate it. One whose head is influenced by alcohol is capable of any dangerous indignity and evil irreverence.

The women also joined in the drinking and revelry. What becomes of a nation whose women resort to drinking? What happened to '*apple pie, the flag*, and model motherhood'?

"When Cyrus heard that the Babylonians were celebrating a festival in Babylon in which all the Babylonians drank and revelled the whole night, . . . [he] opened the ditches into the river, . . . and the passage through the city became passable . . . as soon as the noise and clamor began, . . . the king commanding to see what the matter was, ran out throwing open the gates . . . As soon as they found the gates loose, broke in; mastered him, (the king), they that were with him were likewise killed . . . Cyrus sent a body of horses up and down through the streets, bidding them killed that they found abroad. They that had stayed at home were to stay in."[13]

Lucky for those who stayed home
away from the wine bash!

"Can you discover any parallel between Belshazzar serving wine to a thousand guests, among whom must have been numbered the leaders of his kingdom, . . . and the annulment of the Eighteenth Amendment in our own country?"[14]

13. Xenophane, Cyclopedia, 370 BC.
14. Smith 1935.

Nebuchadnezzar had defied God by taking the Temple Vessels, though there is no evidence that he drank from them. But the reveling Belshazzar knew no bounds.

What about those who drink alcohol in the observance of the Lord's Supper?

Daniel 10:2-3 (Nonalcoholic):

> In those days I Daniel was mourning three full weeks. I ate no pleasant bread, neither came flesh nor wine (grape juice) in my mouth, neither did I anoint myself at all, till three whole weeks were fulfilled.

Ferrar Fenton translation, *The Holy Bible in Modern English*, reads: "Flesh or 'fruit' did not enter my mouth."

While stated in the negative, the indication is that Daniel quit drinking wine because of the mourning. Earlier he had refused to drink the king's wine. If, after three weeks, he drank, it was probably the unfermented wine or grape juice (Daniel 1:8).

There is no evidence that Daniel ever drank alcoholic wine.

"No one has a right to decide that Daniel in his old age, habitually consumed the kind of [generic] *yayin* which the royal Preacher had designated 'a mocker'[15]

HOSEA

Hosea 2:8-9 (Nonalcoholic):

> For she did not know that I gave her corn, and wine (*tirosh*) (grapes), and oil, and multiplied her silver and gold, *which* they prepared for Baal. Therefore will. I return, and take away my corn in the time thereof, and my wine (grapes) in the season thereof, and will recover my wool and my flax *given* to cover her nakedness.

Hebrew *ve-tiroshi be-moado,* and my vine fruit in its appointed time.

Teachout gives for wine "harvested grape juice" in *VSS* 8 and 9.

15. F. R. Lees & Dawson Burns 1868.

Fenton translates the word wine in this instance as "drinks."

Baal

Samaria did not appreciate that her blessings were from God and did not give Him credit; therefore these blessings would be taken away.

Alcoholic wine does not have a season; grapes have a season.

Tirosh means grapes, fresh grape juice, stored juice or vineyards as a possession. Here they are presumably solid grapes.

Tirosh conveys God's desire to bless. It should never be connected with alcohol. "One of the facts which is most apparent about the Biblical usage of the word *tirosh* is that it speaks of a commodity which is not only approved by God but which is a key aspect of the blessings which he desires to bestow upon his people."[16]

Hosea 2:22 (Nonalcoholic):

> And the earth shall hear the corn, and the wine (*tirosh*) (grapes), and the oil; and they shall hear Jezreel.

Fenton translates this as "the corn, the fruit, and the oil."

Wine, in this case, is referred to as a necessity and a blessing which *tirosh* usually does.

The writer seems to be saying that the earth shall hear of the needs of the Jezreelites and will produce the grain, the fruits and the oil. *Tirosh* and *yitshar* have the same relation to earth as *dahgan* (corn), not alcohol.

Hosea 3:1 (Nonalcoholic):

> THEN said the LORD unto me, Go yet, love a woman beloved of *her* friend, yet an adulter-

16. Teachout 1980.

ess, according to the love of the LORD toward the children of Israel, who look to other gods, and love flagons of wine (*ashishah*) (raisin cakes).

Flagon—a container of liquid with a handle possibly two pints.—Webster. Flagon incorrect with todays meanings. *Ashishah* is raisin cake.

LXX [Codex A] Cakes (made) with raisins.

Fenton, *NASB, NIV,* and *Tanakh* translate this word as 'raisin cake'. Similar are 'cakes of raisins'—Revised Version, 1901, and Revised Standard Version, 1960.

Commentators who use later translations are not concerned with this antiquated use of *ashishah* as wine, for in these later translations there is no mention of wine.

Hosea still loves his adulterous woman, though she loves to be loved by others. Israel is portrayed as an adulterous woman. Her interest is in less demanding gods, as well as in worldly high living which is symbolized here by her love for raisin confectioneries. But he still loved her and wanted her back.

Hosea 4:11 (Alcoholic and Nonalcoholic):

Whoredom and wine (*yayin*) and new wine (*tirosh*) (possession of grape juice) take away the heart.

"Grape juice." Analytical Coincordance to the Bible, Young p.1058. "Hebrew *tirosh,* new wine.." Strongs Comparative Concordance, p.251.

Funk and Wagnall's *Dictionary*: "Must, unfermented juice of the grape, new wine." (1969). *Young Index Lexicon, "Tirosh,* new wine, sweet wine." p.50. Ferrar Fenton, 1907. Tirosh, "Possession of grapes."

Tirosh (always nonalcoholic) is the Hebrew word translated *new wine* in this verse. Nonalcoholic—See Genesis 27:28. It may seem strange that it is found in the same sentence as whoredom and *Yayin,* which could be an alcoholic wine for drinking. *Yayin* is used often as a symbol of God's wrath and judgment. This chapter deals with the sin of whoredom, as the worship of other gods, and the resulting judgment of God on the people of Israel.

Sin is often the extreme use or wrong use of a legitimate blessing. The Scriptures often use the word whoredom to refer to turning to other gods, or not remaining true to the God of Abraham. Their 'marriage vows' to God were broken, resulting in spiritual whoredom against God.

The Westminster divine (1651) say: The meaning of this verse is that their abundance makes them run into all riot." Lees p. 219.

A wise old saying is: Too much of a good thing is a bad thing. So, apparently, one can over indulge in most anything, including good, nutritious, fresh, sweet grapes. It could be idolatry, in the sense that anything, even a grape possession that is put before a full devotion to God, is an idol. The abuse of a good thing can take away the heart, including possessions, if possessions of grape juice, grape syrup or vineyards are put before God. The love of possessions, stores of possessions of grape juice take away the heart, or understanding.

Tirosh, new wine or fresh juice, is here in the same verse with whoredom and wine (*yayin*) but it does not mean they are of the same ilk! Whoredom is not literally intoxication, neither are they the same as *tirosh*, that valued possession. To write that whoredom and intoxicating wine and new wine take away the 'heart,' would be tautological. The terms are symbolical of different things.

Dr. William Patton, in his book *Bible Wines*, adds that the abundant possession of *tirosh* or sweet grapes was a symbol of prosperity. Prosperity often leads to sinful pride. "*Tirosh* may represent luxury, and in this application, dishonesty, formed a portion of the tithes, rapacity in exaction, and perversion in their use, is fitly charged with taking away the heart."[17] Certain interpreters imagine that only alcoholic drinks take away the heart; but we know from the Bible that ambition, worldly pleasures, pride and love of possessions, and other things, take away the heart.

Ezekiel 16:49 brings this idea of prosperity causing separation from God, and pride, to the fore:

> "Behold this was the iniquity of thy sister Sodom, pride, fullness of bread, and abundance of idleness was in her and in her daughters, neither did she strengthen the hand of the poor and needy."

So, a paraphrase of Hosea 4:11 might be rendered: "Whoredom and drunkenness and possessions of grape products take away the heart of my priests."

Tirosh is mentioned 38 times, but not once is there a mention of an Israelite drinking it. It was stored. Later it would be prepared for drinking. While stored it belonged to someone, it was a possession.

As noted earlier, *tirosh* has been at times translated as possessions, and this is confirmed by linguist Dr. S. Lee. Professor Davidson, in his *Analytic Hebrew Lexicon,* also supports this view. Ferrar Fenton also agrees that *tirosh* sometimes means possession, rather than strictly a beverage.[18]

TLB paraphrases verse 11:4 "Wine, women and song have robbed my people of their brains."[19]

Teachout translated it as "Harlotry, wine and even the freshly pressed grape juice of the harvest have taken away their allegiance."[20]

I suggest this possible rendering: "Wanton idolatry, alcoholic wine and grape prosperity turn the heart from God." I cannot see any indication, that new wine is alcoholic. It never is. But if it were, it would be an added condemnation of alcoholic wine drinking. Writes Samuel Bacchiocchi, "They are condemned . . . regardless of the quantity used . . . spiritual apostasy."[21] No room here for moderation. For other notes on *tirosh,* see Genesis 27:28.

It has been said, this indicates *tirosh* is alcoholic, not so. No documentation.

Wine skin bottles

Hosea 7:5 (Alcoholic):

> In the day of our king the princes have made *him* sick with bottles of wine; he stretched out his hand with scorners.

A more accurate translation would be this: At the king's birthday party, the princes made the king sick with *Chemah*: alcoholic, poisonous wine, and he joined hands with scorners.

"It is not for kings to drink (alcoholic) wine," Proverbs 31:4. "They made our king sick . . . with the poison of wine". *Tanakh,* the Jewish translation, 1985. The *NIV*, "Princes have made *him* sick."

Wine is a mocker, betraying kings and princes. It carries its own punishment with intoxication, poison and sickness. But, the abstainer has cool sobriety and health.

17. 1871.
18. The Bible in Modern English 1872.
19. c.1971.
20. 1979.
21. Bacchiocchi 1989.

Hosea 7:14 (Nonalcoholic):

> And they have not cried unto me with their heart, when they howled upon their beds: they assemble themselves for corn and wine (*tirosh*) (grape juice), and they rebel against me.

Lee, "For corn and vine fruit they assemble." NIV, "New wine." Fenton translates as "corn and fruit." The phrase "corn and wine" is used similarly to our English term meat and drink, or simply something to eat, provisions in general.

Tirosh is never connected with alcohol, see Genesis 27:28.

With torture and sickness, they still continue to gather God's blessings of corn and fruit, but without gratitude or repentance. They gathered to beg help from idols, rather than to acknowledge that their blessings, corn and grapes, came from God, the God of their forefathers, Abraham, Isaac, and Jacob.

Hosea 9:2 (Nonalcoholic):

> The floor and the winepress shall not feed them, and the new wine (*tirosh*) (grapes) shall fail in her.

Fenton translates: " 'Juice' shall be wanting you." Lee: "Wine-fruit shall fail." *NIV, NASB*, "New wine."

God warned Israel that His blessings, including grape juice, would be withdrawn if they continued to rebel against Him and failed to acknowledge His authority. God would not tolerate idolatry in His people.

Fermented wine could not possibly come out of the wine press of fresh grapes. Israel's hot weather could cause fresh juice to ferment rather quickly, but not that quickly! For some to say that this refers to alcoholic wine is to reveal very little, if any, knowledge about the laws of fermentation. God does not make fermented wine. Fermented wine results from what man does in crushing grapes and processing the juice over a period of time, with proper temperature, without sunlight.

Tirosh usually means grapes or dehydrated grape juice. Grape juice is a food, never alcoholic. See notes on Genesis 27:28 for more on *tirosh*.

Hosea 9:4 (Nonalcoholic):

> They shall not offer wine (grape juice) *offerings* to the LORD, neither shall they be pleasing unto him: their sacrifices *shall* be unto them as the bread of mourners; all that eat thereof shall be polluted: for their bread for their soul shall not come into the house of the LORD.

"Grape juice." Young p.1058.

Because of Israel's sins, they would be forced from Israel itself and taken to foreign lands where they could not offer any offering to God. They would be prisoners of war, captives, slaves in strange lands.

The Israelites were not to drink fermented drinks, (Proverbs 23:31), "Their wine *is* the poison" (Deutronomy 32:33), nor to offer them as drink offerings. "No . . . offering . . . shall be made with leaven." (Leviticus 2:11). Then would God expect fermented juice or wine to be part of the Sacrament of Communion? Reformed alcoholics have started drinking again after taking alcoholic communion.

Hosea 14:7 (Nonalcoholic):

> They that dwell under his shadow shall return; they shall revive *as* the corn, and grow as the vine: the scent thereof *shall be* as the wine (grape juice) of Lebanon.

"Grape juice." Young p.1058.

Their return to their own homeland is assured. The prophecy is certain. They shall grow as the grapes. Luxuries as well as the necessities of food, drink, shelter and clothing would once again be theirs. Homes would again be lovely. The aroma of grape juice would be fragrant. No longer would the malodorous stench of alcoholic breath be rampant. Prosperity in daily needs is God's blessing for those who "dwell under His shadow." Grape juice is a blessing for those who dwell under his wing. Fermented wine is a curse to those who do not choose God's canopy of protection. So Hosea begs his people to return to God, to be forgiven, loved, cared for, and prospered.

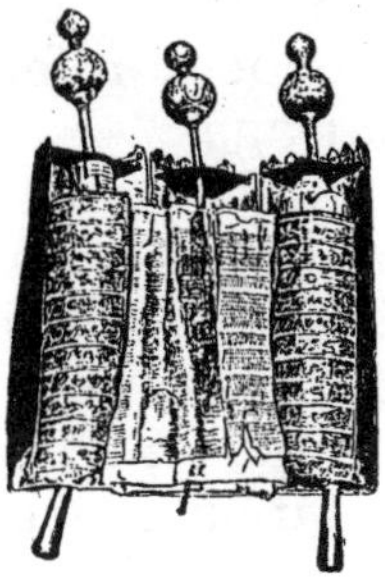

Ancient scroll

Notice "grow as the vine." Wine does not grow. Grapes grow.

"The scent of the boiling of Lebanon wine was almost universal."[22]

JOEL

Joel 1:5 (Alcoholic and Nonalcoholic):

> Awake, ye drunkards, and weep; and howl, all ye drinkers of wine (*yayin*), because of the new wine (*asis*) (grape juice); for it is cut off from your mouth.

The Hebrew word here translated "drinkers of wine" is *yayin*, in this case fermented wine, the wine of drunkards. But for 'new wine' the Hebrew word is *asis*, grape juice, a food that is healthful and pleasant to the taste. The prophet is telling them that there will be no more wine. Joel, because of the brevity of his book was a Minor Prophet, but one with a major message for straying Israel. He was one of the first great prophets to prophesy of the insect evils to come upon Judah because of her sins.

Joel 1:10 (Nonalcoholic):

> The field is wasted, the land mourneth; for the corn is wasted: the new wine (*tirosh*) (grape juice) is dried up, the oil (*Yitzer*) languisheth.

New wine, "must, expressed unfermented juice of the grape." Funk and Wagnalls.

According to William Ritchie, *tirosh* here means grapes, as bottled liquid does not dry up.[23]

The first part of Joel's prophecy deals with destruction by insects of the grape vines, the vineyards, so necessary to their economy. No grape juice would be available since the grape harvest was destroyed by insects. Some scholars see in this a double prophecy, including the coming judgment on the Chaldeans—their destruction.

Locust
(Acridium Peregrimum).

Tirosh vine fruit, and *Yitzer*-orchard oil, are both unprocessed produce. It would take processing to turn vine fruit into fermented products. With knowledge today of the Hebrew language, there should be no confusion over the approval or disapproval by God of alcoholic wine. He disapproves its use entirely. *Tirosh*, a food, is never alcoholic.

Fenton's version reads: "Its 'drink' from the Lord's house is gone."[24]

Joel 2:19 (Nonalcoholic):

> Yea, the LORD will answer and say unto his people, Behold, I will send you corn, and wine, (*tirosh*) (grape juice) and oil, and ye shall be satisfied therewith: and I will no more make you a reproach among the heathen:

22. Sir John Bowring, Bible Commentary.

23. Reynolds 1983.
24. Fenton 1903.

Dr. Fenton's translation, "I will send you the corn and the fruit."[25] Lee "vine-fruit, and the orchard fruit" (1970).

In this chapter, although the "day of the Lord" comes, He will not allow total destruction of the land. There is hope among the people in spite of the punishment about to come upon them, because of their turning away from God. Eventually, "Behold, I will send you corn and wine" (vine fruit). However God does not send alcoholic beverages. These are an evil creation of man. God assures his people of His unfailing love, discipline them for their disobedience, He would once again let their land produce, and they would reap their harvest of grapes. Fresh, pure grape juice would flow, and refreshing drink would once more be available to them. *Tirosh* is always nonalcoholic. See Genesis 27:28.

Joel 2:24 (Nonalcoholic):

> And the floors shall be full of wheat, and the fats shall overflow with wine (tirosh) and oil (vats).

Fenton translates it thus: "Your stores shall pour out their fruit."[26] *Tirosh* is never connected with alcohol.

The Hebrew word used in this reference is *tirosh*, the refreshing, always nonalcoholic sweet juice from the vines.

Not only would there again be fresh grape juice, but an abundance of it. The vats would overflow. A real restoration was promised. What the locusts would eat, would eventually be restored.

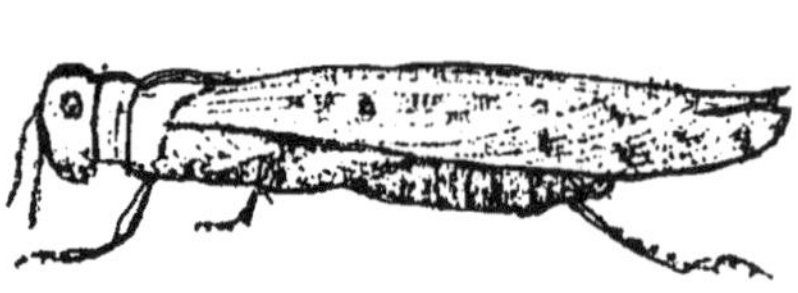

Locust
(Oedipoda migratoria).

25. Fenton 1979.
26. Fenton 1872.

Joel 3:3 (Alcoholic):

> And they have cast lots for my people; and have given a boy for an harlot, and sold a girl for wine, that they might drink.

The time period is a bit vague in this reference.

Some Bible scholars suggest this is a prophetic reference to the final days of our age.

Addiction to alcohol causes moral maladjustment to say the least! Children traded like a piece of property! Boys traded as prostitutes. Girls traded for a bottle of wine. Imagine the anguish caused to children, all to satisfy those who had made drink their god!

Joel 3:18 (Nonalcoholic):

> And it shall come to pass in that day, that the mountains shall drop down new wine (*asis*) (fresh grape juice), and the hills shall flow with milk, and all the rivers of Judah shall flow with waters, and a fountain shall come forth of the house of the LORD, and shall water the valley of Shittim.

Lee translates, "Drop down fresh juice" LXX, "Drop sweetness." Vulgate, "Drop sweetness."

Asis, translated new wine, means to tread down—freshly expressed juice; therefore nonalcoholic.[27]

This prophecy relates to the time period following the captivity. "The mountains shall drop down new wine," is a poetic expression of God's abundant blessing to be showered once again on His people. The land would once again be fertile and productive.

Joel's prophecy reads like an elegant poem. Some believe this book to be possibly the earliest recorded prophecy. Why then was this little book relegated to the back of the Minor Prophets? When the Canon was formed, the Ma-

27. Bible Encyclopedia 1909.

jor Prophets were placed first. They were labelled major because of the volume of the material, not because their messages were more important.

AMOS

Amos 2:8 (Probably Alcoholic):

> And they lay themselves down upon clothes laid to pledge by every altar, and they drink the wine of the condemned in the house of their god.

Verses 6, 7, and 8 of this chapter enumerate the revolting, repulsive, oppressive, and idolatrous sins of Israel. They were unmerciful to the poor. They indulged themselves in the idolatrous worship of Astarte, which involved public prostitution. Fathers and sons prostituted the same maid. Regarding "clothes laid to pledge," Deuteronomy 24:19-13 sheds light on this strange custom. The poor were allowed to pledge something, generally an article of clothing or blankets, in faith or honor, promising to repay a debt on something borrowed. God specifically required the one accepting the pledge to return it to the lender the same day, so "he may sleep in his own raiment." Here, in Amos 2:8, it seems the early instructions had been all but forgotten. The lender was not returning the pledged items. Wines were paid as security, for a loan. They were drinking this wine given as security. The fines had been unjust, possibly a means of procuring more wine to drink. Drinking these wines, in the temple of their gods, was their method of declaring what they felt was acceptable practice. After all, they offered the wine to their gods; don't some Christians use alcoholic wine in communion?

But God, the true *Elohim*, whom they had been taught to worship, had plenty to say in condemnation of such practices. Such behavior was sin and it must be punished.

Amos 2:12 (Probably Alcoholic):

> But ye gave the Nazarites wine to drink; and commanded the prophets, saying, Prophesy not.

Numbers 6:3 declared in no uncertain terms just what were the rules for the Nazarites. Part of the rules included these words: "He shall separate himself from wine and strong drink." Peer pressure causes many weak people to give in and accept a drink that is alcoholic, or take drugs that may ultimately kill. In my own childhood, others, unsuccessfully, tried to get me to take a drink with them. Ridicule, even in childhood, is hard to take. It is easier for many to join in the drinking rather than lose face and be ridiculed. We must instill into our children strength enough to resist and say a resounding "NO!" More power to former first lady, Nancy Reagan, who, in her campaign against drugs, encouraged kids to say "*NO TO DRUGS*." Alcoholism among junior high and senior high students is fast reaching epidemic proportions. Alcoholism is our number one drug problem.

Conformity is becoming a serious problem, even among Christians. Christians involved in office parties find themselves pressured to take a drink, to "share" in the lives of co-workers. "Being at one with my fellow workers," seems to be the thinking pattern now. Christians have been known to believe that "joining in" will cause the other to listen to their testimony of faith in God. However, it has the opposite effect. The non-Christian sets standards for Christian conduct much higher than that which the Christian sets for himself.

The Living Bible paraphrases Romans 12:2 so succinctly:

> "Don't copy the behavior and customs of this world, but be a new and different person with a fresh newness in all you do and think. Then

> you will learn from your own experience how his ways will really satisfy you."[28]

It's easiest to resist temptation with sound Christian training—and witnesses.

Amos 5:11 (Nonalcoholic):

> Forasmuch therefore as your treading is upon the poor, and ye take from him burdens of wheat: ye have built houses of hewn stone, but ye shall not dwell in them; ye have planted pleasant vineyards, but ye shall not drink wine (grape juice) of them.

"Grape juice." Analytical Concordance to the Bible, Young p.1058.

"The inference would naturally be that the wine was really contained in the vineyards, not needing the process of fermentation to produce it, but only pressure to educe it."[29] Fresh, no time to ferment, therefore nonalcoholic.

Because of their mistreatment of the poor, God told them, through Amos, that they would not reap the benefit of their own harvest. Though they planted vineyards, they would not reap a harvest, thereby having no grapes from which to receive fruit juice. A negative regarding even fresh grape juice.

In this case, because of their leaving God, their enemies would drink the grape juice from the vineyards.

Amos 6:6 (Alcoholic):

> That drink wine in bowls, and anoint themselves with the chief ointments: but they are not grieved for the affliction of Joseph.

Gold Bowl

"Woe to Zion!" declares the prophet. He then lists the sins being committed in the daily lives of the people. This reference concludes with a description of their drinking problem: drinking wine by the bowlful. Along with this, they anointed themselves with expensive ointment. I wander if this expensive ointment could have been something like a breath freshener used to cover their alcoholic breath? They expressed no concern about those in their communities who were in need, thereby failing to live up to God's directives for their lives.

A wino becomes so enslaved by alcohol that he will spend his last dime for drinks regardless of whether he has food to eat, or a place of shelter. His least concern is for others.

"To drink large quantities of wine was customary among eminent topers . . . To swallow gallons of liquor at one sitting was a feat held in great esteem, without reference to the intoxicating quality of what was consumed."[30]

Amos 9:13 (Nonalcoholic):

> Behold, the days come, saith the LORD, that the plowman shall overtake the reaper, and the treader of grapes him that soweth seed; and the mountains shall drop sweet wine (*asis*) (fresh grape juice), and all the hills shall melt.

Some do not use the word wine. LXX "Drop sweetness," Vulgate, "Distill sweetness." NASB: "New wine." "From the Hebrew, 'fresh,' 'sweet,' 'pure." *The Popular and Critical Encyclopedia*, 1909, p.1725.

There is no question of the kind of wine referred to here, since even in the KJV, the term *sweet wine* is used for *asis*. In poetical images the prophet holds out hope to the people that happier times are ahead. Agricultural abundance without exhausting the soil is envisioned.

The Hebrew term *asis*, here as elsewhere, indicates a dripping of fresh grape juice. Sweet wine is a better term than merely *wine*; which is the

28. Copyright 1971.
29. Lees 1968.
30. Lees and Burns 1868.

general translation. In 1611, the term *wine* meant also unfermented juice, but it does not mean that now. But with copy cat scholars, most modern versions still term it *sweet wine*. *Asis* certainly is not alcoholic wine, and should not be translated wine in today's parlance.

Amos 9:14 (Nonalcoholic):

> And I will bring again the captivity of my people of Israel, and they shall build the waste cities, and inhabit *them*; and they shall plant vineyards, and drink the wine (grape juice) thereof; they shall also make gardens, and eat the fruit of them.

"Grape juice." Young p.1058.

Drink the wine of the vineyards.

Yayin is the term used here and means the drinking of the juice, whereas *asis* refers to the free-flowing juice from the presses. Originally, the term *wine* was used to translate words having clearly different meanings. Some writers have wrongly concluded that the word *wine* is only in reference to fermented wine, not sweet, fresh juice.

Prof. Teachout translates, "Come buy *grape juice* and milk." We go with Dr. Teachout, and Dr. Van Impe and Roger Campbell here in concluding that the reference is to unfermented juice. The tenor of this verse is bright and cheerful. When the tone of *yayin* is dark, it is usually in reference to a curse.

OBADIAH

Obadiah 1:5

> If thieves came to thee, if robbers by night, (how art thou cut off!) would they not have stolen till they had enough? if the grapegatherers came to thee, would they not leave some grapes?

Obadiah writes as if the desolation has already come. This is in reference to the desolation to be caused by the Chaldean invasion.

Wine, as such, is not mentioned in this one reference in the single chapter book. But grapes held such an important place in the lives and economy of the Israelites, the prophet had to mention them. His mentioning *grapegatherers* and *grapes* would have touched them deeply, because of the value of the grape harvest.

The ordinary thief would leave something behind. Normally a thief steals some things from a home, but not everything. The Prophet is saying that the Chaldeans would come and destroy everything! No grapes would be left.

JONAH

Jonah is the only book in the entire Old Testament that mentions neither wine, grape juice nor grapes. Apparently there was no reason why it should come up in this particular book. Jonah presents a unique subject matter, not actually related to the topic of wine, either sweet or fermented.

MICAH

Micah 2:11 (Uncertain):

> If a man walking in the spirit and falsehood do lie, saying, I will prophesy unto thee of wine (grape juice) and of strong drink (*shekar*) (sweet orchard juice); he shall even be the prophet of this people.

If a man in mind and falsehood do lie, saying I will prophesy—Revised Version of 1885.

Depraved people are willing to accept lies, in favor of alcoholic wine and strong drink.

But before the return of prosperity, through God's blessings, there must first come captivity, punishment for sin and idolatry. Samaria is to be reduced to a heap of rubble, as happened with the coming of Shalmaneser. People do not like to hear of coming doom. Today, as in Micah's day, people have 'itching ears,' preferring to hear about a God who only loves, who does not punish, and who overlooks backsliding in His people.

Unforgiven sin will be punished—God's teaching method.

Is this verse telling us that the preachers of that day, as today, assured the people that drinking alcoholic beverages was acceptable in God's sight? As the verse says, these prophets do lie.

Micah 6:15 (Nonalcoholic):

> Thou shalt sow, but thou shalt not reap; thou shalt tread the olives, but thou shalt not anoint thee with oil; and sweet wine (*tirosh*) (grape juice), but shalt not drink wine (*yayin*).

Fenton translates, "And grapes, but not drink of wine ."[31]

Tirosh is never related to alcohol, and generic *Yayin* are both used in this prophetic message.

This reference is similar in content to the prophecy of Amos. Without God's blessing, there is no ultimate future assurance of even the necessities being available.

Tirosh is referred to as a food, while *yayin* refers to a drink. One refers to a "sweet wine" while the other at times refers to fermented wine. It is strange that some Bible scholars cannot see the difference here. Literally, the prophet says: "Thou shalt tread out the grapes . . . *tirosh* but shall not drink the beverage *yayin* that is a product of the treading process." These should not be translated wine in today's vernacular. In modern day versions, the word *wine* should not be used to mean fresh juice, because it means alcoholic wine today. It was impossible for fresh juice being treaded out to be alcoholic or wine. Fermentation takes a period of time, with exposure to yeast spores, enzymes, and proper temperature. Juice protected by the grape skin does not ferment. When fresh juice is treaded out it is sweet, not fermented, and not wine.

Even "sweet wine" in today's world leaves a mental picture of a certain type of fermented wine, a sugary, intoxicating wine, as opposed to a dry intoxicating wine.

What does Webster say about the word *must*? "Must, new wine, *mustus*, fresh, the juice pressed from grapes or other fruit before it has fermented."[32]

Is it so much easier to say incorrectly "sweet wine" than grape juice?

31. The Bible and Wine 1907.

32. New World Dictionary 1988.

Study Notes

NAHUM

Nahum 1:10 (Alcoholic):

> For while they be folden together as thorns, and while they are drunken as drunkards, they shall be devoured as stubble fully dry.

An intoxicated person is both perplexed and unsteady. While in such a state, he or she shall endure the judgment of the Lord. Wine is not mentioned here, but the people were certainly aware of the degeneracy brought on by alcohol, fermented fruit juice. One could not likely be "drunken as drunkards" without having consumed alcoholic wine or alcoholic strong drink. Sweet grape juice, freshly, extracted, will not intoxicate. It rejuvenates.

HABAKKUK

Habakkuk 2:5 (Alcoholic):

> Yea also, because he transgresseth by wine, he is a proud man, neither keepeth at home, who enlargeth his desire as hell, and is as death, and cannot be satisfied, but gathereth unto him all nations, and heapeth unto him all people:

It is believed this was a direct reference to the haughty Nebuchadnezzer. Because he transgresseth by wine. Here the evils from wine are listed.

Alcoholic wine tends to lead to selfishness and pride. Nebuchadnezzer was an ambitious king, proud and powerful, but one who could not rest, and was often inebriated by wine and marred by his excesses. He was headed for tragedy because of his pride; for four years he imagined himself to be a beast, and ate grass (Daniel 4:33).

Habakkuk 2:15 (Alcoholic):

> Woe unto him that giveth his neighbor drink, that puttest thy bottle to him, and makest him drunken also, that thou mayest look on their nakedness!

A thorough study of wine cannot be made without reference to drunkenness. Did being drunk cause them to dance around naked? Worse, "Look on nakedness" means licit sexual intercourse. See Levitious 20:17 and 18. Drunkenness, at least causes vulnerability.

ZEPHANIAH

Zephaniah 1:13 (Nonalcoholic):

> Therefore their goods shall become a booty, and their houses a desolation: they shall also build houses, but not inhabit them; and they shall plant vineyards, but not drink the wine (grape juice) thereof.

"Grape juice." Young's Analytical Concordance, p.1058.

Fenton translates: "If they plant orchards, they shall not feast on their 'fruit' " (1872).

Again, this is a reference to fresh juice straight from the extracted grapes. Though it was a sweet, refreshing beverage, they would not get to enjoy it.

This prophecy is similar to those of Amos 5:11 and Micah 6: 15.

The sins of the people result in God's wrath and punishment, but again, he holds out a promise of forgiveness and peace and prosperity. However at the first, they shall not get to drink the grape juice from their vineyards. Their treasures shall become spoils of war for the enemy. They shall not enjoy the blessing of the fruit of the vine. Pure grape juice, unadulterated, is a blessing from God, as opposed to alcohol, which is a curse.

HAGGAI

Haggai 1:11 (Nonalcoholic):

> And I called for a drought upon the land, and upon the mountains, and upon the corn, and upon the new wine (*tirosh*) (grape juice), and upon the oil, and upon *that* which the ground bringeth forth, and upon men, and upon cattle, and upon all the labour of the hands.

Ferrar Fenton translates thus: ". . . on the 'fruit' and on the oil." Lee: "Vine-fruit" 1868.

Tirosh is the Hebrew word used in this verse, a food, always nonalcoholic. New American Standard Bible, "New wine" and New International Version, "New Wine."

This does not refer to an artificial procedure which results in alcoholic wine or fermentation, but to the growing produce of the soil, grapes.

Whether as a threat, a punishment, or a blessing, the fruit of the vine is definitely prominent. In this case, the threat of taking away the grapes worked.

Haggai 2:12 (Nonalcoholic):

> If one bear holy flesh in the skirt of his garment, and with his skirt do touch bread, or pottage, or wine (grape juice), or oil, or any meat, shall it be holy? And the priests answered and said, No.

"Grape juice." Young's Analytical Concordance, p.1058.

The grape juice is listed with other food things, therefore nonalcohol.

ZECHARIAH

Zechariah 9:15 (Nonalcoholic):

> The LORD of hosts shall defend them; and they shall devour, and subdue with sling stones; and they shall drink, *and* make a noise as through wine (grape juice); and they shall be filled like bowls, *and* as the corners of the altar.

"Grape juice, Young p.1058.

The Lord does not defend alcoholic wine drinkers. The alters were holy, no poisonous wine.

They would celebrate their victory with a feast, and drink, and shout and become ecstatic, as if they had been drinking refreshing, invigorating grape juice.

The Jonathan translation of this text reads: "Like those who drink wine" are refreshed.

Incense altar

Zechariah 9:17 (Nonalcoholic):

> For how great *is* his goodness, and how great *is* his beauty! corn shall make the young men cheerful, and new wine (*tirosh*) (grape juice) the maids.

Tirosh is the word used here for wine. *NASB* and *NIV*, translate "New Wine." "Must, pressed from grapes before it has fermented, new wine." Webster.

The young men would be gladdened by the bountiful harvest of grain, and the young women would be happy in their preparation of drink from the abundance of grapes.

"The bloom and lusciousness of the vine-cluster better harmonized with the beauty and sweetness of the Jewish virgin than the masculine attributes of the rougher sin." (Lees p.246).

Zeahariah 10:7 (Nonalcoholic):

> And *they* of Ephraim shall be like a mightly *man*, and their heart shall rejoice as through wine (grape juice): yea, their children shall see *it*, and be glad; their heart shall rejoice in the LORD.

Grape juice: Young Analyical Concordance, p.1058.

Rejoice and be glad, as opposed to, don't even look at the alcoholic wine. Proverbs 23:31.

MALACHI

Malachi 3:11 (Nonalcoholic):

> And I will rebuke the devourer for your sakes, and he shall not destroy the fruits of your ground; neither shall your vine cast her fruit before the time in the field, saith the LORD of hosts.

While Malachi 3:11, gives the promise that the vine shall not lose its fruit, the preceeding verse in Zechariah 10:7 is the last mention of wine in the Old Testament. In the first usage wine is a curse, in the last reference it is a blessing. There are two opposite meanings according to the context, as there are with many words. The word "fast" has nine meanings: To anchor solidly, or the opposite, to move speedily, and seven other meanings.

CONCLUSION

We have covered the verses where wine is mentioned 234 times in the Old Testament along with some related words. We have endeavored to determine by exegesis and context, where possible, and as related to the Bible's overall teaching, as to whether alcoholic wine or nonalcoholic for most mentions of the word wine.

The first mention of wine in the Old Testament begins with drunkenness. The last mention of the vine ends with God giving victory over the enemy, and the vine is to have lasting fruit and is to be a blessing. May it be so!

CHAPTER ELEVEN

New Testament Commentary

On Each

Use of The Word Wine

The Gospels

"If I am right, your chapters are valid and sound, and your basic conclusions are legitimate. My attempts at exegesis over the years have often pained me to realize how much cultural conditioning influences and modifies our grasp of the truth. Every generation needs folk like you to set the record straight and 'by all means to save some!'" -- Wilbur T. Dayton.

Wilbur T. Dayton, B.D., M.R.E., M.A., Th.D.
Asbury Theological Seminary
Professor Emeritus
Chairman, Biblical Literature
Union Biblical Seminary, Yeatmal, India,
Houghton College, former president
Wesley Biblical Seminary
Greek professor
Vice President
Author
many books and articles

CHAPTER ELEVEN THE GOSPELS

ALCOHOLIC WINE IS NEVER COMMENDED

Context here means not only the immediate surrounding subject matter, but also how the subject relates to the entire Bible's teaching.

This commentary on wine in the New Testament will probably often be used to look up specific verses. It is therefore necessary to have some repetition of material to cover similar verses.

The usual Greek word translated "wine" in the Authorized Version in the New Testament is *Oinos*. When other Greek words are used, they will be indicated. When no other Greek word is indicated, the word referred to will be *Oinos*.

The word *Oinos*, like its counterpart *Yayin* in the Old Testament, is a generic term. It can mean alcoholic or nonalcoholic wine, depending on how it is used, and this is determined by the context, exegesis, or as it relates to, and is consistent with Bible teaching.

Says Ralph Earle, Distinguished Prof. Emeritus of Nazarene Theological Seminary, "In both the Hebrew (OT) and the Greek (NT) the same word is used for both fermented and unfermented juice, so it cannot be insisted that an alcoholic beverage is meant," Earle 1988-89 Peloubet Sunday School Notes.

Dr. Ralph Earle

Dr. Ralph Earle is one of those who originally inspired me to write this book. He is a graduate of Eastern Nazarene College (B.A.), Boston University (M. A.), and Gordon Divinity School B.D. and Th.D., He has also taken postdoctoral studies at Harvard and Edinburgh universities.

In more recent years he has served on the fifteen-man Committee on Bible Translation, the governing body for the New International Version of the Bible. Part of the time as chairman.

Chapters 11 through 14 of this book, as in the Old Testament, present a verse by verse New Testament commentary on every verse that mentions the word wine and also 35 related words; such as winebibber, drink, fruit of the vine, vinegar, etc.

Must by dictionary definition, is unfermented grape juice.

See endnotes for documentations. Some ancient books do not have dates or addresses.

"Drugs? I never use drugs—only alcohol."

MATTHEW

Oy'nos (Gr. οινος), the Greek generic term for wine, from the Hebrew yah'yin

Popular and Critical Encyclopedia 1907, p.1726

Matthew 9:17—(Also in Mark 2:22, and Luke 5:39)

Neither do men put new wine into old bottles: else the bottles break, and the wine runneth out, and the bottles perish: but they put new wine (grape juice) into new bottles, and both are preserved.

Nonalcoholic

"Grape juice," Young's Analytical Concordance, p.1058.

New wine, *oinon neon*, fresh from the press. Must, is without fermentation. All three of the above Gospel references refer to grape juice, says *Young's Analytical Concordance*, "New Wine, sweet wine, grape juice" 1910, p.1058.

This first mention of "wine" in the New Testament is nonalcoholic. "Neither do they pour fresh grape juice," translates the British Ferrar Fenton (1907).

This verse is part of Jesus' answer to the Disciples of John the Baptist, when they asked why the Disciples of Jesus did not fast as they and the Pharisees did. Jesus replied that His teaching could never be put into the old dogmas of the Scribes and Pharisees. A completely new bottle, or wine skin, was required. A new and different dispensation was underway, and rules and methods must also undergo a complete change.

Bottles of Skins

Bottles are translated *wine-skins*. In all the later versions: *New wine* (Greek *oinos* with adjective *neos, new*) is fresh grape juice. Fermented wine would not be called "new."

The common opinion seems to be old leather loses its elasticity, and as the grape juice would ferment, it would cause the old leather bottle to crack.

First, it should be noticed that such a view admits labeling *grape juice* as *new wine* when no fermentation is indicated. For, if it had fermented, there would be no danger of pressure of expansion.

Where did this imagined *stretch* come from? It is not to be found in any of the three gospel references.

No Skin Would Stretch Enough

None of the containers of that day, whether glass, skins, or earthen ware, would have been able to cork up the fermentation pressure once it started. The tremendous carbon dioxide pressure would shatter a new skin about as fast as an old one. As Thudicum and Dupre have pointed out, "A *must*,* one fifth sugar, develops 47 times its volume of carbonic acid, equivalent to a pressure of 34.3 atmospheres. This would be ten times the pressure of the boiler of the high pressure required by a steam engine" (p.478). Webster defines *must*, as new wine, before it has fermented.

At wineries, the fermenting is done in open vats. If fermenting grapes were enclosed, the CO_2 gas would explode.

Fermenting is largely completed before alcoholic wine is put in bottles. Carbonation is then often added to give bubbles.

Regarding this same point, *Chamber's Cyclopedia*, 1750, says, "The force of fermenting wine is very great, and would be able, if closely stopped up, to burst through the strongest cask." Job's comforter, Elihu, understood this tremendous pressure for he said, "Behold, my belly, like wine, hath no vent; like

* *Must, mustum*, "The expressed unfermented juice of the grape or other fruit" Funk and Wagnalls, 1989.

new bottles, it is rent" Job 32:19. Notice the comparison of "new bottles rent," not "old," as usually assumed.

The real meaning had to be that a new, clean skin must be used. If grape juice were put into an old wine skin that had contained fermented juice, the residue of yeast would start the ferment and break the skin whether old or new. But if new fresh grape juice, which already had the pulp and enzymes filtered out, was then heated and put into a new, unused skin, this could be kept permanently with no fear of fermentation and subsequent pressure.

Columella (12:41), an almost contemporary of Matthew, in describing the common practice of preserving unfermented wine, placed equal stress on its being put into a new, unused amphora.

Amphora, a small neck and small bottom.

Stretching has nothing to do with it. New skin would *never* stretch enough to take care of the pressure of fermentation. It is not scientifically possible for leather to stretch sufficiently according to the rules of physics.

New Clean Bottles Needed

All of this confusion comes from not translating *oinos* as "grape juice," as it should be in this case. The misunderstanding creates some strange logic, for instance, from the *Interpreter's Bible*: "These wine-skins were usually from whole goat hides, the neck and feet being tied. Naturally an opening was left for the escape of gas . . . of course, freshly made wine was put into new wine-skins; old wine-skins would burst under pressure" (R-Z 850, 1962).

Naturally, our question is, how could the skin burst under pressure if an opening were left for the escape of gas?

Matthew 10:42 (Nonalcoholic):

> And whosoever shall give to drink unto one of these little ones a cup of cold water only in the name of a disciple, verily I say unto you, he shall in no wise lose his reward.

Ancient Cretan scroll cup

(The wine maker kept things bottled up until he finally blew his cork.)

When Jesus spoke of giving a drink to others, or to himself, it is noteworthy that He always spoke of water, here He said, *cold water*, not wine. It was "fruit of the vine" at the Last Supper, not wine. For me, Israel's water is good drinking water. From north to south of Israel, I found no fault in it, except for some fruit juice, I drank nothing but Israel's water. Moses promised, "a good land, a land of brooks of water, of fountains . . ." (Deut. 89).

Matthew 11:19 (Nonalcoholic):

> The Son of man came eating and drinking, and they say, Behold a man gluttonous, and a winebibber, a friend of publicans and sinners. But wisdom is justified of her children.

Phillips translates, "Came enjoying life" (Copyright 1958).

'Winebibber' (oinopotas) or wine drinker was translated as "drunkard" in later versions, *NIV; NASB*. Jesus was derided as "winebibber" by his enemies. Since the charge was by His enemies, it had little merit, as did the comment made by the enemies of John the Baptist (who were now the enemies of Christ), that John had a devil.

A description by an enemy is likely to be false, and the truth can often be discovered by reversing an enemy's condemnation. Therefore, Jesus did not think it necessary to deny the assertion that John had a demon, or that He, Himself, was a glutton or a sensualist. If this charge indicated that Jesus drank wine, then it also indicates that He was a drunkard, glutton, sensualist, and a revolter against Roman rule.

Actually, His enemies knew that Jesus was not a drunkard. So they fabricated the charge of John's demon-possession to try to destroy his moral influence. As enemies of John, they also tried to destroy Jesus' influence, trying to discredit both. If we put any credence to the charge of a desperate enemy then we would believe anything. We would believe that Jesus was also a blasphemous person, and that he perverted the nation, for so He was charged before Caiphas' high court.

"But wisdom is justified." True wisdom is justified by its works; is honored by its children. Jesus' thought is, those who know me need no denial; those who hate me will receive none.

The glutton and drunkard's knees buckled, but his belt wouldn't buckle over his beer belly.

Matthew 15:11,20 (Nonalcoholic):

> Not that which goeth into the mouth defileth a man; but that which cometh out of the mouth, this defileth a man.
> These are *the things* which defile a man: but to eat with unwashen hands defileth not a man.

Let us consider the context. This is Christ's response to the question posed by the Pharisees in verse two: "Why do thy disciples transgress the tradition of the elders? For they wash not their hands when they eat bread."

Answering that question, Jesus defended his disciples for not washing their hands before eating. The requirement of washing hands before eating did not derive from Old Testament Law, but from one of the many traditions of the elders. It was therefore not God's law, but man's religious rules relating to matters of unclean foods. Jesus declared that true uncleanness related to moral defilement, not mere formalism. It was "not what went into a man's mouth—unclean food—that defileth him, but what came out of his mouth" (Earle, Wesleyan V. 4, p.71).* His answer had nothing to do with alcohol.

Some have implied that Jesus thereby permitted a person to drink alcohol. But this is contrary to Jesus' clear intent; it would mean that He was permitting moral defilement.

Then we need to be careful of what comes out of the mouth. Those under the influence of alcoholic drink have little control. Our influence on others is of prime importance. We should not contribute to the downfall of those who cannot hold their liquor. The only safe way is to be an example of one who is totally abstinent.

---

*Earle, Ralph, *Wesleyan Commentary.*

Study Notes

THE LORD'S SUPPER— (THE PASSOVER FEAST)

Nonalcoholic

Matthew 26:27,28,29 Also Mark 14:23,24,25 Luke 22:18,20

And he took the cup, and gave thanks, and gave it to them, saying, Drink ye all of it;

For this is my blood of the new testament, which is shed for many for the remission of sins.

But I say unto you, I will not drink henceforth of this fruit of the vine, until that day when I drink it new with you in my Father's kingdom.

No Basis For Alcoholic Communion

To use The Lord's Supper as a basis for serving alcoholic wine in communion, or any place else, is a groundless and ridiculous misunderstanding of our Lord's action. In this instance, no reputable scholar should use the word *wine*, for the text clearly calls it the "fruit of the vine" ("genneematos tees ampelou").

The Savior here does not use *oinos*, the usual Greek word for wine, whether alcoholic or not alcoholic. He deliberately used a word that was clear rather than a generic word that could be interpreted either way. He said, "the fruit of the vine," and so it is properly translated. No scholar could translate it as wine, for fruit implies being fresh and unspoiled (by fermentation). Here are scholars' translations: "fruit of the vine" Revised 1881, also Revised Standard Version 1946, NASB 1973, NIV 1978, NKJV 1983; and similarly "product of the vine" Goodspeed 1934; "produce of the vine" Weymouth 1902 and Moffatt 1934; "juice of the grape" TCNT. There is no translation as wine in Matthew 26:29.

Also, the Apostle Paul avoided *oinos* which, because of its two meanings, could be interpreted incorrectly. The drink was not alcoholic wine. Paul calls the juice, as used by Christ, "the 'cup' *protirion* of blessing which we bless, is it not the communion of the blood of Christ?" I Corinthians 10:15. He again quotes the exact words of Christ, "This 'cup' is the New Testament in my blood" I Corinthians 11:25.

"There is no positive proof that the fluid used by our Lord in instituting the sacred communion was alcoholic; it is nowhere expressly called wine."[1]

With no basis or precedent for doing so, it is difficult to understand how or why some churches began the practice of using fermented wine in their communion services. Especially since it is forbidden in the very Bible from which they teach. The only extraneous precedent dates back to some heathen religions that used "the spirits" in their worship. So apparently, what we have in our day is a carry over from a pagan practice, from Rome's god of wine, Bacchus. This has influenced the Roman Catholic Church and its successors.

"Here's to Bacchus."

It is the church that blundered by allowing pagan practices in Christian worship. The heresy has lived. It is important to correct this practice.

1. The International Standard Bible Encyclopedia 1939.

If the use of an alcoholic beverage is required in a sacred ceremony, it is certainly acceptable in secular use. Both are contrary to Scripture.

Ancient Abstinent Minded Christians

There were always Christians who believed that it was wrong to use fermented wine in communion or otherwise.

"Hardly any churches but the corrupted, intolerant, and persecuting churches of the West ever introduced any other practice than that of the abstainer."[2]

The southern African and some Asian eastern churches have not been so influenced. These use grape juice or juice from raisins.

The Christians of St. Thomas claimed to have received their Gospel from St. Thomas the Apostle. They celebrated the Lord's Supper with juice from raisins "softened one night in water" (Barbosa, p.282).

In Europe, in the fourth century, some churches were using unfermented juice; some even used water when it was too difficult to get grape juice (Thayer 79ff).

St. Thomas Aquinas, the thirteenth century Catholic scholar, said, "Grape juice has the specific quality of wine, and therefore this sacrament may be celebrated with grape juice."[3]

St. Thomas also alluded to Pope Julius who in his *Epistle to the Egyptians* stated, "But if needful let the bunch of grapes be pressed into the cup, and let water be mingled with it."[4]

Most of the confusion of today as to whether the term "wine" used in our English translation of the Bible refers to alcoholic or nonalcoholic wine, stems from the mistranslation of Greek and Hebrew terms, according to the present meaning of the word "wine."

Current Abstinent Communion

Presently, it is mostly the highly liturgical churches that use alcoholic wine in the observance of the Lord's Supper. It is very unusual to find an evangelical church with alcoholic communion. Most teach abstinence.

"To abstain from using or trafficking in substances known to be destructive of physical and mental well-being such as alcohol beverages and tobacco, and from using drugs for other than proper medical purposes."[5]

Some churches now offer communicants a choice of alcoholic or nonalcoholic in communion.

Plain water is used regularly in St. Louis by one group today, as the author has witnessed.

Alcoholic Communion Makes Alcoholics Become Drunks Again

Dr. Dayton Biblical Seminary

Dr. Wilbur Dayton 1/6/90 sends this from the *Weekly Bulletin* of the Cherokee Heights, United Methodist Church, Napier at Pio Nono:

"Dr. Thomas Welch was the son of a Methodist minister and a dentist by profession in Vineland, New Jersey, more than a hundred years ago. He also was the Communion Steward for the First Methodist Church. One Sunday a visitor with a weakness for alcohol was staying at the Welch home. Unfortunately the wine used for communion at the church that morning set the man off on a drinking binge.

2. Nott, 1863, p.227.
3. Nott.
4. Lees.

5. The Discipline of the Wesleyan Church 1988.

Dr. Welch, himself a teetotaler, was quite upset. He felt wine was wrong;and if it were wrong to use it for a beverage, it was wrong to use it as a sacrament in the church. He set out to find a substitute. In September of 1869, he and his wife and son picked about forty pounds of ripe grapes, pressed them, pasteurized the juice and bottled it.

"For weeks, the family listened for the exploding bottles which would signify their failure, but none occurred. When Dr. Welch opened the bottles and tasted the sweet, unfermented wine (as it was called), he offered it to the pastor to try out in the church. The unfermented wine was an instant success, and Dr. Welch began selling it to nearby churches. By 1880, the name was, 'Dr. Welch's Grape Juice.' "

We all know the rest of the story. Thanks to Dr. Welch and his concern, problem drinkers are not tempted at the Lord's table in many churches. The Wesleyan Discipline clearly states about the observance of the Lord's Supper, "That the pure, unfermented juice of the grape be used." We all know the rest of the story.

"Follow doctor's orders—drink only sweet kinds of wine. They won't make your head heavy.

One man's concern about a stumbling block in the path of another human being, is a lesson for each of us to make an effort to reach out and touch another life in a caring way.

Worship Leads to Alcoholism

Once an alcoholic, always an alcoholic. It certainly is terrible when a reformed alcoholic goes to church, takes communion, is overcome by temptation and is out of control again. Backsliding happens when actual fermented wine is served in Communion services in some churches. Geisler has seen it happen.[6]

"Lead us not into temptation" is for churches, too.

Lead us not into temptation

This writer, during an early pastorate in a ritualistic church, had to face this issue of an alcoholic wine in Communion. We faced it head on and absolutely forbade the use of alcoholic wine in the Communion service. The spirituality improved and the church grew.

Today there are some Synagogues where fermented wine is used. Since Mosaic Law forbids this, they use a very strange, contradictory type of reasoning. Most noteworthy Maimonides, Bartenora, and other rabbies, in allowing intoxicating wine, defend their position by supposing that it is not fermented.

They say, "It is an hypothesis of Jews that the water of fruits does not ferment; hence the prohibition does not apply to pure water and wine."[7] This is

6. 3/82 pg. 53.
7. Lees 1868.

no more strange than reasons given for using fermented juice or alcoholic wine in a Christian service. Or, the rabbies might be right, *pure* grape juice, (without the pulp), does not ferment.

No Wine At The Passover

There is no Biblical mention of a beverage for the Passover. The preparation for the celebration of the Passover Feast was not the occasion for the use of fermented wine for religious purposes in the entire Old Testament. On the contrary, during the Passover celebration, all leaven or yeast was forbidden for seven days. It was sometimes called the *feast of unleavened things.*

There is no mention of meat at the Lord's Supper. Jesus Himself was the slain Passover Lamb.

Peabody, in his essays on the Lord's Supper, writes, "The writer has satisfied himself, by careful research, that in our Savior's time, the Jews, at least the high ritualists among them, extended the prohibition of leaven to the principle of fermentation in every form; and that it was customary at the Passover festival, for the master of the household to press the contents of the 'cup' from clusters of grapes preserved for this special purpose."[8]

Jewish rabbi, Dr. S. M. Isaacs said, "In the Holy Land, they do not commonly use fermented wine. The wines are preserved sweet and unfermented. The Jews do not, in their feast for sacred purposes, including the marriage feast, ever use any kind of fermented drink."[9]

Gesenius, the eminent Hebrew scholar, says that "Leaven applied to the 'wine' as readily as to the 'bread' "[10] This is correct since yeast is the cause of fermentation in both alcoholic beverages and in bread.[11]

Dr. Leibers writes in *Turner's Chemistry*, "Ferment or yeast is a substance in a state of putrification." Freedom from petrification was predicted as a peculiarity of the Messiah. ". . . neither wilt thou suffer thine Holy One to see corruption" Psalm 16:10. Acts 13:37 expresses the direct fulfillment of the Psalm, by stating, "But he, whom God raised again, saw no corruption." All, I believe, admit that the unleavened bread which had no fermentation or putrification was the proper emblem of the body of Christ, which "saw no corruption." For the same reason, there was a necessity that the fruit of the vine should be unfermented that it might be the fit emblem of the great Sacrifice which "saw no corruption." Thou shalt not offer the blood of my sacrifice with leaven (Exodus 34:25).

". . . with all thine offerings, thou shalt offer salt", (Leviticus 2:13). Salt was offered as an ingredient because it prevented corruption, killed yeast fungus, and preserved the item into which it was placed. Jesus then would not disregard such a positive command. He would not admit leaven into the element which was to perpetuate the memory of the sacrifice of Himself, of which all other sacrifices were but types. As said John R. Rice, "Fermented wine, with microbes of decay, would not picture the perfect blood of a sinless Christ."[12]

Alcoholic Wine—Not Fruit of the Vine

Neither alcoholic wine nor vinegar can any longer be specifically called the "fruit of the vine." Both have added vinous and acetous yeast spores which have totally changed the nature of the

8. Fields 1870.
9. Patton 1871.
10. Patton 1871.
11. Thayer 1869.
12. Rice 1955.

grape juice. There is a complete decomposition of the original juice formula.

Chemistry is completely changed by the addition of yeast to grape juice. There is no more similarity than there is between barley and beer. The following chemical change takes place:

$$C_6 H_{12} O_6 \text{ becomes } C_2 H_5 OH + 2\ CO_2$$

Or to put it another way, the contrast between the vitamin and mineral rich grape is shown by *McLennon in Propaganda vs. Facts*, p.59:

General Grape Content:
- 2.8% albumen
- 83.7% carbohydrates
- 2.3% mineral salts
- 1.2% acids and extractives

Fermentation destroys:
- 98.5% albumen
- 98.0% carbohydrates
- 47.0% of acids and extractives
- 76.0% of mineral salts

The decay has taken the life away. Alcoholic wine is so changed from the original grape juice that the two have almost nothing in common.

"Hey this is delicious $C_6H_{12}O_6$!"

New—Not Aged

. . . until that day when I drink it new with you in my Father's Kingdom (Matthew 26:29).

Before further discussion regarding the falsity of assuming that Christ was referring to alcoholic wine, let us note again the key word "new," when He referred to the next time He would partake with them. He specifically indicated the beverage would be new, not aged. Freshly crushed grape juice would be "new. " Alcoholic wine is aged, and by definition and composition, not new.

By this statement, did Christ intimate that in His Father's kingdom there would be intoxicating wine?

THE LORD'S SUPPER

He said, "Drink ye all of it; For this is my blood of the New Testament, which is shed for many for the remission of sins" Matthew 26:27,28.

Ye cannot drink the cup . . . of the Lord's table, and of the table of devils (I Corinthians 10:21).

Unfermented Grape Juice Was Available

It has been taught that there were no fresh grapes at the time of year when Christ held His Last Supper with His disciples. Not so! Josephus states in reference to the fortress at Masada, that there were "all kinds of pulse (*legume*) and dates, heaped up together. These fruits, all fresh and full ripe, were in no way inferior to such fruits newly laid in, though they had been there little short of 100 years when the place was taken by the Romans."[13]

13. Josephus.

"They have the secret of preserving grapes, sound and juicy from one season to another."[14]

"Unfermented wines were made and preserved for years. Even some old wines were elaborately treated in order to free them from any intoxicating power."[15]

How about eggs that were buried in Pompeii nearly 2000 years? They were fresh and edible. Keeping food from spoilage depends on many factors.

"No, I didn't say you're well preserved. I was talking about the grape juice"

MEANS OF PRESERVING GRAPE JUICE AS NONALCOHOLIC

See chapter 6 for a detailed discussion on each of these eight means:

1. Boiling the juice (boiled juice will not ferment)
2. Filtering out the enzyme laden pulp
3. Excluding air, yeast spores from the air
4. Excluding water (no water, no fermentation)
5. Cooling and subsiding of the pulp
6. Preserving by salting
7. Fumigating to kill yeast with sulphur
8. Soaking or boiling raisins

Besides, one of their most favored drinks was freshly squeezed grape juice.

Inconsistency of Using Fermented Wine

. . . whosoever eateth leavened bread from the first day until the seventh day, that soul shall be cut off from Israel (Exodus 12:15).

Ross J. McLennon, in *Propaganda vs. Facts*, observes, "They insist that the bread used in the communion must be unleavened bread or bread made without yeast because they claim that yeast is the symbol of impurity. To some it seems rather inconsistent to insist on unleavened bread for the communion service and then insist that intoxicating wine be used which is made by the addition of yeast or bacteria cells to grape juice."[16]

Drinking alcoholic wine is far worse than using leavened bread, for the yeast and alcohol are burned away in the baking. In alcoholic wine, the leaven remains.

Fermentation is the result of active yeast. Let us clarify this with a synonym for yeast: "Leaven—a substance as yeast to produce fermentation."[17] "Leaven, or yeast, was prohibited because it was an emblem of corruption . . . It was used figuratively to denote false doctrine." (See Matthew 16:11.) Also it was compared to "impure conduct, " (See I Corinthians 5:6-8) (Dickson, copyright 1950, p.133). It was for this reason that all yeast was excluded from alter offerings to God, Leviticus 2:4.

Matthew 27:48 (Nonalcoholic):

. . . and took a sponge, and filled *it* with vinegar, and put *it* on a reed, and gave him to drink.

This verse is in harmony with Mark 15:36, Luke 23:36 and John 19:28-30. It

14. Swinburn.
15. Pliny the Elder 67 A.D.
16. McLennon 1978.
17. Webster 1965.

is one of the very few that are in all four gospels.

Since we are using the Authorized Version we have no problem here. But some questions might arise for those who use some other versions which translate as "sour wine." Such translations give today's readers the wrong idea. Wine is today understood as an intoxicating beverage. Vinegar is not intoxicating. The *NIV* translates as "wine vinegar" (copyright 1978). Wine vinegar is that found on grocery shelves, generally used in cooking, with no alcohol or stigma attached.

The word vinegar comes from the Latin *"vinaigre,"* meaning soured wine. This rendering might have served in an earlier day when wine was used as a generic term, but not today when wine is understood as intoxicating. In vinegar, the alcohol has been transformed into acid, so there is no more alcohol in it. Using vinegar as an anesthetic would be similar to giving a patient in surgery a dill pickle. (See Mark 14:36, notes.)

There was a Talmud tradition of a society of ladies in Jerusalem, that supplied execution bound criminals a drugged drink (Lees 1870).

(We need a pickle that is harder to get into and easier to get out of.)

MARK

Mark.2:22 (Nonalcoholic):

> And no man putteth new wine (grape juice) into old bottles: else the new wine doth burst the bottles, and the wine is spilled, and the bottles will be marred: but new wine must be put into new bottles.

"Grape juice, oinos" (Young's Analytical Concordance, 1910, p.1058.)

Fenton translates "new wine" as "fresh unprepared grape juice," (1907). Young's *Analytical Concordance, Lexicon*, "new wine" translates as "grape juice" (1910, p.1058).

"Grape juice must be put in new skins!" Dr. Reynold's, The Purified Version.

Old wine-skins could not be used because they likely would have a residue of ferment, causing the juice to ferment, swell and burst the bottle. Please see Matthew 9:17 for lengthy discussion.

Mark 7:15

> There is nothing from without a man, that entering into him can defile him: but the things which come out of him, those are they that defile the man.

Jesus is speaking here in reference to eating with unwashed hands, and so this verse does not refer particularly to wine. Some wrongly suggest it implys that drinking alcoholic beverages are not harmful. (See Matthew 15:11,20 notes.) To maintain that position, one would also logically approve the drinking of poison as not being harmful either. In several places, the Bible calls wine poison. Deuteronomy 32:33

"In some people, small amounts of alcohol cause profound dilation of blood vessels that can lead to red noses, flushing, headaches, and lightheadedness."[18]

Mark 14:23,24,25 (Nonalcoholic):

> And he took the cup, and when he had given thanks, he gave it to them: and they all drank of it.
>
> And he said unto them, This is my blood of the new testament, which is shed for many.
>
> Verily I say unto you, I will drink no more of the fruit of the vine, until that day that I drink it new in the kingdom of God.

(All the chief MSS, except A, omit *ho*, 'the' cup) NASB's 'a cup' would be our choice.

18. Gott, Peter H, The Daily Ledger, Noblesville 9/26/1992, p.5.

No reference here to *wine*. Dr. John R. Rice writes:

"The cup the disciples drank at the Lord's Supper is nowhere called wine, but 'the fruit of the vine.' We believe it was simply grape juice. Even if the word wine had been used, wine in the Bible means grape juice whether fermented or unfermented. Fermented wine with microbes of decay, would not picture the perfect blood of a sinless Christ."[19]

Dr. Rice personally told this author the same. See Matthew 26:29 notes.

Mark 15:23 (Alcoholic)

And they gave him to drink wine mingled with myrrh: but he received it not.

(*Piein*) (To drink, is absent from Codices aleph, B and C. So absent in NARB and NIV). He did not drink. "I will drink no more of the fruit of the vine, until that day I drink it new in the kingdom of God" (Mark 14:25).

From the *Encyclopedia Americana*: "Myrrh was used in making incense and other perfumes and as a medicine. It was one of the wise men's gifts to the Christ Child. The Myrrh of the Bible is thought . . . to have been a mixture . . . derived from various substances."[20] So it was offered to Christ at birth and death.

It was customary to give a stupefying potion to criminals being executed in order to help alleviate their sufferings. Myrrh was an added "narcotic" (Zodhiates, Hebrew-Greek Key Study Bible 1986, p.4669).

(See notes on Proverbs 31:6.) This expresses the one possible practical use of alcoholic wine. But when Jesus tasted it, He would not drink, Matthew 27:34; 31:6. Christ as an abstainer refused even this kindness.

1) He would meet his sacrificial death fully conscious.
2) He would continue abstinence. He was now performing the essential work of Eternal High Priest (Hebrew 10:22-28). High Priests were forbidden at the time of sacrifice to drink an intoxicant "lest ye die" Leviticus 10:8-11. Christ was that sacrificial High Priest who offered Himself as the meat sacrifice.

Mark 15:36 (Nonalcoholic):

And . . . filled a sponge full of vinegar, (*oxos*) . . . and gave him to drink, . . .

Christ refused the first sponge of alcoholic stupefying potion which was offered Him. The second, *oxos*, actual vinegar, contained no alcohol, this He received.

He likely wetted His parched lips, so He could cry out with a loud voice, "It is finished!"

COBRA
Asp

In spite of what some authors say, there is no evidence that Jesus ever drank poisonous alcoholic wine. On the contrary, He would not partake of that which He condemns in other parts of His word, for example, ". . . their wine is the poison of dragons, and the cruel venom of asps" Deuteronomy 32:33. To have been bitten by an asp (cobra) brought immediate death.

19. John K. Rice 1955.
20. Vol. 19, 1964.

See Matthew 27:48, for more on vinegar.

LUKE

Luke 1:15 (Nonalcoholic):

> For he shall be great in the sight of the Lord, and shall drink neither wine nor strong drink; and he shall be filled with the Holy Ghost, even from his mother's womb.

John was probably a Nazarite from birth. The Nazarites drank no alcoholic wine, and didn't touch grapes or grape products, according to Numbers 6:1-21. It is appropriate here to note the pairing of two concepts which are Biblically related in Ephesians 5:18. Not drinking wine fits well with being filled with the Holy Spirit. "And be not drunk with wine, wherein is excess; but be filled with the Spirit." John's mother was probably also an abstainer. Young's Analytical Concordance, "grape juice," 1910, p.1058.

"Here's to Mom, who made me what I am today—an alcoholic."

Jesus said, "Among them that are born of women, there hath not risen a greater than John the Baptist." Not only did he abstain, but in his mother's womb he was filled with the Holy Spirit. This is so contrary to some modern day, liberated mothers, who give birth to alcohol syndrome babies. These are handicapped babies, who probably would have been born normal and healthy, had the mother abstained from alcoholic drinks. Some babies are born as "alcoholics" and must go through withdrawal. This alcoholism becomes genetic. Even "when the child of an alcoholic parent is raised apart from the afflicted parent, the child still faces four times the risk of developing alcoholism, than a child whose biological parents were not alcoholic . . ."[21]

Matthew Henry, referring to Samson's abstaining writes, "Perhaps Samson's mother was to refrain from wine and strong drink, not only because he was designed for a Nazarite, but because he was designed for a man of strength."

Have you been drinking?
Your baby seems to be drunk."

"Not only does alcohol kill the brain cells of pregnant women, but one drink penetrates the placenta and destroys brain cells in the fetus. Much of this results in a great percentage of mentally retarded children for society to support."[22]

See notes on Judges 13:4,7,14.

Many are also born with handicaps due to the mother's drinking. How sad to see, as I have seen, an 11-year-old

21. Dr. Smith 4/27/1988.
22. Lees 1869.

boy born of an alcoholic mother, not toilet trained, and unable to eat by himself.

There have always been devout Christians who were for abstinence, especially for women. Dr. Jack Van Impe, in his book *Alcohol: The Beloved Enemy*, 1980, quotes Kotulak, "Every drink a pregnant woman takes hits her fetus with a chemical sledge-hammer." A "Hooray, I'm Pregnant" glass of champagne may permanently harm the fetus. A researcher in the field, Dr. Kenneth Lyons Jones, estimates 10 percent of babies born to "moderate drinkers" may have alcohol related problems (p.57). Alcohol is statistically the greatest cause of moron babies, next comes cocaine, crack.

". . . visiting the iniquity of the fathers (mothers) upon the children, and upon the children's children, unto the third and to the fourth generation" (Exodus 34:7).

According to Dartmouth anthropologist, Michael Davis, "Any alcohol a mother consumes passes into the bloodstream of a fetus, which promptly gets drunk." He asks, "You wouldn't give a kid a bottle of gin the day after birth, why give it one the day before?"[23]

"Beginning in November, 1989, federal law required all alcoholic beverages to carry warnings about birth defects and other hazards of drinking."[24]

"Some babies smell like powder, some like cheap wine,"[25]

For years society has tended to approve of moderate drinking for expectant mothers despite warning from older civilizations. It wasn't until the 1970's, that the old warning was rediscovered by a University of Washington team.

In their survey, "The results were striking." Children from the drinking mothers had shorter noses, flatter midface areas, and smaller heads, indicating smaller brains. The average IQ ranged from 60 to 70; some were as low as 30.

While children from heavy drinkers were the worse, there were bad results from women who had no more than two drinks a day (Van Impe, p.46-47).

60 year old alcoholic male | 68 year old control male

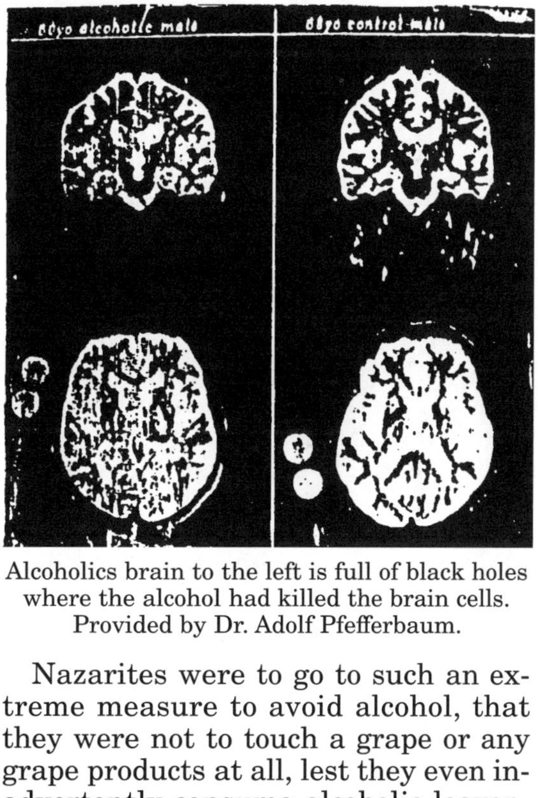

Alcoholics brain to the left is full of black holes where the alcohol had killed the brain cells. Provided by Dr. Adolf Pfefferbaum.

Nazarites were to go to such an extreme measure to avoid alcohol, that they were not to touch a grape or any grape products at all, lest they even inadvertently consume alcoholic leaven.

See Samson's mother, Judges 13:4.

Remember that even Greek and Roman women were not allowed to drink alcoholic beverages. How much more should Christian women abstain!

Luke 5:37,38 (Nonalcoholic):

And no man putteth new wine (grape juice) into old bottles; else the new wine (grape juice) will burst the bottles, and be spilled,

23. The Broken Cord, Harper and Row.
24. TIME 8/28/1989.
25. Charles Turham with Ellzabeth Schaffer in Newsweek 7/31/1989.

and the bottles shall perish. But new wine (grape juice) must be put into new bottles; and both are preserved.

(Interestingly, Codex Aleph omits *neos*, new.)

Young's *Analytical Concordance, Lexicon*, (1910)—"grape juice" in new bottles., 1910, p.1058.

Fenton translates: "No man pours fresh grape juice . . ." (1907).

"Grape juice must be put in new skin bottles." Dr. Reynolds, The Purtified Version.

Assyrian Glass Bottles
(from the British Museum Collection).

Fresh unprocessed grape juice must be put in clean containers that have no yeast. Otherwise, if there was residue of yeast, there would certainly be fermentation that would subsequently break the bottles. Jesus had to start with a clean slate, cleansed from the myriad of strictly Pharisaic rules, which included the one regarding eating with unwashed hands. As says Dr. Jack Van Impe, "The primary message of this parable does not concern wine but Salvation." (Please see Matthew 9:17, with notes.)

Luke 5:39 (Alcoholic):

No man also having drunk old *wine* straightway desireth new: for he saith, The old is better.

(Codex Aleph omits, *neos*, new. Codex D *repeats* old.)

This is a metaphor. Christ evidently is still speaking of new wine as nonalcoholic and comparing it with old alcoholic wine. He is not stating as a fact that the old is better, but says that the "*drinker*" of old fermented wine says that it is better. The alcoholic drinker is addicted and thinks it is better, because it temporarily dulls his craving for alcohol. The more alcohol is drunk, the more the craving for strong alcohol.

Dr. Van Impe says in his book *Alcohol: The Beloved Enemy*, 1980, "Try to sell grape juice on skid row, and you will probably have no takers." For them, the old poison is better. But for Paul, the new is better. Christians who would use this verse for drinking are making themselves Pharisaic.

The writers of today, such as Dr. Fort, in *Alcohol our Biggest Drug Problem*, 1913, and others, realize that addictive alcohol is our biggest drug problem. It is also so easy to get; and so often leads the way to other illegal drugs. Jesus is not commending the using of an addictive drug.

Verses 34, 35 tells us that Christ's disciples did not fast, a strictly Pharisaic rule. Christ was teaching that one must make a complete break from hypocritical Pharisaism. The Pharisees prefer the "old wine," the ceremonial laws, better for the Pharisees. But there must be a new, clean bottle, containing no trace of a contaminant which could precipitate fermentation. Old habits die hard. It is easier to fast than to be born again. It is easier to fast than to love the Lord and love your neighbor as yourself.

Dr. Elton Trueblood, in his book, *The Humor of Christ*, believes this verse indicates Christ's dry humor. After giving the *new* a big buildup, He recognized human nature: no one wants to change anyway. The old is "better" for them (Trueblood 1964, p.96).

Luke 7:33 and 34 (Nonalcoholic):

And John the Baptist came neither eating bread nor drinking wine; and ye say, He hath a devil.

> The Son of man is come eating and drinking; and ye say, Behold a gluttonous man, and a winebibber, a friend of publicans and sinners!

"Grape juice," Young's *Index Lexicon to the Old and New Testament.* (1910, p.1058).

Most scholars today translate winebibber as drunkard. John a Nazarite, did not partake of the grape in any form, but lived a continent, self-denying life. The ridiculous charge of having a devil stemmed from the comments of John's enemies. The wise and knowledgeable knew otherwise of John.

For Jesus, their comments were so absurd they did not even deserve a refutation. Jesus did not drink alcoholic beverages.

"Here is a glutton and a drunkard" (NIV).

If, as some say, Jesus here admits drinking alcoholic wine, then Jesus admits also to being a drunkard and a glutton. A glutton and a drunkard were to be stoned to death (Deuteronomy 21:20). Also, if we put credence in the enemies' comments, then Jesus by not denying it, accepts that John the Baptist had a devil. Jesus was not admitting to being a drunkard and a glutton. It is not logical to conclude from this that Jesus drank alcoholic wine and was a drunkard.

The Rechabites and the Nazarites were commended for not drinking wine. Could Jesus, the sinless one, have a lower standard? Would He who had it written in Proverbs, "don't even look at it," change His mind and partake? Would He present Himself as stung as by an "adder?" Proverbs 23:32. Actually, these criticisms of enemies mean nothing.

I presume these were the same accusers that employed false witnesses at Jesus' trial. Did their accusations mean Jesus was a revolutionary to challenge Rome? Neither did accusations of being a drunkard mean Jesus admitted drinking alcohol.

Nowhere is it stated that Jesus drank wine. He did however, specifically drink "the fruit of the vine."

Often, in order to find the truth, you can take the accusation of an enemy and realize that the opposite is true.

Luke 10:34 (Nonalcoholic):

> And went to *him*, and bound up his wounds, pouring in oil and wine (grape juice), and set him on his own beast, and brought him to an inn, and took care of him.

"Grape juice" Young's Concordance, 1901, p.1058.

Except for sterilizing instruments, and diluting some medicines, modern physicians find little medical use for alcohol.

In going through modern medical material, I find no place where alcohol is recommended for cuts. It might have antiseptic value, but alcoholic wine could burn the flesh of an open sore. Grape juice mixed with oil to form an emollient could be a soothing salve, with a healing effect. Pliny (23-70 A.D.) gives a recipe for making a salve of sweet wine, *gleukos*, and oil (Natural History) Book 15, Ch7 (1). Also, Columella, another contempory of Christ, gives a recipe using *mustum* and oil (12th book, Chapter 51).

Alcohol dehydrates and hardens flesh; it is used to harden and preserve flesh organs in the laboratory.

Luke 22:18,20 (Nonalcoholic):

> For I say unto you, I will not drink of the fruit of the vine, until the kingdom of God shall come.
>
> Likewise also the cup after supper, saying, This cup is the new testament in my blood, which is shed for you.

This is in reference to the Lord's Supper. Jesus used the term "fruit of the vine" and the "cup." Never, ever, did He say wine, "oinos." He purposely did not

"A LARGE UPPER ROOM."

use a word that could be interpreted as alcoholic. It is noteworthy that nowhere in the whole New Testament is the word *wine* used in relation to the Last Supper.

A teacher brought an alcoholic beverage to class and put a worm in it. Immediately the worm became fried well done. She asked, "What does that teach you about drinking alcohol." One boy answered, "If you have worms, drink alcohol." (Please see notes on I Timothy 5:23.)

All synoptic gospels use the same Greek word: "*Poterion*" for the cup, and *gennematos tes ampelou* for "fruit of the vine." There is not the slightest hint of alcohol. This is also "the cup" for Paul in I Corinthians 11:25.

To say that fermented wine is the product of the vine is just as incorrect as to say that limburger cheese is the product of the grass that the cow eats. Both require a process of fermentation, one by yeast, the other by rennet and bacteria.

As noted in Matthew 26:29, there is no reference to a specific beverage for the Passover in the Old Testament. However, after Old Testament times, a practice developed for a Passover beverage. The most popular beverage was grape juice. This juice must exclude fermentation. ". . . even the first day ye shall put away leaven (yeast) out of your houses: for whosoever eateth leavened bread from the first day until the seventh day, that soul shall be cut off from Israel" Exodus 12:15. This was to be followed for the Passover celebration for "all generations."

"The Rabbis seem to have interpreted the command respecting ferment as extending to the wine as well as to the bread of the Passover. The modern Jews, accordingly, generally use raisin wine."[26] Raisin wine is nonalcoholic.

"The *Thora* (law) does not only forbid the use of leaven during the days of Passover for any usage whatsoever, but also to have it in possession for this time . . . it must not remain in Jewish possession" (Schlessinger).

"During the prohibition period in the United States (1920-1933) the federal government permitted the manufacture and sale of wine for sacramental purposes. Conservative as well as Reform rabbis in the country maintained that as far as Jewish ritual was concerned, there was no need of this special privilege."[27]

There is absolutely no scriptural reason for using Biblically condemned alcoholic beverage in communion services. It was not even proper for the Jewish Passover. We can only conceive it to be a pagan-influenced carry-over of the worship of Bacchus, god of wine. (Please see Matthew 26:29 with notes. Also, I Corinthians 11:19-22.)

Luke 23:36 Nonalcoholic:

And the soldiers also mocked him, coming to him, and offering him vinegar,

Vinegar is neither wine, nor alcoholic. The chemical reaction is as follows:

CH_3 CH_2 OH_2 + 0 + bacterial enzymes equals CH_3 COOH + H_2O

Note the H_2O. The resultant acid equals 4 to 5 percent, the usual cooking strength; the rest is water. (Please see Matthew 27:48 and Mark 15:36 with notes.)

26. Encyclopedia Britannica, 8th Edition 1849, p.333.
27. Universal Jewish Encyclopedia, 1943.

JOHN

John 2:1-4

Jesus Turns Water into *GRAPE JUICE*
John 1:11

Nonalcoholic

AND the third day there was a marriage in Cana of Galilee; and the mother of Jesus was there: And both Jesus was called, and his disciples, to the marriage. And when they wanted wine, the mother of Jesus saith unto him, They have no wine (grape juice). Jesus saith unto her, Woman, what have I to do with thee? mine hour is not yet come.

"Grape Juice," Young's Concordance, p.1058.

There are both modern and ancient scholars who have wondered if this story of Jesus turning water into grape juice was not a strictly "allegorical" or "spiritual" study to show the superiority of the Gospel to the Law (Dummelow, 1936, p. 77). If it was an allegorical element later introduced by John, the synoptic gospel writers were possibly not aware of it.

The German scholar Bultmann questions whether it is to be understood literally because the chronology of Jesus seems to make the journey from Cana to other locations of His ministry in the suggested time periods unlikely. (Bultmann 1971, p.218).

J. N. Sanders also questions if this was an actual wedding (Sanders, 1817, p.109). There is disagreement as to the site. Some wonder if there was such a place.

Dodd writes of it as symbolic: "The good wine has been kept until the time of the incarnation of the logos: when the transformation occurs 'the hour has come.' "[28]

It is true that John was capable of symbolism, as we see in the book of Revelation. However, Dr. Teachout believes "The gospel account here is a single straight forward narrative detailing actual events," (Personal note to the author).

I would like to use, in the discussion of this verse, the words of my beginning Greek Professor, the late Dr. Byron Osborne, who was also the founder of Malone College (Canton, OH) and president emeritus. He wrote to me:

"The Greek word **Oinos**, translated wine in the New Testament, has reference both to unfermented and fermented grape juice." For devout Christians this fact settles the question of Jesus making unfermented wine.

If this passage really is an historical section of Scripture, then it is most important for our study. Why is this? If Jesus made fermented wine to be wine served to guests, then it's all right for his followers to do the same. It would give Christ's sanction to an alcoholic beverage and would therefore set an example for others who want to drink alcoholic beverages.

Wilkerson makes this point:

"If it was good enough for Jesus, then it should be allowed to any teenager."[29]

The word *Oinos* used here is a generic term that can mean either a sweet or alcoholic drink. For us today, wine uniformly means an alcoholic beverage. In itself, the Greek word *Oinos* gives us no clue. We must discern by means of the internal or contextual evidence and moral likelihood.

For Christ to make poisonous, addictive wine, He would be going against all of His Old Testament prohibitions of wine use: Leviticus 10:9, Numbers 6:3, Deuteronomy 32:33; Judges 13:4,7; I Samuel 1:14; Proverbs 20:1, 21:17, 23:30, 23:31, 31:4, Isaiah 5:11, 5:22, 28:7, Jeremiah 35:6,14, Ezekiel 44:21, Hosea 7:5, Habakkuk 2:5, Haggai 2:12. Therefore, the greater context of the

28. Dodd 1963.

29. Wilkerson David 1978, *Sipping Saints*, Fleming H. Revell.

whole Old Testament forbids such an interpretation.

John 2:3 (Nonalcoholic):

And when they wanted wine, the mother of Jesus saith unto him, They have no wine (grape juice).

"Grape juice," Young's Concordance, 1910, p.1058.

With Jesus' mother seeming to have some authority, and Jesus Himself coming, this should read, "They have no more grape juice."

Jesus and His disciples were wedding guests. Jesus had already been proclaimed to be the Messiah by Andrew, and the Son of God, the king of Israel, by Nathanael. Perhaps Jesus' presence was responsible for a larger than expected crowd. The punch bowl got empty too soon.

John 2:4

. . . Woman, what have I to do with thee?

If this sounds harsh, let us take other translations of the Greek *ti emoi kai soi.*

"Dear woman, why do you involve me?" NIV. (Dear is not in the Greek text).

Woman was sometimes used to address a Queen.

According to Earle, this is simply "A gentle suggestion of misunderstanding: 'I shall see to that: it will be better that you should leave it to me' "[30]

Moffatt (Copyright 1935) translates: "What have you to do with me?" (Gordon, (1944,3) renders: "What have we in common?" Gordon also translates *methuo* in verse 10 as "intoxication." That section is rendered in the *NIV* as "The guests have had too much to drink." I can't have anything to do with this type of thing." So at the opening of His ministry, Jesus Christ showed His aversion to alcoholic wine, and those drinking it. Dear woman, You are concerned with earthly wine while I, as the true vine, have another kind of wine in my concern.

Allan B. Kraft in his study of the Douay, concludes that at one time Christ acted as a Nazarite.

John 2:5

His mother saith unto the servants, Whatsoever he saith unto you, do *it*.

While these four verses do not mention wine by name, they are part of the story and do indicate some interesting aspects.

Cana was just a few miles from Nazareth. Since Mary took the authority to order the servants, it is assumed that this was a wedding of a close relative.

Mary had full confidence that Jesus would miraculously provide. There is no reason to believe the mother of Jesus would be expecting Jesus to supply alcoholic wine. She put her faith on the line.

John 2:6

And there were set there six waterpots of stone, after the manner of the purifying of the Jews, containing two or three firkins apiece.

In Matthew 15:2 we learn of the "tradition of the elders" in washing their hands before eating. Also Mark 7:3,

30. Earle Ralph 1987, *Word Meanings*, Beacon Hill Press.

"For the Pharisees, and all the Jews, except they wash their hands oft, eat not, holding the tradition of the elders." So possibly these pots were there for the guests to perform that purification rite.

There seems to be no actual knowledge of what a firkin was. Various authors give different amounts: ten gallons, two pints (Adam Clarke); it totals sixty gallons (William Patton); one hundred sixty gallons (Field). Van Impe and Campbell use the more usual figure of one hundred twenty gallons.

Whatever the amount, it was certainly enough to make the whole gang dead drunk if it were, as some claim, alcoholic. Would Jesus do that? Of course it was not alcoholic. God gave a sentence of death for disobedience, drunkenness, and gluttony. "He will not obey our voice; he is a glutton and a drunkard. And all the men of his city shall stone him with stones, that he die: so shall you put away evil from among you" Deuteronomy 20:21,22. For Jesus to make a beverage that would cause further drunkenness is unthinkable. It would be absolutely incongruous. "God offers superabundance of all good things conversely, for his people to enjoy is the message in this miracle." Butler, Dr. Charles, J.

Incongruous—some say where laws are made.

John 2:7

. . . Fill the waterpots with water. And they filled them up to the brim.

Like "Filled the hunger with good things." If we truly hunger for the Spirit, He will fill us to the brim.

John 2:8

Draw out now, and bear unto the governor of the feast.

How He must be saddened when people have taken His courtesy in supplying grape juice, and made it into an excuse for drinking forbidden alcohol. (Remember: "Look not upon the wine," Proverbs 23:31. "Wine is the poison of dragons and the cruel venom of snakes." Deuteronomy 32:33. (We use the *NIV* © 1978 here instead of *KJV*.)

John 2:9-10

When the ruler of the feast had tasted the water that was made wine (grape juice), . . . the governor of the feast called the bridegroom, And saith unto him, Every man at the beginning doth set forth good wine ("grape juice," Young); and when men have well drunk, then that which is worse: *but* thou hast kept the good wine (grape juice) until now.

That was made "grape juice," Young's Concordance, 1901, p.1058.

"When the master of the feast tasted the water that had become grape juice." Dr. Stephen Reynolds, The Purified Version.

Good Wine, Every Man at the Beginning Doth Set Forth

The Jewish philosopher Philo, a contemporary of Jesus, wrote a passage that has been interpreted to indicate what was "good." "The custom being setting forth the sweetest at the beginning, then when the drinkers had blunted their taste, the "older' " intoxicating, inferior wines were given the guests, finishing up with bowls and goblets of all the largest sizes that they can get, and drinking the wine unmixed in huge draughts."[31] Note the contrast between sweet and older intoxicating wine. Similar statements are made by Athenaeus and Diogenes.

There are evidences to show that the pure grape juice, "the good wine," was preferred by many. Horace, born 65 years before Christ, indicates, "there is no wine sweeter-than *Lesbian*; that it was like nectar, and more resembled ambrosia then wine; that it was perfectly harmless and would not produce intoxication."[32] Virgil, the poet, in 70 B.C., commented on the boiled wine allowed to women: "The use of this inspissated (condensed) juice became general."[33] Boiled grape juice will not ferment.

Plutarch, born A.D. 60, in his *Symposium* says, "Wine is rendered old or feeble in strength when it is frequently filtered. The spirit or strength being thus excluded, the wine neither inflames the brain nor infests the mind and the passions, and is much more pleasant to drink."[34]

Volney, after describing the unfermented and boiled wines of Syria, adds: "Such are the wines of Lebanon, so boasted by Greek and Roman epicureans."

Commentator Adam Clarke here translates the "good wine" as "moral wine," and "perfectly pure and nutritive." Conversely, bad wine, alcoholic wine, would be immoral wine.

This shows how historically wrong are those who say "Jesus' " wine was alcoholic. He gave not the "older intoxicating wine" but the good wine.

The verdict of the ruler of the feast was pronounced only upon tasting; it shows that its sweet superior qualities, commended themselves immediately to the taste. Alcohol does not improve the taste of a beverage. It is bitter. It is not drunk primarily for taste. It is drunk because it deadens the forepart of the brain. The troubles of reality are minimized and one temporarily feels good. It does not increase joy, but gives that illusion. In this case the ruler, by taste, said immediately that it was good; not by later intoxicating effect.

The carbon dioxide that accompanies alcoholic wine does give a zest to the drink, just as carbonation does to pop. Pop is not as appetizing after the carbonation is gone; the carbonation in wine and in soft drinks is the same. In grape juice there is no need for carbonation, with its questionable health effect to some on the stomach. There is delicious satisfaction in healthy sweet grape juice. I have never known of one to advise abstinence from grape juice.

Jesus Transformation, Water To Grape Juice, Is Yearly

This transformation takes place every year. It was simply a speed-up of the process that God yearly uses to make grape juice. St. Augustine was possibly the first to suggest this interpretation. Since then, this same interpretation has been adopted by many commentators (Chrysostom, p.117). With this interpretation, we have the answer as to whether Jesus did or did not turn that water into wine of the alcoholic variety. This was new, fresh grape juice, not that which is "poison" and "stings like an adder" as alcoholic wine is referred to in the Old Testament. "Their wine is . . . the deadly poison of cobras" *NIV* © 1978 Deuteronomy 32:33.

So this should be translated, "The water that was made grape juice." "It . . . symbolized the beginning of Chris-

31. Field 1882.
32. Anti-Bacchus.
33. Georg 1293, Patton 1871, p.44.
34. Patton 1871.

tianity with its endless, joyful supply of God's grace."[35]

Cop: "What have you been drinking?"
Drinker: "Water."
Cop: "Your breath smells of alcohol."
Drinker: "Lord, you did it to me again, turned water into wine."

Alcohol Is Man Made

God never created a drop of alcoholic wine within the grape! If left on the vine, grapes do not ferment, they dry up as raisins. If the skin is broken, they rot. Dry raisins do not ferment. Fermentation is a process of decay by using Biblically frowned on yeast, or fungus. Jesus made the real thing, not a derivative, not what the Scripture condemns as a mocker and defrauder. Jesus rather made delicious, nutritious grape juice.

A minister had a debate with Clarence Darrow. Darrow said he had some grape juice which he put on the porch for a period of time. Eventually it fermented and he called it wine, declaring that God made it. The minister replied, "I put some eggs away and they rotted. But I didn't eat them." Most likely Darrow would no more drink the decaying stuff on the back porch than the minister would eat the eggs.

35. Earle 1987.

The destructive decay in winemaking does not come of itself.

Alcoholic wine is man-made, by careful manipulation of the elements, extracted juice, sugar, yeast, time, ten to fourteen days, the proper temperature and proper amount of moisture. Dr. Richardson (p.178) describes alcohol as ". . . an artificial product devised by man for his purposes."

Wine-making takes much effort. "In the successful manufacture of wine, great discretion, unremitting care and wide experience are essential."[36]

Pure filtered grape juice, like that found in your refrigerator, will not ferment. The bulk from around the seeds and skin, contain the enzymes necessary for fermentation. (Also, pure apple juice filtered of all bulk will not ferment.) My personal experiments with grapes have verified this scientific fact. I grow grapes.

36. Universal Cyclopedia.

Study Notes

NONALCOHOLIC

Vs. 10-When Men Have Well Drunk

The Revised Version and the New English Bible translate "when men have drunk freely." Phillips renders it as "have had plenty to drink." *The Living Bible* says, "when everyone is full." But the *NIV* says, 'had too much to drink,' which is close to Gordon's version, "became drunk." Gordon translates *methuo* as intoxication.

Well drunk of water or a nonalcoholic beverage means one thing, but when speaking of an alcoholic drink it is entirely different. So Teachout writes, "These guest would thus have already become intoxicated if they were drinking wine." p.373

People drink intoxicants to get intoxicated. Since alcohol has about as much volatility as any other substance, it immediately saturates the system, including the brain. So as Edgar J. Goodspeed says in *An American Translation*, "They had 'drunk deeply' ", they were as Tyndale said, "Dronke." In the same vein, Reynolds translates *methusthosin* as "had become drunk." Dr. Stephen M. Reynolds, The Biblical Approach to Alcohol, p. 95.

Such wine is in contrast to what Matthew Henry calls "Moral wine."

Would Jesus then give them more alcohol?

"It has always been very offensive to me that anyone would attempt to use as an argument for drinking and drunkenness that Jesus drank fermented wine. Frankly, I do not believe that he did."[37]

Could Jesus, "Knowing that even ten ounces of alcohol (two glasses of wine per day) would risk the lives of unborn children, turn water into fermented wine and serve it to an expectant mother, had she been in attendance at the wedding of Cana? No! A thousand times no!"[38] As Dr. Teachout has stated (in personal correspondence), "The Greek verb here translated as either drink freely or become drunk, literally means to drink deeply. The beverage that is imbibed then, will determine whether drunkenness results. If they had already been drinking intoxicating wine, or if Jesus had given them some of the same except better (as some claim) then he would have been guilty of causing deeper levels of drunkenness in participants. That would truly be sin by God's holy standards. Therefore it is impossible to believe that Jesus made intoxicating wine without accusing Him of sin!"

Ross J. McLennon, in *Propaganda Vs. Facts*, 1978 asks, "Would Jesus, attending a wedding, create 60 or more gallons of intoxicating wine which wine has a history of breaking up more families than any other item?"[39] There is not the slightest shadow of evidence that this beverage made by Christ, and offered to all men and women present at the feast to drink, was alcoholic.

(Contrary to popular notions, if you pinch a grape it does not give out a little wine.)

John 2:11

"AND HIS DISCIPLES BELIEVED ON HIM"

In coming to the rescue, Jesus put his approval on marriage festivities. But the real ground of justification was convincing evidence of his benevolence and power, for "they believe on him."

However, such belief could not have resulted had they seen Jesus encouraging the guests to drink more alcoholic beverages, which would certainly have resulted in drunkenness. He came not to hold out the allurement of sensuality. He came in part as a "Man of Sor-

37. Spann 1989. President Wesley Biblical Seminary, 8/25/89.

38. Dave Wilkerson 1978.

39. Ross J. McLennon 1978.

rows" whose requirement was that His followers deny themselves, take up their own cross and follow Him, that they might have a more abundant life," that 'my' joy might be in you."[40]

The disciples believed on Him because He made the moral and good wine, pure grape juice. Jacobus said of the wine made by Christ, "All who know of the wines then used will understand the unfermented juice of the grape. The present wines of Jerusalem and Lebanon as we tasted them, were commonly boiled and sweet, without intoxicating qualities such as we have here called wines. Those were the best wines which were the least strong."[41]

It is a noteworthy fact that the Arabic translators of the Old and New Testaments, about the middle of the eighth century, read "the wine, the new," signifying in relation to this verse, that it is new wine unfermented.

Leon C. Field, the writer of the *Methodist Quarterly Review*, like Adam Clarke, states that the Greek word actually indicates not just "good" but "that which is morally excellent."[42] The term is suggestive also of Theophrastus'* characterization of unintoxicating wine as "moral wine." This is really what we would expect from Jesus, rather than poisonous immoral wine.

Christians have been properly horrified to hear a statement like this: "Jesus had an affair with Mary," as was suggested in the movie, *The Last Temptation of Christ*. It would be just as much out of character for the Son of God to create intoxicating wine, something that so often wreaks havoc on those who drink it and on innocent people around them. It has absolutely no potential for good. Christ would have gone against all the Biblical admonitions against alcoholic beverages, had He made such. This would have made the very Son of God to be a hypocrite!

John 4:46 (Nonalcoholic):

> So Jesus came again into Cana of Galilee, where he made the water wine (grape juice). And there was a certain nobleman, whose son was sick at Capernaum.

"Where he made the water grape juice." Dr. Reynolds, The Purified Version.

The nobleman or government official apparently knew Jesus had turned water into the best "wine" of all, grape juice that is. He surely must have believed that such a person could also heal his son. So the need was presented to Jesus who took care of that need as well.

John 19:30 (Nonalcoholic):

> When Jesus therefore had received the vinegar, he said, It is finished: and he bowed his head, and gave up the ghost.

Jesus, who had refused the alcoholic wine presented to Him as He hung on the cross, received the vinegar. The wine would have dulled or numbed the senses, alleviating His suffering to an extent. The nonalcoholic vinegar cooled His parched lips somewhat and relieved His burning thirst without beclouding His mind or His thinking capacity, so He could cry out, "It is finished."

This vinegar offering is related in all four Gospels. Unfortunately, some versions translate as wine or wine vinegar, though vine vinegar is not alcoholic. It is used for pickles, etc. (See Matthew 27:48, Mark 15:23, and Luke 23:36 for more on vinegar.)

(A pickle is a cucumber that is soured because it was jarred.)

40. Adam Clarke 1842.
41. Nott 1863.
42. July 1882.
* *Theophrastus succeeded Aristotle* as head of the Perepaletic *school three centuries* before Christ. Like Aristotle and Plato he *believed in conditional prohibition* of alcoholic beverages.

"And he bearing his cross went forth into the place of a skull is called in the Hebrew Golgotha." John 19:17.

Mt. of Olives. "When Jesus therefore had received the vinegar, he said, It is finished: and he bowed his head and gave up the ghost." John 19:30.

CHAPTER TWELVE

THE BOOK OF ACTS

Here The Bible is Made Plain

Text by text, a clear, simple explanation concerning Wine and Its' Use.

Ernest H. J. Steed, Ph.D.
Director, International Commissions for the Prevention of Alcoholism and Drug Dependency

Vice President
American Council on Alcohol Problems

Executive Director
Narcotics Education, Inc.

Chairman, American Council on Smoking and Health

Delegate,
Research Status,
World Health Organization

Author, *Winds of Change*

CHAPTER TWELVE
ACTS OF THE APOSTLES

ACTS

Acts 2:13 (Nonalcoholic):

> Others mocking said, "These men are full of new wine."

Glyoo'kos (Gr. Γλεύκος*),must* in common usage,'sweet' or 'new wine.' It only occurs once.
Popular and Critical Encyclopedia, 1909 p.1726.

(*Gleukos*) (glucose)* (grape juice).

"Gleukos, from glukus, sweet. Musk, sweet wine." 1098, Zodhiates 1986, p. 1675.

"Ben ful of must," Wycliffe, 1380 A.D., is correct, as we translate, *gleukos* is must—unfermented.

GLEUKOS, in some ancient and dependable *Lexicons and in all Greek literature* — means **SWEET JUICE**. Young's *Index Lexicon of the Old and New Testament Concordance, 1910*, says in *Index Lexicon to the New Testament*, page 72— "*Gleukos*, New Wine I"; and in the *Concordance*, page 1058 is: "Wine 12, sweet or new wine, *gleukos*."

James Strong in his *Exhaustive Concordance* agrees. In the *Greek Dictionary of the New Testament*, p. 20, 1098: "*glyoo'kos*; akin to 1099; sweet wine, i.e (prop.) must (fresh juice)". So far so good, but for some unknown reason, he begins to contradict himself. It is no longer fresh juice, "but used of the more saccharine (and therefore highly inebriating) fermented wine:—new wine." We would like to know the basis for the switch. Further, "akin to 1099," 1099 says, "*glukus, glyoo-koos*; of uncert affin; sweet (ie. not bitter nor salt); sweet, fresh." This is far from being fermented. Alcohol is bitter.

*$C_6H_{12}O_6$ *(nonalcoholic) "sweet syrup", Webster's New World Dictionary, 1980.*

Another anachronism is from Vine's *Expository Dictionary of New Testament Words*. It says, "*Gleukos* denotes sweet 'new wine' or must, Acts 2:13. The accusation [?] shows that it was an intoxicant and must have been undergoing fermentation for some time. In the Sept. Job 32:19. "Here *glucose* is used to translate *yayin*, an apparently old, fully fermented liquor. So, what happened to sweet "new wine" or must? The dictionaries define must as unfermented.

"Consistency, thou art a jewel."

How does Brother Vine get so much confusion? First it is must, sweet juice, and then a switch to "an apparently old fully aged liquor." Vine should show some kind of process from fresh, sweet, to alcoholic, if indeed, he claims that there was a change.

Dr. Teachout and Dr. Reynolds agree that *gleukos* is always nonalcoholic. They say Vine confuses an ability of *gleukos* to become alcoholic, just as must often can. As must they retain their nonalcoholic state. If must became alcoholic, it would no longer be must; and if *gleukos* became alcoholic, it would no longer be *gleukos*. Vine confuses the first state with the latter. Teachout quotes the Septuagint on this verse. "And my belly is like a skin full of grape juice closed up and beginning to ferment . . . (Teachout, p. 367). If it fermented, it would no longer be *gleukos*. Fermentation could be stopped at any time with sulphur from the yokes of pigeon eggs. (See Fumigation Chapter 6) *Gleukos* never means alcoholic.

We must remember that the word wine for hundreds of years before this, and to about the last hundred years or so meant both fermented and unfermented fruit juice, as cider does. (See Chapter Five.) Donnegan's Lexicon, "renders *gleukos*, new unfermented wine-must. From "*glukus* sweet wine made by boiling grapes." (Patton, p.94).

T.S. Green's Lexicora, "*gleukos*, the unfermented juice of the grape, must; hence, sweet new wine" Acts 2:13. ibid p. 94.

Kitto's Cyclopedia, "*Gleukos*, must, in common usage sweet or new wine, It only occurs once in the New Testament (Acts 2:13)." Professor C. Anthon says, "The sweet, unfermented juice of the grape is termed *gleukos*" Vol. ii p.955, 1845.

"Calmet observes that the ancients had the secret of preserving wine *sweet* through the whole year." Clarke's Commentary Vol. 5, p.695, 1842. (See Chapter 6 for Preservation.)

Smith, in his *Greek and Roman Antiquities* says, "The sweet unfermented juice of the grape was termed *gleukos* by the Greeks and *mustum* by the Romans—the latter being properly an adjective signifying new or fresh." Kitto ii. 955; A.-B. 217, Patton, p.48.

Gleukos is related to the Hebrew *asis*, which also is nonalcoholic. BDB translates *asis* as "sweet pressed out juice" or KKB—"freshly pressed out, sweet, not yet fermented".

Notice the translation into the English words *new wine* which means unfermented. Ordinarily, the Greek word *GLEUKOS* is from *glykys*, that in English is glucose. This means musk, 'sweet new wine', 'grape juice', 'sweetness'. In all of my studies of the ancients' writings *Gleukos* has always meant sweet nonalcoholic juice. No exceptions!

Check glucose in English dictionaries. *Funk and Wagnall's Standard Dictionary 1969*, "sucros 1. Less sweet than cane sugar. 2. The thick yellowish syrup used in confectionery baking, etc. Gk. *glykys*, sweet." There is no reference to alcohol. *Webster's New Twentieth Century Unabridged 1965*, "Gr. *Glykys* 1. sweet, a variety of sugar less sweet than cane sugar. 2. . . . 3. a syrup obtained in the preparation of grape sugar." There is no fermentation in sweet syrup! No reference to fermentation!

For further confirmation see *Green's Lexicora*, T.S. Green, *Thayer's Lexicon*, also *Kitto's Cyclopedia* ii 955, and *Greek and Roman Antiquities*, Smith. (1868, p. 754). Besides Josephus applies the word to fresh grape juice, "pressed by the Archi-oinoos into the cup of the royal Pharaoh,"[1] or "*Gleukos* does not intoxicate." Also the Lexicon by Liddle and Scott. *Clarke's Commentary*, "Rather sweet wine, . . . Hesychius and Snidas, *Gleukos* . . . distills from the grape before pressed." (1842 Eng. Ed. Vol. 5, p.695).

Young's Analytical Lexicon "Sweet or new wine, *gleucose*." (1910, p. 1050). Patton quotes Hippocrates, "*Gleukos* is less calculated than other wine, *Oinodeos*, to make the head heavy."[2] Hippocrates b. 460 B.C.: "The sweet unfermented juice of the grape was termed *Gleukos*". *Dictionary of Greek and Roman Antiquities, Art Vine*— "As in Acts 2:13 it refers specifically to unfermented grape juice."[3] Therefore, we should translate; 'full of grape juice' which comes closer to Zodhiates' 'provender' or food. The NASB says, "Full of sweet wine." Sweet wine is nonalcoholic. Alcohol is bitter.

The N.E.B. says simply "have been drinking". This is the only time that we find *Gleukos* in relation to drinking in the Authorized Bible. It has no bearing on the meaning of the generic words *Yayin* and *Oinos*. **Gleukos never means alcoholic.** Those who say it does, misinterpret the facts.

Some would rather take seriously the joking of the critics than the seriousness of Peter. "Thayer's well known lexicon (p. 118) 'must, the sweet juice pressed from the grape.' " Dr. Butler, 1994.

1. p.18.
2. Nott, London Ed.
3. Bacchiocchi, 1989.

Aristotle, born 384 B.C., writes of Gleukos as one of the two kinds of wine: "For some kinds of wine, *oinos*, for example, 'must' *gleukos* solidifies when boiled."[4] Alcohol boils away.

Grape juice was boiled, which killed the fermentation enzymes. To save space, at times the juice was boiled to a thick syrup then "necessary to mingle water with it previously to drinking." The Popular and Critical Bible Encyclopedia, 1909, p. 1725.

In Meleoralogica, 387 (b.9.13), Aristotle again refers to Gleukos as a grape juice, "Though called wine (*oinos*) it has not the effect of wine, for it does not taste like wine and does not intoxicate like ordinary wine." Notice, wine does not always mean alcoholic. See Chapter Five. Root beer is not alcoholic beer.

By the way, Must has two meanings, as wine does. It ordinarily means something that is required, or vital.

Others Making Sport of Them

(New Testament in Basic English)*

Acts 2:15

Not drunken as ye suppose.

Not a fact but your supposition — to assume, to guess, to think.

No doubt the jesters were familiar with the abstinence of the Christians and were playfully sarcastic in their remark. Dr. Elton Trueblood writes on *The Humor of Christ*, as to why Bible humor is not realized and appreciated. Trueblood says: "The general misunderstanding is very great, and also because much of the relevant evidence is so deeply hidden by accepted presupposition, that it will not be recognized apart from some analysis."[5] My father's old, 1913 *Funk and Wagnall Dictionary* gives 'burlesquing' for mocking; *Webster* says 'sport'. In other words, don't take the jesters too seriously.

We approach the Bible so seriously that we can't laugh when Jesus jokes about pulling a speck from another's eye when we have a plank in our own. Nor do we see the humor of the jester in suggesting that the Christians were drunk on grape juice, for in no place in all literature is *Gleukos* equated with alcohol. But serious Bible scholars have turned somersaults trying to make it so.

The jesters were saying, "They have had too much grape juice to drink"! We apparently have difficulty seeing the humor in such a flip remark in a serious exegetical study.

Assuredly, there is absolutely no basis here for thinking the Christians were drinkers of alcohol, as some have assumed. Russell concluded that this was a sarcastic, humorous remark, "Disciples known to drink only unfermented grape juice, in their exuberant enthusiasm appeared intoxicated."[6] That this was not a serious reasoned accusation is pointed out by Patton. First, drinking alcoholic wines could never teach men languages. Second, every man heard them speak in his own language and the listeners were probably not drunk either.

Thayer suggests, "If a professed teetotaler should get drunk, it would be the greatest irony for his foes to say, 'See your teetotaler, intoxicated on cold water' "[7] So here, Christ's enemies meant that the apostles were drunk on grape juice. Carter and Earle call it "irrational" intoxication. (Wesleyan Commentary p.34).

Ironsides tells of a missionary who spoke French, Italian, Spanish, Portu-

---

4. Meteoralogica 1868.

* 26 Translations—Rev. Bryan E. Mathis, Mathis Publishers, P.O. Box 621, Moss Point, MS 39563.

5. 1964.

6. Russell 1963.

7. Thayer 1869.

guese, and other languages. He would go to a port of the city where sailors gathered. He could distinguish sailors from their caps or otherwise, and would speak to the various ones in their own language. "More than once, I have seen persons come up and say, 'What is the use of listening? He is drunk, you can't understand a word he says'."[8]

"The phrase 'these men are full of grape juice' is a joke. Now I get it!"

"We do hear them speak in our tongues the wonderful works of God." All heard in their own tongue. Possibly the miracle was in the hearing rather than in the speaking. As always, God gives His messages to those who will hear it. There were those who did hear it. There were also those who would not hear it, mockers rather than hearers of the Word. To them it was nonsense, and they said, "These men are full of grape juice".

Peter's answer that they were not drunk because it was only the third hour of the day was not an admission that they might have become drunk later, but he was answering the mockers in their own character. Especially on the Sabbath, and festive occasions, and even at some other times, the Jews did not eat or drink until after the third hour of the day. (Barnes, Thayer p.15).

Even those who drank alcoholic wine, considered it indecent to drink alcoholic wine in the daytime. Even drunkards didn't get drunk that early in the morning. Peter deflated the scoffers.[9]

They were teasing "You temperance people are drunk." They didn't believe it. Why would some give more credence to the skeptical joking of unbelievers than to the seriousness of truthful Peter? Peter said they were not drunk. So that settles it. They were not drunkards. They were blessed, exalted, and empowered by the Holy Spirit. There is absolutely no basis here to suggest, at this period Christians were not abstainers. They were not wine drinkers.

Eusebius, was called the Christian representative of the era of Constantine. He quotes Hegesippus as saying, "St. James, the Lord's brother, did not drink wine." Traces of this may be perceptible in I Peter 1:13, 4:3, and in II Peter 1:6.

Some earlier commentators say that Peter and Jesus' brothers had a strong sympathy with the Nazarites, the Rechabites, and the Essenes, all of them strict abstainers. The Bible commended them for not using, not for not abusing. *Abusing wine* is not found in the Bible; neither is moderation of alcohol. The Bible either condemns its use or commends its use. It never commends the use of alcoholic beverage.

Alcohol has one good use, to preserve organs in the laboratory, "If you want to keep a dead man, put him in whiskey, If you want to kill a living man, put the whiskey in him."[10]

Acts 24:25 (Nonalcoholic):

> And he reasoned of righteousness, temperance, and judgement to come, Felix trembled, and answered, Go thy way for this time; when I have a convenient season, I will call for thee.

Some translate temperance as self-control.

8. Van Impe 1980.

9. Bruce 1986.

10. Thayer 1869.

Paul did not limit his teaching of temperance to the Christian community. Temperance is too important to be limited. The effects of alcohol limit righteousness on the part of rulers. In preaching to Felix, Paul was in line with Proverbs, Proverbs declared, in 31:4, "It is not for kings to drink."

With half of our highway deaths caused by alcohol we need legal protection from our rulers for the innocent. In our democracy it is our responsibility to do what we can to get the best rulers.

The Greek root of temperance, is *temo*, *temno*, *tempo*, to 'cut off' that which should not be retained. The Temperance movement would cut out alcohol for abstinence, even prohibition. So temperance does not mean being temperate in drinking. Alcohol is poison. To take poison into the temple of God would be sin to me, so different from some of my Christian friends.

It takes self-control to not drink when others are putting festive occasions pressure on one to "take a snort." But the only safe way is to have abstemious behavior. The word abstemious is one of only two words in our language that have all the vowels, a, e, i, o, u, in order. The other word is facetious.

Devout Christians are abstentious followers of Christ. To me arguments for drinking alcohol are facetious arguments.

Overlooking Jerusalem. The author taking a respite from his researching at the Hebrew University.

Entering into Egypt for further research.

CHAPTER THIRTEEN

A COMMENTARY ON EACH USE OF THE WORD WINE IN THE EPISTLES

Christian
Theological
Seminary

Dear Dr. Hansen:

Your research is impressive and thorough. I am unable to provide any critical judgment on your conclusion.

I want to wish you the best as you continue your work.

Sincerely,

Calvin L. Porter
Professor of New Testament

CHAPTER THIRTEEN THE EPISTLES

THE BOOK OF ROMANS

Romans 13:13

Let us walk honestly, as in the day; not in rioting and drunkenness, not in chambering and wantonness, not in strife and envying.

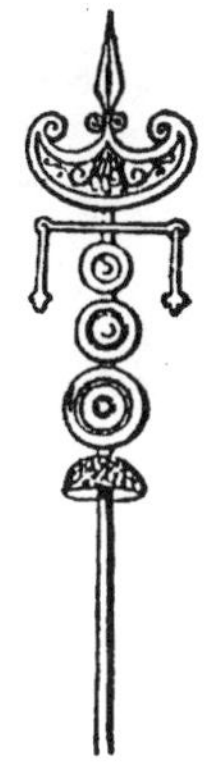

Roman Insignia

"As in the day," Christians are not of the nightclub set of bad company, of rioting, chambering, strife and envy. Drunkenness was common in Rome.

Alcohol is addictive. Few moderate drinkers expect or want to become alcoholics or drunkards. Drunkards ordinarily come from moderate drinkers. They do not come from abstainers. "No drunkard shall enter into the kingdom of God" (I Corinthians 6:10).

What's your income?
In the wee small hours.

Roman 14:17

For the kingdom of God is not meat and drink; but righteousness, and peace, and joy in the Holy Ghost.

Paul, in relation to meat and drink, is speaking strictly in regard to that offered to idols. He is not referring to the type of drinking that leads to drunkenness that he mentions earlier, in chapter 13:13. He is not saying the kingdom allows alcohol drinking. Please check the next addressed verses, Romans14:20-21.

Romans 14:20-21 (Nonalcoholic):

For meat destroy not the work of God. All things indeed are pure; but it is evil for that man who eateth with offence.
It is good neither to eat flesh, nor to drink wine (grape juice), nor *any thing* whereby thy brother stumbleth, or is offended, or is made weak.

"Grape juice," Young's Concordance, 1910, p.1058.

It is thought that there were Rechabites and possibly Nazarites among the early Christians. They feared fermentation so much that, to them, even drinking unfermented grape juice was sin. Paul might have had them in mind, advising against the drinking of grape juice, if it caused them to be offended. Rechabites, like the Nazarites were commended in the Old Testament for not drinking. They did not plant vineyards.

So Paul, not wanting to discourage Jewish Christians and lose them, pleaded that nothing be done to discourage them. Still, his practice of living, so as not to offend anyone, is an excellent way of life.

Let us not take this verse out of context. This is not a matter of expediency. Paul is not implying that he would drink an alcoholic beverage, forbidden in the Old Testament, if it did not offend someone. One type of sin is using a blessing to excess, such as gluttony regarding food.

This verse deals with following or not following the Mosaic ordinances and ritualistic laws. The converted Jews had a deep veneration for the whole law of Moses. The converted Gentiles, under grace and never under Law, felt no responsibility to follow Jewish holy days, or to refrain from prohibited foods. To them Paul implores, let's go easy and not offend these Jews.

"To encourage another person in any way to indulge in the use of the narcotic is spiritually criminal," so says

Roy C. Smith. One out of ten moderate drinkers become alcoholics, they drink more than they want to. "For the sake of these weaker ones, even for the one out of ten, we should personally abstain. Further, as Christians, we should work to show social opinion in favor of not drinking."[1]

As Geisler says, "A believer should ask himself, "Will my drinking cause anyone else to sin? Would it cause someone else to stumble?' " Some, including Geisler, have seen it happen. He has seen reformed alcoholics return to addiction after taking wine in communion. (Geisler, A Christian Perspective on Wine Drinking, 1982, p.53).

"The Orthodox Church in Norton, Massachusetts, discontinued the use of fermented wine several years ago. A drunkard in the place was reformed, and subsequently he was converted and joined the church. At the Lord's Supper, however, he did not dare to taste the intoxicating wine, for fear of 'self destruction'. He partook of bread but not of the wine. The church looked at the matter. One member said, "It is wrong to tempt our weak brother for whom Christ died." They voted to put away the temptation; and that church has used no fermented wine since."[2]

This verse should never be used to suggest that God normally approves of alcohol.

I CORINTHIANS

I Corinthians 5:11 (Alcoholic):

> But now I have written unto you not to keep company, if any man that is called a brother be a fornicator, or covetous, or an idolater, or a railer, or a drunkard, or an extortioner; with such an one no not to eat.

1. Hull 1989.
2. Thayer 1869.

Lead us not into temptation.

Do not keep company with a drunkard, don't even eat with him. He may be called 'a brother', but actually he is not. Do not give approval of his conduct. But try to win him to the gospel, as did Christ in associating with sinners for that purpose.

I Corinthians 6:9,10 (Alcoholic):

> Know ye not that the unrighteous shall not inherit the kingdom of God? Be not deceived: neither fornicators, nor idolaters, nor adulterers, nor effeminate, nor abusers of themselves with mankind, Nor thieves, nor covetous, nor drunkards, nor revilers, nor extortioners, shall inherit the kingdom of God.

A preceding verse, (vs 5:11) tells us not to keep company with drunkards, to not even eat with them; but through the power of the gospel all such sinners can be washed, justified and sanctified. This verse and similar ones need to be emphasized today. This study is a part to that end. Abstinence is the only safe way for the former drunkard to remain free of drink and return to the state of sobriety. He needs an example and influence from his Christian brothers. Abstinence is safe.

However, in extreme cases of alcoholism, the help of God, and sometimes of physicians, is needed. Some alcoholics have died in withdrawal.

I Corinthians 9:25 (Nonalcoholic):

> And every man that striveth for mastery is temperate in all things.

One of Webster's definitions of temperance is "total abstinence from alcoholic liquors" (1980). Funk and Wagnall's Dictionary: "total abstinence from intoxicants." (1969).

The Greek word here translated temperance is *eqkrateia*. One of the meanings given in Donnegan's New Testament Lexicon and in Robinson's New Testament Lexicon is "total abstinence from alcoholic liquors." To be consistent with the Old Testament, Paul would have meant: Abstain from alcohol.

So the *Revised Standard Version* reads: "Every athlete exercises self-control in all things." Temperate is not mentioned.

The New English Bible (1961) states it as: "Every man goes into strict training." Funk and Wagnall's *Unabridged Dictionary* (1913): "Total abstinence from intoxicating beverages."

Weymouth comes close to the Old Testament teaching: "But every competitor in an athletic contest practices [abstinence] in all directions."

> Physician, "It's best you quit drinking."
> Patient, "I do not deserve the best, what have you got for second best."

I Corinthians 10:21 (Nonalcoholic/ Alcoholic):

> Ye cannot drink the cup of the Lord, and the cup of devils: ye cannot be partakers of the Lord's table, and of the table of devils.

Patton says, "If their cup contained that which was intoxicating, it was, as Paul declares, the devil's cup. Not the Lord's cup."[3] Notice Paul always uses the word *cup*, never a word that could denote alcoholic wine. (see John 2:10-11). "Let us keep the feast not with old leaven" (yeast), (alcohol). (I Corinthians 5:8).

I Corinthians 11:20-22 (Nonalcoholic):

> When ye come together therefore into one place, *this* is not to eat the Lord's Supper. For in eating every one taketh before *other* his own supper: and one is hungry, and another is drunken. What? have ye not houses to eat and to drink in? Or despise ye the church of God, and shame them that have not? What shall I say to you? shall I praise you in this? I praise *you* not.

I have read that this verse shows that alcoholic wine was used by the early church in their observance of the Lord's Supper.

"Not so," says the Apostle Paul in the preceding verse. "*This* is not the Lord's Supper" (v. 20.)

If this is a party, "Have ye not houses to eat and drink in?"

The commentator Matthew Henry calls it a *debauch* (Vol.6, p.563).

> Drink to another's health,
> and spoil your own.

Drinking alcoholic wine was one of the immoralities that precipitated the writing of Paul's Epistle. It was linked to the divisions that so concerned Paul. In verse 23, he shows the proper respect for the sanctity of the Lord's Supper, using the term *the cup*, which could not be translated as alcoholic wine. **In no place in the Bible is the word wine used in reference to the Lord's Supper.**

There is a sense that the Lord's Supper is an extension of the Passover. It was established before the ceremonial law at Mount Sinai. But this is a new dispensation, as Paul points out in the 24th verse where he says, "This cup is the New Testament."

The Scriptural Passover had no reference to a beverage. Even leavened

3. Patton 1871.

"Dang—I can't find permission to drink alcohol anywhere in here."

bread, in which the alcohol is destroyed by baking, was not allowed on anyone's premises for seven days, on penalty of being cut off from Israel. So there could have been no wine made alcoholic by leaven, at a legitimate observance.

There is no mention of meat at the Last Supper, for Christ is the Lamb slain from the foundation of the world.

No leaven, no yeast, no alcohol was allowed. Dr. Reynolds believes that since baking kills yeast, regular bread may be allowed in the sacrament. Letter to author, 1994.

The only explanation for using alcohol at the Lord's Supper can be that the use of alcoholic wine was borrowed from the pagans. It infiltrates the sacred observance with poison. The wine gods of Dionysus and Bacchus, though very liberal in most things, demanded very strict adherence to worship at their required drinking festivals. The current word "spirits" stems from the supposed supernatural power of the mind altering drug alcohol.

The seriousness of this intemperance is shown by the fact that some got sick and some even died (vs. 30). Drinking alcoholic wine then, as today, was deadly dangerous.

Even today we still have around us some of the pagan lesser gods involved in intoxicants. In a religious book published in Los Angeles in 1978, we read: "After the mission was fulfilled, the demigods by the will of the Lord, relinquished their corporated bodies by fighting amongst themselves by the madness of intoxication. The demigods are accustomed to drinking somarosa beverage, therefore drinking of wine and intoxicants are not unknown to them."[4]

In the mythology of Egypt, Osiris, the King of the gods, established the laws and institutions for Egypt. One of his claimed religious benefits was the bringing of sacred wine to the people.

Among the Aztecs, wine was an important part of the worship of their tribal deity, known as Huitzubapchtli.

The Christian Church developed in a pagan environment where wine was an integral part of pagan worship. Both the Roman Catholic Church and the established Church of England assimilated much from the pagan environment, including allowing the use of wine in the Mass.

The Puritans, influenced by pietism, strove to purify the forms of worship and Christian living. The result in evangelical churches was the shift toward the use of grape juice instead of wine in the observance of the Lord's Supper, and incidentally toward personal abstinence.

I Corinthians 11:25 (Nonalcoholic):

> After the same manner also he took the cup, when he had supped, saying, This cup is the new testament in my blood: this do ye, as oft as ye drink it, in remembrance of me.

Touto to poterion—this cup which I now give to you.

This agrees with Christ's word: *the cup*. If the reference had been to an alcoholic drink, the generic term wine (*oi-*

4. Prabhupadec 1978.

nos) could have been used. In the light of the evident Scriptural opposition to alcoholic wine, it is difficult to even conceive how Christ or Paul could have meant an alcoholic beverage. They carefully avoided *oinos*, the word usually used for alcoholic wine.

It would be difficult to use this verse as a basis for stating that the Scriptures teach moderation in the drinking of alcoholic wine, for nothing in the context refers to wine.

If there is no basis for fermented communal wine in the Scriptures, where did this idea of fermented communal wine come from? Just as the Israelites were influenced by their environment and combined licentious worship of Baal with their own traditions, so was the early church affected by its pagan environment. This was particularly true of the Roman Church. The civilization of the West is largely influenced by the Roman Church.

In Roman mythology, Romulus and Remus, founders of Rome, were of the genealogy of the Roman gods Venus and Mars. These gods were of the general family of the ruling god Jupiter (identified with the Greek god Zeus). Bacchus, the god of wine and fertility, was the adopted son of Jupiter/Zeus. Sessions of drunkenness characterized the worship of Bacchus. Alcohol, a mind-controlling drug, was equated with a godly spirit. So even today, alcohol products are labeled as spirits. (Not godly, but demonic).

The Roman Church developed in this pagan environment, allowing the spirits of wine for its communion. There is no Scriptural justification for alcohol's use at the Lord's Supper, but it is nevertheless still used for that purpose today in some churches. When in Rome don't do as the Romans do.

"Within the pale of the Oriental Churches, where Christianity was earliest established, and has, in many respects, been preserved in greatest purity, we find proofs of the long established use of unfermented wine at the Lord's Supper."[5]

In Acts 8:27 we have the story of the Ethiopian eunuch, treasurer to Queen Candace, who was converted after listening to Philip. Possibly this was the beginning of the church in Ethiopia, known as the Abyssinian Church. These churches in their communion used the unfermented bread and the juice of crushed bunches of grapes. (Fields, 1882, p.677).

There were also other churches which were not in a position to be so strongly influenced by Roman paganism. Bishop Gobat of Jerusalem indicates that their church used unfermented wine in communion "from the earliest times." Dean Stanley said the same of the Coptic Church, which he called "the most primitive and conservative" (Renaudot, Lit. Orient; call.i, p.193 Leon C. Field, p.678).

Tischendorf writes in *Travels in the East:* "Instead of wine they used a thick juice of the grape." The cooking of grape juice kills the enzymes and leaven (yeast); the resulting thick liquid will not ferment.

The Christians of St. John, along the Jordan Valley, claim to have received their gospel from the Apostle John. They used juice from dried grapes steeped in water for their communion (Travels in Persia, London, p.60, 1677 Field, p.678). The Christians of St. Thomas on the Malabar Coast south of India, an offshoot from the ancient Christian Church of Persia, follow a like custom. Bishops Osorius, Brerewood, Ross and Nelson all give the same information. (Field p.678). The Nestorians of Western Asia also used this juice from dried grapes. (F 678).

The list continues. It appears that the early churches which were not influ-

5. Fields, 1882.

enced by Rome never had a thought of using fermented wine in communion.

BOOK OF EPHESIANS

Ephesians 5:18 (Alcoholic):

> And be not drunk with wine, wherein is excess; but be filled with the Spirit;

"Grape juice," Young's, 1910, p.1058.

Kai mee methsekesthe oino, and be not surcharged with wines.

"Do not get drunk on wine, which leads to debauchery." NIV

"Do not besot yourself with wine that leads to ruin."[6] Monsignor Ronald Knox, *The New Testament in Language of Today*.

Notice none of the above use the word excess.

The translation of *asotia* as *excess* is as incorrect for today as is the use of *charity* for *love*. Recent translations do not use the word excess here. "Wherein is excess"; the Greek is *estin asotia*. *Asotia* can be translated many ways: "riot," in *ASV*, "debauchery", *RSV*; "wild living," by Beck. "The dissipation that goes with it," in *NEB*.

There is no reference here to degree, the word excess is gone; there is no allowance for any drinking. Simply, don't get drunk. As amplified elsewhere, "No drunkard shall inherit the kingdom of God" (I Corinthians 6:10). Today, the word *excess* has no place here, as these scholars agree. The point of the verse is to draw an antithesis between wine and the Holy Spirit. Patton quotes Olshausen, "Man feels the want of a strengthening through spiritual influences from without: instead of seeking for these in the Holy Spirit."[7]

> A fool and his money are saloon parted.

So there is really no allowance here for a Christian to drink wine in any amount. The verse is a clear directive not to drink alcoholic wine, which leads to the sin of drunkenness, but rather to be filled with the Holy Spirit.

Why didn't Paul say, "Don't drink alcoholic wine"? Because the word has two meanings. We would not say to a group of abstainers, "We are going to have cake and nonalcoholic punch." The Ephesians knew Paul's aversion to alcohol and knew perfectly well what he meant, and so should we.

In the first 20 verses of this chapter, there is no permissiveness except walking with the Spirit and living a circumspect life. As Paul sums up in *Galatians* 5:16, "Walk in the Spirit, and ye shall not fulfil the lust of the flesh."

In short, the key is not in the amount that a Christian should drink, which is none, but in substituting the fullness of the Holy Spirit instead. To be caught up in the idolatry of Bacchus excess, which is idolatry, is simply to substitute wine as a replacement for God.

In the life of the Christian, *it must be one or the other*. It is God or something else. Jesus quoted *Deuteronomy* when He said, "Man shall not live by bread alone, but by every word that proceedeth out of the mouth of God." (See Matthew 4:4 and Deuteronomy 8:3).

The Psalmist put it in the first person, "As the hart [deer] panteth after the water brooks, so panteth my soul after thee, O God." (Psalm 42:1). This is an exhortation in favor of being filled with the Spirit.

The Greek and Roman gods of wine and revelry were Dionysus and Bacchus respectively. Worshipers at feasts in honor of these gods got drunk, but this was not considered excess. It was the thing to do. Paganism has its influence on Christianity today.

Paul contrasts this drunkenness with being filled with the Spirit. So far as Paul was concerned, it was not a matter of how much, but of one or the

---

6. Knox.
7. Patton 1871.

other. A matter of quality rather than quantity. The Christian was to completely turn from such debauchery, and instead was to be filled with the Holy Spirit.

"The excess does not, then, so much apply to the quantity of wine used as to the mental and moral condition of the person, since *asotia* denotes such entire dissoluteness of mind and heart."[8]

Get under the influence — God's influence

At least translators agree that the Greek word used here does not mean "*moderation in drinking*." Unfortunately, regarding alcohol, the so-called Christian teaching has all too often been based on moderation rather than on total abstinence. Yet moderate drinking has always been the first step to drunkenness.

One of the very few recent in-depth studies on wine has been undertaken by Robert P. Teachout. He did an exhaustive, exegetical study of wine in the Old Testament for a Doctor of Theology dissertation from the Dallas Theological Seminary, 1979. He gave his conclusion in the last chapter. His position is that the modern English word *wine* should only be used in translations to refer to alcoholic beverages. Reference to nonalcoholic juices should be translated *grape juice* in modern English Bibles.

From Dr. Teachout's thesis, titled *The Use of 'Wine' in the Old Testament*, we quote the following: "There are two basic positions which have been taken historically regarding the divine attitude toward wine. One position, which has become quite popular with the more scholarly, is that God never approved of wine at all. This latter view was that of the godly prohibitionists of the last century and has had a small following up to the present day.

"The first viewpoint to be discussed is that God has always approved of the moderate use of wine for believers. As long as wine is not imbibed to the point of intoxication, it is asserted, the Bible permits the godly to drink it.

"While it is recognized that this conviction is held in all honesty, it is incorrect in that it is based upon a superficial exegesis together with a faulty use of logic." (pp 314-316).

"A partial understanding of truth, or overemphasis of one truth to the neglect of another, can bring about devastating conflicts. This is essentially the difficulty with the position that God approves of wine in moderation."[9] To deduce a positive from a negative is very poor logic. What is positive is to be filled with the Spirit.

Where is moderation in drinking alcohol allowed? I cannot find any instance of it. Where is drinking any alcohol encouraged? I cannot find any reference to it when it is realized that there are two meanings for the word *wine*.

One out of 10 moderate drinkers become alcoholics; we've heard it for years. (See Chapter 1, pp.137, 138). Now we hear, "One out of three Americans drink more than they should."[10]

How much alcohol is moderation? What is the rule? Who determines how much? Where is it written? As Professor Teachout shows, God gave very specific directions, such as the fourth part of an hin of wine for a drink offering. (Exodus 29:40). All commands regarding the tabernacle, vestments, etc., were specific. If God intended an alcoholic beverage to be drunk moderately, would he not say what moderately meant?

"Recently, one of my students, a converted alcoholic, told me how she

8. Patton 1871.

9. The Use of "Wine" in the Old Testament 1979.

10. CBS news on *48 Hours*, July 6, 1989.

became a drunkard. Her Christian parents taught her how to drink moderately. At parties, birthdays, and when company came, everybody took a social drink. It was served at meals. She admired and loved her parents. They despised drunkenness, yet they had a bar in the house. This young lady started to go to teenage parties and began to drink socially with her crowd. That led to drinking in clubs. Soon she was getting stoned with her boy friend in parked vans. Finally, when problems began to pile up, she began to rely heavily on alcohol. She ended up in a mental institution—a hard-core alcoholic."[11] Wilkinson

The Bible grants no permission for the use of any alcoholic wine.

Only God can satisfy a person's thirst. There is no substitute. Historically, all cultures have had objects to worship outside themselves. Our new religion of secularization has torn our youth away from our Judeo-Christian moorings, fostered on alcohol—and drug-related sprees of teenage pregnancies and suicides, and caused our prisons to overflow faster than new ones can be built. Yet the inner thirst is not satisfied. We need the only true thirst quencher. "He that drinks of the water that I give shall never thirst again."

"Let your fullness be not that of wine, but of the Spirit which you have received by faith in Christ."

THE BOOK OF PHILIPPIANS

Philippians 4:5

> Let your moderation be known unto all men. The Lord is at hand.

This is the only time "moderation" appears in the *King James Version*. It means gentleness. It does not appear here in other translations. There is nothing in the verse to relate it to wine.

Here again, the *King James Version*, because of its archaic language, is misleading. The Greek word here translated as "moderation" is *epieikes*, which literally means "gentleness."

The *New King James Version* says: "Let your gentleness be known to all."

Phillips translates it: "Have a reputation for gentleness."

Dr. Jack Van Impe and Roger F. Campbell, in *Alcohol: The Beloved Enemy,* 1980, state: "The word translated moderation here means gentleness and has to do with our attitude toward others . . . ."

This verse must not be used to condone the drinking of alcoholic beverages in moderation. This verse poses no threat to teaching total abstinence.

A moderate drinker could stop if he would,
an alcoholic would stop if he could.

THE BOOK OF COLOSSIANS

Colossians 2:16

> Let no man therefore judge you in meat, or in drink, or in respect of an holy day, or of the new moon, or of the sabbath days:

Ee en posei—or in drink. Codex B has *kaienposie*.

Again, if we examine the context we discover Paul is writing about the ceremonial laws, which were a foretaste of things to come. He said that these were established to look forward to the body of Christ. The ceremonial laws now were nailed to the Cross. So Paul advises to let no one judge you for not abiding by the ceremonial laws of eating, drinking, and the new moon.

Paul says these things looked forward to Christ coming. But Christ did come. So don't get bothered, Paul says, by some Judaizer judging you for not putting the drink offering on the altar.

Therefore, the use of the word "drink" in this verse, does not mean

11. Wilkinson, p.15 in Sipping Saints.

that drinking wines in moderation is nobody's business but our own. This verse has nothing to do with drinking alcohol.

THE BOOK OF I TIMOTHY

I Timothy 3:2

> A bishop then must be blameless, the husband of one wife, vigilant, sober, of good behavior, given to hospitality, apt to teach;

Vigilant from the Greek word, *nephalion*. Donnegan's Lexicon renders "vigilant" as "abstemious, that abstains especially from wine." The language is imperative, "must be."

The word was first used literally to describe drink which was "unmixed with wine." The ancient Greeks used to give to the Muses offerings of water, milk, and honey. It was forbidden to mix wine with these. The prohibitions went a step further: the wood burned with the sacrifices must not include twigs of grape vines. There must not be the slightest contact with that which might cause drunkenness. Compare this to the use of wine in some Christian sacraments.

Applied first to materials, *nephalion* was used later to refer to persons. The meaning then was "abstaining from wine."[12]

Sober-Sophron-sober, literally sane, sound mind, curbing one's desires and impulses, self controlled.

I Timothy 3:3 (Nonalcoholic):

> Not given to wine, no striker, not greedy of filthy lucre; but patient, not a brawler, not covetous;

The Greek phrase translated "not given to wine" is *me paroinos*. It could mean "not to be near wine." *The Living Bible* (1971) translates "not a drinker." Phillips renders: "neither intemperate." The NEB (1961) says "not given to drink." *The American Revised Version* (1919) translates "no brawler." Earle says, *me* means "not," *para* "beside," oinos "wine": to not sit, down beside wine.

As the priests of the Old Testament were to abstain from alcoholic wine in the tabernacle, so in the New Testament, the bishops, as religious leaders, were to abstain from even being in the presence of alcoholic wine. Paul is very specific regarding the conduct of a bishop. A bishop should have the highest of standards. This does not mean that a lay person could be given to wine, be a striker, greedy of filthy lucre, a brawler and covetous. These are all evils that any conscientious Christian will shun. But clergyman must especially beware. "Drinkers of fermented wine were not allowed to hold an office in the early Christian Church."[13] Not given to wine does not mean some alcoholic wine is all right, any more than not being a brawler means that some brawling is all right.

The law book of the Ante-Nicene Church contained this order: "If any one of the clergy be even eating in a tavern, let him be suspended, unless he is forced to be at an inn upon the road." (Section 54).

Years ago at a Quaker temperance gathering, along with some other ministers, I took a pledge not to eat in a restaurant where alcoholic beverages were served.

I Timothy 3:8 (Nonalcoholic):

> "Likewise must the deacons be grave, not double-tongued, not given to much wine, not greedy of filthy lucre;"

"Grape juice," Young's, 1910, p.1058.

Two Kinds of Wine

Why didn't Paul condemn all wine? Simply because wine then meant all

12. Earle 1987.

13. Van Impe.

grape juice, alcoholic or not. If alcoholic wine was meant here, to be true to the Old Testament, Paul would have said, "not given to *any* wine."

The unfermented juice without the bitterness of alcohol was much more pleasant to drink. Said Plutarch, born A.D. 60, "The strength or spirit being thus excluded, the wine neither inflames the brain nor infests the mind and the passions, and is much more pleasant to drink."[14]

Once again we must go to the context for interpretation regarding which kind of wine was referred to, alcoholic or nonalcoholic. What is the context of this chapter? The general theme is that of self-control, summed up in the tenth verse where he says: ". . . then let them use the office of a deacon, being found blameless." "Without reproach" can be used instead of "blameless."

Could This be Alcoholic Wine?

Would this also imply self-control in the use of alcohol? The answer is certainly not, on two counts:

1. From the evidence of all other texts, any amount of alcohol is wrong.
2. Nowhere in Scripture is it indicated how much would be right and how much would be wrong. Alcoholic beverages in any amount are wrong!

"Not given to much wine," *me paraoinos* in the Greek, is used only here and in Titus 1:7; *me* means "not", para means "beside" *oinos* means "wine", *para oinos* then means, literally, not to be beside wine. Some translate "not to be near wine." The translation of "not given to much wine" might have made sense four hundred years ago, but not today. Patton translates as "not to be beside or near wine" (p.114). He comments, "This looks considerably like 'total abstinence' (p.111) (see Titus 1:7). Teachout also considers that the verse to a position standing near wine rather than any degree of wine imbibed. (1983, 71). Actually, a literal interpretation says nothing about any amount.

"Excessive drinking, even of unine-briating drinks, was a vice prevalent in the days of St. Paul, and corresponded to gluttony, the common, excessive use of food."[15]

Paul is guarding against such vices as overeating and overdrinking even in acceptable food and beverages. So Paul admonished the believers to be moderate even in drinking grape juice. Proverbs 24:13 advises, "My son, eat thou honey because it is good." But too much of a good thing is a bad thing. And in the next chapter, Proverbs 25:27, Solomon advises, "It is not good to eat much honey."

In Ulysses' poem, "You were all the day glutting yourself with whole milk."[16]

Too much milk disagrees with many people. Too much honey can lead to diabetes in some people. The same with too many grapes or too much grape juice. I know of a man who was limited to twelve grapes per day by his physician.

There was a preference for a filtered nonalcoholic drink. Fermentation or potency was altered by a system of filtering out the pulp with its enzymes. There were in that day those who could and would drink unfermented juice all night because they could do so without becoming intoxicated.

I Timothy 3:11

Even so must their wives be grave, not slanderers, sober, faithful in all things.

Ferrar Fenton omits *sober* from his translation.

The word *sober,* translated from the Greek-word *sophrona*, is also used in

14. Bible Commentary 1868.

15. The Bible Commentary.

16. Athenaus 192 A.D.

verse two. A better rendering would have been temperance, meaning abstinence. (Patton, 1871 p.111). Today, the word *sober* means 'not drunk.' In the English of King James' time, it meant diligent, temperate or abstinent. Donnegan's Lexicon renders sober, as "abstemious, that abstains especially from wine."

This translation of abstinence agrees with the ancient classical writers. For the ancients knew the poisonous effects of alcohol on the fetus and children of drinking mothers.

"The best known causes of behavioral birth defects are those caused by alcohol . . . there is no safe dose because even an isolated drink has been shown to act on the fetal nervous system, suppressing normal breathing movements."[17]

Even when the physical facial and head features are not distorted, there is an inward suffering for so many who have had an alcoholic parent or parents.

"They didn't cause it, but they feel they are to blame. They feel helpless and hopeless, ashamed and confused. Who are they . . .? They're the children of alcoholics—some of the loneliest people in the world; [without help] they become very unhappy adults—even alcoholics themselves."[18]

You cannot drink yourself sober.

"The old Roman law of the twelve tables prohibited intoxicating wine to women who by inference were permitted to drink any other drink."[19] The prohibition of women drinking intoxicating wines was enforced by the severest penalties. "Plato, Aristotle, Plutarch, and others have noticed the hereditary transmission of intemperate propensities, and the legislation that imposed abstinence on women had unquestionably in view the greater vigor of the offspring (healthy minds in a healthy body)."[20]

Matthew Henry, in the case of Samson's abstaining mother, writes, "Perhaps Samson's mother was to refrain from wine and strong drink, not only because he was designed for a Nazarite, but because he was designed for a man of strength."

Dr. Lee over 100 years ago, comments, "Not only does alcohol kill the brain cells of pregnant women, but one drink penetrates the placenta and destroys brain cells in the fetus. Much of this results in a great percentage of mentally retarded children for society to support."[21]

Robert Alsop, a Friends minister in southern France, wrote to Dr. Lees in 1861. "It is proverbial that if a young woman is known in the habit of using it (alcoholic wine) she is unlikely to receive proposals of marriage."[22]

Women ought to realize that there was little freedom in the world for them until Christ. Thousands of years of experience have shown the disastrous effect of alcohol on their offspring. But now we have liberated women: liberated them to ignore Christian principles; liberated to drink; liberated to bear imbecile children.

In a Moslem country, I saw women working hard in the fields, tilling the soil, while their husbands were playing cards in town. A missionary friend of ours Ann Kuhn, remarked that she saw the same type of culture in a non-Moslem country in Africa where she worked. The women did all the hard labor — back-breaking work — while

17. Patton, 1871.
18. Together we can make it.
19. Lees, Patton, 1871.
20. Lees, Patton, 1871.
21. Lees 1871. See notes on Judges 13:4,7,14.
22. Patton 30.

their husbands, for the most part, spent their days drinking banana beer and engaging in idle chatter. Christ brought liberty to womanhood.

I Timothy 5:23 (Nonalcoholic):

> Drink no longer water, but use a little wine (grape juice) for thy stomach's sake and thy often infirmities.

"Grape juice," Young's, 1910, p.1058.

Many scholars question the authenticity of this verse as to whether it should be in the New Testament. James Moffatt's translation omits this verse entirely. In a marginal footnote, he says the words are "either a marginal gloss or misplaced." The Living Bible also questions it for it is enclosed in parenthesis. In Letters to Young Churches, Phillip also enclosed it in parenthesis. It is also questioned by Weymouth, who enclosed it the same way.

Fenton: "Use a little grape juice." The Revised Standard Version: "No longer drink only water." (1952). Goodspeed: "Stop drinking nothing but water." (1923). F. R. Lees: "To drink water for the Greeks, as among ourselves, a special signification for not using inebriating drinks." (p.371).

Says Dr. Ralph Earle, "This verse has posed a problem for many Christians . . . The important thing to note is that *oinos* is used in the Septuagint for both fermented and unfermented grape juice. Since it can mean either one, it is valid to insist that in some cases it may simply mean grape juice and not fermented wine.

"Probably the question cannot be settled on the basis of Greek words, but rather on moral and scientific principles. Does fermented wine have medicinal value? The present writer once put this question to a noted surgeon, the head of a department in a university medical school. His answer was an emphatic *no*!

"The possibility is still open that the apostle referred to unfermented grape juice, which of course is good for a weak stomach."[23]

It is evident that Timothy was a teetotaler. Possibly he maintained the habits of a Nazarite—never touching grape products, and living a life as a person set apart, dedicated to the Lord.

Says Dr. Samuele Bacchiocchi of Andrews University: "The advice implies that Timothy, like the priest and Nazarite, had abstained until that time from both fermented and unfermented wines, presumably in accordance with the instruction and examples of Paul.

"Thus, the apostle may well be clarifying his position by telling Timothy that keeping himself pure did not require him to drink only water. He could rightly use some grape juice to alleviate his stomach problems and frequent ailments."[24]

The use of the term "often infirmities" possibly indicates a peptic ulcer. Says W. B. McKnight, M.D., "They tend to be chronic or recurring, and may heal in a short period, only to recur . . ."[25] If this were an ulcer, Paul had to mean nonalcoholic grape juice. An ulcer is an open sore. Did you ever try putting alcohol on an open wound? One of the first things that the physician prescribes for an ulcer is to cut out alcohol.

The danger of alcoholic wine to the stomach was well known by the ancients who lived shortly after Christ. "Pliny, Columella, Philo, and others state that many of the wines of their day produced, 'headaches, dropsy, madness, and stomach complaints' "[26] Modern physicians say the same thing.

On the contrary the same Pliny recommends nonalcoholic wine as a remedy. "For all the sick, wine is most use-

23. Word Meanings 1987.
24. Wine in the Bible, 1989.
25. 1963, p.187.
26. Patton 1871.

ful when its forces have been broken by the strainer."[27] The strainer strained out the pulp and skins which carried the enzymes, without which there could be no fermentation. So grape juice was medicinal. (Pliny lived at the same time as Christ. He was the Ben Franklin of his day. He was an accomplished scientist, historian, a prolific writer of health, zoology, botany, and physiology, practiced law, and was the Roman Secretary of Defense).

Baronites is quoted by Fenton as saying, "The practice of abstinence was so widespread among early Christians, and prized so much, that in some places scandal was given if a Christian were seen to depart from it, and drink intoxicating wine."[28]

"A neighbor of mine was aware that the only time his ulcer would bother him was when he drank wine. At the time of World War II, when it came time for him to report for the draft physical, he drank heavily the week before. He failed his physical because of his stomach ulcer, but was told to report back six months later. He acted so sad, but preceding the next physical he tanked up again. The ulcer flared up again and he was classed 4F, unfit for military service." (reported by Ronnie Bruce, 7/4/1987).

Writes my retired physician, "I am opposed to internal use of alcohol in all except those medications that require a solvent. Alcohol as a primary medication is totally unnecessary today and medically contra indicated because in the alcoholic one more dose of the Beloved Enemy would be harmful. There is a wide range of sedation on the market which will perform in a superior manner without the alcohol side effects."[29]

The Meadowbrook Veterinary Clinic gives a warning against detergent shampoos that contain ethyl alcohol. The shampoo can be absorbed through the skin and be extremely toxic, possibly fatal to pets.[30]

The Apostle Paul, one of the wisest men that ever lived, would not prescribe something that would have a debilitating effect on Timothy's stomach. Dr. Luke, the beloved physician, who would have been aware of the effects of alcohol on a sore, was at Paul's side at the time, and was possibly his penman.

Grape juice or nonalcoholic wine is known to be healthful, unlike alcoholic wine, which the Bible calls poison. At the same time that the Apostle Paul was prescribing wine for Timothy, Pliny said, "The wine whose strength is broken by the filter is useful for all the sick."[31] Around the same time, Columella says of the filtered wine that it is "firm, durable and healthy to the body."[32]

Chief Justice Swift, on an ambassadorial trip, found "nonalcoholic wine to be a precious balm for repeated seasickness."[33] Seasickness is a stomach disturbance. I myself have found that grape juice helps. Crossing the English Channel, in a storm on a ship, I was the only one down for breakfast.

The Ethiopian Version renders this verse as: "for the pain of thy liver and for thy perpetual diseases."[34] If it were a liver problem, Paul, with Dr. Luke at his side, would certainly not prescribe an alcoholic beverage, since the liver is the organ which, after the brain, is most susceptible to alcohol damage.

"Alcohol is used in the pathologist's laboratory to fix or harden tissues that are being prepared for microscopic examination. Because the liver must 'break down' alcohol, exposure of its

27. Ibid.
28. Gordon.
29. Ridgeway, 1984.
30. Meadowbrooke Veterinary Clinic.
31. p.113.
32. Nott, 1863. p.213.
33. Patton p.48.
34. Lees, Patton 1871.

cells to this fixing action can produce permanent changes that eventually impair the normal functions and structure of that organ."[35]

35. The Family Doctor 1963.

There was an author of the African church, which translated I Timothy 5:23, "for the pain of your liver." Whatever alcohol is not excluded from the breath, goes to the liver. Overcrowding of the liver results in cirrhosis of the liver, often causing death.

STUDY NOTES

THE BOOK OF TITUS

Titus 1:7,8

> For a bishop must be blameless, as the steward of God; not self-willed, not soon angry, not given to wine, no striker, not given to filthy lucre; But a lover of hospitality, a lover of good men, sober, just, holy, temperate.

"Not given to wine" is *me paranoinus* in Greek, it could mean "not to be near wine," or, as Ralph Earle translates: "stays by wine."[36] Teachout compares this to Paul's admonition in I Corinthians, "not to even eat with a drunkard." "The bishop must not be in the company of drunkards at their drinking parties."[37] "The passage says nothing about how much wine is allowable without sin. Instead . . . of not consorting with the wrong kind of company."[38] The New English Bible translates "must be no drinker." (Copyright 1961).

As Timothy was in charge of various sections of the mainland, so Titus was in charge of the churches on the island of Crete. Paul's instructions to Titus were the same as to Timothy. The bishop must set the example, in being abstinent of alcoholic wine, even not to be near it.

The preceding verse, Titus 1:6, connects rioting with 1:7, including wine. A little alcohol is no more to be tolerated than a little rioting.

Alcoholic wine can prepare one for a new wardrobe; hospital gown, that is.

Titus 2:3 (Nonalcoholic):

> The aged women likewise, that *they* be in behaviour as becometh holiness, not false accusers, not given to much wine, (grape juice) teachers of good things;

"Grape juice," Analytical Concordance to the Bible, Robert Young, L.L.D.

Weinstein refers to Acts 2:13, *glukus,* new sweet wine, "The Roman ladies were so fond of it, that they would first fill their stomachs with it, then throw it off by emetics, and repeat the draught."[39]

In verse two, Titus is exhorting men to be sober, in Greek *neophalion,* abstinent in respect to wine.

For verse four, Patton quotes from Polybius' fourth book, "Among the Romans, women were forbidden to drink (intoxicating) wine. They drink however, what is called passum, made from raisins which drink, very much resembles *aegosthenian* and *Cretan gieucose* (sweet wine)," Nott, London Ed. p.80. Patton p.121.

The Greek word *egkrates* means self-controlled, discreet, sober. To imply that one has to drink deeply of a large quantity before God would disapprove would be comparable to claiming that it is necessary to sin over a long period of time before a given prohibited action violates the holiness of God.

We must not forget that the word *wine* was used as we use the words cider or punch. It could mean either alcoholic or nonalcoholic grape juice or grape juice boiled down into syrup. Compare this with I Peter 2:11, where the writer says, "Beloved, I beseech you as sojourners and pilgrims, to abstain from fleshly lusts, which war against the soul."

So Paul was probably speaking of the excessive use of grape juice.

Paul uses the word "temperate," one meaning of which is abstinent, so Moffatt translates "abstemious." (Moffan, 1922).

Too much of a good thing becomes a bad thing, even grape juice.

"Teacher's of good things;"

"Train up a child in way he should go" Proverbs 22:6

36. Word Meanings, 1987 p.413.
37. Teachout, 1986.
38. Ibid, p.71.
39. Bible Commentary, p.378.

The hand that rocks the cradle rules the world.

An innocent drink can be converted into a curse by excess. "The Danish government found it necessary to prohibit the sale of coffee to the inhabitants of its Greenland Colonies because the women robbed their husbands to ruin to obtain that bean to drink its decoction in incredible excess, during the absence of the men upon their fishing voyages."[40]

Our easy attitude toward alcohol is very strange in light of the strong teachings against such drink in the Bible. On the contrary, the Koran has such little teaching about alcohol, but many Moslem followers are strong abstainers. The Koran states: "They ask concerning wine and gambling. Says: In them is great sin, and some profit for me; but the sin is greater than the profit."[41]

One of the reasons Christian missionaries' teaching is so resisted by Mohammedans is their fear of the intrusion of alcohol from the Western decadent and drunken Christian countries. (See Judges 13:4,7,14).

THE BOOK OF I PETER

I Peter 4:3 (Probably Alcoholic):

> "For the time past of our life may suffice us to have wrought the will of the Gentiles, when we walked in lasciviousness, lusts, excess of wine, revellings, banquetings, and abominable idolatries:"

We have here again that King James favorite word "excess", which may indicate to some that alcoholic wine is O.K. if not taken to excess.

Since the word wine can mean both nonalcoholic and alcoholic, it is possible the reference is to drinking grape juice to excess. There are historical statements showing how this was done, since this could be done excessively without intoxication. (See I Timothy 3:8 notes).

More likely here the reference was to alcoholic beverages, but translators do not agree on the translating as "excess". The recent 1978 New International Version translates as "drunkenness," as does the New English Bible, Copyright 1962, the Twentieth Century New Testament, Taylor's Living Letters, the Living Bible, etc.

Whatever the meaning, this is a reference to "the time past of our life." "Be ye therefore sober," vs.4:7. The safest way to being sober, it cannot be argued, is to be abstinent.

Before conversion, there were continual debaucheries of drunkenness, but now "Live according to God in the spirit" (vis. 4:6).

Regarding the word 'excess,' Dr. George W. Crane, professor at Northwestern University said, "Alcohol is a traitor to every human being, for it lends itself so easily to excess, that one cannot expect to be temperate in its use. When we consume alcoholic beverages we do not have to become intoxicated before our mental faculties and the speed of our reactions are affected."

Oinophlugia occurs only here. It is a compound of *'oinos'*, or 'wine' plus *'phluo,'* to overflow. A debauch is to overflow with wine. If one leaves wine alone by total abstinence, then he or she cannot possibly have a problem with 'excessive use of it' which surely is an overflow! Five to ten percent of all moderate drinkers eventually become alcoholics. (See I Corinthians 9:25, Ephesians 5:18, I Timothy 3:11) See also chapter 1, pp.137, 138.

Dr. Jack Van Impe and Roger F. Campbell have made an in depth study of alcohol in the Bible. They have written a scholarly and thought provoking book, *Alcohol: The Beloved Enemy;* in Appendix B, they give a quick reference list of where every occasion wine is

40. Fenton.
41. Quran sii 219 p.93.

listed in the King James Version. They give the Greek word from which wine is translated. They also supply, for most of these references their opinion as to whether the meaning is for unfermented or fermented. You would notice that it almost always agrees with our reasonings.

CHAPTER FOURTEEN

A COMMENTARY ON EACH USE OF THE WORD WINE IN REVELATION

"Dear Dr. Hansen,

Your research concerning wine is very impressive. There is nothing that I can add."

D. Elton Trueblood, Ph.D.
Seminary Professor at Large
Earlham School of Religion
Author books published by
Main line Publishers
Including *The Humor of Christ*
Harper and Row
Wider Quaker Fellowship
Founder and Director

CHAPTER FOURTEEN THE BOOK OF REVELATION

REVELATION

Revelation 6:6 (Nonalcoholic):

> And I heard a voice in the midst of the four beasts say, A measure of wheat for a penny, and three measures of barley for a penny; and *see* thou hurt not the oil and the wine (grape juice).

"Grape juice," Young's Concordance, 1910, p.1058.

The oil and the wine, *"to elaion kai ton oinon,"* both are nutritious foods. In the famine, both were necessary for very survival; alcohol was not. Grapes can be boiled to a syrup for preservation, so *"hurt not."* Alcohol boils away. Therefore, this is nonalcoholic.

This is in reference to the grape vines and the olive trees, that could have been destroyed, so there would not have been any harvest. Grapes and olives were important crops, and many people depended on them for their livelihood. Conservation was necessary. Van Impe and Campbell describe this as unfermented.

Revelation 14:8 (Alcoholic):

> And there followed another angel, saying, Babylon is fallen, is fallen, that great city, because she made all nations drink of the wine of the wrath of her fornication.

This is an allusion to a custom practiced by impure women. They gave intoxicating love potions, here called wine of wrath, to those whom they wished to seduce. The ancient Romans extended their idolatrous religion of the wine god Bacchus as far as their extension of conquest. Here God calls it, "wine of the wrath of her fornication." It is "pleasure promising allurement of Babylon the Great-not-God who offers (*pleasure*) to the nation." Dr. Butler, C.J. in personal correspondence.

Revelation 14:10 (Alcoholic):

> The same shall drink of the wine of the wrath of God, which is poured out without mixture into the cup of his indignation;

Again, this is a metaphorical use of the word *wine*, a symbol of God's wrath. Alcoholic wine is in contrast to other references, where grape juice is meant, and is a blessing.

Alcoholic wine in the Bible represents sin, corruption, and the wrath of God; but bread, oil, and milk are never used as symbols of God's wrath. The nutritious grape juice, a *blessing*, is changed by yeast; the leaven, to be non-nutritious, alcoholic, and poison, a curse, the appropriate symbol of wrath. Even the leaven or yeast, which creates the excretory alcohol, is often used as a symbol of evil in the Bible. "Neither with the leaven of malice and wickedness, but with the unleavened bread of sincerity and truth" (I Corinthians 6:8). Now from the Dead Sea Scrolls we learn that those who called themselves The Children of Light are thought to have lived long lives with great energy in their old age. Not only did they abstain from alcohol, but they did not even use yeast in their bread. (Bruder Woodbridge Press).

Revelation 16:19 (Alcoholic):

> And the great city was divided into three parts, and the cities of the nations fell: and great Babylon came in remembrance before God, to give unto her the cup of the wine of the fierceness of his wrath.

Wine once more represents the wrath of God. Can this be the same thing that is represented in so many places as a blessing of God, or in Deuteronomy 14:26, where God encourages the Levites, the religious leaders, to buy wine? Could it be the cup of the Lord's Supper? We say "NO". There were two wines, fermented and unfermented.

Revelation 17:1-2 (Alcoholic):

> And there came one of the seven angels which had the seven vials, and talked with me, saying unto me, Come hither; I will shew unto thee the judgment of the great whore that sitteth upon many waters: With whom the kings of the earth have committed fornication, and the inhabitants of the earth have been made drunk with the wine of her fornication.

With verse one, the awful state of religion in subjection to the great whore is represented by the wine of her fornication. Lovely stuff, this wine! Alcoholic wine is often one of the bad four letter words of the Bible. Often, as here, it is directly related to evil. Rather than glorified loveliness, wine is often in a class with adultery, fornication, whores, drunkenness, and debauchery.

Revelation 18:3 (Alcoholic):

> For all nations have drunk of the wine of the wrath of her fornication, and the kings of the earth have committed fornication with her, and the merchants of the earth are waxed rich through the abundance of her delicacies.

In both the Old and New Testaments, wine and fornication are linked together symbolically. Is it not true, literally? Is this for the saints? See Revelation 14:8, 14:10 and 16:19.

Revelation 18:11 and 13

> . . . no man buyeth their merchandise anymore:
> And cinnamon, and odours, and ointments, and frankincense, and wine, and oil, and fine flour, and wheat, and beasts, and sheep, and horses, and chariots, and slaves, and souls of men.

Babylon is fallen; she is no longer a market for the above.

Wine, wrath, fornication. These five previous wine verses have to do with wine as the wrath of God for the punishment of sin, particularly idolatry. Can anyone honestly claim that this stuff is the same as that which Christ made at the Cana wedding?

Bread, milk, and oil are never used as a symbol of the wrath of God. It is the spoiled, nonnutritious, excretory poisonous alcohol that is the appropriate symbol of wrath.

We have tried to make it very easy to find the meaning of the wine words in the Bible. But for lightening fast knowledge use the appendix in *Alcohol: Our Beloved Enemy*, by Dr. Van Impe and Roger Campbell. They will quickly and in Biblical order, give you the source of the word and if fermented or unfermented.

UPDATE

On the fourth day of August 1991, a Washington (UP) Article was published to the effect that people who had only two or less drinks of wine a day had a lower death rate than abstainers. I did not give it much attention because it contradicted all of the other information that we had on longevity.

As of now, April 1997, the University of Wisconsin Medical School's Professor John D. Fotts, Ph.D. and his associates have made a new discovery. It is, that the flavonoids that are found in the stems, skins and seeds of grapes, as well as, some other fruits and vegetables, help clear the blood-clotting platelets from the arteries. It is the beneficial flavonoids, not the alcohol found in red wines that help lengthen life, (The National Good Templar April-May 1995, p.8). (Dr. Potts, in 1944, was the first to demonstrate that aspirin helps guard against heart disease by turning down platelet activity).

I have a vision of a new reformation. A time when the Church of Christ shall shed its last vestige of the paganism of Bacchus the god of wine. When people shall cease worshipping mind twisting drugs, and instead shall worship the pure, holy, innocent Christ. A vision of when the whole church shall purify itself, and be free of drunkenness, and of the nonbiblical invention of moderation of harmful drugs.

We hope that wading through this drug, wine, and grape juice treatise will keep you dry.

Two hundred twenty eight wine words are in the King James Version. Approximately half are nonalcoholic.

Alternatives

Mock Champagne.

Mix 2/3 cup of chilled lemon lime with carbonated water and 1/2 cup of chilled white grape juice. Pour into champagne glasses. Makes two servings.

Order for cocktails.

Tonic water, fruit juice and club soda or bottled water; order with traditional cocktail garnish.

Quit drinking.

Lose weight. Alcohol adds calories with scarcely any nutrition.

Avoid hazardous waist.

Study Notes

ENDNOTES

CHAPTER ONE

1. Joel Fort, M.D., *Alcohol Our Biggest Drug Problem*, 1973, p.100—By permission, McGraw Hill, Inc.
2. Eugene H. Methvin, *Let Us Pray, Reader's Digest*, November 1992, Pleasantville, N.Y. 10570, p.75.
3. Kenneth Hamilton, *God is Dead*, Erdmans, Grand Rapids, MI, 1966, p.77.
4. Robert Schwebel Ph.D., *Saying No is Not Enough*, Newmarket Press, New York, 1989, p.12.
5. Dr. James Dobson, *Focus on the Family Bulletin*, (USPS 00-877) (Vol. 4, No. 7) Published monthly by Tyndale House, Pamona, CA 91799. Also, *Parenting Isn't for Cowards*, 1989.
6. Jay Strack, *Drugs and Drinking*, Thomas Nelson Publishers—Nashville, Camden, New York, 1985, p.171.
7. Dr. James Dobson, *Parenting Isn't For Cowards*, 1987, Tyndal Publishing House, p.86.
8. Ibid, p.88.
9. Jodi Freeman M.Ed., *How to Drug Proof Children*, The Think Shop, Inc., P. O. Box 3754, Albuquerque, N.M., 1989.
10. Harold B. Voth, M.D. and Gabriel G. Nahab, M.D., Ph.D., *How to Save Your Child from Drugs*, Paul S. Erikson, Publisher, Middlebury, VT, 1987, pp.4 and 5.
11. Driver and Swann—*Seventh Report To Congress*, Seventh Special Report to Congress on Alcohol and Health from the Secretary of Health and Human Services, Jan. 1990.
12. Galen C. Bosley Sc. D., *Ministry Magazine*, May, 1986, Review and Herald Publishing Association 125 01 Columbus Pike, Silver Springs, MD 20904-1608, p.14.
13. Earnest H. J. Steed Ph.D., LL.D., *Winds of Change*, Pacific Press Publishing Association, Boise, ID, 1987, p.13.
14. Ibid, p.11.

CHAPTER TWO

1. Stephen Schall, Headed Research at Ohio State University, funded by Central Ohio Chapter of American Heart Association 1983.
2. *American Health Journal*, January/ February 1990.
3. Robert Barnett, *The Proper Cup, American Health Journal*, p.95, 1990.
4. Lois Costomiris, author *Rail Fences, Rolling Pins and Rainbows*, 23330 Millcreek Road, Cicero, IN 46034.
5. Jay Strack, *Drugs and Drinking*, Thomas Nelson Publishing, Nashville, Indiana, 1985, p.70. It's good.
6. Washington, AP, 10/22/1981.
7. *The World Health Organization and the Addition Research Foundation*, Vol. 2, p.297.
8. H. L. Henderson, et al, *Archives of Otolaryngology*, 95, 1972, pp. 248-251.
9. P. W. Fleischman, et al, J. R. Baker, and Rosenkrant 291-295, *Toxicology and Applied Pharmacology 47*, 1979, pp.557, 566.
10. M. Fink, *Annals of the New York Academy of Science*, 1976, pp.282, 387-398.
11. R. G. Heath, et al, Biological Psychiatry, Tulane University, Oxford: Pergamon Press, 1980, pp.657-690.
12. Harold B. Voth, M.D., *How to Save Your Child From Drugs*, Paul S. Erikson, Publisher, Middlebury, VT., 1987.
13. D.E. McMillan, *Science* 1970, pp.501-503.
14. A. E. Abel, *Federation Proceedings*, 1972, 31:505.
15. Oxford, Third International Union of Pharmacoloogical Science, 1984.
16. R. D. Harbison, *Toxicology and Applied Pharmacology*, 1941, pp.413-414.
17. R. M. Vardaris, *Pharmacology, Biochemistry and Behavior*, 1976, pp.245-254.
18. P. L. McGreer and A. Jakubovic, *Marijuana: Biological Effects*, Makas, G.G. and Paton, Oxford Pergamon Press, 1979, pp.519-520.

19. Curtis L. Jarrezek, *Marijuana, Time for a Closer Look*, Healthstar Publications, P. O. Box 8426, Columbus, Ohio 43201, 1980-81.
20. Herbert Zinn, *Our Wonderful World*, Founding Editor, Grolier, Inc., New York.
21. W. B. McKnight, M. D., *The Family Doctor*, The Southwestern Company, Nashville, Tennessee, 1963, p.462.
22. Harold B. Voth, M.D. and Gabriel G. Nahab, M.D., Ph.D., *How to Save Your Child from Drugs*, Paul S. Erickson, Publisher, Middlebury, VT, 1987.
23. Lyle Alzado, Los Angeles' Raider, with Nat'l Football's Dr. Forest Tennant.
24. Bill Ashpaugh, *Powerlift*, Impact Books, The Benson Co., Inc. 365 Great Circle Rd., Nashville, TN 37228, 1981.
25. Maurice Zolotow, May, 1985.
26. Wesleyan Church Discipline, Section (8), Wesleyan Publishing House, Indianapolis, IN, 1992.
27. U. S. Department of Agriculture, Handbook #456, U.S. Government Printing Office, p.31.
28. Statistical Abstinent of the U.S. Plate 1262, p.149.
29. *World Book Illustrated Home Medical Encyclopedia*, Childcraft International Inc. Merchandise Mart Plaza, Chicago, Ill., 60654, 1980, pp.427-428.
30. Dwight Janerick, Yale epidemiologist, *Newsweek*, 6/11/1990, p.59.
31. Geoffrey Cowley, *Newsweek*, 6/11/1990;59.
32. Lewis Kullur, M.D., Chairman of the Department of Epidemiology at the Pittsburgh School of Medicine.
33. Charles L. Barber, M.D., quoted by Dr. John R. Rice, in *Tobacco*, Sword of the Lord Publishers, Wheaton, Ill.
34. *American Heritage Dictionary*.
35. Frank A. Oski, M.D., *Readers Digest*, condensed from the New York Times, 1/12/1984.
36. Stan Fortenberry, *From Valium to Victory*, Praise Books, Harrison House Publishers, Tulsa, OK., 1989.

CHAPTER THREE

1. U. S. Dept. of Health, Education and Welfare.
2. Joel E. Fort M. D., *Alcohol: Our Biggest Drug Problem*, McGraw-Hill Book Co., College Division, 1221 Avenue of the Americas, New York, NY, 1973, by permission.
3. Sam Rhine, Geneticist at Noble Centers and Genetic Education Center, quoted from the *Noblesville Daily Ledger*, December 18, 1986, pp.1 and 16.
4. National Institute on Alcohol Abuse and Alcoholism, *Highlights from the 1981 National Drug and Alcoholism Treatment Unit Survey*, Rockville, MD, NIDA/NIAAA, 1989, p.278.
5. John H. Mendelson, M.D. and Nancy K. Mellow, Ph.D., Seventh Special Report to Congress. January 1990, p.7, from *The Diagnosis and Treatment of Alcoholism*, N.Y., McGraw-Hill, 1985, pp.1-20.
6. Ronald Schiller, *A Reader's Digest* Gallup Survey 1/85, Vol 9, No. 4, pp.11-15.
7. *Newsweek*, April 30, 1979, Newsweek, Inc. 251 West 57th St., New York, NY 10019.
8. V. E. Pollock, The EEG after alcohol in men at risk for alcoholism, Art. Gen, *Psychical*, 1983, pp.40-857-864.
9. Gabriel Nahab, M.D., Ph.D., Along with Harold B. 16th, *How To Save Your Children From Drugs*, Paul S. Erikson, Publisher, Middlebury, VT, 1987, p.48.
10. W. B. McKnight, M.D., *The Family Doctor*, The Southwestern Co., Nashville, TN, 1963, p.463.
11. Boston University of Medicine, Journal of Studies on Alcohol, January 1982, Vol. 43, No.1, pp.81-87.
12. Albert Q. Maisel, *Reader's Digest*, "Alcohol and Our Brain: Some News For Social Drinkers", 1970, p.5.
13. Geriatric Society Journal of September 1983, Vol. 31, No.9, pp.540-543.
14. Summers, Alcohol Health and Research World, Vo. 9, No.4, pp.4-7.
15. *Ministry Magazine*, May 1986, 12501 Old Columbia Pike, Silver Springs, MD 20904.
16. Louis W. Sullivan, M.D., U.S. Secretary, H.H.S., *Seventh Special Report to Congress*, January 1990, p.viii.
17. Sixth Report to Congress, Alcohol and Health, p.61.

18. National Highway Traffic Safety Administration, *Drunk Driving Facts*, Washington D.C.
19. W. R. Miller, *Seventh Special Report to Congress*, 1990.
20. R. E. Miller, *Seventh Special Report to Congress*, 1990.
21. Manning, et al, *The Taxes of Sin*, "So Smokers and Drinkers Pay Their Way?" JAMA 261(11), 1989, pp.1604-1609.
22. Ronald Schiller, *Reader's Digest*, The Readers Digest Association, Inc., Pleasantville, N.Y., 10570, December 1985.
23. *Newsweek*, April 29, 1991, 251 West 57th St., New York, NY 10018-1894.
24. E. Vingilis, et al, *Currents in Alcoholic Research* and *Prevention of Alcoholic Problems*, Hons Huber Publishers, Berne, Switzerland, 1985, pp.118-124.
25. Kenneth Woodward, *Newsweek* 11/20/1992, Newsweek, Inc. 251 West 5th Street, New York, N.Y., 10019-1894, p.71
26. U. S. News and World Report, Sept. 10, 1981, p.6.
27. Tufts University, Diet and Nutrician News Letter, March 1986, Vol. 4, No.11, pp.4-7.
28. H. L. Ross, Deterring Drunken Driving, *J. Stud in Alcohol*, 1985, pp.122-128.
29. R. Kingston, et al, Effects of Maines 1991 and Mass. 1982 D.U.I. legislation. American Journal Public Health, 1987, pp.593-594.
30. H. L. Ross, Deterring Drunken Driving, *J. Stud in Alcohol*, 1985, pp.122-128.
31. U.S. Department of Agriculture, Handbook 456, U.S. Department Printing Office, p.31.
32. Mothers Against Drunk Drivers (MADD).
33. Decker and Associates, P. L. Graitcer Decker, M.D. and W. Schuffner, JAMA, *Seventh Special Report to Congress*, 260(24), 1985, p.235.
34. Maine State vs. Lafleur, April 1, 1952, Maine Court decision.
35. Maine State vs. Lafleur 4/1/1952.
36. Driver and Swann, H. E. Driver and P. F. Swann, Alcohol and Human Cancer Review, *Anticancer*, Res. 7: 309-320, 1987, In the *Seventh Special Report to Congress*, January 1990, p.130.
37. Yale University Press, *Drinking in College* (New Haven University Press 1953, p.14. Study by Robert Strous and Seldon D. Bacon.
38. Ronald K. Seigle, *Intoxication: Life in Pursuit of Artificial Paradise*, U.C.L.A., School of Medicine, L.A. $19.95 Dutton, 1989.
39. Grossman M., *Control Issues in Alcohol Abuse Prevention; For States and Communities*. JAI Press, Greenwich Conn, 1987, also 1988 p.169-188.
40. C. E. Phelphs, "Death and Taxes", *Journal of Health Economics*, 7:1-24, 1988.
41. Thomas F. Pogue and Larry G. Sgontz, "Taxing to Control Social Costs: The Case of Alcohol" *The American Economic Review*, University of Iowa, Iowa City, IA., Guest Commentary, January 1989.
42. Saffer and Grossman, "Drinking Age Laws and Highway Mortality Rates", *Economic Inquiry*, 25:403-417, 1987.
43. Joel Fort, M.D., Fort Halfs, San Francisco, CA, *Alcohol, Our Biggest Drug Problem*, 1973, p.100. Permission granted by McGraw-Hill, Inc., 1221 Avenue of the Americas, New York, NY 10020.

CHAPTER FOUR

1. *The Catholic Encyclopedia*, McGraw Hill, 1967.
2. D. James Kennedy, Ph.D. and Jerry Newcomb, *What if Jesus had Never Been Born*, Thomas Nelson Publishers, Nashville, 1994, p.209.
3. *The Illustrated Science and Invention Cyclopedia*, H. S. Stuntman, Inc. Westport, CT, 1983, p.2681.
4. *Journal of the Rev. John Wesley*, J. M. Dent & Sons Ltd, New York, 1906, pp.5-6.
5. Elijah P. Brown, *The Baseball Evangelist*, Fleming H. Revell Co., New York, 1914, p.209.
6. D. Leigh Calvin, *Prohibition in the United States*, George H. Doran Co., 1926, pp.268-269.

7. Mabel Willebrandt, *The Inside of Prohibition*, Bobbs Merrill Co., 1929, p.243,
8. Ibid, p.344.
9. Father J. J. Curan, *Deliver Us From Evil*, W.W. Norton and Co., Inc., N.Y., 1976, p.186.
10. Bishop Leniham Norman H. Clark, *Deliver Us From Evil*, W. W. Norman and Co., Inc., N.Y., 1976, p.187.
11. Irving Fisher, *Prohibition at Its Worst*, p.44, *The Noble Experiment*, 1932, p.142.
12. Samuel Crowther, *Prohibition and Prosperity*, John Day Co. 1930, p.57.
13. Herman T. Feldman, *Prohibition, Its Economic and Industrial Aspects*, D. Appleton and Co. 1927, pp.118-124.
14. Whitney Williams, *Survey Graphic*, February 1, 1931.
15. Herman T. Feldman, *Prohibition, Its Economic and Industrial Aspects*, D. Appleton and Co., 1927, p.254.
16. Dr. J. M. Doran, quoted in *The Amazing Story of Repeal*, by Fletcher Dobyns, Signal Press, Evanston, IL, 1940, p.393.
17. Mark Moore, *The National Statesman*, N.Y. Times, June 1990, p.1 and 2.
18. Edward Freschi, Pres. Holeproof Hosiery Co., Milwaukee, WI., *Propaganda Vs. Facts*, Ross J. McLennan, Sane Press, Okla. City, OK, 1978, p.127.
19. George M. Verity, President, American Rolling Mill Co., Middleton, Ohio., ibid, p.127.
20. Prof. Henry Farnam of Yale University, "The Law of the Land and Our Moral Frontier", *Propaganda Vs. Fact*, Ross J. McLennan, 1978.
21. W. S. Stone, Ground Chief, Brotherhood of Locomotive, ibid pp.127-128 Engineers, Cleveland, OH.
22. H. F. Miller, *An Economist Looks at Prohibition from Propaganda Vs. Fact*, Ross J. McLennan, Sane Press, Oklahoma City, OK, 1930, p.123.
23. A. Carlson Brisbane, *Brisbane, Propaganda Vs. Facts*, Ross J. McLennan, Sane Press, Okla. City, OK, 1978, p.250, ibid p. 124.
24. December *Survey Graphic*, Art. The Prohibition Question.
25. A. Carlson Brisbane, *Brisbane, Propaganda Vs. Facts*, Ross J. McLennan, Sane Press, Okla. City, OK, 1978, p.250.
26. Jack Van Impe, M.D. and Roger F. Campbell, *Alcohol: The Beloved Enemy*, Jack Van Impe, Ministries, 1980.
27. May, *Psychiatrist*, June Magazine, Jack Van Impe, 1980, p.89.
28. Professor Henry W. Farnam, of Yale University. *The Laws of the Land* and *Our Moral Frontier. Propaganda Vs. Fact*, Ross J. McLennan, 1978.
29. Norman H. Clark, *Deliver Us From Evil*, W. W. Norman and Co., Inc. N.Y., 1976, pp.145-146.
30. Professor Henry W. Farnam of Yale University, *The Laws of the Land* and *Our Moral Frontier", Propaganda Vs. Fact*, Ross J. McLennan, 1978.
31. Louise Burgess, *Alcohol and Your Health*, Charles Publishing, Los Angeles, September 1973, p.153.
32. Ibid, p.152.
33. Fletcher Dobyns, *The Amazing Story of Repeal*, Signal Press, Evanston, IL 60201, 1940, p.18.
34. Ibid, pp.22-23.
35. Ibid, p.22-23.
36. Ibid. p.24.
37. Jack Van Impe, M.D., and Roger F. Campbell, *Alcohol: The Beloved Enemy*, Jack Van Impe Ministries, 1980. p.91.
38. Assemblies of God, *Abstinence*, Gospel Publishing House, Springfield, MO, General Presbytery of Assemblies of God, 1985.
39. Ibid, p.1.
40. Ibid, p.1.
41. Southern Baptist Convention, Resolution No. 9 on Alcohol.
42. Bible verses are given I Corinthians 3:16-19, Romans 2:12 and 6:12.
43. Church of Brethren, 1976, Report of Study Committee of Annual Conference.
44. General Assembly of the Christian Church (Disciples of Christ) No. 56, 1971.
45. The Church of Christ, *Keep Your Body* by Joe E. Barnett, Christian Tracts, Pasadena, TX, p.8.
46. *Thinking and Acting Together*, Barry L. Callen, the Executive Council of the

Church of God and Warner Press Inc., Anderson, IN.
47. Discipline of the Church of the Nazarene.
48. Friends Church, *Faith and Practice*, Western Yearly Meeting of Friends Church. Book of Discipline, 1974, pp.86 and 87.
49. King of Glory Church, Luthern, 4, p.17.
50. p.96.
51. A336, p.48.
52. *The Amazing Story of Repeal*, Fletcher Dobyns, Signal Press, 1974, p.225.
53. The Discipline, 1992-365:8.
54. The Discipline, 1992, 410:4.

CHAPTER FIVE

1. Robert P. Teachout, Ph.D. Thesis, Dallas Theological Seminary, *The Use of Wine in the Old Testament*, Copyright Robert Teachout 1980, University Microfilms International, Ann Arbor, MI 1986. Used by permission. Preface.
2. Jack Van Impe, M.D. and Roger F. Campbell, *Alcohol: The Beloved Enemy*, Jack Van Impe, Ministries, Box 3, Royal Oaks, MI 48060, 1980, p.111. Used by permission.
3. Joseph Wechsberg, *Cyclopedia Americana*, Americana Corp. New York 22, NY, Art Wine, Vol. 29, p.36, 1963.
4. Odyssey Book *ix*, p.44, Quoted by E. Nott, 1863, London Edition.
5. Plato, Laws 2.674 a-b, Robert P. Teachout, Ph.D. Thesis, Dallas Theological Seminary, *The Use of Wine in the Old Testament*, University Microfilms International, used by permission, 1980, p.65.
6. E. Nott, Former President of Union College London edition. Quotes Columella, *The Wines of the Ancients*, Sane Press. London Edition 213; A-B, 216 "Vinum dulce sic facere oportet," *Lectures on Temperance*, 1863, p.78.
7. Ibid, p.80.
8. Leon C. Field, *Methodist Monthly Review*, April 1892, p.299. Ref 00648.
9. William Patton, D.D., *Bible Wines or Laws of Fermentation*, Sane Press, 101 N.E. 23rd St., Oklahoma City, OK 73105, 1871, p.49.
10. E. Nott, quotes Columella, *The Wines of Ancients*, Sane Press, London Edition 2B; A-B, 216 "Vinum dulce sic facere oportet." 1863, p.180. Also, William Patton, quotes Delphin Notes Car. libi 006 ii. By permission. 1871, p.44.
11. Ibid, p.41.
12. Georgi, *Aut dulcls muste Volcano decoguit humoren, ect.* lib 1, line 295. Parts are quoted from *Bible Wines* by William Patton. By permission. 1871, p.44.
13. Liber i ode XVIII, Line 21, Patton, p.42.
14. Frederick R. Lees, Ph.D. and Dawson Burns, M.R., *The Temperance Bible Commentary*, Library of Congress HV518V4, London, 1868, p.374.
15. Prochus, *The Works and Days of Hesiod*, Line 611, Quoted by Leon C. Field in *Methodist Quarterly Review*, April 1882, p.299.
16. Pliny, the Elder, *Natural History*, translated by H. Rackham, *The Loeb Classical Library*, Cambridge, MA. 1960. Also *Bible Wines*, William Patton, Sane Press, Oklahoma City, OK, 1871.
17. Frederick R. Lees, Ph.D. and Dawson Burns, M.R., *The Temperance Bible Commentary*, Library of Congress HV518V4, London, 1868, p.374.
18. Ibid.
19. Papius, Pliny, the Elder, *Natural History*, translated by H. Rackman, *The Loeb Classical Library*, Cambridge, MA. 1960. Liber XXIII, Cap 24, p.168, *Bible Wines* by William Patton, 1871, Sane Press, Oklahoma City, OK 73105. Kitto iii 955; A-B, 217, Smith Antiquities, Anit-Bac.
20. James A. Wesley, *Was Jesus The Lil' Ole' Winemaker?*, WesPress Publications, P.O. Box 2107, Apache Juntis, AZ, 1983.
21. *The Century Dictionary and Cyclopedia*, Vol. VIII, The Century Co., NY, 1899.
22. William Patton, *Bible Wines* or *Laws of Fermentation*, Exposition, Quoter of Delphin Notes Car. lib i ode ii by Permission, Sane Press, 101 NE 23rd St., Oklahoma City, OK, 1871.
23. James A. Wesley, *Was Jesus The Lil' Ole' Winemaker*, WesPress Publica-

tions, P.O. Box 2107, Apache Juntis, AZ, 85220, 1983.
24. Leon C. Field, "Jesus, A Total Abstainer", *Methodist Quarterly Review*, Jan., 1992.
25. W. W. Bauer, M.D., Editor *Today's Health Guide*, The American Medical Association, 1965.
26. Stephen Reynolds, Ph.D., Princeton University, *Alcohol and the Bible*, The Challenge Press, P.O. Box 5567, Little Rock, AR, 72215, 1983, p.13.
27. Ibid., p. 16.

CHAPTER SIX

1. Pliny, the Elder, *Natural History, The Loeb Classical Library*, Cambridge, MA., 1960, 14.26. There are copies in the Library of Congress, where I did some research.
2. Lucius Junius Columella, Moderatus Roman writer on *Agriculture* of the middle of the first century, 50 A.D. 12:20-8.
3. Cato, The Elder, Marcus Porcius, *The Loeb Classical Library*, Cambridge, MA., 1960. *De Agriculture*, 191 B.C., p.148.
4. Ibid, p.23.
5. Ibid, p.109.
6. Ibid, p.110.
7. Ibid, p.23.
8. Lucius Junius Columella, Moderatus Roman writer on *Agriculture* of the middle of the first century, *The Loeb Classical Library*, Cambridge, MA., 1960, 12.20.1.
9. Ibid, 12.20.6
10. Samuele Bacchiocchi, *Wine of the Bible*, Biblical Perspective 4569 Lisa Lane, Berrien Springs, MI 49103, 1989, p.112.
11. Flavius Josephus, *The Works of Antiquities of the Jews—Wars of the Jews*, 91 A.D., Translated by William Whiston, A.M. 1871 Porter and Carts, Philadelphia, PA, *Wars of the Jews*, p.872.
12. Lucius Junius Columella, Moderatus Roman writer on *Agriculture* of the middle of the first century, *The Loeb Classical Library*, Cambridge, MA., 1960, 12.10.3.
13. Helen Peffer Oakley, *The Encyclopedia Americana* International Edition Americana Corp. 575 Lexington Ave., N.Y., 1969, Vol. 29, p.314.
14. Lucius Junius Columella, Moderatus Roman writer on *Agriculture* of the middle of the first century, p.134, *The Loeb Classical Library*, Cambridge, MA., 1960, 12.46.6.
15. Ibid, 12.46.5.
16. Ibid, 12.44.3.
17. Pliny, the Elder, *Natural History, The Loeb Classical Library*, Cambridge, MA., 1960, 14.3.16.
18. Ibid.
19. Samuele Bacchiocchi, *Wine in the Bible*, Biblical Perspective 4569 Lisa Lane, Berrien Springs, MI 49103, 1989, pp.107, 108.
20. Georg Ebers, Professor of Egyptology at Jena and Leipzig. *Durch Gosen Sum Sinai, Hours With the Bible*, 1872, p.480.
21. *Biblicotheca Review*, January 1881, p.112.
22. Appleton, *American Cyclopedia*, Art Fermentation, 1963.
23. "Fermentation", *Encyclopedia Britannica*, 1894, IV Edition (Chicago: The Werner Co. Art.), *Fermentation*, p.94.
24. Ibid, p.95.
25. Amphora—A Greek and Roman narrow mouthed vessel with handles on both sides; made of either wood or earthenware; earthenware was easier to make both air and water tight.
26. Cato, *De Re Rustica*, 120. Leon C. Field, *Methodist Quarterly Review*, April 1882, p.296.
27. Pliny 14:9. Ibid.
28. Plutarch 2 N-26. Ibid.
29. Geopnica 6:16, *Smith Dictionary of Greek and Roman Antiquities.*
30. Donovan, *Domestic Economy*. Anti Bacchus p.162 Patton p.24.
31. Columella, liber XII, Cap. 29, Nott and Anti Bacchus 216.
32. Lardner's Cabinet Encyclopedia, Contains *Domestic Economy*, p.162. Donovan, p.24, 1849.
33. Tieberg, *Letters on Chemistry*, Temperance Bible Commentary, London Edition, 1871, p.25.

34. Amerine A. Maynard, "Wine", *Encyclopedia Britannica* (NY), Worlds Fair Edition, 1963, p.44.
35. Archbishop Potter, *Grecian Antiquities*, Edinburgh Edition, 1813, Vol. 2, b. 1674, p.360.
36. Aristotle, E. Nott, London Edition, p.80 and F. R. Lees and D. Burns, *Temperance Bible Commentary*, London, 1868, p.295.
37. Aristotle, E. Nott, London Edition, 1868, p.30.
38. R. Laird Harris, Faith Seminary Professor, "Wine and Strong Drink", *The Bible Today*, March 1944, p.138.
39. Georgi, *Out dulcis muste Volcano decoguit humoren, etc.*, lib. 1, line 295. Parts are quoted from *Bible Wines* by William Patton. By permission.
40. Anti-Bac, p.221. William Patton, *The Wines of the Ancients*, 1871, p.41, Oklahoma City, OK, Sane Press.
41. *The Popular and Critical Bible Encyclopedia and Scripture Dictionary*, Ed. Rev. Samuel Fellows, M.A.,D.D., LLD Vol III p. 1724, (Howard Severance Co. Chicago, 1909).
42. Adams, *Roman Antiquities*, (Edinburgh, 1791), p.29.
43. *Kittos Cyclopedia*, 1845, Vol. II, p.477.
44. Leiber Chemist, 1817, Nott's Lecture 1863, p.30.
45. F.R. Lees and D. Burns, *Temperance Biblical Commentary*, London, p.17, 1868.
46. Dr. William Glaisher, *Dictionary of Classical Literature and Antiquities* from the German, 1882.
47. William Patton, *Laws of Fermentation, Wine With Water*, 1871, p.50.
48. F. R. Lees, "Captain Treat", *Lee's Works*, 1868, p.50.
49. F. R. Lees and D. Burns, *Temperance Bible Commentary*, 1861.
50. E. Nott, Former president of Union College, London Edition 213, A-B 216 Quotes Athenaus, *Wines of the Ancients*, Oklahoma City, OK, Sane Press.
51. Volney, *Travels in Egypt and Syria*, and also Volney, *Travels in Syria*, Vol. 2, 1788, ch.29.
52. E. Nott, Nott's Lectures, London Ed., 1863, p.81, quoted in *The Wines of the Ancients*, Oklahoma City, OK, Sane Press.
53. Samuele Bacchiocchi, *Wine in the Bible*, Biblical Perspective, 4569 Lisa Lane, Berrien, MI 49103, 1989. $12.95 post paid.
54. Horace, Car, lib i ode ii Deljin Notes 65 B.C., *Wines of the Ancients* p.35.
55. E. Nott, 1863, *London Edition* 213; A-B, 216 "Vinum dulce sic facere oportet."
56. In Nott's *Lectures on Biblical Temperance*, London Edition 213; A-B, 216.
57. Columella, liber xii, cap 29, Nott, Forster and Huffman, Loeb Classical Library, Cambridge, Mass. 1955, and Anti-Bac p.216, Patton 1871, p.37.
58. *Kittos Cyclopedia* ii, John Kitto, D. D., 1843, 1845, 955. Roman Antiquities, Carr, T.S., (p.39).
59. Nott, *London Edition*, 1848, p.80 (p.44), Patton.
60. Dr. F. R. Lees, *Temperance Bible Commentary*, London, 1868, p. 282.
61. Ibid.
62. Ibid.
63. Ibid.
64. *Columella, The Loeb Classical Library*, Cambridge, MA., 1960, 12.37, Leon C. Field, Methodist Quarterly Review, April 1882, p. 291.
65. Pliny, *National History, The Loeb Classical Library*, Cambridge, MA., 1960, 14.11, April 1882, p.291.
66. Geopon VI: 16, Columella 12:41, *Smith Dictionary of Greek and Roman Antiquities, Art-Vinum.*
67. *Encyclopedia Britannica*, 1894, IX Edition (Chicago: The Werner Co. Art.), Fermentation, p.92.
68. Wilkinson, *Ancient Egyptians* i. 45. *Methodist Quarterly Review*, April 1882, p.291-292.
69. Virgil 70 B.C., Georgics 2, pp.210-245.
70. Ibid.
71. Pliny, 14:22. Lees *Bible Commentary*, 1868, p.34.
72. Delphin Notes i. II *Viva Liques, Veteres Nempe Mustum Prinsquam Ferbuisset Per Saccum Taties Cola Bunt, etc.*
73. Pliny, *The Loeb Classical Library*, Cambridge, MA., 1960, 14.22-47, "Ut Plus Capiamus Vini Sacca Frangimur Vires."

74. Plutarch Sympos 8:7. A.D. 60 Lees *Bible Commentary*, 1861, p. 278.
75. Horace Car lib i ode ii, *Laws of Fermentation*, Patton, 1871, p.36.
76. Millers, *Gardener's Dictionary*, Article Wines, Dr. Lee's Works, Vol. 2.
77. Adams, *Roman Antiquities*, defaecabantur—to strain, purify.
78. Nott, *London Edition*, 1863, p.82, (p.40).
79. Carr, T. S. (Kitto, Cyclopedia), 1845, London Vol. 2:956, 1863, (p.40).
80. Kitto, Sir Edward Barry, 2:956, Kitto's Encyclopedia Vol. II, Kitto Cycolepedia 1i, 955, *Roman Antiquities*.
81. Count Dandalo, *The Art of Preserving the Wines of Italy*, first published at Milan, Italy, 1812, Nott in Patton, p.40, *Bible Wines*.
82. *Encyclopedia Americana*, Vol. 24 (Americana Corp. 1963), p.43.
83. Dictionary of *Ancient Greek Civilization*.
84. *Encyclopedia Americana*, Vol. 29 (Americana Corp., 1963), p.43.
85. Prof. W. Ditmor, "Fermentation", *Encyclopedia Britannica* 9th edition (Chicago: The Warner Co., 1894) 9th Ed., p.95.
86. *Encyclopedia Britannica*, 1894, IX Edition (Chicago: The Werner Co. Art.), *Fermentation*, p.93.
87. Lucius Junius Columella, Moderatus Roman Writer on *Agriculture* of the middle of the first century, 50 A.D.
88. E. C. Delevan, *An American Travelling in Italy*, confirmed by Rev. B. C. Duff, *Travel Through the South of Europe*, also Nott, *London Edition*, 1868, p.57 and Lees, 1869, p.278.
89. Norman, M. D. Kerr, FLS. *Wines of the Bible—An Introduction to Their Study*, National Publication Depot, 337 Strand W.C. London, 1885.

CHAPTER SEVEN

1. Charles J. Butler, B.D. and St. M. Faith Theological Seminary M. A. Temple (Religion) University, Ph.D., Temple University, MBA St. Joseph U. Taught Systematic Theology Faith Seminary Clark, Presbytary, N.J.
2. Frederick Richard Lees and Dawson Burns, *The Temperance Bible Commentary*, Library of Congress HV418V4, 1868, p.11.
3. Robert P. Teachout, *The Use of Wine in the Old Testament*, Copyright 1980 University Microfilms International, Ann Arbor, MI, p.287.
4. Jack Van Impe with Roger F. Campbell, *Alcohol: The Beloved Enemy*, Jack Van Impe Ministries, 1980, p.175.
5. Jerry Hull, *NO! The Positive Response to Alcohol*, Beacon Hill Press of Kansas City, 1989, pp.41-42.
6. Jack Van Impe with Roger F. Campbell, *Alcohol: The Beloved Enemy*, Jack Van Impe Ministries, Box J, Royal Oak, MI, 48060, 1980, p.175.
7. Geoffrey Chaucer, *The Pardoner Tale*, 1395, The College Survey of English Literature, Harcour Bruce and Co., New York, 1947, p. 197.
8. William Patton, *Bible Commentary*, Sane Press, 101 N.E. 23rd St., Oklahoma, City, OK, 1871, p.58.
9. Samuele Bacchiocchi, *Wine in the Bible*, Biblical Perspective, currently available from author at $12.95 postpaid, 4569 Lisa Lane, Berrington Springs, MI, 1989. p. 81.
10. Bill T. Arnold, Ph.D., Professor Old Testament, Wesley Biblical Seminary, 12/01/1989.
11. Robert P. Teachout, *WINE, The Biblical Imperative Total Abstinence*, 1983, p.25, Trinity Baptist, 6034 Beech Daly Rd., Taylor, MI, 48180.
12. Ibid.
13. William M. Thayer, *Communion, Wine, and Bible Temperance*, National Temperance Society and Publishing House, N.Y., 1869, p. 917.
14. F. F. Bruce, *The International Bible Commentary*, Guidepost, 1986, Carmel, N.Y. 10512.
15. William Patton, *Laws of Fermentation*, Sane Press, 101 North East 23rd St., Oklahoma City, OK., 1871, p.83.
16. *Deuteronomy 21:20,21*.
17. Stephen M. Reynolds, Ph.D, *Alcohol and the Bible*, The Challenge Press, P.O. Box 5567, Little Rock, Arkansas, 1983, pp.24-25.

18. *The International Standard Bible Encyclopedia*, 1939, Vol. 2, pp. 879-880.
19. Analytical Concordance of the Bible, Robert Young, 22nd Edition, p.273, *Strong Drink*, p.273.
20. Frederick Richard Lees and Dawson Burnsa, *The Temperance Bible Commentary*, Library of Congress HV518V4, 1868, p.32.
21. *The Popular and Critical Bible Encyclopedia*, Vol. 1, The Harvard-Severance Co., Chicago, 1909, p.546.
22. Ibid.
23. Ibid.
24. Ferrar Fenton, *The Bible and Wine*, 1907, p.52.
25. Arnold D. Peiskers, *The Wesleyan Bible Commentary*, Vol. 1, William Erdmans Publishing Co., Grand Rapids, Michigan, 1967, p. 319.
26. Rev. J. R. Drummelow, M.A., *The One Volume Commentary on the Holy Bible*, Macmillan Publishing Co., New York, 1936, p.91.
27. Alexander Heidel, *The Gelgamesh Epic and Old Testament Parallels*, The University of Chicago Press, Chicago, Phoenix Books, 1963, p.87.
28. W. G. Lambert, *Babylonian Wisdom Literature*, Clarendon Press, Oxford, 1960, p.150.
29. Robert P. Teachout, *Wine The Biblical Imperative*, and *Total Abstinence*, 1983, p.45.
30. Teachout, 1979, p.180.
31. Ferrar Fenton, *The Bible and Wine*, 1907, p.3.
32. Ibid.
33. F. F. Bruce, *The International Bible Commentary*, Guidepost, 1986, Carmel, N.Y., 10512.
34. Samuele Bacchiocchi, *Wine in the Bible*, Biblical Perspective, 4569 Lisa Lane, Berrion Springs, MI, 49103, 1989, p. 227.
35. Ferrar Fenton, *The Bible and Wine*, 1907, Ferrar Fenton MRAS, MCAA, etc. and John Abbey, Second Edition, Published by S. W. Partridge and Co. London.
36. Dr. Stephen M. Reynolds, *Alcohol and the Bible*, The Challenge Press, P.O. Box 5567, Little Rock, Ark, 1983, p.15.
37. Norman L. Geisler, *A Christian Perspective On Wine Drinking*, Notes 1982, p.55.
38. Samuele Bacchiocchi, *Wine In the Bible*, Biblical Perspective, Berrion Springs, MI, 1989, p.233.
39. Dr. Jack Van Impe and Roger Campbell, *Alcohol the Beloved Enemy*, Jack Van Impe Ministries, 1980, p.5.
40. Ferrar Fenton, *Complete Holy Bible in Modern English*, 1872, p.3.
41. *The Living Bible*, copyright 1971, Tyndale House Publishers, Wheaton, IL 60187.
42. *The International Standard Bible Encyclopedia*, p.879.
43. Robert P. Teachout, *Wine, The Biblical Imperative: Total Abstinence*, 1983, p.25.

CHAPTER EIGHT

1. Charles J. Butler, B.A. Bob Jones U. B.D.; Faith Theological Seminary; S.T.M. Faith Theological Seminary, Old Testament; M.A. Temple U., Ph.D. Temple U. 1994.
2. F. R. Lees and D. Burns, *The Temperance Bible Commentary*, London, 1868, p.71.
3. Polybius B. 205 B.C.
4. F. R. Lees and D. Burns, *The Temperence Bible Commentary*, 1868, p. 442, written one hundred years ago.
5. Jack Van Impe with Roger F. Campbell, *Alcohol The Beloved Enemy*, 1980, from Ronald Kotulac, "The Chemical Sledgehammer alcohol lined to birth defects" Chicago Tribune, September 13, 1977.
6. Centers for Disease Control, By UPI February 13, 1987.
7. Sam Rhine, Geneticist at Noble Centers and the Genetic Ed Center, quoted from the *Noblesville Daily Ledger*, December 18, 1986.
8. Ibid.
9. Charles Turham with Elizabeth Schaffer in *Newsweek* July 31, 1989, Newsweek, Inc. 251 West 47th Street, New York, N.Y. 10019-1894.
10. *The Popular Critical Bible Encyclopedia and Scripture Dictionary*, Rev.

Samuel Fellows, D.D., L.L.D., Vol. III, Chicago, IL. 1909, p.1724.
11. Liebig, *Chemistry of Agriculture*, 3rd. Edition.
12. F. R. Lees and D. Burns, *The Temperence Bible Commentary*, 1868, Prelim XX Note, 13a Footnote p.XX.
13. *The Living Bible*, paraphrased, large print edition, copyright Tyndale House Publishers, Wheaton, IL 60187, 1971, p.932.

CHAPTER NINE

1. Robert P. Teachout, Ph.D., Thesis, Dallas Theological Seminary, *The Use of Wine in the Old Testament*, University Microfilms International, 1979, p.292.
2. Adam Clarke, *Clarke's Commentary*, Abington–Cokesbury Press, N.Y., 1842, Vol. 3 p.549.
3. Robert P. Teachout, *The Use of Wine in the Old Testament*, Copyright by the author 1979, p.269.
4. F. F. Bruce, General Editor, *The International Commentary*, also H. L. Ellison and G.C.D. Howley, Guide Post, Carmel, N.Y., Marshall Morgan and Scott Publications, Ltd., 1986.
5. Leon C. Field, *Methodist Quarterly Review*, January 1882, p.294.
6. Jack Van Impe, *Alcohol: The Beloved Enemy*, Jack Van Impe Ministries, Box 3, Royal Oak, MI 48068, 1980, p. 106.
7. Stephen M. Reynolds, Ph.D., *Alcohol And The Bible*, The Challenge Press, P.O. Box 5567, Little Rock, Arkansas, 1983, pp.12-14.
8. Princton University, Adam Clarke, *Clarke's Commentary*, Vol. 3, Abington–Cokebury Press, N.Y. 1842, p.768.
9. Luke 12:15, *The New International Version*, NIV, Zondervan, Grand Rapids, MI.
10. Robert P. Teachout, *The Use of Wine in the Old Testament*, University Microfilms International, Copyright by the author, 1983.
11. Ibid, p.67.
12. Ibid, p.160.

CHAPTER TEN

1. Joel Fort M.D., *Alcohol: Our Biggest Drug Problem*, McGraw-Hill, Inc. 1221 Avenue of the Americas, New York, NY 10020, 1973. By permission.
2. Winton H. Beaver, *Ministry*, July 1983. Review and Harold Publishing Associations Hagerstown, MD, p.5.
3. Ibid.
4. Stephen M. Reynolds, Ph.D., Princeton University, *Alcohol and the Bible*, The Challenge Press, P.O. Box 5567, Little Rock, Ark, 72215, 1983, Ch.5, p.20.
5. *Temperance Bible Commentary*, F. R. Lees and D. Burns, London 1868, p.168.
6. William D. Patton, *Bible Wines or Laws of Fermentation*, Quoter Delphine Notes Car lib i ode ii, Sane Press, 101 NE 23rd St., Oklahoma City, OK 73105, 1871.
7. Kenneth Taylor, *The Living Bible*, Tyndale House Publishers, Wheaton, Illinois, 1971.
8. Robert P. Teachout, Th.D., Thesis, Dallas Theological Seminary, *The Use of Wine in the Old Testament*, University Microfilms International, 1980, p.180.
9. William M. Thayer, *Communion, Wine and Bible Temperance*, Published in *Bibliotheca Sacra*, January 1869 and by the National Temperance Society, N.Y. 1869.
10. *Bible Commentary*, p.198, Letters on Chemistry Tieberg, by F. R. Lees and D. Burns, London 1868.
11. Robert P. Teachout, Th.D., *Wine the Biblical Imperative Total Abstinence*, 1986, p.36.
12. *The Temperance Bible Commentary*, F. R. Lees and D. Burns, London, 1868, p.202.
13. Xenophane, Cyclopedia, 370 BC.
14. Roy C. Smith, *Is It Too Much To Ask*, Chicago, Signal Press, 1935.
15. F. R. Lees & Dawson Burns, *The Temperance Bible Commentary*, 1868, pp.215, 216.
16. Robert P. Teachout, Th.D., Thesis, Dallas Theological Seminary, *The Use of Wine in the Old Testament*, University Microfilms International, 1980, p.198.
17. William D. Patton, *Bible Wines*, Quoter Delphine Notes Car lib i ode ii, Sane Press, 101 NE 23rd St., Oklahoma City, OK 73105, 1871.
18. *The Bible in Modern English*, 1872, p.2.

19. *The Living Bible*, c. 1971.
20. Robert P. Teachout, Th.D. Thesis, Dallas Theological Seminary, *The Use of Wine in the Old Testament*, University Microfilms International, 1979, p.191.
21. Dr. Samuel Bacchiocchi, *Wine and the Bible*, Biblical Perspective, 4569 Lisa Lane Berrien Springs, MI 49103, for book send $12.95 post paid, 1989, p.241.
22. Sir John Bowring, *Bible Commentary*, p.224.
23. Stephen M. Reynolds, Ph.D., Princeton University, *Alcohol and the Bible*, The Challenge Press, 1983, p.20. May be purchased from IOGT, 9926 Cedar Ave. Minneapolis, MN 55407.
24. Ferrar Fenton, *Complete Holy Bible in Modern English*, 1872.
25. Ferrar Fenton, *The Bible and Wine*, 1872, p.8.
26. Ibid.
27. Bible Encyclopedia, 1909.
28. *The Living Bible*, Tyndall House Publishers, Wheaton, IL, Copyright 1971.
29. F. R. Lees and D. Burns, *The Temperance Bible Commentary*, London, 1968, p.231.
30. Athenaus, *The Banquet of the Learned*, 192 A.D., F. R. Lees and D. Burns—*The Temperance Bible Coimmentary*, 1868, p.231.
31. *The Bible and Wine*, Ferrar Fenton and John Abbey, S.W. Partridge & Co., London, E.G., 1907, p.8.
32. New World Dictionary, Collins, 1988.

CHAPTER ELEVEN

1. *The International Standard Bible Encyclopedia*, Art. "Strong Drink", T. K. Cheyne & J. Sutherland Block, 1939, pp.879-880.
2. Nott, *The Wines of the Ancients*, Sane Press, Oklahoma City, OK, London Edition, 1863, p.227.
3. Ibid.
4. Frederick Lees and Dawson Burns, *Temperance Bible Commentary*, London, 1868, p.280.
5. *The Discipline of the Wesleyan Church*, Wesleyan Publishing House, Indianapolis, IN 1988, pp.30-131.8.
6. Norman L. Geilser, *A Christian Prospective on Wine-Drinking, Biblical Sacra*, January-March, 3/82, p.53.
7. Frederick Lees and Dawson Burns, *Temperance Bible Commentary*, London, 1868, p.53, p.280.
8. Leon C. Fields, *Methodist Monthly Review*, January 1870, p.187.
9. William Patton, *Bible Wines* or *Laws of Fermentation*, Sane Press, Oklahoma City, OK, 1871, p.83.
10. Ibid, p.84.
11. Rev. William M. Thayer, *Communion, Wine and Bible Temperance*, Published in *Bibliothesa Sacra*, and by the National Temperance Society and Publishing House, N.Y., January 1869, p.71.
12. John R. Rice, *Sword of the Lord, The King of the Jews*, Grand Rapid, MI, Zonderran Corp., 1955, p.436.
13. Flavius Josephus, *The Works of Antiqutics of the Jews—War of the Jews*, translated by William Whiston, A.M. Porter L. Carts, Philadelphia, PA, Chapter 8, p.872.
14. Swinburn, *Travels*.
15. Pliny, the Elder, *Natural History*, translation by H. Rackham, *The Loeb Classical Library*, Cambridge, MA, 1960, p.278.
16. Ross J. McLennon, *Propaganda Vs. Facts*, Sane Press, Oklahoma City, OK, 1978, p.60.
17. *Websters New Twentieth Century Dictionary of the English Language*, Unabridged, 1965, Rockville, House Publishers, NY.
18. Peter H. Gott, *The Daily Ledger*, Noblesville 9/26/1992, p.5.
19. John R. Rice, *The Kings of the Jews*, Grand Rapids, MI, Zondervan Corp., 1955, p.436.
20. *Encyclopedia Americana*, Vol. 19, 1964, International Edition, American Corporation, p.665.
21. James Smith, M.D., Researcher at Schick-Shadele Hospital speaking at a two day conference on alcoholism at the University of Notre Dame, South Bend, IN, April 27, 1988.
22. Frederick Lees, *Text Book on Temperance*, JN Stearing, NY, 1869, p.442.
23. Michael Davis, *The Broken Cord*, Harper and Row.

24. *TIME*, 8/28/1989, Time Inc., NY, p.60.
25. Charles Turham with Elizabeth Schaffer, *Newsweek*, 7/31/1989, Newsweek Inc., 251 West 57th Street, NY.
26. *Encyclopedia Britannica*, 8th Edition, Vol. 17, 1849, p.333.
27. *Universal Jewish Encyclopedia*, 1943, Vol. 10 quoted in *The Bible and it's Wines*, Eurny, Charles, Wesley, Prohibition National Committee, Kalamazoo, MI, p.529.
28. C. H. Dodd, *Historical Traditions in the Fourth Gospel*, Cambridge University Press, London American Branch, NY, 1963, p.223.
29. David Wilkerson, *Sipping Saints*, Fleming H. Revell Co. Old Tappen, NJ, 1978, p.21. By special permission.
30. Ralph Earle, *Word Meanings In The New Testament*, Beacon Hill Press Of Kansas City, 1987, p.83.
31. Leon C. Field, *Methodist Quarterly Review*, Jan. 4, 1882, p.472.
32. Anti Bacchus, *Bacchus and Anti-Bacchus*, Quoted by William Patton in *Wines of the Ancients*, Oklahoma, City, OK, Sane Press, p.220.
33. Georg Virgil, lib. i line 1293, Parts are quoted from *Bible Wines* by William Patton, 1871, Sane Press by permission, p.44.
34. William Patton, *Bible Wines*, Sane Press, Oklahoma City, OK, 1871, p.74.
35. Ralph Earle, *Word Meanings In The New Testament*, Beacon Hill Press of Kansas City, 1987, p.83.
36. *Universal Cyclopedia*, p.9228.
37. Harold Spann, President of Wesley Biblical Seminary, Jacksonville, MS, 39286, 8/25/1989.
38. David Wilkerson, *Sipping Saints*, Fleming H. Revell Co., Old Tappen, NJ, 1978, p.23.
39. Ross J. McLennon, *Propaganda Vs. Facts*, Sane Press, Oklahoma City, OK, 1978, p.71.
40. Adam Clarke, *Clarke's Commentary*, Vol, 5, 1842, p.527.
41. Dr. Rev. E. Nott, *Lectures on Biblical Temperance*, London Edition, 1863, p.222.
42. Leon C. Field, *Methodist Quarterly Review*, July, 1882, p.474.

CHAPTER TWELVE

1. Josephus, Flavius, B.37 A.D., The Works of Antiquities of the Jews and Wars of the Jews, translated by William Wluston, A.M., Porter Carts, Philadelphia, P.A., b. 37 A.D.-D. 100 A.D.
2. Nott, *Notts Lectures on Biblical Temperance*, London, Ed., p.78, Patton, *Bible Wines*, 1871, p.43.
3. Samuele Bacchiocchi, Ph.D., 1989, p.180, *Wine in the Bible*, Biblical Perspective, 4569 Lisa Lane, Berrien Springs, MI, 49103.
4. Aristotle, *Meteoralogica Passion* IV, London, 1868.
5. Elton Trueblood, *The Humor of Christ*, Harper and Roe Publishers, San Francisco, 1964, p.10.
6. Emmet Russell, Art. "Dine", *The Zondervan Pictorial Bible Dictionary*, Tenny, NC 1963 ed.
7. Rev. William Thayer, *Communion, Wine and Bible Temperance*, Published in *Bibliotheca Sacra*, and by the National Temperance Society and Publishing House N.Y., January 1869.
8. Dr. Jack Van Impe with Roger F. Campbell, *Alcohol: The Beloved Enemy,* Jack Van Impe, Ministries, Box J, Royal Oak, MI, In Canada, Box 1717 Postal Station A, Windsor, Ontario, N9A, 6Y1, 1980, p.131.
9. F. F. Bruce, *The International Commentary*, 1986. Also H. L. Ellison and G. C. C. Howley, *Guide Post*, Carmel, N.Y., Marshall Morgan and Scott Publications, Ltd.
10. Rev. William Thayer, *Communion, Wine and Bible Temperance*, Published in *Bibliotheca Sacra*, and by the National Temperance Society and Publishing House, N.Y., January 1869, p.66.

CHAPTER THIRTEEN

1. Jerry D. Hull, *NO! The Positive Response to Alcohol*, Beacon Hill Press of Kansas City, Copyright 1989, p.50. Used by permission of the publisher.
2. Rev. William M. Thayer, *Communion, Wine and Bible Temperance*, published in *Bibliotheca Sacra*, Jan. 1869, pp.70-71, and by the National Temperance

Society, NY, 1869, National Temperance Society and Publishing House, NY.
3. William Patton, *Bible Wines*, Sane Press, Oklahoma City, OK, 1871, p.107.
4. *By His Divine Grace*, A. C. Bhaktwedanta Swami Prabhupadec, Bhaktwedanta Book Trust, 3764 Watseka Ave., Los Angeles, CA, 1978, p.167.
5. Leon C. Fields, quotes from Stanley in *Christian Institutions*, Harpers Ed, 1882, p.43.
6. Monsignor Ronald Knox, *The New Testament in Language of Today*, Knox.
7. William Patton, *Bible Wines*, Sane Press, Oklahoma City, OK, 1871, p.108.
8. Ibid.
9. Robert P. Teachout, *The Use of Wine in the Old Testament*, University Microfilms International, Ann Arbor, MI, 1980.
10. CBS news on *48 Hours*, July 6, 1989.
11. David Wilkerson, *Sipping Saints*, Fleming H. Revell Co., Old Tappen, NJ, 1978, p.15. Used by permission of the publisher.
12. Ralph Earle, *Word Meanings in the New Testament*, Beacon Hill Press, Kansas City, MO, 1987, p.390.
13. Jack Van Impe and Roger Campbell, *Alcohol: The Beloved Enemy*, Van Impe Ministries, Royal Oak, MI, 1980.
14. Frederick Richard Lees and Dawson Burns, *The Temperance Bible Commentary*, London, 1868, p.278.
15. Ibid, p.368.
16. Athenaus, *The Banquet of the Learned*, 192 A.D.
17. William Patton, *Bible Wines*, Sane Press, Oklahoma City, OK, 1871, p.45.
18. *Together We Can Make It*, St. Anthony's Medical Center, Hyland Center's Kid's Group, 10020 Kennedy Rd., St. Louis, MO 63128.
19. Frederick Richard Lees, *Lees' Works*. See William Patton, *Bible Wines*, Sane Press, Oklahoma City, OK, 1871, p.440.
20. Ibid, p.72.
21. Ibid, p.442.
22. Ibid, p.30.
23. Ralph Earle, *Word Meanings in the New Testament*, Beacon Hill Press of Kansas City, MO, 1987, pp.396-397. Used by permission of the publisher.
24. Samuele Bacchiocchi, *Wine in the Bible*, Biblical Perspective, Berrient Springs, MI, 1989, p.245.
25. W. B. McKnight, M.D., *The Family Doctor*, The Southwestern Company, Nashville, TN, 1963, p.187.
26. William Patton, *Bible Wines*, Sane Press, Oklahoma City, OK, 1871, p.112.
27. Ibid.
28. Earnest Gordon, *Christ, The Apostles and Wine*, The Sunday School Times, Philadelphia, PA, p.30.
29. Personal letter to the author by Alton H. Ridgeway, M.D., 1/8/84, Route 3, East Bend, NC.
30. Meadowbrooke Veterinary Clinic, 3233 Westfield Rd., Noblesville, IN 46060.
31. Phiny, the Elder, *Natural History*, translation by H. Rackham, *The Loeb Classical Library*, Cambridge, MA, 1960, p.113.
32. Dr. Rev. E. Nott, Aristotle, *Lectures on Biblical Temperance*, London Edition, 1863, p.213.
33. William Patton, *Bible Wines*, Sane Press, Oklahoma City, OK, 1871, p.44.
34. Frederick Richard Lees, *Lees' Works*. See William Patton, *Bible Wines*, Sane Press, Oklahoma City, OK, 1871 p.373.
35. W. B. McKnight, M.D., *The Family Doctor*, The Southwestern Company, Nashville, TN, 1963.
36. Ralph Earle, *Word Meanings in the New Testament*, Beacon Hill Press of Kansas City, MO, 1987, p.413. Used by permission of the author.
37. Robert P. Teachout, *The Use of Wine in the Old Testament*, Copyright by Robert Teachout University Microfilms International, Ann Arbor, MI, 1986, p.69.
38. Ibid, p.71.
39. F. R. Lees and D. Burns, *Bible Commentary*, Letters on Chemistry, Tieburg, London, 1968.
40. Ferrar Fenton, *The Bible and Wine*, 1907.
41. Quran sii, *The Holy*, published by American Trust Publication, for the Muslin Student Association, 2nd Edition, 1977, p.93.

INDEX